A permanent adaptable setting for *The Cradle Song.*

PLAY-MAKING AND PLAYS

PLAY-MAKING AND PLAYS

THE DRAMATIC IMPULSE AND ITS EDUCATIVE USE IN THE ELEMENTARY AND SECONDARY SCHOOL

BY

JOHN MERRILL

HEAD OF THE DEPARTMENT OF ORAL EXPRESSION
FRANCIS W. PARKER SCHOOL, CHICAGO

AND

MARTHA FLEMING

LATE ASSOCIATE PROFESSOR, DEPARTMENT OF SPEECH
AND ORAL READING, SCHOOL OF EDUCATION
UNIVERSITY OF CHICAGO

NEW YORK

THE MACMILLAN COMPANY

1930

ACKNOWLEDGMENTS

The authors acknowledge indebtedness to D. Appleton and Company for permission to use the play "Mr. Wolf Makes a Failure," which is adapted from *Uncle Remus, His Songs and His Sayings*, by Joel Chandler Harris; to Charles Scribner's Sons for permission to use the play "Old Pipes and the Dryad," which is adapted from *Fanciful Tales*, by Frank Stockton; to the American Book Company for permission to quote from *Psychology*, by John Dewey; to Mr. John Duncan for the use of the story "The Woodman and the Goblins"; to Mrs. Edith F. Flint of the University of Chicago for the use of "The Knighting of Richard Neville."

CONTENTS

PAGE

INTRODUCTION xiii

PREFACE xvii

PART I
THE DRAMATIC IMPULSE

CHAPTER

I. Universality of Dramatic Impulse and Expression   3
II. Dramatic Work of Little Children   16
III. Stories Suitable for Children's Plays   19
IV. Dramatic Work of the Junior High School . .   26
V. The Use of the Dramatic Impulse in the Senior High School   30
VI. The Qualifications and Training of the Teacher of Drama   35
VII. The School Drama and the Professional Stage .   44
VIII. Results of Dramatic Training   52

PART II
THE EDUCATIVE USE OF THE DRAMATIC IMPULSE

IX. Little Children's Plays and Their Sources   . .   63
X. Poetry in the Dramatic Training of Children   .   76
XI. World Literature as a Source of Children's Plays   83
XII. Animal Tales   94
XIII. Junior-High-School Plays and Their Sources   .   100
XIV. The Literary Drama in the Junior High School   104
XV. Production of *The Nativity* in the Eighth Grade   116
XVI. The Drama Course in the Senior High School   .   123
XVII. Play-Making in the High School   141
XVIII. The Literary Play in the High School   . . .   145
XIX. Presentation of Shakespeare's Plays   163
XX. Costuming and Setting   179

vii

CHAPTER   PAGE
   XXI.   Stage Lighting 193
  XXII.   The School Theater 202

                        PART III
NOTES ON AND ILLUSTRATIONS OF ORIGINAL PLAY–MAKING[1]

 XXIII.   The Harvest Feasts 213
 XXIV.   Dramatic Presentation of a Corn Husking in the
             Middle West 222
  XXV.   A Thanksgiving Exercise in Pageant Form . . 226
 XXVI.   The Pine-Tree Shillings 233
XXVII.   The Woodman and the Goblins 243
XXVIII.   Mr. Wolf Makes a Failure 260
 XXIX.   The Magic Gifts 265
  XXX.   The Box of Pandora 321
 XXXI.   The Bremen Town Musicians 336
XXXII.   Rip Van Winkle 345
XXXIII.   The First Thanksgiving Day in America . . 365
XXXIV.   Old Pipes and the Dryad 375
 XXXV.   The Knighting of Richard Neville 391
XXXVI.   The Departure 397

                        PART IV
                      BIBLIOGRAPHY

Full-Length Plays 411
Collections of Short Plays 481
List of Short Plays 483
Books Related to the Art of the Theater 542
Valuable Periodicals on the Art of the Theater . . . 558
List of Publishers 559

[1] The examples given in this volume are taken from work done at the Francis W. Parker School, Chicago, and at the School of Education of the University of Chicago.

LIST OF ILLUSTRATIONS

A permanent adaptable setting for *The Cradle Song*   *Frontispiece*[1]

PAGE

The second scene of *The Cradle Song* 7
The Hillman and the Housewife 17
A scene from *A Midsummer-Night's Dream* 23
Quality Street: the scene in the tent 32
A setting for *The Will* 33
A setting for *A Night at an Inn* 38
A Midsummer-Night's Dream 45
Snow White 48
Another scene from *Snow White* 53
Snow White: the scene in the home of the Dwarfs . . . 54
A setting for *Catherine Parr* 59
A setting for *The Florist Shop* 77
A non-realistic setting for *The Florist Shop* 84
The Cat That Walked by Himself 96
A setting for *The Red Turf* 109
A scene from *The Turn of the Road* 122
A scene from *Cathleen Ni Houlihan* 129
A scene from *Aria Da Capo* 133
A scene from *Aria Da Capo* 138
A scene from *Overtones* 146
A scene from *Androcles and the Lion* 152

[1] The illustrations in this book have been made from photographs of stage settings used at the Francis W. Parker School, Chicago. None of them — with the possible exception of the Frontispiece and a few others — gives an adequate idea of the appearance of the stage when lighted for a performance. They were taken in most cases by flashlight, which destroys all sense of illusion and of beauty. To visualize correctly the illustrations, one must imagine the transformation made by an appropriate lighting such as is seen in the picture of *The Cradle Song.* But even here in a time exposure the result is misleading and ineffective because of the absence of correct values and of color.

ix

PAGE

The Admirable Crichton, Act IV 155
The Admirable Crichton, Act II 157
A setting for *Master Pierre Patelin* 160
The Closet Scene from *Hamlet* 164
An Elizabethan setting for *Hamlet* 167
A setting for *As You Like It:* the lawn before the Duke's
    palace 171
A setting for *As You Like It:* Oliver's garden 171
A scene from *The Merchant of Venice:* a public place in Venice 173
A setting for *The Merchant of Venice:* a room in Portia's home
    at Belmont 174
A setting for *The Merchant of Venice:* a court of justice at
    Venice 176
A setting for *The Merchant of Venice:* Portia's garden . . 176
A setting for *Tom Pinch* 182
Another setting for *Tom Pinch* 185
A setting for *Lucky Pehr* 194
A scene from *Mr. Sampson* 205
A setting for Act I of *Tilly of Bloomsbury* 212
A scene from *Master Pierre Patelin* 220
A setting for *A Thanksgiving Exercise* 229
A scene from *The Servant in the House* 234
The Admirable Crichton, Act III 244
Cat costume for *The Woodman and the Goblins* . . . 253
A setting for the Prologue of *Androcles and the Lion* . . 266
A setting for Act I of *Androcles and the Lion* 288
A setting for the first scene of Act II of *Androcles and the Lion* 297
A setting for the second scene of Act II of *Androcles and the
    Lion* 312
A setting for *Lucky Pehr* 322
A setting for *Lucky Pehr:* the scene in the woods . . . 336
A setting for *Lucky Pehr:* the scene in the street . . . 344
A setting for *Lucky Pehr:* the scene at the seashore . . 364
A scene from *Twelfth Night* showing an apartment in the
    Duke's palace 374

PAGE

A setting for *Old Pipes and the Dryad* 379
A setting for *Twelfth Night* showing a room in Olivia's house 390
A scene from *Twelfth Night:* a street 398
A setting for *Twelfth Night* showing Olivia's garden . . . 406

LIST OF DIAGRAMS

PAGE

1. — Stage arrangement for *The Cat That Walked by Himself* 97
2. — Arrangement of the battens used in Act III of *The Admirable Crichton* 158
3. — Stage arrangement for *Master Pierre Patelin* . . . 161
4. — Curtain arrangement for *Twelfth Night* 177
5. — Light plot for *The Merchant of Venice*. Scene I: a public place 200
6. — Light plot for *The Merchant of Venice*. Scene VIII: Portia's garden 200
7. — Plot of the various places on the stage 274
8. — Stage arrangement for *The Magic Gifts*. Acts II, IV, and VI 275
9. — Stage arrangement for *The Magic Gifts*. Act I . . 275
10. — Stage arrangement for *The Magic Gifts*. Act III . 276
11. — Stage arrangement for *The Magic Gifts*. Act V . . 277
12. — Stage arrangement for Act I in a recent production of *The Magic Gifts* 279
13. — Stage arrangement for Acts II, IV, and VI in a recent production of *The Magic Gifts* 280
14. — Stage arrangement for Acts III and V in a recent production of *The Magic Gifts* 280
15. — Stage arrangement for *The Box of Pandora* . . . 323
16. — Stage arrangement for the Greek games 325
17. — Stage arrangement for a recent presentation of *The Box of Pandora* 326
18. — Stage arrangement for *Rip Van Winkle:* the scene in the village 349
19. — Stage arrangement for *Rip Van Winkle:* the scene in the mountains 350

INTRODUCTION

Expression is without doubt the most fundamental of all human powers, and of the various kinds of expression, dramatic expression is probably the earliest to appear. In its simplest form, dramatic expression is identical with language, and the first attempts at language both for the child and for the race were not logical nor freighted with information. They were rather revelations of the inner feelings and, so far as they were directed to communication, simply aroused similar states in others.

Language functioning in this way does not confine itself to words. Actions, looks, and other signs accompany the words and are sometimes more important than the sounds. And always the sound itself is the soul of the word and vibrates with feeling not because it is a noun or a verb or any part of speech, or because it has an abstract sound capable of being spelled or repeated with accuracy, but because it is something that is alive and part of the whole life of the person who speaks and of the person who hears. A word said at one moment is not the same as that word said at another moment, because the life has changed, the dramatic situation is different, and the expression as a whole is a new creation.

It would appear, then, that about the worst way to teach children to express themselves or to use language with force, beauty, clearness, or effect is to teach them grammar prematurely. Language is first of all a living art and not a logical mechanism. When logic uses language, it inserts itself into something already created and produces analysis and gives information, modifying the art of expression no doubt, stiffening it at times, but never able to cut itself loose from the art which is its foundation.

To teach children to express themselves, to make them able to seize their own feelings and images in all their intensity and with all their accompaniments of action, look, breath, and tone, and to interpret the feelings and images of others is fundamental to all further education whatsoever. Whether this is done with an emphasis on speech or whether the center is writing or painting or whatever other art, the medium chosen reveals itself as a kind of language and expresses the dramatic situation in which it comes to birth.

It is, therefore, not only a new thing in education which the authors of this charming and useful book have brought to pass, it is an old and everlasting thing in human nature. We neglect it at our peril, and much of the waste in our schools and in our society is due to the lack of this spiritual nourishment. The fine insight shown by the authors will help to warn us of many a pitfall and particularly of those so common ones where the teacher substitutes his own interpretations and his own way of expressing and doing things for the actual interpretations and actual creations of the children themselves.

The teacher often feels at a loss to know where to look for any criterion of excellence. In human relations, expression objectifies itself and naturally leads to communication. This is not a separate act; it is a necessary part of the expression and consists in the building up by other people of a responsive expression in their own minds. The reaction of this on the original expression acts as a criterion or guide — although by no means an exclusively determining criterion — of its value and effectiveness. It is the practice of the authors to have plays produced, first, of course, for

PREFACE

Behold the Child among his new-born blisses,
....
See, at his feet, some little plan or chart,
Some fragment from his dream of human life,
Shaped by himself with newly-learnèd art;
    A wedding or a festival,
    A mourning or a funeral;
      And this hath now his heart,
    And unto this he frames his song:
      Then will he fit his tongue
To dialogues of business, love, or strife;
    But it will not be long
    Ere this be thrown aside,
    And with new joy and pride
The little actor cons another part;
Filling from time to time his "humorous stage"
With all the Persons, down to palsied Age,
That Life brings with her in her equipage;
    As if his whole vocation
    Were endless imitation.

— WORDSWORTH.

The day is past when the dramatic impulse can be ignored
in any educational scheme. This impulse is present in every
human being, and, like every good tendency, it needs careful
nurture if it is to bud, blossom, and bear good fruit. There
can be little argument about the fact that the dramatic
impulse should be utilized in some vital way in education
and, by proper direction, made to do its part in developing
and cultivating bodily control, mental discipline, and social
consciousness. Thus it may help to lead the way to effici-

ency, æsthetic appreciation, and spiritual development. The fundamental importance of the correct educative use of the dramatic instinct can be appreciated only when we realize the significance of the child-actor's imaginative excursions into the world of reality and into the realm of fancy as he makes and acts his little dramas. These experiences leave indelible impressions on the child's mentality and constitute the core of his developing consciousness of self. Wordsworth expresses all this in a later part of the ode already quoted:

> The thought of our past years in me doth breed
> Perpetual benediction . . . .
>   . . . for *those first affections,*
>   *Those shadowy recollections,*
> Which, be they what they may,
>   Are yet *the fountain-light of all our day,*
> Are yet *a master-light of all our seeing.*

The purpose of this book is to discuss the principles and the pedagogy underlying the correct use of the dramatic impulse in the elementary and secondary schools. The plays included in this volume are given as illustrations of the play-making process and of its educative value, and not because of any superiority which they may or may not possess as plays.

During the past twenty years, the direct use of the dramatic impulse in the education of young people has made great advances. There is hardly a school in the land where children do not "give plays," and this in spite of the popularity of the moving picture, which provides a vicarious and frequently unprofitable means of gratifying the dramatic impulse. In most schools, dramatization and play-acting are carried on, whether properly directed or not. The play-acting is either in the form of a school play or in the more restricted form of dramatizations conducted by classes in connection with literature they study. Almost everywhere the emphasis is mainly upon the final performance rather than *upon the education that comes from making a play and from preparing the play for presentation.*

In this book, the authors hope to contribute some advice and help, born of years of practical experience, to those who are seriously considering the drama from the standpoint of the development of the child as he makes and acts the play, quite apart from any effect it may have upon the audience at the final performance. The authors desire to help to bring nearer the day when the child's first dramatic impressions and experiences — the "first affections," the "shadowy recollections," the "master-light of all our seeing" — shall be not haphazard and undirected but selected and educative; shall be not "what they *may*" but what they *should* be.

JOHN MERRILL
MARTHA FLEMING

PART I
THE DRAMATIC IMPULSE

Each man to himself and each woman to herself, is the word of the past and present, and the true word of immortality;
No one can acquire for another — not one,
Not one can grow for another — not one.
The song is to the singer, and comes back most to him,
The teaching is to the teacher, and comes back most to him,
The murder is to the murderer, and comes back most to him,
The theft is to the thief, and comes back most to him,
The love is to the lover, and comes back most to him,
The gift is to the giver, and comes back most to him — it cannot fail,
The oration is to the orator, the acting is to the actor and actress not to the audience,
And no man understands any greatness or goodness but his own, or the indication of his own.

— WALT WHITMAN, from *A Song of the Rolling Earth*.

PLAY–MAKING AND PLAYS

THE DRAMATIC IMPULSE AND ITS EDUCATIVE USE IN THE ELEMENTARY AND SECONDARY SCHOOL

CHAPTER I

UNIVERSALITY OF DRAMATIC IMPULSE AND EXPRESSION

IMPORTANCE OF DRAMATIC EXPRESSION

IN considering the dramatic impulse and its use in education, we must of necessity think first of the child himself, his needs and tastes, and then of the place of each subject and the office of each mode of expression in the development of that child and in the realization of all his possibilities. We must study the manifestations of the dramatic impulse from the kindergarten through the elementary grades, noting the steps by which the simple dramatic play of the younger child develops into the original drama of the high-school student, and we should look into the play-making and play-acting processes and their educative results.

Before we can discuss the dramatic impulse, however, we must know something of the drama of to-day, of its scope and function in modern life. In our complex life, the drama has established its claim and has become a tremendous force to be reckoned with by the sociologist, by the schools, and by the church. The latter no longer regards the theater as an outcast and actors as vagabonds, but looks upon them rather as great powers for good or evil and has joined hands with them as teachers of the ethics of life. Many schools have already seen that dramatic training is of fundamental use in education and of great value in giving mental, emotional, and physical discipline. Whether we admit it or not, the stage has become a great influence in the lives of the people and promises to be one of the dominating powers of our time. Never has the field of the drama been so wide, for on our stage almost every human problem and every phase of life are represented. Never, indeed, has the theater been so popular. The reason for this is that the theater answers man's universal demand to have his feelings moved, the monotony of his life broken up, and his nobler self started into action. The drama is, therefore, unescapably in the social life of the children and must be considered in their education.

Yet it is not upon the stage alone that dramatic expression plays its part; it is an important factor in the everyday life of each individual. Dramatic art is based initially on the fact that the inner life of the individual is revealed by words, tones of voice, facial expressions, bodily movements, and actions. The meaning of these signs each person is more or less skilled in reading. Indeed, all life is an incessant exercise of the dramatic faculty. We estimate the inner lives of one another by means of these outward expressions; by sympathetic, imaginative understanding we are able to imitate them and thus to put ourselves in another's place and in a measure to partake of his experiences. Imitation is the door through which the actor on the stage and in life enters into the inner lives of other persons, whether these persons be real or creations of the imagination. Whatever other function the dramatic impulse may have in the development of the individual, the beginnings of dramatic art seem bound up in the tendency to imitate, as exhibited in greater or less degree by all human beings and especially by children.

In all imitation, before we can have action, we must naturally have thought. Therefore, we can easily see that drama is fundamentally a mode of thinking based upon the power of each individual to enter into another personality. It presupposes the ability to put oneself in another's place and to see, to think, and to feel with that person. Its exercise, then, involves an estimate of values in the individuals about us and an instinctive recognition of their personalities and their rights.

Jesus, like every other illustrious leader of men, had the dramatic temperament — imaginative, emotional, sympathetic. Every great teacher of children has become a great teacher because he has had dramatic sympathy enough to put himself into the child's place. Pestalozzi, Froebel, Parker, such men as these could "live with little children," understand them, sympathize with them, love them, in imagination see life in the child's way, and thus know what is worth doing from the child's point of view.

THE DRAMATIC IMPULSE IN PRIMITIVE PEOPLES

The dramatic impulse clearly observed in primitive peoples and little children manifests itself in imitations, impersonations, dramatic plays, and dances. To-day it is difficult for us to realize what the dance meant to early peoples, because its modern representative has degenerated until it has lost its true significance. It was an expression of their most intense feelings, associated with some idea or event which to them had great meaning. With it they celebrated their great occasions, such as seedtime and harvest, victory in war, and compacts of peace. It was rhythmical and usually accompanied by singing, by speech, and by rude, wild gesture. The participants repeated over and over syllables, words, and phrases that they had heard, imitating tones and inflections of voice, and accompanying and illuminating all by gesture. Some were simply expressions of the love of movement — forms of gymnastics, full of the mere joy of being alive. Many of the primitive dances which still survive are mimetic like the Frog Dance, the Butterfly Dance, and the Kangaroo Dance of Australia. Eyre speaks of seeing this last so wonderfully done that it would have brought thunders of applause from a European audience.[1] Such expressions are a great delight to the performers themselves and often signify their sympathy with the universal joyousness of nature.

The primitive tribes have also given pantomimic representations of the great human passions — love, hate, jealousy — or illustrations of their ideas of life, death, and immortality. Love and battle, or conflict of some sort, are the two most important events in primitive human life, and so afford the two principal subjects of pantomimic dances. The motive in the dances which give representations of human passions seems to be the pleasure of expressing emotion or arousing it in others. These performances of primitive peoples are, of course, more purposeful and also more consciously and thoroughly organized as dramatic expression than is the child's dramatic activity; but both contain the same elements — action, gesture, tone-coloring, and speech. These are only a few of the many instances that may well lead us to believe that dramatic expression is instinctive in the human soul and that it is the common property of the human race.

[1] Grosse, *Beginnings of Art.*

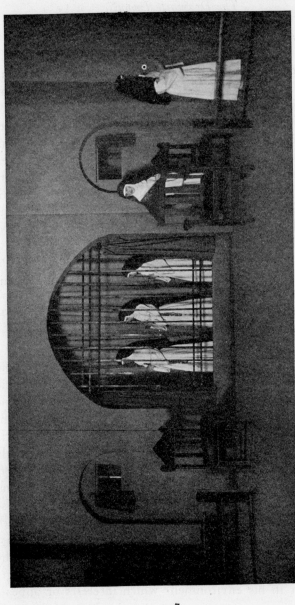

The second scene of *The Cradle Song* was quickly made ready. (See frontispiece.) A grille was placed in the large arch; windows were fixed in the two smaller arches; and a gray curtain was drawn to hide the blue cyclorama and to serve as a background for the small inner room.

THE DRAMATIC IMPULSE IN CHILDREN

In the case of the child, the dramatic impulse appears very early. During the first year and a half or two years of his existence, he is learning to control his body; he is absorbed in learning its uses and in ascertaining something of the coördination of its movements. He reaches and stretches, pushes and pulls; and these seemingly aimless activities are executed with great zeal. His sense of gratification is probably due to his feeling of his own power and to his consciousness of himself as the cause of the various motions of his limbs and body. In these lower stages of culture (in both the primitive peoples and the primitive individual — the child) the desire to copy seems irresistible. During his second year the child often begins to imitate and pantomime — that is, to use his body as a medium of expression. At this stage he has only partly mastered the technicalities of speech, and therefore he resorts frequently to pantomime, because it is easier for him.

These various imitations, reflex, spontaneous, unconscious, purposeful, associated, and dramatic, so overlap and combine that it is difficult to say where one leaves off and another begins. Broadly speaking, reflex imitations are the responses made to some movement or sound to which there is a physiological tendency to respond. We yawn, we laugh, we cry, without volition of our own, simply because others do these things in our presence. Purposeful imitations are made in order to get the mental experience which gives rise to the act. They are nearly exact reproductions of the act observed, and by means of them the child gains a vast amount of knowledge, many subjective experiences, and the power of performing a large variety of actions. He selects this or that in his environment which interests or appeals to him and, by employing one or more of these various imitations, gets the mental experience associated with the object of his interest. Thus he studies and experiments with material, gets at the secrets of his world, and develops his own intellectual, physical, and emotional power. The following incident will serve as an illustration of a child's study and expression:

One evening as the family of little Marjorie, who was about four years old, was entertaining guests in the front of the house, from somewhere in the back came groans and moans of agonizing pain. Everybody rushed out to see what was the matter and Marjorie was found slowly and apparently painfully climbing up the back stairway.

"Aunt Jessie goes upstairs just this way, and now I know how she feels," announced Marjorie.

Aunt Jessie was a suffering rheumatic, and her niece by assuming the actual physical actions of Aunt Jessie was experiencing in a degree her aunt's inward state.

In the child's thought, dramatic imitation is largely taken up with the idea of an action; his attention is centered upon the conception of which the act is an expression, rather than upon the outward similarities between this conception and the act. Indeed, he often invents new forms for the expression of the original idea, and many times uses symbols and make-believe objects. So a chair may in turn become a horse, a soldier, or a bridge. Such procedure is the distinctive characteristic of the little child's play and may be ranked as his most dramatic. A solitary child will use thimbles, spools, clothespins — almost any object — and pretend that they are people. He makes the inanimate objects act, and he feels keenly the situations and emotions of each. They are as effective for his purposes as the realities which they represent. We may see then that the child is constantly "reading back" from the signs put forth by those about him to the idea symbolized. He enlarges on this idea, puts his own personality into it, and then expresses it in his own way, thus creating a new idea and a new form of expression — both educative acts. In this way he gets at the essentials of every process in his environment which appeals to him. From the dramatic standpoint particularly, purposeful and dramatic imitations stand out as pre-eminently important.

Memories of what one did as a child, or why one did it, are brittle things upon which to lean for scientific information, but for what the testimony might be worth, a class of teachers was asked to write down their recollections of the dramatic plays of their childhood and also any observations they had made on the plays of other children. A few of these are here noted:

Philip was very often an engine, and when this was the case, he made the noises of the whistle and the bell. Again he was either one or both of these; and at the same time the whole engine. Sometimes he was the entire train and at the same time the brakeman calling the names of the stations.[1]

My brother and I used to play that we were wild animals. Our cave was under the table, or sometimes it was made of chairs turned sideways. Often one of us would be a hunter and shoot a bear. The other played the part of the bear. Then the animal would be carved and eaten, and immediately thereafter would return to life, to become another bear. Sometimes we were lions and sometimes wolves.

A little three-year-old girl once said to me: "Now you be Mama and I'll be Papa, and I'll go to town while you stay home and get dinner." She then proceeded to hitch up a chair for a horse,

---

[1] Read Mark Twain's *The Adventures of Tom Sawyer*, Chapter II.

and a very unmanageable one it proved to be, judging from her efforts to keep it under control. After some moments I made a remark to her, to which she answered indignantly, "Don't talk to me! Don't you know that I'm four or five miles away — almost up to Ottawa!"

Most of the stories told me were Bible stories, and I had a feeling that they were a thing apart from everyday life. I never hesitated, however, to play church and Sunday school and once added the Lord's Supper to my church service, being in turn minister and congregation. This last innovation seemed a great success to me, but those in parental authority forbade a repetition under severe penalty.

I do not remember dramatizing before I was old enough to read for myself. Then we read stories for the sole purpose of acting them out. We never played if anyone could see us or hear us — we were rather afraid that someone would make fun of us. From the age of ten to fourteen, we played whenever we could go to some part of the house where we should not have an audience. We often performed the same thing over and over for three or four hours at a time, and every day at that. Our favorites were *The Swiss Family Robinson*, the *Elsie* books, and stories of girls with high-sounding names who went to boarding schools and got into all kinds of mischief.[1] We were apt to be five different characters in a single hour. When we studied our real school lessons, we pretended we were girls at boarding school. I shall always remember the intense pleasure we derived from these impersonations. I often wondered whether other children played in this way and was surprised when I first learned that it was natural for all.

This passion of the child for acting out, by means of his own body, phases of life that he observes, and adding to

---

[1] It seems a pity that these children had not been introduced to great world literature, so that they would not have been forced to resort to the mediocre stories which comprised their literary equipment.

these his own interpretations and contributions, is one of the deepest-seated emotions in the human soul. He will add to his rendition new and individual touches and even new situations and conditions; he will stretch his own personality to include other lives; and living in an assumed character for days at a time, he will take on the actions, voice, and speech of another, and so appropriate to himself another self. A three-year-old child assumed for three days a personality to which she gave the name "Rosebud," and would not answer to any other name, except to say, "I'm not Jean; I'm Rosebud!" Professor James has noted this same tendency:

For a few months in one of my own children's third year, he literally hardly ever appeared in his own person; it was always "Play I am so-and-so, and you are so-and-so, and the chair is such a thing, and we will do this or that." If you called him by his name H——, you invariably got the reply, "I am not H——, I am a hyena" (or a horse-car, or whatever the feigned object might be).

Wordsworth likewise has shown a profound understanding of child psychology when he wrote the lines quoted in the foreword of this volume:

> As if his whole vocation
> Were endless imitation.

Thus the entire social life of his community is material for the little actor's appropriation, and he will reproduce the life about him with startling accuracy. Often with uncanny truthfulness he shames his elders by seeing through the signs they put forth into their hearts and spirits. "The child does not hear what you say, he sees what you do."

Dramatic Play is the Child's Mode of Study

Each small individual then takes hold of whatever in his own environment most appeals to his capacities and to his tastes; he studies it by means of his imitations and dramatic plays, and thus experiments with his materials and gets at the secrets of his own world. His educability seems somehow bound up with this propensity and ability to imitate, to adopt the actions or feelings of whatever attracts him in his surroundings, to do the things he sees others do, and so learn to think and feel and act as does the society into which he is born. All this "playing" is, then, the little child's mode of study; it is based on the imaginative reconstruction of how the people around him are thinking and feeling. He is interested in people and what they do; he can think, at this age, only in personal terms, so that human life, human interests, and human actions are for him the core of an educative curriculum. Therefore, this study of the life about him gives the child wide and varied experiences; it leads to a great number and variety of physical actions; and, consequently, it makes towards adaptability and plasticity — qualities which were never more worth cultivating than at the present time. Thus we may assert that the habits resulting from the intensity of this dramatic impulse react to determine the emotional life of the person.

Now psychologists agree that conscious dramatic play begins about the age of three and is at its height at about the age of seven. The educational problem is not, then, the introduction of the dramatic into the schools — for wherever there is a child, there are dramatic doings — but it is, rather, to get hold of the tendency in some vital, well-organized way, to direct it to something ahead, and to make it a source of mental discipline, bodily control, social consciousness, efficiency, and artistic pleasure. Noting the universality of this instinct and observing also the widespread love and delight of old and young in histrionic performances, it is evident that this most spontaneous, deeply-rooted, usable mode of study and expression cannot be ignored in education, and that to overlook it is a tremendous waste of power. Indeed, so fully is this fact realized to-day that there are few educational schemes that do not at least claim to recognize the dramatic in some form or other as a means of training as well as a factor of the modern school curriculum.

This discussion has gone as fully as the compass of the book permits into the psychology and pedagogy of dramatic expression, in order to make clear that play-making is one of the most highly developed forms of child expression, and to emphasize the fact that through the exercise and the training of this faculty, the child realizes himself and develops his consciousness and efficiency to the highest power. From the previous pages it will be seen that in its very nature dramatization by the children is not only a perfect embodiment of the project method, but that the play is an ideal project in which the motive is constantly present as the task progresses and in which the motive cannot in any way be separated from the task at hand.

The "project method" is much more than a method: it is a principle of living, and can perhaps be defined from one avenue of approach as *working for a purpose that is consciously appreciated and held as an ideal by the individual himself*. The project method, then, must necessarily be part of the educative process if the latter is life and if the schools are to be related to life. Therefore, no form of education should be neglected that involves this mode of procedure so fully as does play-making. Now the development of purposeful action and initiative in the individual is education's most significant function. This function play-making fulfills, because in it purpose and initiative are bound to be constantly stimulated and developed, for the process always begins with an idea, which develops into an ideal. This in turn calls forth constant purpose in action and initiative in working out ways of expressing the idea.

Play-making, furthermore, is essentially a socialized project, yet one in which individual motives necessarily operate at the same time and in perfect harmony with the social. Thus it reproduces perfectly the complex that obtains in the activities of real life. Herein it differs from the proposition ordinarily assigned; for in classes where each individual initiates his own task, there is no common bond to unify the whole, and any attempt at coöperation is forced or extraneous. Play-making, on the other hand, because of its very nature meets all requirements.

CHAPTER II

DRAMATIC WORK OF LITTLE CHILDREN

If we consider dramatic work throughout the school as a unit, its discussion will necessitate a long look ahead for kindergarten and primary teachers and a long look in both directions for teachers of the higher grades. Thus only, however, can we get the perspective which reveals the significance, distinction, place, and educative value of children's plays, and we shall, therefore, watch the play-making process from the first year of school through its development into the highly organized drama of the high school and of the art theaters. This comprehensive, unified view of the various stages of dramatic development will certainly bring to us a sense of the fitness of little children's demands for play-making and play-acting. The whole history of literary development gives dignity and significance to children's delight in repetitions of rhymes, jingles, poems, and stories, and in dramatic performances. Out of such crude beginnings have grown all great poetry, story, and drama. These activities of boys and girls are not to be regarded as ends in themselves, but as the germinating seed of a fruit that is to be borne — the child's developing appreciation.

Little children act solely to gratify the dramatic impulse. There is no preparation to interfere with their delight in the acting; the story is told to them, and then they play it. The speeches, if there are any, are spontaneous, short, and to the point. There is no learning of lines; the situations themselves are the great stimuli to fitting language. The child lives the story, his very naturalness makes him free in pantomime and in language, when he needs it; but his words rarely become fixed. Both action and speeches change at

The second grade presented their own dramatization of *The Hillman and the Housewife* at a Halloween party. The audience was seated along three sides of the room. The children acted their play within the hollow square. The selfish housewife's home was in front of the stage; the steps leading to the stage were the rocky hillside where the hillmen lived. Two chairs represented a fireplace and chimney; two bowls served as properties. Costumes were permitted because of the importance of the occasion. There was no artificial illumination. The stage was decorated for the party and not especially as a background for the play.

every playing, if the child is constantly thinking and creating. This is an ideal condition, for too much talk will spoil any dramatic presentation.

In the upper second grade and in the third grade, however, the plays the children make begin to take on written form. At this age they are able to read for themselves some of the literature which they propose to dramatize, and they enjoy doing so. Moreover, they like to see their speeches in black and white, so that both they and others may have the pleasure and profit of reading them. The stories dramatized become longer and more complex and the personal contributions of the children more important, because their inclination and ability to use speech in their plays have increased.

In the fifth and sixth grades, or at about that time, children begin to appreciate character and its significance in social life. They have, moreover, acquired a better idea of plot and a better control of language. Therefore, they sense quickly the purpose of the story or play and appreciate the logic or the order and arrangement of the incidents that tell the story. So most children at this period begin to make an imperative demand for well-organized, well-written stories and plays, especially if they have been constantly in touch, from the kindergarten up, with good literature.

As an illustration of this point, an actual conversation overheard between a boy and a girl may be cited. They were planning to write a story, and the conversation drifted to a comparison of *Treasure Island* with one of the Henty books. The listener felt that much had been accomplished when the boy said, "There is a reason for the wild happenings in *Treasure Island*, but the other book is a jumble of things and situations — there is no plot. I mean to have a plot in my story." He had evidently recognized, even if unconsciously, the orderly and artistic construction of Stevenson's tale and would be satisfied with nothing which fell below the standard his awakening critical faculty had set him.

CHAPTER III

STORIES SUITABLE FOR CHILDREN'S PLAYS

THERE are, of course, no literary plays for primary children, so we must be content to give them literature in story form and let them make their own plays. At this period they enjoy stories and are quick to see whatever dramatic possibilities they contain. The tale out of which a play is to be fashioned must of course be actable. Some of the most childlike folk stories cannot be presented, or are difficult to act out, even with regular theater appliances. Such is *Beauty and the Beast*, because of its complexity and the abundant use of magic in the action of the story. The same is true of *Cinderella*, in the Grimm version; therefore the story is better told than acted. The suitable narrative must have a simple plot with one thread of interest which reaches a climax and has a happy outcome. It should fit the children's degree of experience and it should gain by dramatization. In it there must be no confusion between right and wrong, in the sense in which the children understand these terms; there must be no subtlety of character and not much development of character — just good people and bad people in clash and struggle. And the former, who have the sympathy of the children, must always come out ahead. Here life and all its affairs must be conducted justly, honorably, and beautifully; for a vivid, lasting impression is made upon the child by what he acts out and also by the literature that he studies closely in making his play.

The acting of stories constructed along lines as severe as those the drama demands gives to the children a feeling for the technique of the drama as well as for the story. The presentation of these stories is really thinking them, seeing the characters move in a certain environment under certain conditions and limitations. To be of use the child's story must be the work of a craftsman; it must be shaped and woven together with skill; it must be clear-cut and short, as well as interesting from beginning to end. Its art then is closely akin to that of the drama. In both there is one predominating incident, one preëminent character, and much compression of material. A run of incidents in the order in which they occur does not make a literary story. There must be a set purpose; and from the beginning the material and incidents must be such as will make this clear. The selecting and planning, and the skillful arrangement and interweaving of details for this definite purpose give a story or play a pattern, called *plot*. The plot excludes all nonessentials and concentrates upon that which is absolutely necessary for the working out of the problem set up. A story or drama should leave, therefore, one direct impression. This unity is as necessary to a child's story or play as it is to a composition for mature minds. Andersen's story, *The Ugly Duckling*, is a beautiful illustration of the principles here set forth and an excellent story for use in the sixth grade. Its symbolism makes it particularly suitable material for these older children.

To accomplish this result, the child's story and drama must conform to the technique of the best short stories and the best literary dramas — it must have a beginning, a middle, and an end.

The beginning of any well-constructed story or play states definitely and clearly the situation, presents the characters, introduces the conflicting force, defines the difficulties, and sets forth the real problem so sharply that it cannot be misunderstood. The beginning, or exposition, shows the causes of things that are going to happen in the story or play. Next follows the logical and progressive development growing out of the premises stated in the exposition. The rising action culminates in an inevitable crisis. The descending action begins as soon as the resolving force begins to act. The end is a conclusion, or dénouement, that leaves the audience satisfied with the outcome.

The child's literature and his play should present such phases of life and such experiences as are right and proper for him at the time. For example, one would not offer children of the primary grades the problem of Ibsen's *Doll's House*, or that of Shakespeare's *King Lear*, but they may be asked to follow the fortunes of the wondering, investigating youngest brother in the old story of *Boots and His Brothers*, where nothing is needed but the tale itself to show the final reward of a tireless search into the causes of things and the inevitable penalty of a selfish, shiftless love of ease. Here are set up an ideal of persistent endeavor and a philosophy of life entirely possible of realization in the actual world. To study this story, make a play of it, and act it, is an education in ethics. Indeed some such narrative is the only concrete way of approaching this subject. Children cannot grasp truth when it is merely stated as such.

Therefore, the atmosphere and the hero of the play must be above moral reproach, or else there is an offense to taste, which destroys unity. The child has a very keen feeling of right and wrong and he has an absolute and abiding faith in the final winning out of righteousness. To be sure, he will not concern himself deeply with the finer details of the two; but for the large and elemental virtues and vices — the

essential things in character — for truth, honor, justice, fair
play, and loyalty, he has an unerring sense. In his play
then, lying, disloyalty, unfairness, or coarseness should never
be successful in the end. Naturally, children want a happy
ending to their stories and certainly to their plays. Indeed,
the conventional fairy-story ending "and they lived happily
ever afterwards" is preferred by many grown-up people as
well as by the children. Poetic justice is a child's ideal;
it is the only kind of justice that exists for him, and therefore in his story the good should be rewarded and the evil
punished. If there must be a disastrous ending, it should
be well prepared for, so that it is felt to be necessary and is
realized to be the only conclusion possible under the circumstances. For example, in Grimm's *The Cat and the Mouse
in Partnership*, children know that a mouse foolish enough
to set up housekeeping with her hereditary enemy is bound
to come to some extremely bad end.

Children have a great love of the marvelous. They
believe in enchanted woods; they make terms with the
spirits of the earth and air and water, and "exchange civilities
with the unseen world." The fairies are to them, as
Mr. Yeats says, "only little stitches that join this world
to the world beyond." But the wonderful and the supernatural may be overdone with children. These elements
must be used with economy and discretion, and to be effective and harmonious they must be called in at the supreme
moment, when they alone can turn the tide. The good fairy
in *The Sleeping Beauty* steps in at just the right moment to
change death to the sleep of a hundred years. The fairy
godmother in *Cinderella* comes in when there is no other help
for the lonely, suffering little maiden.

The presence, of course, of too much of the magical elim-
inates many stories from the play-making list, because of

A scene from *A Midsummer-Night's Dream.*

the obvious difficulty of representing the supernatural on the stage, even with the best stage appliances, and also because a child who lives too much in an imaginative world of unearthly beings and events loses his capacity for the thrill which mysterious unknown powers give. Too much of the magical creates an undue excitement, strains nerves, and wastes energy.

In dealing with blood in children's stories and plays, it must be remembered that these little people have not had the experiences which make violence and death the terrible things that they are to older persons. The sight of gore does not "take hold" of the average child. Because he cannot imagine the tragic results of cutting off heads, it seems to him simply an artistic way of getting rid of extremely undesirable, troublesome, and wicked people who undeniably deserve expeditious elimination. Furthermore, if a happy ending demands it, in the children's world of poetic justice heads grow on again. Yet like everything else that goes with a good story, blood, when it appears, must be an intrinsic necessity of the circumstances; otherwise, the unity of the story's design is destroyed. Also, a very sound purpose may sometimes be served by the introduction of the terrible into children's stories. Not infrequently it happens that a vicarious experience of fear, say like *Little Red Riding Hood's* [1] in her encounter with the wolf, may take the place in a measure of a real apprehension and is easily overcome without the dire results of reality. Indeed that elusive something which man has never been able to explain about the pleasure of tragic literature with its perpetual appeal to the heart and to the intelligence suggests that in some way the children's intuitive delight in terror and blood is in the

[1] It is taken for granted that the folk version of *Little Red Riding Hood* is used. Here the Grandmother is discovered safe and sound inside the wolf.

order of nature and must work both ethically and artistically toward the cleansing, beautifying, and fortifying of the individual life.

Not in its turn to be ignored is the humorous. Many of the old folk tales have in them this element. Nonsense is a natural product of the mind, a sort of mental play. Thus a comic story like *Hans in Luck* has a place in the children's training. There was no sense, no logic, in the exchanges Hans made, so they are incongruous and therefore comic. The story builds up a sense of the relation and agreement of things, by showing us the nonsense of disagreement and lack of relation. It helps also to show harmony and relevancy, and so promotes organization of a concordant mental world.

Observation of work through the grades and the attitude of people toward literature in later life would seem to prove that literary taste is either made or marred in the elementary school. Therefore it is plainly of supreme importance that the literature selected for study and for play-making should be of the finest quality, that during this period the children, from the kindergarten up, should come in touch with world literature, not only to establish a literary taste, but to collect therefrom a mass of beautiful poems and stories upon which to draw for future pleasure and inspiration.

CHAPTER IV

DRAMATIC WORK OF THE JUNIOR HIGH SCHOOL

BY the time boys and girls reach junior high school, they are moving out of the realm of childhood into the more complex occurrences of the world, and they are beginning to look outside themselves. Now society begins to make its first claims upon them, for "it is the time of new talk." Religion also exerts a mysterious call; civic life becomes full of interest; college or their own calling in life is looming up. In other words, there has developed a new attitude towards their environment, with its fresh, absorbing interests. Yet this period is also one of much perplexity and doubt. In this uncertainty the acting of a part in a drama may intelligently transform the new and puzzling thoughts into beauty of sentiment. It may provide a healthy, sane outlet for emotion, and thus bring intense feelings under the control of the intellect and will, through the release of these feelings in speech and action. Expression of thought and feeling deepens and intensifies impressions. It exorcises such demons as anger and hate and brings sanity and peace in their place. Denied expression, these sensations will spend force blindly in some abnormal way at the expense of the individual.

This is the time, then, to introduce young people to the literary drama, because it is the most complete art representation of social life, and because the problems, characters, and situations it presents are those that satisfy these new interests. Children at this age are vitally concerned in every phase of life, and the drama with its complex human

26

society gives them the freedom of the world. It brings out the real meaning of a bit of life or literature, gets to the kernel of human experience and gives it out in a form most appealing to boys and girls. In the play, actions are traced back to motives and are seen in the light of cause and effect; we know *what* happens and *why* it happens. Character is revealed in the light of completed action, and the insistence and fatality of dispositions become manifest. At this period, the play is a most subtle means of teaching morality and ethics, not only by implication, but by actual presentation of the abstract values involved in the most concrete and vital form. Thus it gives a chance for perspective, a rare thing in real life. Such study leads to a better understanding of the ethical forces at work among us than the individual can get from his own environment. At this time, art expression of some kind is an absolute necessity because it affords a beneficent cleansing and freeing of the mind. Now tragedy makes its first great appeal. Comedy, which requires finer intellectual perceptions and more knowledge of life and people, is not so attractive, since children cannot understand the fine discriminations and subtleties involved in the perception of the incongruities which make this latter form.

In this respect, they are like young writers. In an address delivered in Chicago, Lady Gregory, speaking of the Irish Players and commenting on the difficulties encountered by youthful aspirants and actors in composing and producing comedies, remarked that she, herself, would plan to write a merry piece only to find her characters taking matters into their own hands and developing a most doleful situation. Such observations rather point to tragedy as most valuable in the dramatic training of the upper grades.

About the time they enter the eighth grade, the children are becoming too critical to be completely satisfied with their own productions. As a rule, they want better English than they can write and better art than they can originate.

This, therefore, is the time to take up the study of the literary plays and, in particular, the intense study of one Shakespearian drama. Still, if the children's dramatic training has been continual, the chances are that they will not only wish to act plays, but will occasionally write plays which show marked creative power. In their study of both literature and history, they will often want to utilize dramatization, if only of little scenes such as the one in *Ivanhoe* where the castle is attacked and Rebecca, as she watches the fight, reports it to Ivanhoe. This will be especially true if the boys and girls have approached their English literature in the dramatic spirit, if they continue to study literary drama, to receive dramatic training, and to have the privilege of acting occasionally. At this time a teacher may perhaps have the joy of discovering an artist whose gift is for the world.

It must be evident that there is an abundance of literary material for play-making. Indeed so rich is the field that the danger lies in paying too much attention to it and neglecting the other modes of expression, which should be given increasingly more attention.

Play-making itself is a form of composition, the elements of which can be taught. It affords an opportunity for originality and for getting that mastery over material which comes with creative power and is the first step in the appreciation of any art. A playwright must have the most intimate knowledge of all that concerns his idea; he must have the power of selecting from all the matter gathered that which serves his purpose, and he must have the discrimination and courage to reject everything else. Therefore, from the first he must have the power of seeing the play as a whole and of knowing how to relate the parts to that whole. Principles of dramatic construction are learned only by actually fitting the play to the necessities of the time and the space in which it is to be given. The teacher at this stage of the students' development should hold them definitely to drama form; for left to themselves they may lose the natural order and fail to secure a definite point. Looseness of structure and lack of organization result from looseness of thinking and show that there has not been the concentration of thought required in the construction of any play. There is also a tendency on the part of the children to multiply scenes until the shifting and changing takes up more time than the acting, and the frequent curtains, with waits between the scenes, cause confusion to both producer and audience. Here, then, the teacher may step in with questions, suggestions, and criticisms which lead to the discovery of the impracticability and even the ridiculousness of some of their plans, and which help to mold the play into a restrained form fitted to the subject and to limited conditions. In this way, school dramatics may teach the beginnings of dramatic analysis. Expression is disciplined by technique, and the teacher should be as free here to aid as she is in other subjects.

The subsequent play must, of course, satisfy the requirements of the common sentiment of the audience, as well as those of art. It must correspond to ideas of life held by the audience. Thus, the popular play merely makes concrete the estimate of some phase of life into which a large number of people can enter, because the individual or the audience can understand only that which is related to his own experiences or knowledge.

> No man understands any greatness or goodness
> But his own or the indications of his own.

CHAPTER V

THE USE OF THE DRAMATIC IMPULSE IN THE SENIOR HIGH SCHOOL

THE farther one advances in elementary and secondary schools, the more practical the work becomes. Emphasis is laid more and more upon the cultivation of the intellect, with an ever increasing stress upon the utilitarian side of life. Less and less cognizance is taken of the æsthetic, emotional, and spiritual nature of the individual. Thus, with material needs and desires urging their claims everywhere, there is little fear that educators will fail to strive to equip young people physically and mentally to meet the demands made by the economic world. The great danger is that they will neglect the more vital needs of life by their failure to look beyond the present to the development of the real individual.

Literature, because of its very nature and scope, is, when wisely chosen and presented at the right time and in the right manner, one of the great factors in the larger education of man — true education that deals with the things which count because they are built on the rock, Truth, and so endure. If one's acquaintance with literature is to be worthwhile, his study of it must be dramatic in spirit and he must be moved to give some expression to the thought received, for the effort to make others see and feel truth and beauty enhances one's own perception of them. The urge of the author's thought and feeling was so potent that it naturally demanded and found an outlet. If the reader really appreciates the true message of the literature, he too will wish to react to his feelings, and unless there is some adequate expression, the impression is weak and transitory. I do not mean to suggest that every piece of literature should be dramatized, or that every drama is to be acted; but I do mean to say that imaginative literature should be approached in a dramatic frame of mind, and that it should be given vocal expression. Every impression, to become permanent and valuable, must have a motor expression.

Legitimate dramatic expression, in the high school as in the grades, is indissolubly connected with the study of literature and is the natural outgrowth of this study. Too frequently this subject has been taught as if its main purpose were training in English or philology, or to get over the ground necessary to meet college requirements. I once heard Dr. Richard G. Moulton say to a class of university students: "In most subjects, all you need is facts. Facts are the most barren things in literature. The emotional nature must be aroused or you are outside literature. The soul must be stirred to love or to hate."

The first step is to abandon the purely academic method of study that has so long been applied to the few literary plays that have been considered in the high schools. Dramas are written to be acted and can no more be realized fully without production than pages of printed musical symbols can be enjoyed thoroughly until they are given expression through some musical medium. The drama, to be truly understood and appreciated, must be studied as one studies drawing or chemistry — by the laboratory method. As one comes to appreciate the laws of perspective through his own attempts to execute a drawing, and as through actual performance of chemical experiments one comprehends the science of chemical action, so one can best acquire dramatic appreciation by participation in the actual making of a play, by dramatizing some part of a great piece of literature, and by producing some play of worth. The drama is an objective form of art and must be studied as such. It is as easy to understand drama without conceiving and portraying a character, or designing a costume, or striving to evolve a suitable setting as it is to learn to cook solely through the study of the rules for cooking.

Quality Street: the scene in the tent.

In all this there is no desire to make actors or play producers of the students of the secondary schools, any more than there is any desire on the part of the instructors in the manual-training shop to make carpenters of those who learn the significance of tools and their use through first-hand experience. The aim is the development of a genuine love for the fine art of the drama. The laboratory method of teaching is essential to the development of a real appreciation; this depends upon understanding, which, in turn, grows out of intimate acquaintanceship.

It is not necessary or advisable, with the needs and purposes of the secondary schools in mind, actually to produce any number of plays. The great object is to learn the significance of drama through the only medium by which this

This setting for *The Will* was inexpensive but effective. The background was formed of gray flannel hung from an arc of iron piping. The effect of a fireplace was secured by the use of andirons and the red glow of the fire (see left of the picture).

knowledge can be gained; that is, through the actual preparation of a real drama. The play need not be a long one, but it must be one that has artistic merit. There can and should be much pleasurable acting, before the class, of scenes and short plays done without special costumes or setting; but the full and real value of the study is lost unless there is in the school experience of every high-school student at least one play prepared as carefully as young people are capable of doing, and presented with beautiful settings, wisely chosen properties, harmonious costumes, and adequate lighting. The play may be done before the entire school with distinct profit to all. And where there is the desire frequently expressed to do the play for more people, this natural longing should at the appropriate time have its gratification.

It is a great mistake, and one productive of many evils, to allow the players to charge an admission fee. Why should the dramatic department need public financing any more than does the mathematics department? The purpose of the school is not a commercial one, and the studies pursued are certainly of sufficient merit to make their maintenance worthy of the school.

One of the great reasons for the failure of the schools to realize the educative value of drama study lies in the fact that dramatic training has been reserved for those who seem to have a special gift for it. This is contrary to the purpose of elementary and secondary education, which is to give every child a general education, universal in aim and in spirit, in order that he may the better understand life, secure a fuller development, and have sufficient background to know in what subject he can best specialize when he takes up the work of the university or of life. Indeed, for his fullest development and enjoyment, every high-school student should have the advantage of a course in drama given by some one who has a real appreciation of the drama in all its aspects and phases.

CHAPTER VI

THE QUALIFICATIONS AND TRAINING OF THE TEACHER OF DRAMA

WHO then is to be placed in charge of school dramatics? To do ideal work, a person must be highly gifted and highly trained and must be selected, as music and art instructors are chosen, because of special gifts and special training. First, the teacher of dramatics must be a real teacher; and such an individual is difficult to define and even more difficult to find. Perhaps the most reliable means of judging the teacher's natural power is by expert personal observations of his actual functioning with the children. In this way, intangible and almost indefinable personal qualities may be seen, heard, and appreciated.

No matter how much natural teaching power a person may possess, and no matter what his education may be, he should have had some general teaching experience as a preparation for this highly specialized form of teaching. In this way, he will have a practical knowledge of children, of the other subjects of the curriculum, of modes of expression other than the dramatic, and the place of his own subject in the general educational scheme. His general education should be broad, thorough, and in accordance with the most advanced thinking, and he should have an accurate, up-to-date working knowledge of psychology — especially applied psychology, for this is his starting point and it enables him to make full use of himself and his own methods. He should be also a student of advanced ideals of education and he should be familiar with the most modern methods of teaching.

His personal technical preparation should be a training in voice, speech, carriage, and gesture, with special attention paid to harmonious coördination, to grace — which means economy of energy and ease in movement — and to genuineness in expressing thought and feeling. Children are quick to feel insincerity or falseness of any kind, and to react to them. Body, voice, and speech are the mediums of dramatic expression, and self-consciousness seems to creep more easily into these than into painting, modeling, or making, where the medium is non-personal. The primary reason, then, for demanding teachers who have trained, musical voices, who speak pure English, and whose bodily movements are harmonious is that the children will consciously imitate and adopt these forms of expression for their own.

It is a well-known fact that teachers as a class are not marked by distinction of speech or musical qualities of voice. Hamilton Mabie once said in a lecture that he had had to flee from many schoolrooms to rest his ears and his soul from the terrible voices that he heard there. He wondered what moral effect these had, and how children hearing them could remain good-natured. They do *not* — always. The power of the voice and its tones, intonations, and inflections cannot be overestimated in considering the qualifications and training desirable for the teacher of dramatics — in fact for any teacher. One may be accurate and clean-cut in speech, yet dull and prosaic. Reading may be perfectly clear but lack that final grace which, as the product of dramatic sympathy and trained voice and speech, makes music to the ear.

As a means of gaining this grace and artistic effectiveness, no better method can be recommended than sympathetic oral reading of imaginative literature. Such expression cultivates in the reader, as well as in the hearers, a subtlety of hearing that will soon demand and create new effects in speech. If training along such lines were more emphasized, we might begin to notice our own and one another's voices, until in the end poetry and rhythm might come nearer to common life. It is an artist-teacher we want, not an elocutionist.

Of course the teacher should have sufficient dramatic ability to enable him to act with the children and thus teach acting by acting, and he should also be able to criticize constructively. He should possess dramatic sympathy and imagination, qualities which do not always accompany ability to act. So important are the foregoing qualifications that it may be truthfully said that it would be far better to have no teacher of dramatics in the school than to have one who does not understand the dramatic impulse and has not the intellectual and emotional endowments which will enable him to guide and train it. Indeed, it must always be remembered that a teacher endowed with the basic qualities, even though poorly trained, may make a better instructor than one poor in the appropriate natural gifts, no matter how well prepared the latter may be. Play-making and acting are each an art, and to teach them demands even more skill than does the teaching of most other subjects.

If a teacher is deficient in emotional power, or if he undervalues feeling and does not see its direct relation to thought and, therefore, keeps back its expression, the children will soon learn to think that feeling should be concealed, and habits of inhibition will be initiated and established, with all the evil consequences that follow repression of normal and legitimate emotion. The danger of a teacher of this sort will be appreciated when we remember that the child reflects not only what we *are*, but also what we *idealize;* and he

A setting for *A Night at an Inn*. The screens forming the walls of the room were of natural-tone burlap; the curtains were of maroon velours. Beyond the window was the deep blue of the sky. The major light came from without the window. As the play progressed the light waned, and when the jade idol entered the only illumination on the stage came from the fire on the hearth and from the one candle on the table; pale moonlight streamed in through the window.

judges us from his conscious or unconscious observations of our conduct and from his interpretations of our expression. Thus an unexpressive teacher brings about pupils with ideals of repression as part of their standards of conduct, so that the inhibitive process goes on from bad to worse, and the individual is rarely himself. With his own self subdued, he exists in bondage to the will of another, does not live in the light of liberty, and knows nothing of the joys of freedom. Unrestrained action is almost beyond his comprehension. What kind of a citizen will a child so environed by fear and external force grow to be? The teacher must be chosen because of what he is himself and what he will allow the children to do and to become.

A sense of humor will help a teacher over many a rough place. Teaching dramatic reading and acting, play-making and play-staging — all this is hard work, and without the gift of humor, the instructor will some day be overcome by the irritability of fatigue. For the sake of the health of his own body and the preservation of his own soul, he must be keenly alive to incongruities, be able to laugh and help the children to laugh with him, and so consciously train them to a delicate and discriminative appreciation of wit, humor, and comedy. It is obvious that a sense of humor is demanded for the appreciation of many forms of literature, but it has a much deeper significance than this. It implies an instantaneous appreciation of the incongruous — that delicate sense of the ridiculous essential to the "feeling" of fine emotional distinctions in dramatic work or in the speech or the performances of the children or, indeed, of himself. It implies, too, the ability to judge oneself impersonally and to smile or, upon provocation, even to laugh at oneself. A real sense of humor also confers upon its possessor the ability to change his point of view rapidly and constantly, which is fundamentally necessary in acting of any kind, and even more necessary in playwriting. Overseriousness misses many an opportunity of forcing truth home in a most effective way, especially in dramatic work.

Always, of course, the teacher of dramatic work should be distinguished by the qualities which mark the man or woman of good breeding. His manners should be the expression of a delicate courtesy which comes from real kindness of heart and which has its basis in a true consideration for others. The finest ideals of truth, righteousness, justice, and sincerity of spirit must motivate his every act, because, from the very nature of the work and the special fascination of dramatics for the children, they will tend to imitate this leader. Therefore, too, instinctive knowledge of child psychology and of the child heart and a genuine love for young people must mark him.

In addition he must have unbounded enthusiasm and love for his calling and faith in its value, a fact which will go far toward giving him inspirational power. It is a significant truth, and one of the supplementary reasons for having dramatic work in the schools, that the teacher of dramatics comes very near, in a special sense, to the child and to his ideals. The imaginative experiencing of life together in literature, and especially in dramatic literature, develops confidence, understanding, and sympathy, and makes the teacher a powerful influence in molding and training the child's mental and emotional habits. Under the influence of a sympathetic leader a pupil often develops in dramatic work a "mental set" towards ethical living that lasts a lifetime.

As a general principle, the teacher of dramatics should know from a practical standpoint as much as possible about acting and the technique of the drama and the stage. The

deeper he is able to go into the refinements of stage management, the more artistic effects he can produce, even with
simple materials.   However, no matter how extensive this
training, sincerity and simplicity must always be the key-
notes of his work with the children, in whatever acting he
himself incidentally does with them, and also in whatever
interpretation of literature is necessary in connection with
dramatic expression.

In the application of the teacher's knowledge and personal
training to his actual work with the children, it must constantly be borne in mind that his office is not to teach how
to act, but how to *study*.   His task is not to direct but to
stimulate, to stir imaginations, and to lead by questions and
suggestions and by acting to more accurate observation,
and to more complete and truthful expression.   The child
must get the spirit of the piece and act it as he sees it, not as
someone else directs.   The play and the acting under such
conditions may be crude and childlike, but for this very reason they will be normal and beautiful.

To get the standpoint of the individual child is very often
difficult, because he is inclined to say nothing about the
deepest things within him, and this silence is hard to
break through.   His reserve, no doubt, is partly a subtle
natural reaction to our efforts to shape him into some conventional grown-up model which we repeat until we adults
are so like one another that we are comic.   We forget the
possibilities of differentiation and the exquisiteness of natural
variation.

As to the necessary literary qualifications of the instructor,
it must be evident that one who will have to make selections
for even very young children should have a considerable
knowledge of literature, in order that he may be able to
choose from a large field.   He must also be a lover of letters,

keenly appreciative of the best in books, and he must know not only what literature is good in itself, but what is good for the child at every stage of his growth. All this sounds onerous, but in reality the necessary preparation is not excessively great. What is essential to any literary culture is a certain body of carefully chosen material. This should be world literature — *Robinson Crusoe*, the *Odyssey*, the Bible, the Arthurian legends, and the like.

Assuming a reasonably adequate background, it is absolutely necessary that the teacher of dramatics have a sympathetic understanding of the child's viewpoint, in order that he may choose in poetry, story, and drama, those things to which the child can respond. He must be constantly guided by the form of the literature, by the emotional reactions natural to the individual at his stage of development, and by his capacity to appreciate the ethical ideals presented. He must determine what part of the bulk of literature is related to that which the child has already felt and had knowledge of, or to the experiences which it is possible for him to have imaginatively. Also he must consider how his literary material anticipates and supplements insight which is to come. In other words, the teacher of dramatics must get the child's standpoint *exactly*, with all its limitations, all its latent capacities, all its riches, and its imaginative beauty. He must know literature in this special sense — as material looked at from the child's standpoint. We can only teach effectively what is translatable into terms of the student's own life.

For the sake of final emphasis, it may be well to state negatively the all-important question of point of view. A teacher who cannot tell a story from the child's standpoint, but who must carry over his own grown-up attitudes and emotions, is of necessity artificial. A person who cannot interpret a poem as a child sees and feels it, who cannot reach up to the child's level in simplicity and genuineness, is absolutely unfit for dramatic work in the schools. He has not the sympathy nor the imaginative power to put himself in the child's place in matters of right and wrong, in feeling about poetic justice, in attitude toward fears and blood, or in appreciation of the mysteries of the superhuman and of the unseen world.

CHAPTER VII

THE SCHOOL DRAMA AND THE PROFESSIONAL STAGE

ALL through his work with children and their plays, the teacher of school dramatics must keep in mind the differences between the drama with which he is dealing and that of the professional stage. The motives of both the actors and the stage managers of the former are different from the motives of those of the latter, for education is the essential aim of the one, entertainment the real goal of the other. The professional theater must present a play that meets with financial success; it may be artistic or not, but it must bring in box-office receipts. Therefore, in the commercial play the performance is most important; in the school play it is least important, because the major function of the production is to serve as a motive for the study and work that go into its preparation.

The teacher-manager also, unlike his professional counterpart, is interested primarily in the actors. In the commercial theater a performer is selected for a certain part because he has the temperament and personality which especially fit him to interpret it; indeed, often the play is built around his individuality. In the school play the child is, or should be, selected for a certain part primarily because he especially needs the training which it will give him. The boy or girl who needs a quickening of the imagination, an outlet for some cramped emotion, the opening of the ear to beauties of speech and tone, and who needs above all to acquire self-confidence and belief in himself, is the one who should be chosen to attempt the dramatic thing that will tend to cultivate in him these particular qualities.

Therefore, because both motive and fundamental purposes are so different, the school presentation should not ape the professional stage. Many children are corrupted in

In this presentation of *A Midsummer-Night's Dream*, the flowers were designed and painted by the third-grade children who gave several of the fairy scenes.

their taste by what they see at the theater, and they want to incorporate into their plays the gaudy make-believe seen there, instead of holding to simplicity, chasteness, and sincerity, in such externals as lights, scenery, and costume. Even the very perfection of finish sometimes exhibited in the professional play is out of place in the child's play. Indeed, children should not see much of the professional theater, especially when it deals with grown-up life and its complex social problems, which force upon the children emotional experiences for which they have no intellectual background. The dramatic work the children *do* is of much more importance than what they *see*. It is the expression that counts. It is, therefore, an inspiring thought that the school has within itself the means, and often the opportunity, of completely satisfying the children's craving for dramatic experiences, at least until they reach the eighth grade and the high school.

There is, however, a vital relation between school dramatics and an appreciation of professional productions. The child's education can and should train him to recognize and to enjoy a good play. It should set up standards by which the individual will later on test the productions of the theater, thus safeguarding him, and at the same time the future art of the theater. This is distinctly worth while, because of the great influence of the drama in our social and literary life.

The theater for the child under eleven, speaking approximately, is the auditorium of the school proper. His own plays and his own acting are eminently satisfying to him if he has had the opportunity for self-expression, but if this opportunity is not given him, he will go to any kind of theater or movie that comes within his horizon. This fact lays upon the school the burden, or rather the inspiration, of studying how to handle and satisfy the dramatic instinct of its members. It must know about plays and about children, what they may see, what plays may be given in the schools, and how these plays should be presented. The difficulty of the situation is that very few understand children well enough to write plays for them or know how to direct them in the writing and acting of their own.

Because attending the theater is part of the social life of to-day, children clamor to go, and parents think they must take them. But if children once understand that under no circumstances are they allowed to go to the grown-up play, they readily acquiesce, provided their demand for drama is satisfied by their own productions and their own acting. After the age of eleven, an occasional visit to the theater is profitable if the play is worth while. It would be a great help if there were some one in every town who knew enough about plays and about young people to select and bulletin performances especially suited to them. But most of all, a permanent theater especially for children would help in solving this problem, and it is hoped that there will some day be one in all our cities. The ordinary public auditorium is too large and too ornate; the crowds and the din of the orchestra excite and overstimulate little imaginations. The child's play requires a small hall, an intimate stage, with no abrupt line to separate actors from audience; it needs significant color schemes, beautiful proportions and decorations, simple settings, few performers, short productions, superior music, and reasonable prices. Such a theater should be managed by people who know the child's point of view and his necessities, and who will wisely choose the play and adapt the settings, music, color schemes, size of stage, and size of the audience to him.

As far as the lighting is concerned, the ideal thing for a children's theater would be as often as possible to abolish the footlights, and use instead lights at the top and sides of the stage. If artificial lights are employed, it is advisable at the rise of the curtain to make the transition from the lighted auditorium to the lighted stage very gradual, so as to pass as unobtrusively as possible from the reality to the illusion. This can be accomplished easily if the auditorium lights as well as those of the stage are controlled by dimming devices.

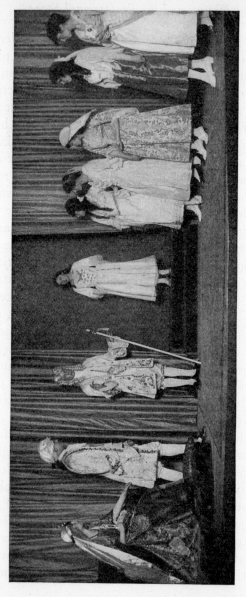

Snow White: Princess Snow White appears before Prince Florimond.

The significant thing about this production was not the staging, lighting, or performance, but the unique purpose which led this twelfth-grade class to select a fairy drama for their class play. They felt that while their parents and friends had numerous opportunities to see plays, there were many children in Chicago who rarely if ever saw a suitable and good play. They, therefore, wished to present a drama which would appeal particularly to these young people. *Snow White* was given several times, and children of all ages and from many parts of Chicago came to see it.

In this theater of our dream, good adult actors would give beautiful, artistic performances, expressive of child life or of phases of mature existence that the children can understand and appreciate, for the children themselves have not sufficient experience and training to present the ideal productions which carefully trained people would give.   It would seem, perhaps, provided financial difficulties could be overcome, that a small theater or hall could be selected in every city and appropriate plays given on Friday afternoons and Saturday mornings, which would help to supplement the school work in dramatics.[1]

The motion pictures also must be seriously considered. Sometimes they present very good historical and literary stories, but in the ordinary theater these are apt to be followed, on the same program, by something absolutely unfitted to the children, showing things which rarely happen in life and which we should not want any one to see if they did happen.   Most moving pictures portray emotions which boys and girls should not know about; they give false ideas and bring a wrong, or at least an artificial, world on the stage and into the young life.   This is a real crime, because what youth sees on the stage is as real to him as his own life.

The following story is repeated here because it shows the "realness" of a play to children: *Faust* was given in one of the outlying theaters of a certain city, and in the process of the play, the hero was dropped into "Hell" through a trap door in the floor.   In the audience was a little boy who had been told many times that he was bad and had been informed also concerning the place where bad boys go.   He believed firmly both in his sin and in the existence of the place to which he was said to be destined.   At this particular performance, the contrivance failed to work perfectly and

[1] The younger children should not attend even this ideal theater.

Faust was left with his head sticking up through the hole in the stage floor. The little fellow jumped up and shouted with a sincere feeling of relief: "Goody, goody, Hell's full!" All was so real to him at the moment that he fully believed that henceforth he could do what he liked without fear of future punishment.

The popularity of moving pictures is one of the strongest reasons for school dramatics. Let us take a look into the mind of the boy or girl who sits watching (perhaps with strained eyes) the illuminated screen. He is living through a process as artificial psychologically as can possibly be conceived. The situation can fairly be compared with a course of study wherein the sole function of the child is to sit quietly and listen to a ceaseless flow of words from the teacher. Such a course of study is not fully educative, for the student is merely the recipient. Similarly at a moving picture performance, the child is merely a recipient, for series after series of impressions race into his brain through the sensitive mechanism of the eye and excite complicated reactions, none of which are allowed to develop into even the most rudimentary form of activity or expression. If the system were devised to paralyze motor response, it could not be more complete. A most interesting evidence of outraged nature's effort to find some way of returning to the normal is the outbreaks of rather hysterical noise with which child audiences punctuate the movies — handclapping and even outcries that are many times enough out of place to show that repressed forces are struggling for expression. The results of dissociation of a mental impression from the motor reaction by which it should be accompanied are too well known and too fully explained in any modern text on psychology to need repeating here. Many of the children of the upper grades do not want to do anything — even applaud. Their one fulfilled desire is to have the idlest possible form of pleasure. Instead of ideas enlarged and developed through correlated actions, we find ideas which have become perverted and sadly set and fixed. This is due to the lack of the normal functioning of the individual in expression. This situation cries aloud for the dramatic class, where without delay action follows thought and emotion, where by means of initiation, construction, and good, honest, happy work with hands and body and vocal organs, motor activity is not only constantly exercised and developed, but is called forth in a natural manner by the motives of the playwrights and actors. As to the thoughts and desires aroused in the child by the picture show itself, it would be a most complicated and almost impossible task to analyze these stillborn ideas and purposes, many of them extremely harmful to the young girl or boy.

The multiplicity of moving-picture houses and the commercial tendencies of the professional stage create a situation that demands children's play-making and acting as an offset, and makes the lack of their dramatics a serious thing. But if playwriting and acting in the school constantly accompany the child's legitimate acquaintance with the movies and the professional theater — and by legitimate acquaintance one means not too frequent attendance at only wisely chosen pictures and plays — not only are the deficiencies existent from the standpoint of the child's training supplied, but school dramatics will even correlate in a way with professional presentations, since children who have had experience in acting in school plays have their own personal experiences as the foundation of a sound critical attitude. Professional acting, critically observed and intelligently discussed, might even help the older children in their own expression.

CHAPTER VIII

RESULTS OF DRAMATIC TRAINING

It may be profitable at this point to consider some of the results that one may confidently expect if the training which has been the subject of this discussion is continued from the kindergarten throughout the high school.

Dramatic expression calls for beauty and quick responsiveness in voice and speech, and vigorous, economical, graceful use of the body. Such expression is the highest form of physical training. Taking part in one good play often does more for an awkward boy or girl than months of formal gymnastics; for acting involves the whole body and necessitates to the highest degree physical freedom and responsiveness. The definite physical training, however, derived from dramatic expression is practice in gesture. Gesture is a universal language, although modified by nationality, temperament, and by individual habits of thought and life. Highly developed it becomes pantomime — a complete expression of thought and feeling by bodily movements without the aid of speech. Pantomime usually involves a finer and more complete coördination of the muscles than does simple gesture. Since in the child's play the thought and the emotion control the body, his efforts at self-expression put him in the way of acquiring physical strength, responsiveness, and freedom in action, and his gesture is sure to be free from self-consciousness and artificiality. His pantomime also is a spontaneous, natural expression through the agency of bodily movement of what he himself sees, hears, and feels;

and through this he develops the finest skill in the technique of physical action. Émile Jaques-Dalcroze, speaking of the human body as a most subtle and complete interpreter of art, affirms, "The body can become a marvelous instrument of beauty and harmony when it vibrates in time with an artistic imagination and collaborates with creative thought." On the other hand learning formal gesture is not the way of skill.

Snow White: the maids of honor tell Astolaine the story of Snow White's parentage.

As the child grows in intelligence and in imaginative and emotional power, his gesture, speech, and voice become more and more controlled and expressive, and the training becomes one in refinement and delicacy of action, with results impossible to secure through any other form of physical exercise. As an illustration of the practical benefits derived from the physical and motor education incidental to dramatic expression, the following incident is given: An awkward, lanky youth, whose muscles did not coördinate, was cast for the dancing master in Molière's *Le Bourgeois Gentilhomme.*

At first he seemed hopeless material, but he so put his heart and will into his part that his tall, slender, flexible body responded, at first only moderately, but then with cumulative rapidity. The result in control, grace, and movement was really marvelous; probably no other form of instruction could have accomplished so much, certainly not in so short a time. Many such developments are promoted under the

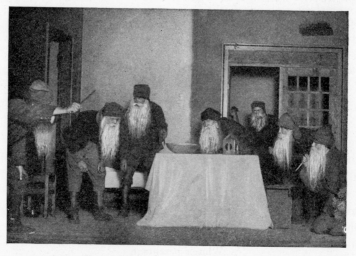

Snow White: the scene in the home of the Dwarfs.

stimulus of acting, and from this and similar experiences one can easily see that dramatic expression and impersonation are important forms of motor education.

More than any other form of literary exercise, dramatic expression tends to develop clear and effective speech. The recitation of poetry is largely a matter of the voice alone, whereas in acting word and motion combine to convey the emotional and intellectual content. Acting thus brings more vivid and complete results, because it is more detailed and utilizes more of the agents at its command. Sympathetic expression of imaginative material by the other members of the class educates the ear of the listeners so that the children begin to notice one another's voices. We grownups are strangely indifferent to voices and to speech effects. We hold up our hands in protest at the least ungrammatical construction, but complacently accept, as if there were no help for it, unmelodious voices, slurred consonants, blurred vowels, and general carelessness and indistinctness of enunciation. Surely it is as much the business of the school to train the child to produce beautiful, effective tones as to elucidate to him the grammatical construction of sentences.

The ability, then, to express an idea by means of speech implies a fine enunciation and pronunciation and a good control of voice. Impersonation and dramatic dialogue, which call for a revelation of character by external agents, clarify thought and modulate tones. The quickening of the imagination which the presentation of the play demands also tends to beautify all utterance. When the time is ripe for training in these modes, the children should be given a chance to acquire permanently a beautiful vocabulary, and to receive practice in the use of the spoken word.

Occasionally a group will ask of their own accord for such drill. For example, members of a seventh-grade class, working on *Julius Cæsar*, had difficulty in making themselves heard across the room. In their anxiety to bring their work up to the highest standard possible, they asked what they could do to help themselves. They knew that their bad habits stood between them and their ideals of freedom and power in expression. It was not difficult to show them then that they did not open their mouths properly and that they spoke with immobile tongues, lips, and jaws. On recognizing where the trouble really lay, they immediately began to practice vigorously exercises for making the faulty speech organs flexible and responsive and for improving their voices. They learned to shape the vowels and to cut the consonants definitely and clearly. Then they sought to give each phrase and thought time to reach the audience, before crowding others on top of it. This work was done entirely apart from their study of the play and, because of the incentive, was never drudgery to them. When the work is properly motivated, as it was in this case, the student, after he has acquired the skill that he needs to accomplish his purpose, straightway forgets the exercises themselves, but unconsciously retains the beauty and power that have been gained. When the teacher's effort is centered not upon exercises as such, but upon the ultimate purpose of the exercises, then these tasks take their proper place as means to an end.

Another important by-product of the intense study of books which play-making demands is skill in reading. A compelling motive is set up by the necessity for knowledge. But since the process is not the conscious motive of the child who is reading to secure knowledge necessary in his play, somehow the attitude of both teacher and pupil is subtly different. For centuries, the technique of reading, or the recognition of words, has seemed so important to the public — and therefore to the teacher — that there has been a danger of forgetting the real office of the book — the effectiveness of motive in learning to read — and the rapidity with which the children acquire skill when they really want something the printed matter has to give.

In the teaching of a foreign language, the dramatic motive affords a valuable aid because it first connects by action the new form of expression with an idea already in the mind. The strange sentence or the unfamiliar word is first combined with gesture in the simplest manner. These soon grow into groups connected by little dialogues, which in turn are followed by short plays, by dramatization of the national stories, and later by drama. Here words as an expression of thought and emotion are repeated over and over as the production is rehearsed. Thus an opportunity arises for learning the idioms and everyday speech of a foreign people. Later the study of a literary play is the best substitute for residence in the country where the language is native, and acting provides a chance for the oral use of the acquired tongue. To listen and speak is the way to attain a new language. Listen to poetry, speak it; listen to a story, speak and act it.[1]

Another value of dramatization is the outlet it gives to children of strong dramatic impulses and the consequent good effect this has upon the entire morale and spirit of the school. Such boys and girls, if denied normal expression, suffer from the lack of any vent to their feelings in the inhibition and rigidity of the classroom, until the overmastering desire to express themselves through their own activities breaks forth in a disorder which is the significantly termed "acting up" or "showing off." Such forms of disturbance can be traced directly to the misdirection of the dramatic impulse. There is nothing bad in all this. Such children are compelled by the pent-up force within them to get into the limelight. To chastise without understanding them and without any effort to provide a wholesome natural channel for the flowing out of this force which torments them when long repressed, is certainly a vicious process for even when suffering from punishment, these imaginative little beings will act the captured criminal with heroism and dignity. These

[1] See Thea J. Scherz "How Dramatization Helps in Teaching a Modern Language," *Francis W. Parker School Studies in Education*, Volume IV.

naturally dramatic children enter with joy into the school play-making and acting, in which they find a natural channel for their misunderstood impulses. Here they can perform until tired and win peace of mind and body by properly exercising and fatiguing the mental and physical activities involved in the drama. There is food for thought in realizing how under these circumstances the entire social attitude of such a child changes and his point of view towards the whole world of school is transformed. He finds that instead of being "cabined, cribbed, confined" by surroundings in which he must play the part of a hunted and stealthy actor, he is transported to a place where the activities which his subconscious self has always whispered to him are good and beautiful are recognized as such, and where he can develop his gift under the guidance of sympathetic teacher-friends who have a fellow feeling with him for the drama.

One of the values of acting is the joy that comes to the doer. This joy results in the fullest realization of all his physical, mental, and spiritual potentialities. The intense delight the child has in his dramatic work is of itself worth while; activity in which a child is happy is of great educative value. The cramping and inhibiting influences of fear are eliminated or modified by his pleasure; this expansion is reflected in all his tasks; and his mental "set" towards all disciplined exertion becomes less an attitude of dislike and fear, and more one of hope, enthusiasm, interest, and ambition. Happiness stimulates growth and expands the whole being until it radiates power. Colonel Francis W. Parker once remarked: "I found that the children were not happy in the school, and I knew that something was wrong with it. That was the beginning of my work as a teacher."

In this setting for *Catherine Parr*, canary yellow sateen formed the background. The side screens, or tormentors, were covered with grayish-green denim. Blue predominated in the oriental rug. On the small table at the back were blue flowers and green maidenhair ferns. The two tall candlesticks at the front of the stage were of dark brown wood and held large white candles. The screens and the border were of grayish-green tapestry.

DAILY ASSEMBLIES

The assembly hall or auditorium is becoming a more and more vital part of the modern school building. It is an open forum for the interchange of ideas. It is the place where the student body gathers for instruction, culture, and enjoyment. Here now and then men and women who have achieved success in their particular field of endeavor come to talk. The artisan tells of his craft, the poet reads his verses, the musician gives his songs voice. Here the school dramas, patriotic exercises, and festivals are given. Here day after day the pupils with great simplicity share with the rest of the school the choicest flower and fruit of work done in the classrooms, the laboratories, and the shops. Thus the students are conscious that the results of the projects they are following, the knowledge gained from the subjects they are studying, will be presented before an audience composed of their schoolmates. A social motive, therefore, actuates them, so they prepare, select, and organize their material in order to present it with clearness and force, and so knowledge is acquired and skill developed. There can be no better training in oral composition and in public speaking than is offered by this use of this school forum, because meeting daily or often gives all the pupils frequent opportunities for addressing an audience.

PART II

THE EDUCATIVE USE OF THE DRAMATIC IMPULSE

CHAPTER IX

LITTLE CHILDREN'S PLAYS AND THEIR SOURCES

THE examples of the child's spontaneous play, to which attention has already been called, indicate the kind of acting that children themselves initiate. Such practical illustrations give hints concerning the choice of material for dramatic treatment; they are something of a guide to the educative use of this impulse, and they suggest the results that may follow its right use. In the instances cited, there is proof that the child's own life affords large opportunity for the exercise of his instinctive power. Little children, therefore, do not need a book, nor do they require worked-out ideas from their teachers. The ultimate material of their study and plays is the social life around them, as they experience it either in reality or in imagination. The people and the activities that enter into their dramatizations should have a meaning in the children's lives and should lead them to a better understanding of the world about them, and a desire for further investigation.

In the kindergarten and primary period, children are so sensitive to sound and to rhythmic movements that many of their plays are largely a gratification of these tastes. The habit of rhyming and of uttering jingles is so instinctive and manifests itself so universally among them that it may be regarded as among their first proclivities. Rhymes and jingles are a child's introduction to poetry, story, and drama. They are little bits of primitive art passed down by word of mouth through many generations — songs, games, riddles, bits of nonsense which by their own simple beauty and fitness have lived through the ages. It is the form of this literature that appeals most to the young boy or girl; the sound, rather than the sense, that attracts them; because it stirs their emotions and builds up their ideals through their feeling for rhythm, for rhyme, for repetitions, and for cadenced musical sentences. It is a noteworthy fact, as all mothers will attest, that the nursery rhyme may have very little intellectual content, but it must be musical and in marked time.

Mother Goose is the poet laureate of childhood. She is of ancient and honored lineage and above the charge of frivolity. One of her great charms is the dramatic possibility inherent in her characters and in her situations. She can always be approached in this spirit; indeed, some of her rhymes can be acted. Take the rhyme of the old woman who lies down to sleep. A mischievous man comes along and cuts off her petticoats, so changing her that even her own little dog does not know her. The result is that finally she doubts her own identity. Here are large dramatic potentialities, either tragic or comic, for lost identity is always a graphic situation.

For everyday use, a number of excellent collections of Mother Goose rhymes, jingles, and poems exist. In 1842, Hallowell of Boston put forth a splendid edition. This is out of print, but one can occasionally find a copy. Andrew Lang's *The Nursery Rhyme Book*, with its analysis and classification of the poems, is also a most desirable little volume. Another excellent and inexpensive edition of Mother Goose is *A Book of Nursery Rhymes*, arranged by Charles Welsh, in which most mothers and teachers will find a sufficient number of rhymes for their needs. Edward Lear's *Nonsense Books*, a most amusing compilation of just the kind of humor that children can appreciate, contain many verses that can be used with little people. They love to hear and to recite the adventures of Mr. Daddy Long-Legs and Mr. Floppy Fly and to follow the wanderings of the Jumblies with the green heads and blue hands, who "went to sea in a sieve," while the "runcible" spoon in "The Owl and the Pussy Cat" makes an irresistible appeal to children, and they would not exchange the coined musical adjective *runcible* for any in the dictionary. There are other poets — among them Christina Rossetti, James Whitcomb Riley, and Andrew Lang — who have written some nonsense rhymes which are so good that they will no doubt some day rank with the Mother Goose melodies. For example, take this of Rossetti's:

> Mix a pancake,
> Stir a pancake,
>> Pop it in the pan;
> Fry the pancake,
> Toss the pancake,
>> Catch it if you can.

or this of Riley's:

> Ringlety-jing!
> And what shall we sing?
> Some little crinkety-crankety thing
> That rhymes and chimes
> And skips sometimes
> As though wound up with a kink in the spring.

These books with a few others constitute a little bookshelf— a library for children. Some of the rhymes are marked by lyric quality, some are little ballads, and some are really miniature plays. They all hold the fundamentals of literature and contribute to the child's pleasure and amusement. In the use of these rhymes, he must not be denied the expression of his likes and dislikes, his right of choice, nor the discipline of choosing for himself from among the rhymes that he knows.

We have seen now how the dramatic impulse manifests itself at first in imitations and impersonations, and in the recognition by the children of the dramatic spirit and situations in the Mother Goose melodies. The same tendency is revealed in the spontaneous use of impersonations and dramatic dialogue.

Here is an illustration of how one Mother Goose rhyme, that contains a real dramatic situation, can be elaborated into the form of a little play by kindergarten or first-grade children.[1]

> Jack be nimble,
> Jack be quick,
> Jack jump over
> The candlestick.

This little poem cannot be motivated until it presents a dramatic situation to the children's minds. First they see only a boy named Jack jumping over a candlestick. If they act out the rhyme without discussing it, the action is largely physical — that is, pantomimic — and with but little dialogue, either original or taken from the poem. If their natural desire to talk about the poem is given free rein, some one will wonder and ask, "Who says, 'Jack be nimble'?"

Then another one will perhaps say, "Why, it's the father sending Jack off to bed."

"Why does he tell him to jump over the candlestick?"

"Because Jack is sleepy; the father wishes to awaken him so that he can find his way upstairs. His father knows that jumping over the candlestick will rouse Jack." And so in some such manner and in some such conversation, the chil-

[1] For further illustrations see "Dramatizing Mother Goose Rhymes," in *Creative Effort: Francis W. Parker School Studies in Education*, Volume VIII.

dren create an imaginary story and connect the rhyme with human experience. After this when they play the little poem, it has a real dramatic quality. One child is the father, perhaps reading the evening paper; Jack sits beside his father dozing; the mother is upstairs preparing Jack's bed. She calls for Jack, but there is no reply. Then she asks the father to send Jack upstairs. The father looks at Jack, sees he is almost asleep, and says:

> Jack be nimble,
> Jack be quick,
> Jack jump over
> The candlestick.

Because it is said with a purpose, this little poem now is given with genuine meaning by the child impersonating the father — he is the father for the time being; he is thinking in personal terms; and only by such thought do ideas evolve and become valuable in one's development. Jack rubs his eyes, picks up the candlestick, makes his way upstairs, and his mother puts him to bed.

In a large class it is not possible each day to give each pupil an opportunity to play a part all the way through, and yet there must be ample opportunities for everyone to express himself through voice and bodily movements; otherwise, his ideas never fully function, but like all fleeting impressions quickly disappear. In order to provide opportunities for all to express themselves, the whole class is frequently invited to "make believe" without leaving their places. Thus, the teacher asks the class to pretend that it is nearly bedtime; that they have played with their toys until they are tired; that they are so sleepy they can hardly keep their eyes open. "Now, let us make believe we are falling asleep," the teacher suggests. The children quickly enter into the game and suit the action to the word. Or the teacher may say, "Make believe that you are Jack waking up." Then, playing with the class, he pretends to be the father, and calls to the children to awaken. They rub their eyes, yawn, and show other signs of waking. Through this playing of an incident of the story, the children develop a sense of characterization, and the self-conscious ones act freely because they have no fear of being observed by their fellows. It is an excellent idea to have half the class act while the other half watches. The teacher may say, "I am going to invite the children on this side of the room to pretend that they are father reading the newspaper. The children on the other side of the room may see which one seems most like a man enjoying his evening paper." In this fashion, and in similar ways, the children — after a group or several groups have played the story as a whole — are led to concentrate upon the parts of the story, and by the general use of pantomimic characterization all are led to study these parts intensively and to give them expression. A replaying of the whole story should follow this detailed work, because the children's last impression should be of the story as a unified whole.

One cannot lay down a set way of leading up to the presentation of a piece of literature. The approach varies with the class, the time, and the teacher. One hesitates to give an illustration, lest some one attempt to follow the letter and lose sight of the spirit. Devices are of slight value, but principles are fundamental and eternal.[1]

[1] The following rhymes are some of those which lend themselves to dramatization: "Hey! Diddle, Diddle," "Hickory, Dickory, Dock," "Old King Cole," "Little Boy Blue," "There Was a Man in Our Town," "Ding, Dong, Bell," "Humpty Dumpty," "Jack and Jill," "Simple Simon Met a Pieman," "The Queen of Hearts," "There Was a Crooked Man," "Three Little Kittens," "Tom, Tom, the Piper's Son," "Jack Sprat," "When I Was a Bachelor."

From the usual list of short stories studied by the kindergarten and the primary grades, children may be allowed a great deal of freedom of choice in the selection of material for their plays. The following are suggested as the type of story suitable for kindergarten:

The Old Woman and Her Sixpence (*English Fairy Tales*, Jacobs)
The Three Billy Goats Gruff (*Popular Tales from the Norse*, Dasent)
The Sheep and the Pig that Set Up Housekeeping (*Tales from the Fjeld*, Dasent)
The Shoemaker and the Elves (*Household Stories*, Grimm)
The Hunchback Weaver (found in almost all folklore)

As an illustration let us look for a moment at the construction of the story of *The Old Woman and Her Sixpence*. This story is built up so like a play that it can be acted by the children with very little adaptation.

Once upon a time an old woman was sweeping her little house, and to her great joy she found a silver sixpence. "What shall I do with my silver sixpence?" she said. "Oh, I know. I'll go down to the market and buy a little white pig." The next day she went to the market and bought a little white pig. She tied a string to one of his hind legs and began to drive him home. On the way, the old woman and the pig came to a fence. Over it there was a stile. The old woman cried to the pig, "Pig! Pig! Get over the stile!" But the pig would not.

Here ends the beginning or exposition of the story. It is clearly marked. The two main characters, the difficulty, and the real problem are set forth so sharply that they cannot be misunderstood. We have the old woman, the sixpence, the purchase of the pig, and the start home. There would have been no complication if the old woman's will had not met with opposition in the will of the pig. At this point begins the real interest which centers in the struggle between these two forces.

The old woman's problem now is to force the pig over the stile. She calls for aid to all within her reach, beginning with her own little dog, but no help comes, and still the pig is master of the situation. At each new failure of the old woman, and with each new character that is brought in, the interest grows. The old woman, at the end of her resources, finally calls on a cat, who makes a condition.

The entrance of the cat upon the scene marks the crisis. This is the middle point, where the action starts to turn and the unraveling of the complication begins. It will not do to destroy the balance here by shortening too much the descending action or resolution, as is done in some versions. The delay is brought about by the conditions made by the cat and the cow. The situation is made acute at the close by the fear that the old woman may not be able to supply the demands of the cow for hay; but just as soon as she finds that she can get it, the beginning of the end of the story is at hand. It closes to the satisfaction of everybody, with something worth doing accomplished, and the old woman and her pig safe and comfortable at home.

The tale is one of action and adventure, full of life and movement, and with a touch of humor in the fact that such a small thing as a little white pig can make so many things happen. The repetitions also move to laughter. The actors are animals perfectly familiar to the children, and yet there is a touch of magic in the fact that all of them talk. The little folk hang breathlessly on the outcome, and are ready to cheer (and often do) when the pig finally succumbs. The little old woman, her small house, her commonplace occupation, and the outdoor scene of the struggle add picturesqueness to the tale — moreover, little pigs are usually attractive to children. Also the interdependence of the various actors, the persistence of the old woman, and the way the whole thing works out when the rat begins to act, are not lost on children, and silently and without notice may teach life-lessons in this concrete form. This is one of those stories which has been told to children since the world was young; yet it is always fresh and captivating. It is only a nursery rhyme, but it is as perfect in plot and construction as a Shakespearian drama. Compare it with *The House that Jack Built*, another cumulative story, in which we find rhyme, rhythm, repetition, and alliteration, just as in *The Old Woman and Her Sixpence*. But in *The House that Jack Built* there is no motive, no plot — the action does not lead to anything, and so we leave it for playtime, and select *The Old Woman and Her Sixpence* for serious study.

Many children's stories are, like *The Three Billy Goats Gruff*, so well organized that they are ready to be acted impromptu, without reorganization into play form. The children play on the floor — possibly they use the kindergarten table as a bridge, with a little chair placed at either end for steps. Some one impersonates each of the goats and some one the big stupid troll. The children use any language that they think necessary to make the meaning clear. The dialogue is not committed to memory but is kept free and fluid.

The Three Billy Goats Gruff has a well-worked-out plot. There is a beginning that introduces the characters and the difficulties, followed by a development, a crisis, a resolution, and a conclusion eminently satisfactory to young readers. The goats are anxious to go to the green hill on the other side of the river to make themselves fat. Over the river there stretches a bridge, and under it lives a big troll, who thinks he owns the passage way. When he interferes with the will of the goats, they are at first afraid of him. Then follows the struggle between the goats and the troll, with the final victory of the former, won by strategy. The conclusion sees the goats on the green hillside, making themselves fat, and so

> Snip, snap, snout,
> This tale's told out.

The Sleeping Beauty (known in Grimm's *Household Tales* as *Briar Rose*), one of the most poetic and artistic of the short stories told to children, is still another which may be played by all primary grades. In the first grade, *The Sleeping Beauty*, especially if accompanied by music, lends itself beautifully to pantomime. The story divides itself naturally into three parts: the Christening, the Enchantment, and the Awakening. Little children do not need to attempt dialogue at all, but may tell the story in movement, keeping time to the beautiful rhythm of the music. Even more appropriate is the story to the second and third grades, where children are capable of handling plots with as many incidents as are to be found in *The Sleeping Beauty*. All the first three grades can well combine to make a dramatization of it for some such gala occasion as the spring festival. A number of the rôles require older boys and girls for their best presentation. Moreover, it will be a satisfaction to the little children and a fruitful source of training, if they play sometimes with their elders. In *The Woodman and the Goblins*, with which we shall deal later,[1] the woodman was played by a third-grade boy, and the little goblins by first-grade children; while the big goblins, the ghosts, and the Halloween spirits were, many of them, from the upper grades. This was

[1] See pages 243–59.

a happy combination enjoyed by all the participants, large and small. In connection with the study of *The Sleeping Beauty*, some of the most dramatic parts of Tennyson's *The Day Dream* can be read, thereby adding to the story the beauty of rhythm and rhyme. For example, let us take the two stanzas describing the awakening, both prime favorites of little children:

> A touch, a kiss! the charm was snapt.
>   There rose a noise of striking clocks,
> And feet that ran, and doors that clapt,
>   And barking dogs, and crowing cocks;
> A fuller light illumined all,
>   A breeze thro' all the garden swept,
> A sudden hubbub shook the hall,
>   And sixty feet the fountain leapt.
>
> The hedge broke in, the banner blew,
>   The butler drank, the steward scrawl'd,
> The fire shot up, the martin flew,
>   The parrot scream'd, the peacock squall'd,
> The maid and page renew'd their strife,
>   The palace bang'd and buzz'd and clackt,
> And all the long-pent stream of life
>   Dash'd downward in a cataract.
>
> *   *   *   *   *   *   *
>
> Across the hills, and far away
>   Beyond this utmost purple rim,
> And deep into the dying day
>   The happy princess follow'd him.

One is not likely to go far wrong when he selects any of the old stories for study and play-making. The physical and social world in these old stories is the normal one for kindergarten and primary children. They are simple, serious, and on the imaginative level of the children, and they have been crystallized by folk repetition into an artistic whole that in many cases is practically dramatic form as far as the construction is concerned.

The Bremen Town Musicians is another story of this kind that the children love, and one that is easily dramatized. Indeed, they will often break up the material it contains and create an almost original production. They always love to act these humorous tales. They enjoy playing tricks on anybody, but stupid people are their favorite victims. These antics are a kind of horseplay, such as the goblins imposed on the woodman in *The Woodman and the Goblins.*[1] As boys and girls move up from the primary to the grammar grades, they should begin to feel the difference between this clumsiness and genuine humor. A little nonsense, however, is a great relief from tension. A bit of fun or a flash of wit often restores mental and emotional balance. Pleasantry acts like a tonic, and humor many times gives the truest and sanest view of life. The manner in which a man gets his fun and recreation is a fundamental test of character. Training young people to enjoy and respect genuine nonsense is an indispensable part of their education.

DRAMATIZATION OF SOCIAL STUDIES

As children grow older, they begin to group themselves together to represent scenes from their history lessons and from the industrial life about them. Primary children play "store" and "railroad" and carry on commercial transactions of all kinds. I have seen a lively bit of bargaining and exchange going on in a third-grade room between two groups playing that they were Scandinavians and Greeks — the classes were studying that year the geography and history of these two countries. Too, the dramatization of all the in-

[1] See pages 243–59.

dustries going on in the immediate neighborhood — farming, lumbering, gardening — occupies much of the children's time.

Dramatic play is the only form of expression that will organize such activities among a group of children. Through this sort of play, they acquire easily and naturally knowledge of the social occupations of the peoples of the earth — such as pottery, textiles, weaving, spinning — and proficiency in the home-making processes that may be observed in the laundry and kitchen, where real things are being done. This is illustrated in the history of New York, as shown in the notes preceding the play of *Rip Van Winkle*,[1] and in the history of New England, as shown in the notes preceding *The First Thanksgiving Day in America*.[2]

The dramatic product in these cases will be unfinished, to be sure, but a teacher must have the courage to accept this crudeness because it is appropriate to the child-producers. Often there is no product to show to outsiders. Indeed, it is a question whether little children's plays should ever be taken out of the kindergarten or primary room to be set up in a new place for others to see.

In any case, the child should be made to feel that his dramatic plays are, as his other lessons are, simply a part of the regular day's work and pleasure. Others may see and study the plays of the little actors in the familiar room. It is difficult for a little child to hold an impersonation before an audience for any length of time, and in a new place he will probably be hopelessly diverted by the new environment; for he will be interested in the new people and things about him and may, indeed, be busy in his mind gathering material for to-morrow's play, to the neglect of his present part.

[1] See pages 345–52.   [2] See pages 365–6.

CHAPTER X

POETRY IN THE DRAMATIC TRAINING OF CHILDREN

POETRY for children is usually in lyric or ballad form. Rhymes, jingles, and simple lyrics are a preparation for the larger heroic ballads and narrative poems found in all folklore, such as *Sir Patrick Spens* and *The Ballad of Robin Hood*. It is not far from these to the longer epics and to romances, such as *The Odyssey*, *Sigurd the Volsung*, the Arthurian legends, and *Sohrab and Rustum*.

Without reflection, it may seem that we are far afield in discussing poetry in connection with children's dramatic work, yet one reason for so doing is that just as rhymes and jingles prepare little tots for the emotional responses involved in art appreciation, so poetry — language in its most artistic form — not only continues the training of emotional responses, refines those aroused by rhymes, and connects them with appropriate intellectual content, but it schools the children in the appreciation of literary form. The voicing of rhyme and meter emphasizes structure and organization, and so prepares the children for the artistic construction of their plays.

In dealing with the lyric, however, there is one difference to be noted. Its form is part of itself, inviolable and inseparable from the content, so that it cannot be adapted or worked over in the way in which the old stories and even the old ballads and epics can often be manipulated. From its style, children get some feeling concerning the organization

In this setting for *The Florist Shop*, spot lights off stage right sent a flood of sunlight through the window and the glass door. The walls were of cream color edged with tan. The furniture was painted a French gray. The cyclorama of blue flannel gave the effect of sky and of distance. In the window was a cement bird bath filled with maidenhair ferns and yellow flowers in a tall glass of deep blue. On the bench were the flowers that the text of the play called for. The cement urn and the Greek bench were in a flood of brilliant, warm light. The footlights and the border lights were used with great moderation.

of material into a stable unit.   They receive not only an emotional enlargement and an outlet for emotion, but they sense the mode of expression itself — the spirit of craft and of technique which literature has in common with the other arts.   At this point the ballad also is valuable to the children because it is a story with a definite plot told in a special literary form.   In both the lyric and the ballad it is true that rhythm and meter and sound serve to bind the thought together — to emphasize organization and thus to prepare the children for the organization of their own plays.

The acting out of rhymes and jingles may be followed by the reading of some of Christina Rossetti's exquisite lyrics.[1] Here again it is the music, not the content, that is emphasized.   A few of those that may be used are *Fly Away, Fly Away Over the Sea, The Wind Has Such a Rainy Sound, The Horses of the Sea, Is the Moon Tired?* and *Boats Sail on the River.*   There are many other lovely verses in Christina Rossetti's *Sing-Song*, inviting to both children and teachers.

After these little lyrics, one feels that it is time for much of Stevenson's *A Child's Garden of Verses.*   These poems are unique, for Stevenson has done that almost impossible thing — gone back to his own childhood and, in most cases, recovered the consciousness of a child and his point of view.   He is thus able to give the child's attitude toward his own life and toward the people that fill it.   In these poems there is perfect structure, musical verse, and a simple, beautiful style.   The verses are lyrics and should be read to the children as such and not as nursery rhymes.   The poems are intensely personal; the lonely and usually companionless child in these poems has not marked dramatic sympathy; he does not readily and naturally put himself imaginatively into some other child's experiences.   He is simply himself, taking peeps

[1] *Sing-Song*, Little Library Series, Macmillan.

about at other children, who are sometimes near at hand and sometimes far away.

Another delightful book which contains many jewels for primary children is *Peacock Pie*, by Walter de la Mare. Many of these poems are distinguished by a naïve and ingenuous expression of childlike thoughts and emotions. A. A. Milne's *When We Were Very Young* and *Now We Are Six* contain many poems that all present-day children love, and *Poems by a Little Girl* by Hilda Conkling is another source of delight to them. Then there are many collections of favorites old and new, some of which every teacher will need to own. Among these are *The Posy Ring*, and *Golden Numbers*, both compiled by Kate Douglas Wiggin and Nora Archibald Smith; *The Home Book of Verse for Young People*, selected and arranged by Burton Egbert Stevenson; *Rainbow Gold*, selected by Sara Teasdale; *This Singing World*, edited by Louis Untermeyer.

Practically all rhymes and poetry should be *read* to children, because in the early years the ear is the pathway to the mind as well as to the heart. A child can hear and understand what he cannot see or read for himself until he is much older, at which time it is too late for both the pleasure and the training of listening. Poetry is written to be voiced, as the play is written to be acted, and only through its own particular form of expression can either of these two forms of literature be adequately studied and expressed.

The response from the children will most frequently come in repetitions of the rhyme or poem, in marches or dances or other forms of action which express the emotion the rhyme or poem contains, in the use of beautiful language, and lovely little bits of dramatic phraseology. However, the return from an art experience is not necessarily expressed in activities such as these: it is sometimes complete in itself. A poem, lyric, or ballad is voiced, and the beauty of tone and movement is felt by those who hear. The resulting pleasure often completes the circuit. Sometimes pleasure is an end in itself.

It is fortunate that beauty of rhythm and music of speech make such an irresistible appeal to the child's emotions; for through the emotions such enlightenment comes that he is enabled to understand and appreciate a whole body of poetry. If the poems he hears are wisely selected and beautifully expressed by the speaking voice, he begins to comprehend not only poetry written for him alone, which is not abundant, but great literature which interprets the large permanent things of nature — day and night, the seasons, the wind, the clouds, the sun and moon. These are real things to him as they are real to us. "The true realism, always and everywhere, is that of the poets: to find out where joy resides, and to give it a voice far beyond singing. For to miss the joy is to miss all." [1]

It is not necessary that children understand all the poetry they hear. Indeed, it would be a pity if they did, because naturally some of the poems will be beyond their intellectual comprehension. You and I understand only in part, each according to his measure. On the other hand, children perceive and appreciate in poetry much which we older people have lost understanding of. Children know more about fairies and springtime and birds and trees than we can dream. Some of the great poetry which makes a universal appeal can be simply read and left to work its own way into the child's consciousness.

One day at a morning assembly when the subject was Kipling and his poetry, the teacher, not knowing in advance

[1] Robert Louis Stevenson, "The Lantern-Bearers," in *Essays by Robert Louis Stevenson*. Scribners.

that the little children were to be present, read *The Feet of the Young Men*, regretting that he had not selected something simple which the young children could understand. A few days later, when the fourth grade was asked to choose a poem which the teacher was to read to them for their pleasure, the almost immediate call was for the poem, *The Feet of the Young Men*. The children liked the big sounds, the sonorous music, the spaces, and the free sweep and movements of large things. They sympathized with "the old spring fret" and the desire to get away to "the other side of the world." Again at a certain morning assembly in May, the old English lyric *Apple Blossoms in the Spring* was read to the school. The first grade was present, and during the next period they asked to be allowed to learn the poem. [1]

Such lyrics as these children will follow lovingly: *Autumn*, from *The Faerie Queene*, Spenser; *I Know a Bank*, *Ye Spotted Snakes*, Ariel's song *Where the Bee Sucks, There Suck I*, Shakespeare; *On May Morning*, Milton; *The Daffodils*, Wordsworth; *The Owl*, Tennyson; *Pippa's Song*, Browning; *Bluebells*, Walter de la Mare; *The Pasture*, Robert Frost; *Stars*, Sara Teasdale; some of the joyful Psalms. These last and the great old hymns of the church make a direct appeal to the poetic instincts of the child, just as the ritual ceremonies appeal to his dramatic instincts. The twenty-fourth Psalm, with its martial tones, touches a responsive note in his heart. The hills in the one-hundred-and-twenty-first Psalm and the green pastures in the twenty-third send a personal call to the little boys and girls so imperative that the

---

[1] It is the author's custom to have each child in the second grade start an anthology of choice poems, dramatic and non-dramatic. The poems are printed on loose leaves by members of the seventh grade printing class, by the school printer, or mimeographed in the school office, and inserted in linen-bound loose-leaf, six by nine inch note books. These individual anthologies have proved most educative, and the pupils of the third and fourth grades have taken delight in adding to them.

teacher is implored to repeat them. The sound and the rhythm, the cadence and the content make a perfect unit and produce a never-to-be-forgotten effect upon these young imaginations. If they are left to their own initiative they will commit to memory most of the poems we have mentioned. This is not a task, but a joy to them.

CHAPTER XI

WORLD LITERATURE AS A SOURCE OF CHILDREN'S PLAYS

THE BASIS OF CHOICE

OUR primary emphasis in this book is, of course, on the training and educative value of the dramatic impulse and tendency. The intention here, therefore, is not to discuss as literature the stories out of which the children's plays are going to be made. It is, rather, to suggest one or more long stories particularly well fitted to this or that grade, and to speak briefly of their suitability for the children's study. Such treatment involves a consideration not only of the stories, but also of the children's needs and tastes, their intellectual interests, and emotional responses, and their attitude towards life. The little actors, in the process of their study of any special story, will have opportunity to decide upon its play-making possibilities and to choose what appeals to them as sufficiently dramatic for this purpose. (See the notes on the play *Old Pipes and the Dryad* [1] for a case where the children not only sensed the dramatic poverty of their story but broke into criticism and really partly rewrote the narrative with a view to increasing its dramatic value.)

When a child reaches the third or fourth grade, his conceptions begin to enlarge. One or more of the long hero tales or romances may then be made the center of his lit-

[1] Pages 375–8.

erary study for about a year.   These narratives are sometimes called *cycles* because the hero goes through many
adventures and experiences, each one a tale in itself.   Around

This non-realistic setting was used for another presentation of *The Florist
Shop*. The stage was hung with apple-green sateen. The flat at the
back of the stage was painted in purple, blue, green, and rose. The table
and stands were violet. The only flowers displayed were those required
by the business of the play.

this cycle as a nucleus, other literature may be gathered —
short poems and folklore bits — which will add to the significance and the beauty of the whole and to the complete-
ness of its effect upon the children.   This procedure gives a

steadiness of purpose and a concentration of attention that short material collected from here and there never provides, no matter how good and suitable it may be, and it dignifies the whole study of literature for both teacher and child. The wealth of material thus assembled gives background for a good play, if the subject matter is dramatic at its core or if the hero has dramatic adventures.

ROBINSON CRUSOE

Robinson Crusoe fits in well at about the third or fourth grade, not because it is a child's story, but because it is full of details that interest and satisfy both grown-ups and children. In presenting the novel one who loves the art of Defoe would not care to change the original work for any simplified edition. The English of Defoe is so fine that it cannot but lose by alteration. The everlasting romance of Crusoe's struggle to secure food and fire, shelter and clothes, makes a universal appeal, but it is the reality, the fullness, the homeliness of these details that constitute their charm for youthful minds. The whole plan of the novel is large, and the study of *Robinson Crusoe* is no doubt one of the fullest literary experiences possible to childhood. It may be remembered that Rousseau in *Émile* calls *Robinson Crusoe* "the one book." Perhaps no other tale so forces home the dependence of the individual upon the community, and the debt he owes to the generations which have left so rich an inheritance for his comfort and pleasure. Then, too, the glimpses of absolute freedom, the outdoor atmosphere, the wonders of the sea, and the ships that go up and down to unite the lands that the waters divide are a never-ending fascination to childish imaginations. Children's interest in the story begins with the shipwreck and does not often extend beyond the rescue from the island and the return home.

Whenever the writer used *Robinson Crusoe* with a class, the children of their own volition studied this story for several months. They discussed it; they read it aloud; they made drawings; and they constructed many articles which they thought might have been useful to Robinson Crusoe. Although occasionally Robinson held converse with himself in short monologues, no one suggested making a play while he was the only character available, for with one character a play would be impossible. After Friday came into the story, however, much pantomimic action took place between Robinson Crusoe and Friday. The rescue of the latter made an exciting, spontaneous bit of pantomime.

To these same classes were also read portions of the story of Jacob, another wanderer, but no attempt was made to dramatize any part of it; it was too complex; it involved too many characters and too many scenes. But the children roamed in imagination over the great pastures and up the mountain sides with the shepherds and the sheep. With the help of other shepherd stories and pictures, they became familiar with the geography and topography of Palestine. Such an experience gives children the background for other Bible stories, and enables them to imagine other Bible characters moving easily in this pleasing pastoral setting.

Attention is called to these two stories to emphasize the fact that the children had perfect freedom in choosing their modes of expression, that play-making was not forced, and that they instinctively felt that these stories could be better studied and expressed by other means than by play-making. One of the great dangers in play-making is forcing the use of material that can better be expressed by reading aloud, story-telling, painting, modeling, or making. Children are usually unerring in their judgment as to what mode of expression will best convey the thought.

David and Goliath

The story of David and Goliath is a favorite with the third grade. It is a splendid offset to *Robinson Crusoe*, because it is dramatic and has in it play-making possibilities which the novel lacks. Like most Bible stories, it should, before being presented to children, be adapted by condensing and by cutting out unnecessary repetitions and details. Occasionally, the incidents in a Bible story have to be rearranged in order to preserve the literary unity, but in this story the original order can be followed. In editing the story as suggested, the Bible language is not changed, although here and there a phrase has to be inserted to link together the incidents. It is the vocabulary, the idiom, and the rhythm of the seventeenth-century English that help to make vivid and beautiful the Bible lyrics and stories. After the defiance of Saul and of the armies of Israel by Goliath and with the introduction of David as the opposing force, the Bible version can be followed with but few changes. The dramatization moves along the lines of the story and the play ends as the story does, with the victory of David, the unarmed boy, over the big giant with his wonderful armor, his sword, his spear, and his javelin. For "David prevailed over the Philistine with a sling, and with a stone, and smote the Philistine and slew him." Here is fulfillment of poetic justice to satisfy the most exacting. It was right, as young minds see right, that the boasting giant should be overcome and promptly beheaded by the boy with a sling and a stone in his hand. There is always great enthusiasm over the acting of this play and great delight in the warlike, defiant speeches.

The dramatic adventures of Joseph, the unknown shepherd lad who came almost to the throne of Egypt, is one of the great pieces of world literature. It gives intense satisfaction and pleasure to children, who are sensitive to form and who love to follow tales of great deeds. The complete narrative makes an excellent play and many of the individual episodes are effective when represented in dramatic form.

The Odyssey

The *Odyssey*, simple, childlike, heroic, and open, is wrought into the world's culture, and for this reason, if for no other, it should be a part of every child's literary training. George W. Palmer's translation is perhaps the best for use with children. Begin with the fifth book, and close with the home-coming of Odysseus. Much of the Palmer version can be read to the children without change. It is a prose rendering and minutely faithful to the Greek original, but the prose is as musical as verse. Nothing is more lovely than these narratives told, read, or recited by a person with a beautiful voice who marks the rhythm of the text.

The *Odyssey* gives great joy to fourth-grade children, as it does to any grade above this. As a background to the wanderings and home-coming of Odysseus, selections from the *Iliad* may be read to the class and discussed. These will explain to the children the cause of the Trojan War and give the account of the fall of Troy. During the experience of the writer, the children have made several Greek plays whose heroes were the warriors of the *Iliad*. A little collection of dramatic studies and plays from this book was published at one time by a sixth grade of The School of Education of the University of Chicago.[1]

[1] *The Wrath of Achilles*, from the *Iliad*, one of the best Greek plays made by the children of the Francis W. Parker School, can be secured for $.08 by addressing the publication department, Francis W. Parker School, 330 Webster Avenue, Chicago. There is an excellent article by Miss Hall òn the "Individual Project Method," in *Studies in Education*, Volume VI, published by the faculty of the Francis W. Parker School, Chicago.

Robin Hood

This story especially fits the children of the fifth grade. The fundamental nobility and sense of justice of Robin Hood and his men far outweigh the tricks they delight in and the skulls they crack. Around the famous outlaw's adventures there may be grouped a number of ballads on the same subject which have like underlying ideals of generosity, gratitude, real manliness, self-reliance, and faithfulness to friends. The idea of fair play is incarnated in all these, for Robin sets himself up in opposition to the unjust laws of the times, and he and his men are generous and kind to the weak and those in trouble. When Robin is defeated in a fight he accepts the outcome cheerfully— a trait which every child admires. The children enjoy, too, the freedom of the out-door life depicted here and the charm of forest and field. *The Merry Adventures of Robin Hood* by Howard Pyle is perhaps the best book on the subject for children's use. To supplement it, some of the old English ballads can be used.

Many of the exploits of Robin and his merry men have been made into rollicking plays that are a joy to fifth graders. *The Shooting Match at Nottingham*, and *The Merry Adventures with Midge the Miller* are the embodiment of boisterous, breezy fun and harmless mischief. An outdoor setting with its sunshine, trees, and grass is ideal for these. It is harmonious with both the external life and the spirit of these merry fellows.

In like manner, the fifth and sixth or even the seventh grade will enjoy *Rip Van Winkle*, with its rich local flavor, its charm of mountain and river, and its story of the sorry trick the mountain spirits played on that ne'er-do-well Rip. The dramatizing of the story is discussed later on in this book.

Sigurd the Volsung

In the sixth grade, at the height of the child's love of heroic achievement, the center of study for a portion of the year may well be the great legend of the Northland, *Siegfried*. William Morris's poem, *Sigurd the Volsung*, may be used, the teacher selecting the portions for study. Here are related in a finished style heroic feats of strength. Here we find the Norse ideals of life and character, their superstitions, their belief in fate, their manliness in meeting what was foredoomed, their frank open-minded honesty, fidelity to spoken word, loyalty to family and kindred, and all the enduring enterprise and daring that made these men explorers and discoverers of new lands. Because of the difficulties of meter and form, the poem should first be read aloud. Then the children may be given the book and each allowed to study what he likes best. Selections well adapted for such treatment are: *The Drawing of Odin's Sword Out of the Branstock*, *The Death of Sigmund*, *The Getting of the Horse Greyfell*, *The Forging of the Sword*, *The Slaying of Fafnir*, *The Getting of the Treasure*, and *The Awakening of Brynhild*. These stories, taken together in proper order, form a unit or *epos* which leaves out much of the blood and horror found in other parts of the story. The children may wish to dramatize their favorite selections and should be allowed to attempt it. Their efforts may be read and discussed in class, where the little playwrights will quickly realize that most of their productions are so difficult to stage that they cannot be used even as the foundation of a play. They learn, however, that some stories are more effective in story form than they are in dramatic, and vice versa. Probably they will finally decide on one, say *The Drawing of Odin's*

Sword Out of the Branstock, as a story on which they can all unite in making a play.

Here is an illustration of what happened in such an instance. The class found at the first rehearsal that the members could not stage the play because of their limited knowledge of the size and shape of the feasting hall of the Volsungs, the arrangement of the furniture, and the placement of the guests. It was necessary for them to go back for more study of the material. The description of the hall they found in the notes in the little book *The Vikings* by Jennie Hall. After much intensive study and after they had overcome numerous difficulties, they composed their adaptation and satisfactorily presented it at one of the morning assemblies. The center of interest in the project proved to be the one-eyed god, Odin, and his drawing of the sword from the Branstock.

THE ARTHURIAN STORIES

The Arthurian group of stories is rich in play-making material. The study of most of these stories, however, can well be postponed until the high-school period, especially those that deal with love in a reflective way, as do Tennyson's *Idylls of the King*. But from Sidney Lanier's *Boy's King Arthur*, his *Mabinogion for Boys*, and *Knightly Legends of Wales* can be drawn selections which make a cycle well suited to the seventh grade. They have a natural center — King Arthur and his court. They give pictures of great knightly enterprises as well as views of the domestic life in the palace. They deal with bold, generous deeds and with acts of gentleness and kindness, and they furnish many a plot for dramatization. In not a few cases an original little play grows out of a situation in one of them; that is, the children break up the material and reorganize it into a new story.[1]   *The Knighting of Richard Neville*, in this book,[2] illustrates a dramatic representation of that ceremony. The rich and brilliant colors of the costumes, the glitter of the armor and jewels, and the splendor of the trappings of the time give pleasure of a fine quality to young people from twelve to fourteen.   They sit silent with awe as one character after another tries to pull the sword Excalibur from the rock, the sword which would yield to none but him whose strength was as the strength of ten because his heart was pure.

There is surely something about these legends that creates not only an atmosphere but a climate wherein the things of the spirit take on value, for the stories so appeal to the imagination that the youth begins to feel that the divine gifts of life are not material pleasures but the joy which comes from intellectual strength, from moral freedom, from beauty and righteous living.   It is worth while to build up such ideals in young lives.

CUCHULAIN

The Celtic story of Cuchulain,[3] recounted for ages by bards in the highlands of Scotland, in Brittany, and in Wales, but told in Ireland by Lady Gregory with much more imagination, is full of wonderful adventures that make splendid material for young people of the seventh, eighth, and even ninth grades to study intensively.   Several incidents in the life of Cuchulain, the mightiest of all the Irish heroes of antiquity, furnish eminently suitable and vitally interesting

---

[1] "Lionel of Orkney," in the *Elementary School Teacher*, September, 1904, is a work of this kind.

[2] See pages 391–6.

[3] *Cuchulain of Muirthemne*, by Lady Gregory, with a preface by W. B. Yeats, published by John Murray, London.

material for dramatization. Theodore Roosevelt, writing in *The Lamp*, and comparing the *Völsunga Saga* with the Cuchulain story said:

However wonderful we may find the *Völsunga Saga* — and it would be a daring iconoclast who should deny the wild poetry of that untamed world in which fought the divine and the mortal on a common battleground — the modern taste for a spiritual and generous type of character is far more wonderfully met in the story of pleasant Cuchulain of the gentle hand and "the kind mouth that was sweet-voiced, telling stories." The great emotions of love and terror and friendship are all there. Except for the marvelous friendship of David and Jonathan, nothing in literature approaches the story of the friendship of Cuchulain and Ferdiad. The story of Cuchulain as told by Lady Gregory exists as a great and permanent work of art; it is told in beautiful language which makes one think of the language of the Bible.

Some day a hand, touched by poetic and dramatic skill, will rearrange and condense these stories; there is in them for older children as full a joy as in the Arthurian legends.

CHAPTER XII

ANIMAL TALES

Their Interest for Children

At some time children should come into contact with the beast stories, old and new. These are folk tales in which the animals' imagined attitude toward people and their imagined reactions to them and with them are shown. Here the beasts talk with one another and with men, just as they do in childish fancy. It is, of course, not the psychology of the animals that is being considered, but that of man, his behavior, and his relation to the beasts. *Why the Bear Is Stumpy-tailed*, the *Three Billy Goats Gruff*, and the *Bremen Town Musicians* are the kind of stories that for centuries have been kept deep in the hearts of the people and have been told and retold about the firesides of their homes. This interest is also found in some of the newer animal stories, as in Kipling's *Jungle Book*, although here the emphasis is upon the imagined psychology of the animals themselves as presented in the story. The upper second and third grades seem to take great pleasure in animal stories and plays. These may be scattered about through their other literature so that the children may not live too long at one time in this imaginary world. It must be remembered that in all this the interest is literary, not scientific, but the real facts of animal life are interesting and the children should be given an opportunity to become acquainted with them; they hold attention and are an anchor to the imagination. They can, therefore, be used as material for the reading hour as well as for the study hour.

The Fable

Most fables are animal stories. Many of them are artistic little creations which present brief views of life and terse bits of philosophy. Some of these fables can be elaborated into plays, but most are too short to hold interest as plays for any length of time, and the children enjoy them simply as stories.[1]

Dramatic Possibilities

Stories from *Reynard the Fox*, if one cares to meddle with this great prose poem of the fourteenth century to the extent of suppressing the satire, will be enjoyed by children as simple animal stories. Many of these stories lend themselves naturally to dramatization. The *Uncle Remus* stories, by Joel Chandler Harris, make splendid material because they represent the traditions of a race told by a great folk-story teller in incomparable form. They also provide excellent material for plays. In dramatizing them, it is remarkable how the little actors ignore the dialect and always translate the language into the English to which they are accustomed. This truth may be noted in the play *Mr. Wolf Makes a Mistake*.[2] Such adaptation does not seem to interfere with the effectiveness of the little plays, for these wonderful narratives bear the translation without appreciable loss.

[1] Among those which lend themselves to dramatization are: *The Wind and the Sun, The Dog in the Manger, The Lion and the Mouse, The Hare and the Tortoise, The Fox and the Crow, The Fox without a Tail, The Town Mouse and the Country Mouse, Androcles, The Ant and the Grasshopper, The Shepherd Boy Who Called "Wolf," The Man, the Boy, and the Donkey, The Hart and the Hunter,* and *The Lion's Share.*

[2] See pages 260–4.

KIPLING'S ANIMAL STORIES AS A SOURCE OF PLAYS

Because of their almost faultless perfection of structure, the vividness and the dramatic character of their language and their style, and their imaginative literary content, Kipling's *Just So Stories* and the *Jungle Book* are

Only an extremely small stage and a very limited equipment were available for this production of *The Cat That Walked by Himself.*

among the great art productions of our time. All the stories are delightfully dramatic, but not all are actable. Those that are capable of presentation are almost in dramatic form as they are printed, so excellent is the form and so abundant and lively the dialogue. In the stories of Mowgli in *The Jungle Book* the children's interest is in Mowgli himself and the conditions of his life among the animals. Kipling's knowledge of the Indian jungle, his creative imagination, psychological insight, and picturesque language, give literary interest to the characters and experiences of Mowgli and his gray wolf brothers.

The third and fourth grades of the Chicago Institute, Chicago, dramatized the story of the adoption of Mowgli into the Seeonee Wolf Pack as it is told in the first chapter of *The Jungle Book*. The play was preceded by singing Kipling's *Hunting Song of the Seeonee Pack* (music by Eleanor Smith).

A small group of ninth-grade pupils, as a project, dramatized from Rudyard Kipling's *Just So Stories*, "The Cat That Walked by Himself." Since the school had a very small stage at the time and a very limited equipment of properties, costumes, and settings, the staging was necessarily simple.

The diagram below gives an idea of the stage arrangement.

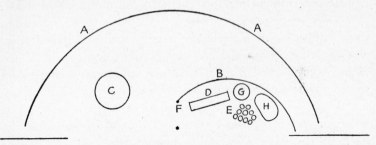

Diagram 1. — Stage arrangement for *The Cat That Walked by Himself.*

A. The green background. *B.* The wall of the cave. *C.* A tree. *D.* A log. *E.* A hearth made of stones. *F.* The entrance to the cave where the dried horseskin is suspended from a stick horizontally placed. *G.* A stump standing on end, with a jar of milk on the top of it. *H.* A bed of skins.

Green curtains made a very attractive and simple background for the stage, and suggested the wild woods. The left portion of the stage was enclosed by brown Canton flannel to indicate the cave. Right center of the stage stood an elevation made of a pile of boxes covered with brown cloth to suggest a high rock. This took the place of the tree into which the Cat climbs at the end of the second act as indicated in the text of the play. The dried horseskin was made of brown Canton flannel and was held in place by being thrown over a horizontal stick at the entrance of the cave. It was weighted at the bottom, and at the top it was held to the stick by a brown cord. This was so fixed that it could be pulled out, by a person hidden behind the cave, at the moment that the action required the skin to fall. The weights at the bottom of the horseskin caused it to drop.

The smoke was feigned by the use of concentrated hydrochloric acid and concentrated ammonium hydroxide. The two chemicals were placed in separate sealed jars connected by a rubber tube; another tube led into the jar of hydrochloric acid, and a third into the jar of ammonium hydroxide. When the stage manager blew into the tube that entered the hydrochloric acid, a perfectly harmless smoke issued from the jar that contained the ammonium hydroxide. This action was worked from behind the cave, care being taken to use a tube sufficiently long to reach from the jar of ammonium hydroxide to the stones that formed the hearth. The milk pot was placed on a thin stick on top of the log at the back of the cave. A person behind the cave, by means of a skillful jerk on a cord tied to the stick under the jar, effected the downfall at the desired moment. A chocolate mouse, drawn across the stage by means of a black thread, made a mouse which the Cat ate with real pleasure.

The man, woman, and baby (the part of the baby was taken by a child from the kindergarten) were dressed in skins. Their bodies were stained. (Brown stain can be secured in liquid form from any reliable dealer in stage make-up and it is easily removed by the use of water.) The animal costumes were made tight-fitting and suggested the beast that was being represented. There were no masks,[1] but the costumes came up over the head like a hood. The face was bare; a few lines of grease paint were used to suggest the features of the animal.

[1] In the plays that have the educational welfare of the child in mind masks should not be used. They are uncomfortable and tend to make the individual self-conscious; moreover, they hide the expression of the actor.

CHAPTER XIII

JUNIOR–HIGH–SCHOOL PLAYS AND THEIR SOURCES

CORRELATION BETWEEN THE DRAMA COURSE AND OTHER SUBJECTS

A SEVENTH-GRADE group which had been studying in their history class the development of the United States during the period between 1787 and 1865 based an interesting dramatization upon their history work. The following is an outline of the program of this dramatization, which was given before the school on the morning of Decoration Day as a memorial service:

Music: *America.*

I. A Session of the Federal Convention.
   Time: Summer of 1787.
   Place: Independence Hall, Philadelphia.
      George Washington presiding. Delegates from eleven of the thirteen colonies present.
   Discussion of the questions:
      1. Shall Slaves Be Represented in Congress?
      2. Shall the Foreign Slave Trade Be Prohibited?

II. The Missouri Compromise (1820). Discussed by two boys in front of curtain.

III. The Compromise of 1850.
   Place: United States Senate.
   Time: Winter of 1850.
      Millard Fillmore presiding. Other senators present; among them Henry Clay, Jefferson Davis, John C. Calhoun, Daniel Webster.

IV. The Kansas-Nebraska Bill.

> Time: Winter of 1854.
> Place: United States Senate.
>> W. R. King presiding. Among others present: Salmon P. Chase, Stephen A. Douglas, Benjamin F. Wade, Charles Sumner.
>
> Music: *Battle Hymn of the Republic.*
> *Fatherland Psalm.*

The delegates to the Convention and the United States senators were impersonated by the seventh-grade boys and girls. They had studied the character and the individuality of each delegate and senator, and in each delineation the attitude of the delegate or senator toward the slavery question was suggested and his own speeches were used whenever possible.

At the close of the session of the Federal Convention, it was necessary to reset the stage for the meeting of the United States Senate. During this time two boys in front of the curtain discussed the Missouri Compromise of 1820, interpreting the attitude and arguments of both the North and the South. As soon as they had retired from the stage, the curtain rose on the Senate, with each boy or girl occupying the seat of the senator whom he or she represented. The presiding officer, Millard Fillmore, opened the meeting and there followed the discussion of the Compromise of 1850. The whole occasion was dignified, solemn, and orderly. In this session of 1850, and also in that of 1854, the great questions connected with slavery, which preceded the secession of the Southern states, were discussed by Senators Webster, Calhoun, Clay, Douglas, Chase, and Sumner. The speeches of such men on the slavery question gave the participants a splendid opportunity for training in impassioned speech, in physical self-control, and in dignified, courteous behavior.

In the delivery of the different speeches, the boys and girls experienced, to a large degree, the emotional attitude and the high idealism of the senators.

A teacher of literature, writing of this subject in the *Elementary School Teacher* (Vol. 4, page 603), remarked:

> The child at this age should have a chance to learn the sonorous and lofty music of impassioned prose. Now, if ever, he has his prime hour of readiness for the orators, both because the subject-matter of the orations appeals to him as never before, and perhaps as it never will again, since he is now for the first time interested in social and political questions of the kind with which the orators deal, and since, as he goes on, he will probably grow less accessible to the emotional appeal made by oratory, and because he needs the artistic enlargement and satisfaction that he gets from the musical flow of eloquent prose.

This program is an ideal illustration of that much abused pedagogical doctrine, "correlation"— the conservation of the child's energy by the use of topics, subjects, and books in their natural setting. The relation between literature, history, and general science has been forced many times. The affiliation between literature and history lies indeed in the spirit rather than in the facts. A story or a play or poem may incorporate some real event, some historical person, as Paul Revere or Julius Cæsar, but these characters have been transferred from their original setting and put into a personal dramatic atmosphere where the action, the human elements, the literary form, are the elements to be emphasized and dwelt upon. The dramatization of an episode in history, even if it is impromptu in the class, transfers not only the incident itself, but the entire associated body of history, from the realm of formal, unreal, memorized material into the child's living experience. Many current events may be treated in this same way.

PLAY-MAKING AS A MEANS OF STUDYING SOCIAL CUSTOMS

Not only history but social customs become more vivid when acted out before young eyes. One year children of the seventh and eighth grades made a study of the corn belt of the Middle West, paying especial attention to Illinois and Indiana. They were greatly interested in the people, the farm life, and the gathering in of the great crops of corn. In this connection, a southern Indiana "husking bee" was described to them. As a "party," this evoked their attention from a social point of view. Two or three days before Thanksgiving, this class requested permission to present a husking bee at the Thanksgiving exercise.[1] Together they sat down, and each contributed to the thought of the whole; they planned the staging and the securing of properties, especially of sufficient corn to make the showing they wished. Each speech, the dialect, the incidents, and the names, they all discussed and decided upon. Naturally they were most enthusiastic, and in one evening wrote the play, concentrating fully upon it. They staged their play on the level floor, in the center of the room, with the audience seated around them. The result was a most interesting representation of a custom that has nearly passed away, and their concrete presentation gave these children a better idea of the people studied, their habits, and the great wealth of corn in the Middle West, than they could have gained from any amount of abstract study.

[1] See *Dramatic Presentation cf a Corn Husking in the Middle West,* on pages 222–5

CHAPTER XIV

THE LITERARY DRAMA IN THE JUNIOR HIGH SCHOOL

SUITABILITY OF LITERARY DRAMAS

To meet the dramatic needs of the pupils of the upper grades a few literary plays are especially suited, parts or all of which can be studied and acted out. *Julius Cæsar* contains just the kind of dramatic struggle most absorbing at this period. Although the characters move in an atmosphere of tragedy, and the end is disaster and death, yet most of this drama can be understood and acted by eighth-grade children. (Costume or stage settings are unnecessary.) The result is a better understanding of the play and a large training in forceful, expressive speech and action. These presentations, even in the junior high school, have in them little of the "show element," as the willingness of the children to act without costumes and stage setting testifies.

Many of the Irish plays fit into school conditions exceedingly well, since they are short one-act dramas which call for the simplest setting. At Dublin where they were originally given, the stage was set with colored curtains or simple screens which harmonized well with the idea of the play. Some performances are deeply religious, such as *The Nativity;* some are serious, like *The Hour-Glass;* some humorous, like *Spreading the News;* and some tricky, like *The Pot of Broth*, the dramatization of an old folk story. The whole body of this literature is clean and wholesome, with nothing morbid or theatrical about it, simply natural and sincere.

INTRODUCTION OF A LITERARY DRAMA

The work leading up to the first reading of any play differs with each drama and with each class. But the general method of procedure is the same. The first reading should be as vividly dramatic as possible, so that the imagination of the pupils may be stirred and their first impression be deep and lasting. It is needless to say that the teacher must do much work preparatory to this introduction. The scenes must be visualized, the characters understood even to the point of actually hearing the tones of their voices and seeing their movements. It is of primary importance that every teacher of literature should be able to read with real dramatic power. Led by the teacher, a round-table or class discussion of the story and of the characters naturally follows the reading of the play. The first day, this should go just far enough to leave the class enthusiastic about the play as a whole.

At the next meeting the pupils are given texts, and after they have had an opportunity to read them over silently, if they so desire, the play is read aloud by the members of the class. Questions arising in the minds of the pupils are voiced and other pupils try to answer them. The questions lead to a detailed study of the text in order to throw light upon the points under discussion. When the class has gained a fair understanding of the whole play and has acquired a certain amount of freedom in reading, it is time to try the play in action. The teacher should have a clear mental image of the general setting, movement, and business of the play before the children are allowed to act. In his preparatory work, the teacher must strive to catch the dominating spirit of the drama and devise setting and furnishings to carry out in line, color, and arrangement this keynote or theme. A good plan is to work out a miniature stage set with furniture of proportionate size and inanimate players which can be moved about as the play is read through.   In this way a fairly definite idea of the most effective arrangement and grouping is obtained. Careful notes must be taken of all that is worked out, so that, when actual rehearsals come, the students' minds may not be distracted by the planning of stage arrangement. This is a problem too complex for young people to solve. This statement does not mean that it is not valuable for them to give expression to their conception of the scenes and their arrangement, but the real work of planning the larger movement and arrangement of the production belongs to the director. At the first informal acting, it is sufficient to set the stage so as to give the actors a fairly clear image of entrances and of the placement of things. At this time no definite action or stage business need be given; the main purpose of this first rehearsal is to leave the young actors free to express as fully as they are able their conception of the part they are playing. At a second rehearsal the main scheme of movement and of business can be made clear. The minor details of action will come individually as the participants grow in understanding of the play and of the characters portrayed.

Selecting the Players

The selection of the players is a difficult problem to most teachers. In a model school, where the group is never larger than twenty-four, it is possible, by having more than one cast, to give each member of the class an opportunity to act. This is the ideal condition, for every child is innately dramatic and needs this training. Two casts give the children an opportunity to see at rehearsals the needs as well as the excellences in the work of those doing the same part that they are to portray. The teacher conducting the class should have the actual choosing of the players. The try-out system, with other teachers and pupils as judges, is a great educational mistake. Only the person who thoroughly knows the children, their needs, their weaknesses, and their latent capacities, can make a wise selection. The outwardly clever pupils, who favorably impress the listener unskilled in the pedagogy of dramatic acting, are often those who should not be chosen for a leading part. We need to remind ourselves frequently that the primary purpose of drama in the school is education and not entertainment. The judicious selection of the players is therefore of greatest importance. It not infrequently happens that the person who at the first acting of the play seems most unpromising, after the long period devoted to arduous rehearsals, shows greater personal growth and does better work than some of his fellows who, through a certain cleverness and self-confidence, seem to promise more at the start. The members of the class may always be asked what part each would like best to play, and the writer frequently has invited his students to make out a list showing what they think would be the best casting of the characters. While this information doubtless aids somewhat in the selection, the final decision must be left to the choice of the teacher, and it will be based largely upon the pupil's intellectual ability to conceive the part, his need for playing it, and somewhat upon his physical fitness for portraying the character. In this connection it should be borne in mind that it is easier to disguise a person's appearance than to change his voice.

LEARNING A RÔLE

The parts once assigned, the players should not be allowed to commit to memory or to read often aloud by themselves until they have a clear understanding not only of the entire play but of every line.   False emphasis and mechanical reading is due to the teacher's permitting the pupil to get the words before he has secured the thought.   The misreading of a line quickly becomes a habit more or less difficult to get rid of.   Interpretation should be fixed before memorizing. One of our leading actors — Mr. George Arliss — in studying a new character goes over the entire play again and again.   He becomes familiar with the entire drama and knows every line that throws light upon the individual that he is to portray.   Should he begin by learning the lines in order, he might find at the end some speech that would change his conception of the entire play.   The whole drama must be visualized fully before any attempt is made to act it. Every speech and situation should be perfectly clear to everyone.   If a player finds difficulty in saying a line, let him put it into his own words, until he has clarified the thought; then he is usually able to give it readily in the author's words.   As soon as the rôles have been distributed, the writer makes it a rule to give the players individual rehearsals in order that he may help them with their particular needs and make sure that they are working with understanding.   When they are perfectly familiar with the thought and with the author's peculiar mode of expression, memorizing is a simple matter and should be the next step.

It is an unwise practice to allow the players, after the first few rehearsals, to use their texts while they are attempting to act.   Mind and body should be free to express themselves in action, and this ease is not possible when one's whole thought is engaged in an attempt to remember lines.   Bodily expression cannot come in any natural way while the players are hampered by the book.   The words mastered, there follows the valuable work of attempting to perfect the

A setting for *The Red Turf.*

players' conception of their rôles, of developing all possible skill in their portrayal, and of trying to weave the work of individuals into an artistic and well-balanced whole. Team work is essential.

It is not necessary in most plays to call everyone to each rehearsal. Special ones for groups having scenes together is an economy of time and effort.

THE PART OF THE TEACHER

The teacher's place is to stimulate, feed, and direct the imagination of his students, to make conditions right for freest expression, and then to leave the players unhampered to express themselves through the medium of the character impersonated. The experienced instructor will not expect more dramatic action than is motivated by genuine thought and emotion. The successful actor is immersed in the part as he understands it and strives to be simple, honest, and direct in carrying out his conception.

REHEARSALS

There is a vast difference between reading a printed page at sight and acting the lines of the play. In the first case the spoken word calls up the image or idea that the word suggests; in the second the idea calls up the word spoken. Every speech must go to the audience thought foremost. Therefore the actor must remain in his part every instant that he is on the stage. A dialogue should be going on in his thought constantly. When not speaking lines furnished by the author, he should be making mental replies or observations. The truthfulness and vividness of this silent dialogue makes or mars his own portrayal. Mr. Louis Calvert, an actor of rare skill and power, actually studied out lines to think while he listened to the speeches of others, and he thought these lines at every performance. Some one has wisely suggested that amateurs should first strive to listen carefully to what is said; second, they should think it over judiciously; third, they should select a reply.

From the time that the parts are memorized, a stage, equipped as fully as possible with setting and properties, should be used. How can the performers gauge their final action when rehearsing in a room that is not of the same size or proportions as the stage where the play is to be presented? How can a king know how to bear a jar supposed to contain precious ointment unless he has the jar when he is rehearsing? Thought should be free from all such external things, and when the time for presentation arrives the handling of properties should have become automatic. Then only is the player in a state of mind to give freedom to action and stimulation to the imagination. There must be many costume rehearsals in order to make the actors feel perfectly at home in their strange clothes.

GESTURE

In rehearsing, formal gesture should never be taught, for the actor should be largely unconscious of his physical movements. Natural gesture proceeds from a desire to express an idea and grows out of the character being portrayed rather than from the line being spoken. A noted English artist once said: "If we have assimilated the character, the gestures will follow inevitably." Nuance of bodily expression and finesse of stage business will develop naturally as the players become more and more identified with their parts, since growth in skill and freedom of movement will follow each effort to portray a rôle. Then, of course, a true actor does not copy. No two persons express their feelings in exactly the same manner. The student must endeavor to feel the emotion and to let it flood his consciousness. At that point the body will respond. "Out of the abundance of the heart" the body as well as "the mouth speaketh." Gesture should always be used sparingly. Amateurs are likely to be restless and are prone to move too much. Thus they register their uncertainty of thought and feeling. A good rule to follow is, do not change your position unless the action of the play requires it. The kind and the extent of a movement depends upon the thought and emotion actuating it.

It may help the actor if he remembers that the listener, in order to get the story being acted out on the stage, focuses his attention. Everything possible should be done to aid him in his effort. Now an unnecessary movement on the part of any actor tends to attract the eyes of the audience. Thinking that this gesture has been made because the unfolding of the story has been taken over by this person, the audience transfers its attention, only to find out that it has been misled. The effectiveness of a dramatic situation is sometimes lost because a performer has made a false or irrelevant movement. On the other hand the actor who is speaking a line and whose right it is to have the attention of his hearers is free to do anything that will help him to reveal the character he is playing. It is the province and duty of his listening fellow actors to help to maintain the spirit and atmosphere of the scene, but they must minimize their physical responses, in order not to attract attention when it should not center upon them. They must accompany the speaker as alertly and as harmoniously as the members of an orchestra accompany a soloist. Honesty, simplicity, coöperation, and reserve characterize the work of every true artist.

There is, naturally, always a period when the results seem crude, inadequate, and uncorrelated; this is the time when the director must have faith born of the knowledge that this is a step in the process of growth, and must wisely refrain from doing the part for the actor to copy. The reason for such an attitude is that the true development of the dramatic instinct goes on within the individual. The instructor then must clarify the player's thinking and lead him on, but he must not coach him. Sometimes at this point it is helpful to make the players do a part of a scene in pantomime. Being deprived of reliance upon mere words, which have become so predominating a factor in the conveyance of thought, they have of necessity to rely wholly upon bodily expression, and this fact helps to free the more or less unresponsive physical agents. Before long the actor will emerge into a period of realism, and from that stage of development the artist-teacher can lead some of the players to enter the first stages of the suggestive realm, the highest in art.

It is not possible to say how many rehearsals are necessary to gain a thorough preparation for a play. They should be repeated until the drama has been as well prepared as is possible for the actors, or as long as they can rehearse with profit to themselves. When their concepts cease to grow, then it is time to stop. The writer has found that, as a rule, at least twenty-five rehearsals are necessary to get a play into really good condition for serious, worthy presentation. Some one in a recent educational journal has told of getting an elaborate production ready in a week and has given as a reason for so doing that a longer preparation would cause the children to become weary of the work. Yet the author has never found that adequate training has this effect. If the play is worth while and it has been decided to present it for an audience, it is deserving of the best the children can give. One must learn to respect art, and hasty, imperfect work is conducive to low ideals and to bad habits of thought and behavior. The work is interesting, provided the students are constantly growing in insight and in the power of expression. Intensive effort carried in extensiveness as far as the pupils are capable of going at that period of their development is essential. The feeling that they have done their best and have given a truly excellent presentation is to them an enduring source of joy and satisfaction.

During the first stage rehearsals, it is the custom of the writer to direct from the center of the stage near the footlights. As the study advances, he moves to the first row in the orchestra. When the actors have become familiar with stage business and have gained some power of characterization, then he stands in the center of the auditorium, and finally, in the back row. This procedure works out most advantageously. The director, during the first days, is in the place where he can be of most help. At the early stages, the acquirement of stage business and the development of characterization are the absorbing problems. Later, the actors are ready and able to attend to the task of projecting their words and of making everyone hear. Then the director is seated in the rear of the auditorium.

As has been stated already, there should be more than one cast, in order to give every member of the class an opportunity to participate. There will be individual variations in the portrayal of a part, but these will be comparatively slight, because the round-table discussions establish the pupils' conception of the play and the characters. The production should be given several times, in order that the students may get the value of more than one performance before an audience; when a person has had the actual experience of trying to impersonate a character and to picture a situation before an audience, he is ready and able to penetrate deeper into the more subtle mysteries of the play and of the character portrayed. The act of expression clarifies vision and sends one back to the literary text of the play for a fuller knowledge. With the second playing comes growth in skill and a deepening grasp of both the individual part and of the play as a whole that was impossible before the first performance elucidated thought and feeling.

CHAPTER XV

PRODUCTION OF *THE NATIVITY* IN THE EIGHTH GRADE

Preparation

The Nativity, by Douglas Hyde, is beautifully written and is of about the length that eighth-grade children or a group of younger high-school students can easily sustain. The characters are about equal in importance, thus allowing everyone an equal opportunity. The setting and costumes give chance for picturesqueness and for beauty.

Before the play was first read to the class, several periods were spent preparing the way by creating an atmosphere and making an intelligent background for the fullest possible understanding and appreciation of the play. This was achieved in part by giving the story of the English drama's origin in the church and a brief description of one of the first dramatic presentations. This account of the rise of the English drama, if told simply with concrete illustrations, is one of great interest to young people. Bits from the old moralities and miracle plays were next read to the class. The instructor read from St. Luke the story of the birth of Jesus, and the children were interested in the account of the coming of the wise men from *Ben Hur* by Lew Wallace, *The Other Wise Man* by Henry Van Dyke, and other stories with the same theme. Copies of the great pictures of the Nativity were displayed about the room, and in their music classes the students heard some of the famous musical compositions that have been inspired by the coming of the Messiah. When it was judged that the class was prepared, the instructor read *The Nativity*, by Douglas Hyde.

STAGING THE PLAY

In the work of designing the costumes of the Nativity play, in arranging the stage, and in evolving effective groupings of the characters, really fine copies of the pictures done by the great artists were frequently referred to. The students were often seen studying "The Star of Bethlehem," by Burne-Jones. They were deeply interested by the way in which the kings expressed in every attitude their wonder and reverence. The shepherds in Lerolle's picture made those playing corresponding parts wish to express awe and humility just as fully. By observing another cast practicing, these young people perceived that those who at the moment of speaking a line felt most deeply and sincerely the thing they were saying, came nearest to having their whole body talk, a truth they found expressed in all great pictures.[1]

The problem of stage setting the class should always talk over freely, for it is *their* presentation, but most young people are so filled with modern, realistic methods of production that they are unable to give much real help. It often takes considerable wisdom and tact to get the young people to feel satisfied with a plan for a sane, artistic setting.

This was true the first time *The Nativity* was prepared. The class was unanimous in its desire for a realistic stable, with large wooden doors opening toward the audience. The director realized that such a setting was out of keeping with the idea of the play. Moreover, the stage was very small,

---

[1] The designing and making of the costumes for *The Nativity* are discussed in *Studies in Education*, Vol. I, "The Social Motive in School Work," published by the Francis W. Parker School, 330 Webster Avenue, Chicago.

and it was necessary to limit expense and to use as far as possible the resources at hand. Realizing that a person convinced against his will keeps a tenacious hold of his opinion, the teacher, like Polonius, "went round to work." He said to the class, "Very well, let us consider how we can carry out your plans." The class looked at the stage and found that it was in truth extremely small. Asked to indicate on the floor with chalk where the stable should stand and where the doors should swing when opened by Joseph, they began to make measurements. Some one soon said, after due consideration, "Oh, we cannot have doors swinging out, because the shepherds and kings would be in the way." All agreed that the stage was too small for swinging doors and actors at the same time. Sliding doors the students found to be impracticable, even if they were really in use at the time of the Nativity.

The actual setting, which grew out of the adaptation of the available material to the space the tiny stage afforded, was wonderfully beautiful and suggestive, and, moreover, it was a great satisfaction to the actors. The rear and sides were hung with soft gray-green curtains, which made a far more pleasing background than could have been obtained by an attempted realistic landscape, which would have failed to harmonize with the spirit and mood of the author. The stable was indicated by two upright logs, some twelve inches in diameter, which supported a similar crosspiece. The silver-gray tones of these weathered logs blended beautifully with the gray-green of the stage draperies. There were no realistic doors, merely curtains of the same material as the background. These opened in the middle and could be pushed back out of sight. The interior of the stable was most simple. On a platform, raised some seven inches so that all might see, was a rude manger. At its left stood a simple bench, on which Mary sat. Joseph stood at the right. Over Mary's head a little to the left hung an old lantern. The placement of the manger, bench, and lantern were nicely calculated so that Joseph at the head of the manger and Mary seated at the foot made a lovely balance of line and mass.

LIGHTING

The lighting was worked out with great care. Light and color express spiritual ideas. Carefully distributed, concealed blue lights gave the appearance of early morning to the portion of the stage in front of the stable. When Joseph drew the curtains at the stable entrance to reveal the mother and child to the kings and shepherds, the audience saw that a brilliant light came from the manger and streamed upon the portion of Mary's face that was turned toward the child. This idea of having the illumination emanate from the face of the Christ Child was suggested by Correggio's "Holy Night." A chiaroscuro effect was gained by the dim light from the old lantern that hung to the left of Mary and cast deep shadows. The idea of having the whole picture dominated by a central high light was the result of a long period of observation by the writer of the methods used at the Royal Opera House in Dresden. A play appeals to the eye as well as to the ear. Therefore, simple artistic effects are always appropriate, provided they help to make the production clearer in its idea and spirit.

LATER PRODUCTIONS

Later other performances of *The Nativity* were given. The school meanwhile had built a more adequate auditorium with a finely equipped stage. The larger space and the more subtle lighting added much to the effectiveness of the presen-

tations.   The description of the play on the restricted, poorly
equipped stage has been given because many people are confronted by the problems of a cramped stage, a poor lighting
system, and limited finances.   Yet when the play was done
on the larger and better equipped platform the same simplicity and unobtrusiveness characterized the staging and the
lighting.   Everything that met the eye and greeted the ear was
planned to serve the one purpose—objectification of the message of the story.   A great curtain of dark green denim hung at
the back and sides of the stage.   The logs used in the earlier
performances were again called into service.   On either side of
the stable, which was placed slightly back of the center, stood
tall fir trees.   These were available because they had been
ordered for the Christmas services and for the Christmas
parties.   At the back of the stable was a curtain of azure blue.
The curtain of gray-green, used on the smaller stage, again
hung between the logs and served in place of stable doors.

   The stage lighting in the performance was intended to sym-
bolize and harmonize with the progressive manifestation of
spiritual illumination, as it is revealed in the unfolding of the
story.   When the play began the stage was in semi-darkness,
suggestive of the state of mind of the two women.   The
moonlight slanted across the trees and fell full upon the
stable portal, where the true light of the world was to be
revealed.   As the play progressed, the morning light replaced
the shadow of night.   While the women told their stories of
grief and sorrow, the dawning was feeble and pale.   When
the shepherds and kings related how the angelic host gave
their message from the skies, how a star appeared in the
East, and how they had searched for the promised King, the
light increased.   Finally as Joseph opened the doors and
revealed the Christ Child, the morning light broke forth and
increased in brightness, until it reached its full effulgence

at the close of the play, when, in the manifest presence of the "Light of the World," kings, shepherds, peasants, and angels all unite in adoration.[1]

---

[1] *Adoramus Te*, by Palestrina (to be found in *Modern Music Series*, Book IV, by Eleanor Smith), was played by a 'cello back of the scenes before the rising of the main curtain. After the lifting of the stage curtain and before any characters came upon the scene, the French Provençal *Cradle Song to the Blessed Child* was sung as a soprano solo back of the stage curtain that formed the entrance to the stable. Before the fall of the main curtain, while all were kneeling in devout adoration, a chorus of girls, accompanied by organ and 'cello, sang *Ave Maria*, by Arcadelt, XVI Century (sung in D major; this is to be had in sheet music). In each case the musicians were unseen by the audience.

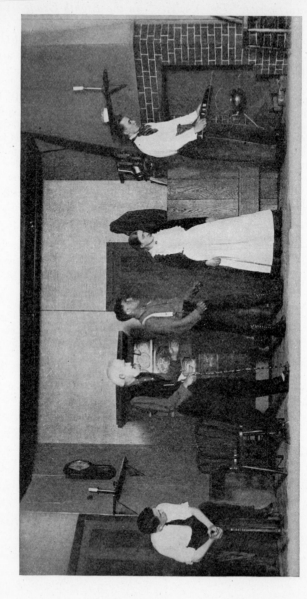

This scene from *The Turn of the Road* shows what can be done even on a cramped and ill-equipped stage.

CHAPTER XVI

THE DRAMA COURSE IN THE SENIOR HIGH SCHOOL

The Dramatic Club

THE dramatic club has been almost the only recognized avenue for the expression of the dramatic instinct in the majority of high schools. But these clubs do not meet the need in any educational or satisfactory manner. The membership is limited, and so the opportunity for the development of the dramatic impulse, which the giving of a play offers, does not come as it should to every member of the school. Moreover, the work of the dramatic organization is frequently unrelated to the work of the school and is often of a very low standard. The work of the dramatic club is objectionable because it is carried on without an adequate background, without the necessary understanding of the first principles of the technique of the art of drama, and without experienced leaders. There may be an occasional presentation of a worthy drama, but more often precious time and energy are spent upon the preparation and presentation of some musical comedy, trivial farce, or meretricious play. This sort of work teaches no lesson — entertainment is the actuating motive. Even so harmless a piece of writing as *The Man from Home* is not of sufficient merit as drama, or as a true picture of life, to warrant the long and serious study that is necessary to prepare a play for stage presentation.

The value to be derived by the few who participate in giving the occasional good drama is lessened also by the manner of study, preparation, and presentation. Frequently a professional coach whose methods are theatrical and non-educative is given charge of the work. He trains for effect and for quick results, and, moreover, he has neither the point of view nor the understanding of pedagogy necessary to impart knowledge of the drama as a fine art. His staging apes the so-called professional standard, is showy, and artistically of little value.

Although the dramatic club offers no solution to the problem, it is an indication of the innate desire of young people for dramatic expression. The department of public speaking and oral English is not necessarily the one to take over the teaching of this subject. It grows naturally out of the study of a piece of literature that is dramatic in its nature and should be taught by an expert — one who knows the technique of drama and of acting.

ORGANIZATION OF THE COURSE

At the Francis W. Parker School, during the senior year of the high school, five periods a week are devoted to the study of the drama. This course comprises both academic and laboratory work; that is, the drama is studied as literature, and the stage presentation of a worth-while play is undertaken and carried out. Every member of the class, regardless of special aptitude, is given some experience in each of the essential aspects of the development. The program is so arranged that the class has two forty-minute periods in succession on Mondays and Fridays and a single forty-minute period on Wednesdays. On Mondays and Wednesdays the class meets as a whole, and the work is largely academic in character. On Fridays the class is divided into groups for the purpose of carrying out the class project — namely, the production of a play. A weekly schedule placed upon the board tells each pupil where he is assigned during the laboratory period. The time of all special rehearsals and all individual or group conferences — and these are numerous — is posted at the beginning of each week. During the one-hour-and-twenty-minute work period on Fridays, one portion of the class remains with the instructor of drama for rehearsal of the play that has been selected. These rehearsals as a rule take place upon the stage where the actual performance is to be given. Another group goes to the art room to draw sketches for stage settings, to make designs for costumes, to plan for needed properties, to make posters, and occasionally to execute miniature stage settings on model stages. Still another goes to the greenroom to work upon costumes. Another constructs in the manual-training shop stage settings and executes properties. As wisdom or occasion may dictate, other units are sent to do other assignments: to the library to look up data of various sorts, to the metal shop, to the print shop, or to the dye room. One small group, without a teacher, spends the double period reading aloud and discussing one of a list of plays chosen for this purpose. Occasionally a selected number chooses to dramatize some short story for the use of the school Forum.[1]

Other projects, frequently chosen by the students themselves, occupy the attention of minor groups. Three girls

[1] The Forum is a society made up of high-school students. It meets once a month for intellectual and artistic culture and for social intercourse. The club is divided into self-determining groups — art, science, debating, literature, music, dance, drama, and others; these furnish the program for the monthly meetings of the society. In the main, the work of the Forum groups is self-motivated and self-directed. The drama group is one of the most popular and furnishes an opportunity for members of the drama class to take the initiative and to put into practice the ideas they have learned in theory.

took as their particular portion of labor the planning and execution of some sort of simple setting to serve as a background for the majority of the one-act plays given by the drama group of the Forum.[1]   They first considered making a set of screens that would be both serviceable and decorative.   Then they decided that curtains would be inexpensive, easy to manage, and appropriate for the majority of plays given.   These could be used as a non-realistic background for outdoor settings; or with solid door and window openings they would furnish an interior setting.   Unbleached cotton cloth was selected as the material.   Blue was finally decided upon as the color.   In order to get a satisfactory shade — not too cold nor too warm in tone — it was necessary to experiment for some time with combinations of dyes. A careful record was kept, that the rules for the combination might be available when needed.   Before the decision as to the exact shade was made, samples of cloth were tried in the stage light.   There was too much material to be dyed at one operation, so it was dyed in convenient lengths.   The careful data kept as to the exact proportions used in producing the sample, and as to the length of time the sample had remained in the boiling pot made it possible to dye the curtains satisfactorily even with a limited equipment.

At first we tried the plan of having the laboratory group work during the second half of the double period on Mondays and Fridays.   But it was found that a single forty-minute period gave too little time for any considerable results. The necessary labor of getting materials ready and of putting them away used up an appreciable amount of time and left too brief an interval for actual accomplishment.   The longer period of one hour and twenty minutes once a week was

---

[1] The Forum plays are given in a small auditorium, on a stage of limited size, where the problem of settings and lighting is reduced to the minimum.

found to be worth more in terms of result than the two forty-minute periods on separate days.

The course aims to accomplish certain definite results, but the order in which these are secured allows flexibility and permits one to meet the particular problem or project of the year. If, for example, it seems wise to give the class a choice in the selection of the play to be presented, then the year may wisely begin by the teacher's reading aloud to the class several plays. If this is the case, the Friday period may or may not be used for laboratory or group work. It sometimes seems better to work intensively for a while with the class as a whole. However, as a general thing, the class does avail itself of the opportunity for group work one day each week. There is always some task to be done in the costume room or some problem to be worked on in the art room; and the making of general articles needed for the stage gives plenty of work to the groups assigned to these activities. An art teacher, a manual-training instructor, and a costumer are always available to take charge of and assist the respective groups during the handwork period. If the play first to be produced — usually two dramas are presented, one in January and the other late in May or early in June — has already been decided upon, as soon as it has been read to the class, it becomes the center of activity. During the laboratory period it becomes the subject of major consideration. The group selected to present the first play is made up of the pupils who must take the college entrance examinations at the end of the year. It has seemed advisable to give these young people their experience in dramatic presentation during the early part of the year. With the completion of any project the units change, so that every pupil has experience during the year in several modes of expression.

The One-Act Play, the First Unit of Study

Discussion as to what constitutes a good play is made the basis for much of the class work of the course. The one-act play, because of its brevity and comparatively simple technique is frequently used as the first unit of study. Such plays as *Riders to the Sea*, by Synge, *The Hour-Glass* and *Cathleen Ni Hoolihan*, by Yeats, *The Rising of the Moon*, by Lady Gregory, *Allison's Lad*, by Dix, *A Marriage Proposal*, by Tchekov, *A Night at an Inn*, by Lord Dunsany, *The Clod*, by Beach, and *The Twelve-Pound Look*, by Sir James Barrie, are presented to the class for study and discussion. Other one-act plays are read aloud by groups during the period of group activity. Still others are given to the class for perusal at home. The plays read in class, at the group meetings, or at home, are used as a basis for class discussion. Such volumes as *The Technique of the One-Act Play*, by B. Roland Lewis, and *The Craftsmanship of the One-Act Play*, by Percival Wilde, are referred to frequently. The class is encouraged to purchase these volumes and to note the most helpful passages. When individual ownership is not possible or convenient, the pupils make notes from the class discussion of the essentials in the technique of the short play and file these notes for future reference. The school library is well supplied with books used in the course.

Study of Longer Plays

A study of the full-length play follows next in the drama course. *How to See a Play*, by Richard Burton, is used as the principal reference book, of which every member owns a copy. Many other texts are also consulted. The one-act and the full-length play are contrasted as to type and technique. Every pupil is given a list of suggested plays and is

A scene from *Cathleen Ni Hoolihan.*

required to be thoroughly conversant with at least one play of each of the following noteworthy dramatists: Shakespeare, Molière, Sheridan, Ibsen, Jones, Pinero, Synge, Gregory, Shaw, Barrie, Galsworthy, Dunsany, and possibly others. Ibsen's *The Doll's House* and Pinero's *The Thunderbolt* are in the possession of each student and carefully studied as examples of modern technique. *The Servant in the House*, *Disraeli*, *The School for Scandal*, and other plays are read outside the class and serve as illustrations of technical excellence: *The Servant in the House* for its use of exposition, *Disraeli* for its skillful manipulation of rising action and of crisis, *The School for Scandal* for its wonderful handling, in the famous screen scene, of the *scène à faire*.[1]

Plays being acted at the theaters are recommended to the class for attendance and are discussed as to theme, technique, staging, costuming, and acting. The teacher makes himself conversant with the plays at the different theaters and is ready to give a reason for his opinions. The class, upon seeing a play at the theater, is eager to discuss the theme, the dénouement, the economy of exposition, and kindred matters relating to the play they have seen. Before the course ends the majority of the class becomes fairly discriminating in its criticisms. A noticeable growth in taste is also evidenced by the plays the pupils choose to witness.

STUDY OF TECHNIQUE

All the work in this study is indissolubly connected with the practical project of the play which is in preparation. Actual contact with the drama as stage material illustrates the uses and fixes the rules of technique firmly in the mind. Principles remain no longer abstract statements; they are

---

[1] The selection of dramas used as illustrative material in the drama course varies.

vital parts of a concrete situation closely connected with the actual problem of acting and staging. Impression is therefore carried over into expression; laws are tested and proved; for the lessons are learned under the guidance of an all-impelling, all-absorbing motive and interest. The work focuses individual interest and later leads naturally to an intensive study of stage lighting, theater architecture, costume, stage setting, and kindred topics.

We are at present in the very midst of a renaissance of dramatic art. An evolution of great import is going on in the theater. Evidences of these changes are to be seen on every hand. Illustrations of the new use of illumination, unit settings, pointillage, *Kuppelhorizont* or dome cyclorama, and wagon stages can be not only read about but observed first-hand. Many of these principles can be applied to the plays being presented by the pupils. Since moving pictures are ubiquitous, the cinema, its place and its technique, should have as much consideration as time allows and as its place among the arts merits.

When the work of the drama course is well under way and many points of contact have been established and many questions aroused (more, in fact, than any one person could himself pursue and find answer for), each pupil makes a special study of some topic that particularly interests him. A bibliography is given by the teacher as a help, and whenever a pupil is ready, he gives a report to the class.

Among the subjects thus treated are the revolving, sliding, and wagon stages; the Fortuny lighting system; the work of Max Reinhardt; the influence of Gordon Craig; the Irish Theater movement; the civic theater or community drama; the little theater movement; the open air theater; pageantry and masques.

Emphasis given to Play Production

The value of the school play is determined, first of all by its value to the player. His needs and capacities must govern the choice of material, the method of work, and the style of presentation. Acting a play is fascinating work, and unless the teacher is wise there is danger of losing perspective of the whole educational problem and of permitting the students' impulsive wants to outbalance their needs. There is grave danger of having too many stage presentations — plays uneducatively prepared and given. It is well that the pupil should have as many types of experience as possible and know from experience the multitude and the variety of things that go to make up a stage presentation. This knowledge can be most easily and satisfactorily gained in the school which has a course specially devoted to an intensive study of the drama, where there is a correlation between the various departments, and where a program is sufficiently flexible to allow at regular intervals group work in rehearsing, preparation of costumes, making of stage settings and properties, and like activities. Many people feel that the pupils should do everything connected with the production of a play. This view does not seem practical, economical, or possible. The making of all the costumes, for example, requires more skill and time than is available. However, the major part of the work can be done by the pupils, and the assistance of some of the parents can oftentimes be secured in helping out at the end.

How the Course Functions

There is no attempt to make a drama course of this sort exhaustive or overmature. Its main purpose is to knit together the isolated facts that have been gathered during

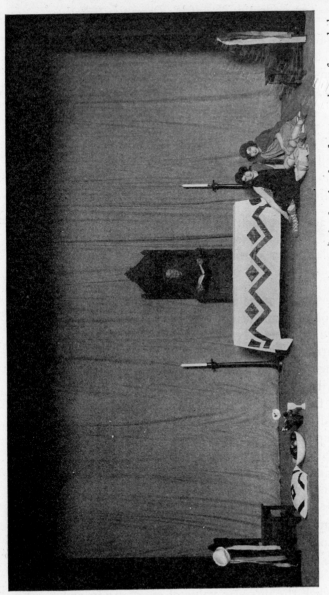

In this scene from *Aria Da Capo*, the regular stage curtains and the first border of taupe velours framed the setting. About eight feet back there was an inner proscenium made of black flannel. The background of gray cotton flannel was left plain in order that the eye might not be drawn away from the area of dramatic action which centered about the table.

the school experience of the children, to give a general survey of the drama, and to furnish those who do not go to college with some exact knowledge on this very important subject. In short, its aim is to give everyone some background for a discriminating appreciation of this fine art and to awaken interest that shall expand, grow, and establish standards that will guide its students in the choice of the plays which they will read and see after their formal school course is done. For, as Tennyson has Ulysses say in his poem of the same name:

> I am a part of all that I have met;
> . . . all experience is an arch wherethro'
> Gleams that untravell'd world whose margin fades
> For ever and for ever when I move.

The regular course in literature needs only to be carried to its logical conclusion to give sufficient exercise of the dramatic impulse. Throughout school experience the study of literature should be dramatic in spirit. There should be a considerable amount of dramatic expression, which is not necessarily a formal play, but yet serves to stimulate imagination, free the agents of speech and gesture, and prepare the children for formal play-giving.

As pupils grow older, they should look upon the plays presented before the whole school as serious pieces of work, demanding a high degree of effort and painstaking and thorough preparation. This attitude means that there will be few stage presentations in the high school. To get the real value out of the production a great deal of time and energy is demanded. If we are to fit youths to become efficient members of society, we must not put an overemphasis on any one subject; therefore, the wise educator should be able to recognize the intrinsic value of every study and be able, through a sane perspective, to give it its due place. The educational pendulum often swings widely from extreme to extreme, because in our enthusiasm, or in our crystallized beliefs, we lose our sense of proportion.

All literature is not to be dramatized, nor is every drama studied to be staged. The presentation of a play represents a social contribution resulting from much thought and long preparation. A play done with costumes and properties before an audience seems to correspond, in a measure, to a picture framed for contemplation. No art teacher would permit a student to frame a rough sketch that he had made. There must be the period of apprenticeship and children should realize that a large appreciation of truth and a considerable degree of freedom gained through practice in expression should precede a formal presentation in costume and with properties. We must elevate the pupil's standards of judgment and hold him to his best. Therefore there should be few plays, as the students mature, and these as carefully worked out as possible. Then they will have that satisfaction and that development of power which comes from a thoroughly painstaking and beautiful bit of work.

TASTES AND STANDARDS

The writer is confident that many young people, through such a course in drama are beginning to see that costumes and scenery alone do not make a play; to appreciate that it is possible to stand before a group of people, and by voice and bearing make a story so real that the listener gets a vivid picture; and to understand that their ability to perceive a thought or an idea vividly is a necessary step which must precede action. Thus they thoroughly enjoy doing scenes from great dramas without scenery or costumes. Let us have as much literary study of this sort as we can afford time for in the high school, let the study be dramatic in spirit, let us have occasional scenes done without special costume, let us have readings, recitations, and story-telling; let us make use of charades, pantomimes, and uncostumed plays, done by one group for another, and by one grade for another, and occasionally let us have a really beautiful and adequate pageant or play in the assembly room, so conscientiously and beautifully done that it lingers in the memory of the school as a standard which it is a high privilege to maintain.

The importance of the occasion should determine the question of scenery and costume, just as it settles what clothes a person shall wear. If the play is a grade exercise, we need merely the suggestion of an accompaniment. If it is for a morning exercise, comparative simplicity again — not too dressed up. If we are presenting a play as a celebration of some festival or as a special occasion, then we may utilize such properties and costumes as will enhance our picture, always keeping in mind the advice of Polonius to his son Laertes:

> Costly thy habit as thy purse can buy,
> But not express'd in fancy; rich, not gaudy.

In its final analysis, the purpose of education is to help one to gain a true consciousness of his real self and to acquire an understanding of his relation to his fellow man. To accomplish this end, education must set the imagination free from the limitations of accidental environment and develop the whole self, physical, intellectual, æsthetic, and spiritual, and thus help man to arrive at the real values of life, the kingdom of Heaven within, the consciousness that he is one with the beautiful and the true. The full realization of this higher self requires therefore more than physical and intellectual attainment; it must include the development of the æsthetic and spiritual nature, and in this attainment the fine arts play a large part. Dr. John Dewey, in a paragraph on the fine arts, writes:

Art is the attempt to satisfy the æsthetic side of our nature. As the æsthetic side of our nature is the feeling of the ideal as such, it follows that art can completely satisfy admiration only when it completely manifests the ideal — whatever that may be. And as we have seen that this ideal is the completely developed self, we may say that the end of art is to create that in which the human soul may find itself perfectly reflected. Or as the essential factor in beauty is harmony — harmony with self — we may say that the end of art is to produce a perfectly harmonized self. The various fine arts are the successive attempts of the mind adequately to express its own ideal nature, or, more correctly stated, adequately to produce that which will satisfy its own demands for and love of a perfectly harmonious nature, something in which admiration may rest.[1]

And in another phrase he says of the drama, "It consummates the range of fine arts."

VOICE PRODUCTION

The professional actor, because of the size of the theater, uses what is ordinarily considered an unnatural voice. He is specially trained in breath control, in range, in enunciation, and in radiation of voice. It is no easy matter to appear to act naturally and at the same time make one's self heard by everyone in a large theater. The ordinary speaker unconsciously gauges the pitch and volume of his voice to the distance between himself and his hearer. On the stage this person (the fellow actor) is not the real listener,

[1] From Dewey's *Psychology* by special arrangement with American Book Company, publishers.

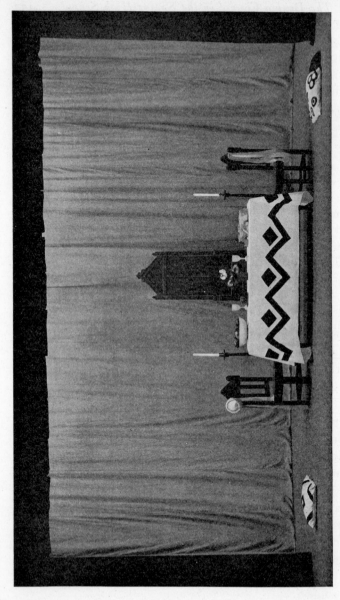

The cushions and table cloth used in this scene from *Aria Da Capo* were designed under the direction of the art teacher; the wooden goblets and the candle holders were turned by the pupils on the school lathes; the chairs were made in the manual-training shop.

138

but the people in the auditorium. It takes a mature physique and a trained technique to make every syllable reach those sitting in the rear seats. Moreover, the effect must be produced consciously. The natural inclination to use no more power than is required to convey one's message to the person on whom the eye is resting has to be counteracted. The amateur's thought — unless the auditorium is, as it should be, comparatively small — is a house divided against itself. He must keep in his part and speak with evident sincerity to the person on the stage, and yet he must consciously strive to make the persons in the back rows of the theater hear. This task requires more skill than the average novice possesses or than there is time to develop; and amateur actors should therefore give their plays in halls of limited size.

A certain amount of voice training, however, can and should accompany the work of preparing a play. It involves very little effort because the motive is impelling. When a person finds that he cannot go through a rehearsal without losing his voice or without at least getting hoarse, he is willing and eager to practice faithfully any exercises that the teacher can prescribe as a counterirritant or as a remedy. Many a household has been astonished to hear a son or daughter, within the privacy of his or her own room, barking like a dog to gain free use of the diaphragm, uttering again and again "mō, mä, mē" — or similar combinations of "m" and vowel sounds to secure forward placement of the voice — or repeating the nonsense combination "most men want poise and more royal margin," as many times as possible in one breath, in an heroic attempt to gain breath control. Training in acting makes young people appreciate, among other things, the necessity for correct pronunciation and for clear enunciation. Careless speech, that to many does not seem especially offensive in ordinary conversation, becomes noticeably bad when spoken in an auditorium, where, to be heard, every syllable must be clearly spoken and not slurred. A musical tone is not only more pleasing than a noise, but it travels farther. Full, resonant tones carry better than loud tones. Indeed in order to express the gamut of feeling and emotion, considerable range of voice is necessary. It is not unusual for an actor to use two full octaves, sometimes more.

CHAPTER XVII

PLAY–MAKING IN THE HIGH SCHOOL

Play-making and the Drama Course

THE writing of plays has its place in the high school, as it has in the grades, and the same general laws and rules apply. Original plays sufficiently meritorious to warrant more than an informal acting before the class are rare. Young people know too little about life and have too few ideas to be able to conceive a plot. There is usually sufficient time during the drama course given in the senior year for the class to attempt to make an original scenario for a one-act play or to dramatize a suitable short story. If an original play is attempted, it would better be a one-act play. The students of a senior class, through their course in drama, should have gained enough knowledge of the technique of the one-act play to make it possible and worth while to attempt that form of literary expression. The students know, among other important facts, that they must have a tense dramatic situation — a *scène à faire* — or there can be no drama in its true sense; and that suspense and not surprise is desirable.[1] They have had practical examples of the way in which the leading dramatists handle the problems of exposition, rising action, and crisis, how they work out dénouement, round out the fable, and avoid an anti-climax. The pupils are well aware that the dramatist is more likely to succeed if he writes about the things of which he has personal

[1] Mr. Lewis states that "suspense is expectancy mingled with uncertainty."

knowledge or experience.   Frequently the dramatization of
a short story, an incident in history, or possibly a portion
of a novel, gives a most satisfactory opportunity for applying
this understanding of dramaturgy and of evolving dramatic
writing that can be presented on the stage with profit.

For Better or Wofse

For instance, a senior class made and presented a dramatization of W. W. Jacobs's short story *For Bett:r or Worse*
— a task which presented many interesting and typical
problems.   The story begins with the chance meeting of
Ben Davis and George Wotton, two penniless old seamen,
in a public room of the "King's Head."   Ben Davis, who
has just returned from foreign parts, tells his friend, George
Wotton, that he has just had the surprise of learning that
the wife he deserted thirty-five years before, has for some
time been living in comfort on money left her by a deceased
mistress.   Ben has returned to England to demand that his
wife take him back and share with him her inheritance.
The two old men start off to find the home of Mrs. Davis.
When at length they reach their destination and gain admittance, an elderly woman appears.   Mr. Davis feels sure
that she is his wife, but on hearing his story, the old lady tells
him that she is not Mrs. Davis, but the housekeeper.   "Mrs.
Davis is away and will not return for some time," she declares.   Ben promises to come back in a week's time and
returns to find a "For Sale" sign in the window.   The old
lady tells him that Mrs. Davis has decided never to come
back to the city and wishes to sell the house.   He learns,
moreover, that he will never get one penny of money.   He
is about to go when his ragged clothing and his look of
misery cause the old lady to reveal the fact that she is Mrs.
Davis and a reconciliation ensues.

To secure the unity of time, place, and action which the one-act play demands, required considerable thought and the exercise of keen discrimination. Many of the class felt that an adequate telling of the story would require at least two locations or scenes; namely, the inn and a room in Mrs. Davis' house. Others were certain that the story could not be presented in dramatic form unless the curtain was lowered to indicate the lapse of time which occurs between Ben Davis' two visits. Some felt that the tale was suited only to the short story matrix and could not be told effectively as a one-act play, but the majority wished to attempt recasting the material in dramatic form.

A tentative plan or scenario was arranged which seemed to meet in a fairly satisfactory manner most of the difficulties. Exactly where to begin the story, how to set up the problem speedily, and how to get in the necessary facts or exposition without slowing up the action unduly, were vital problems which had to be solved when the actual making of the dialogue began. Many changes had to be effected, particularly in the first part of the story. It was decided to have Davis tell his story to Wotton at the Davis house during the interim in which the maid summoned Mrs. Davis. To find a plausible excuse for getting Ben Davis back shortly after his first visit took a considerable period of discussion. Some one at length suggested that he might have lingered opposite the house, in the shadow of a tree perhaps, inspecting the splendors of the house which he hoped to share. It was thought perfectly probable that the old lady might have immediately placed a "For Sale" sign in the window. On the sight of such a notice Ben Davis would doubtless have suspected that all was not as it had been represented. Mrs. Davis had either arrived home unexpectedly, or she had been communicated with by telephone.

Ben Davis in all probability would have sought readmission. The students voted to make these changes of incidents.

The entire class worked on the play, but a voluntary group put it into final shape. It was rehearsed under the sole direction of a few members — pupils who through participation in one of the senior class plays had gained some practical experience — and it was presented at a meeting of the high school Forum. Through the actual presentation of their dramatizations pupils learn in a very practical way where their efforts have failed and where they have proved sound in technique. The test of the cake is in the eating, and the test of the play is in its representation on an actual stage by living actors before an audience.

PAGEANTS

It is perhaps a simpler problem than even this to make a pageant, for its loose construction and large number of episodes make it possible for many groups to write without destroying the unity of the whole. The pageant makes also a most democratic appeal. It has a place even where drama proper is looked upon with suspicion, if not with disapproval. It was with pleasure that the writer saw a Christmas pageant given with special lighting effects and with costumes, in the main auditorium of a conservative Orthodox church in Salem, Massachusetts, where twenty-five years ago such a proceeding would not have been permitted. A discussion of pageants and masques, with their abundant pictorial effects, their application to the celebration of the great recurring festivals, their large spiritual values, and their special technique, are problems that cannot be entered into profitably in this volume. The subject has been treated admirably by such authorities as Percival Chubb, Bates and Orr, Beegle and Crawford, and others.

CHAPTER XVIII

THE LITERARY PLAY IN THE HIGH SCHOOL

THE ONE-ACT PLAY

SHORT plays are especially well adapted to the needs and the ability of high-school students. The school assembly is, of course, the forum where such matters of general interest and profit as the performance of a play naturally find expression. The period set aside for the coming together of all the members of the school is about as long a time as is required to give the average short play. Moreover, beginners have little power of characterization and possess limited ability to sustain an impersonation through the unfolding of a full-length performance. The short play holds the attention of the audience mainly through its story. Inexperienced players, in order to sustain the attention of the audience, have to depend somewhat upon a swiftly moving plot and characters of no great subtlety. The very nature of the short play fits the needs of the high-school student, who has not the power of expression or the mature understanding of life that are necessary to the convincing portrayal of most of the figures of the longer, more complex drama.

The customary single setting for the short play makes it possible also to prepare the scene and to arrange the lighting with a care and attention that are not possible when there are several settings. When it seems desirable to have an audience other than the school — an audience comprised of the parents and friends of the school or the students of other schools — then two short plays preceded by a brief program

For this production of *Overtones*, a background of yellow sateen was used, with old-blue curtains showing beyond the yellow curtains at the place where these parted to form an entrance. Bunch and spot lights with gelatin color filters threw a warm amber light on one part of the sateen curtain and a cold bluish-green on another portion of the curtain. The French gray furniture and the deep-blue wooden vase were made by the class which produced the play.

of appropriate music, or three short dramas, make a program sufficiently long and complex for an afternoon's or evening's entertainment. Every member of the average audience is almost sure to find in a well-chosen and varied group of one-act dramas at least one play that appeals strongly to his fancy.

THE MAID OF FRANCE

The Maid of France, by Harold Brighouse, is a one-act drama with a single setting. The stage directions call for the representation of a square in a French village with a church, houses, and a statue of Jeanne d'Arc in armor. Some of the buildings are in a more or less ruined condition, but the church and the statue are unharmed by German shells. The hour is nearly midnight on Christmas Eve, 1916. The setting and lighting help emphasize the spirit of the play, as the following sketch of the story shows.

A Domrémy peasant has heard that the statue of Jeanne d'Arc comes to life on Christmas Eve. The one great desire of this French private is to hear the voice of the Maid of France, and he is spending his few hours' leave from the trenches waiting for the miracle. As he waits, a flower girl, impressed by his sincerity and his simplicity, gives him a lily of Lorraine to place upon the statue. Then an English private saunters through the square and rests at the base of the statue. To the unbelieving Englishman the *Poilu* confides his great longing, and they fall asleep. As the clock in the tower of the church strikes the hour of midnight, the statue comes to life.

Jeanne is at first surprised and angered to find that English soldiers are frequenting her beloved France. The soldiers awake, and the Englishman vainly tries for some time to explain his presence. At last the French private makes her understand the terrible war that is devastating the country. When she realizes that England has joined France in a great struggle to overthrow military domination, she gives the Englishman thanks and declares, as she steps down from her pedestal and stands between them holding the hand of each: "I am where I would ever be — amongst my fighting men. They have set me on a pedestal and made a saint of me, but I am better here, between you two, both soldiers of France. They will not let me fight for France to-day. Save for this mystic hour on Christmas Eve, I am a thing of stone. But Jeanne lives on. Her spirit fights for France to-day as she fought five hundred years ago. And, in this hour when I am granted speech, I say, 'Fight on, fight on for France till France and Belgium are free and the invader pays the price of treachery.' And you, you English who have come to France, and you in England who are making arms for France, I, who have hated you, I, whom you burnt, I, Jeanne d'Arc of Rheims and Orleans, I give you thanks. My people are your people, and my cause your cause. Vivent! Vivent les Anglais!"

The clock strikes one; a passing cloud shuts the moonlight from her face and she becomes a lifeless statue once more; the two soldiers sleep on at the statue's base. The flower girl returns; the French and English privates awake and at first confuse this modern maid of France, who is standing near them, with Jeanne d'Arc. At length they realize that their experience has been part dream and perhaps part reality. The flower girl wishes the brave fellows, *bonne chance*, and they go back to the trenches uplifted in spirit and indissolubly united in purpose.

In planning the school production, the preservation of continuity was of primary importance; this seemed impossible with the part of the Flower Girl and the part of Jeanne d'Arc played by the same person, as the author intended. An artificial statue was found to be impracticable and unnecessary. The play is short and the person playing the part of Jeanne d'Arc can stand sufficiently still to create the illusion required.

Painted scenery was absolutely discarded because it is

generally inartistic and unnecessary. The stage — which had a depth of about twenty feet and a proscenium opening of twenty-seven feet by fifteen feet — was backed with a cyclorama of Canton flannel dyed a cerulean blue. This curtain of blue was hung from an arc made of iron piping, and in order that it should make a perfectly smooth background, it was tied to a similar arc of piping attached to the floor of the stage. The cyclorama was sufficiently high to render all border strips unnecessary, and extended far enough around to the right and left to make it possible to do away with wings. A sense of great space was thus the result.

A pedestal, with steps leading to it made of wood and painted gray to suggest stone, was placed slightly back of the center of the stage. On each side of the pedestal stood two tall Christmas trees with two shorter ones beside them. The stage was lighted entirely from above by blue light. Jeanne d'Arc, in her suit of bright armor, was the center of interest. In order to hold attention during the first part of the play on the statue as a whole, the light was suffused equally about the stage. It was found through rehearsals — and lighting and setting, as well as actors, need many of these — that a poetic, fanciful atmosphere was best secured when the play was done in a rather dim light. Just as every picture needs its spot of high light, so the stage requires its center. This was secured in the following pleasing and rather novel manner and was made to serve the double purpose of furnishing a necessary note of color and of giving a suggestion of the church from which the music of the midnight mass came while the two privates slept. A cathedral window was painted in color on a lantern slide. The stereopticon was placed off stage left, and the light was focused upon the floor at the base of the statue. This excellent suggestion of the light streaming from the church window gave just the light needed during the conversation of the French private with the flower girl and with the English private and threw the statue sufficiently in shadow to focus the attention where it belonged during the early part of the play. When the clock struck twelve, a spot light off stage right, focused on the face of the statue, was gradually illumined, suggesting moonlight breaking through clouds which had up to this time obscured its rays. The brightest light of the performance came when the play was at its height and was centered on the point of greatest interest.

An old French *Noël* was sung off stage by a dozen boys to the accompaniment of a small organ. The music was introduced solely because it served the effective telling of the story and not as a special feature of the play.

The performance of *The Maid of France* as given by these high-school pupils was a delight to ear and eye. Experience has proved that young people, when properly taught, gain great profit and development from a study of the fine art of drama, and they are able to give performances that are pleasurable and profitable to their fellow students and to older people as well.

LONGER DRAMAS

Pupils, under the enthusiasm aroused by the study of a fine drama, are not infrequently filled with a desire to stage it. This splendid impulse should have due consideration before their request is denied. The expense in time and labor of realizing the thing that they desire must be carefully weighed. High-school students, as the situation now stands, have a very limited time at their command for dramatic projects. In the whole course of their secondary school experience it is improbable that they can be given the time to take part in more than a very few — possibly not more than one — well-prepared and artistically presented dramas. The teacher must count the cost. Is the play under consideration the wisest possible choice? Is it the psychological time to prepare and present a drama? Is the play worth doing? Is it timely, suitable in theme, true in sentiment, helpful and interesting to others? Is it a play that lends itself to stage presentation? Will its cast of characters fit the group that must present it? Are there large royalties or other restrictions in the way? All these and many other questions must be considered. There are numerous plays quite appropriate for silent reading that are not the wisest choice for presentation by students of this age — a glance at the bibliography of plays in this volume will show one the truth of this statement.

It is not always consistent with the best interests of the class that its members should be overurged or forced to choose for presentation one of the classic dramas. The adolescent is interested primarily in the present day, its problems and its achievements. He loves concrete situations, alive with the struggles, hopes, and triumphs of people whom he has some criteria for understanding and judging. Although I never have known a class that did not find the work of preparing one of Shakespeare's plays a thorough joy, nevertheless, I believe it is a mistake to try to force the students to choose something that they do not feel inclined to give. If Euripides, Shakespeare, or Molière be not the dramatists chosen, there are excellent dramas that are well worth every moment of the time that is required to prepare them for satisfactory presentation. For example, one might choose at random the following plays: *The Turn of the Road*, by Mayne; *The Playboy of the Western World*, by Synge; *Trelawny of the Wells*, Pinero; *Androcles and the Lion*, by Shaw; *Abraham Lincoln*, by Drinkwater; *Loyalties*, by

In this scene from *Androcles and the Lion*, the costumes, banners, helmets, spears, slaves' masks, lion's head, the cart, and the painted flats were the work of members of the drama class. Illustrations showing the settings for the various scenes of this play will be found elsewhere in the book.

Galsworthy; *The Servant in the House*, by Kennedy; *The Admirable Crichton*, by Barrie.   Having chosen a play, splendid in content, true in its ethics, faithful in characterization, so well worked out in technique that it is convincing — in short a play that is in all respects worthy of the many hours that must be spent upon it before it can be honestly presented before an audience — the first steps have been taken on the right road — a road that has many bypaths more or less disastrous to the unskilled and the unwise.

There are no hard and fast rules as to when this experience should come in the life of a student: sophomore, junior, or senior year.   It may result best as the natural outgrowth of the study of some particular piece of literature.   There are many advantages, however, in having it come in the senior year as part of definite training in drama and stagecraft. If young people have been educated in a school which recognizes the value of dramatic expression, they have matured sufficiently after twelve years of training to appreciate in a fair degree the place of the stage as a fine art.   They have had considerable practice in expression, vocal and physical; they have acted in an informal way before the class scenes from the dramas under study; they have made into plays episodes in history and literature; they have had work in voice, physical training, and eurythmics; and doubtless every child has taken part in the pageants or festivals of the school.   The preparation of this drama for presentation comes then naturally as a socialized project, in which the pupils put into immediate practice the knowledge that they have acquired in their course in drama and stagecraft.   The course thus becomes of concrete significance and value. Through creative participation thought is clarified, and knowledge functions through experience.   Setting, lighting, costuming, acting, and all the allied activities of the drama become personal interests and the work of such artists as Reinhardt, Craig, Appia, Bakst, Robert Edmond Jones, Walter Hampden, and Mrs. Fiske take on a very real meaning. The student who labors to devise appropriate settings, beautiful costumes, purposeful lighting, and significant stage business, in so doing learns by the one true method — experience.

THE ADMIRABLE CRICHTON

The Admirable Crichton, by Sir James Barrie, is one of the most delightful and one of the most worth-while modern plays for senior high-school or college students to work upon. Furthermore, it never fails, when sincerely and adequately presented, to hold the interest of an audience; for few plays have a theme so pertinent and a love story so sane and wholesome as has this masterpiece of Barrie's.

The stage settings, however, offer a perplexing problem to any group of amateurs limited in money. A reading of the author's descriptions, particularly that of the house on the island, may cause one perhaps to conclude that it cannot be satisfactorily envisaged without great expense. Nevertheless, if one is willing to eliminate every non-essential, and if one will be satisfied to suggest in the simplest way the background and to use only the absolutely necessary properties, the difficulties are reduced, and an artistic, pleasing staging becomes possible without overtaxing the limited equipment available in the average high school. Such a simple setting, provided it is in harmony with the spirit of the play, is not contrary to Barrie's ideas, as will be seen if one reads the introduction to his short play, *The Will*.[1]

For Acts I and IV of *The Admirable Crichton*, a room in Lord Loam's house, simple screens were used, as will be seen

---

[1] *The Will* is a most wholesome play for high-school students to study.

The Admirable Crichton, Act IV.

in the picture shown on page 155. The change to Act II, a scene on a lonely island, was quickly effected because the setting was in place behind the screens when the curtain rose for the beginning of the play. For Act II the blue cyclorama, or *Rundhorizont*, formed the background. Down stage left a great rock (made of beaver board) extended up out of sight and helped to indicate the nature of the island and mask the stage down left. Down stage right stood the front of a rude hut made of unbarked slabs that suggested a hastily erected log shelter. Smaller rocks were placed back stage to mask the line where the blue cyclorama met the stage floor. The height of the cyclorama made the use of borders, other than the first, unnecessary. A bucket, a log, wood for the fire, and a few other absolutely necessary properties completed the equipment for Act II. A judicious use of light and a carefully planned manipulation of the dimmers transformed the simple setting into a picture of excellent proportions and of illusive charm. When night had fallen, the stage, illumined solely by the firelight and the glow of the lantern, gave a sense of the vastness of the island and of the impenetrable depth of the tropical jungle. The frightened refugees creeping back to food, warmth, and shelter, cast great mysterious shadows. Thus the whole effect was far more impressive than could have been secured by paint and canvas.

The interior of the island house with all of its ingenious, quaint equipment, so delightfully imagined and described by the author, and the bane of the stage producer, save a Belasco, was treated in a simple manner that aimed not at realization but at suggestion. Screens, easily put together in any arrangement desirable, formed the background for the house on the island. These screens, similar to those used by Gordon Craig, were covered with natural-tone burlap

The Admirable Crichton, Act. II.

and were built sufficiently high to make a ceiling cloth or border strip unnecessary.

At a more recent presentation of *The Admirable Crichton,* curtains made of unbleached muslin were used to indicate the interior of the house on the island.[1] These curtains were hand-dyed a grayish brown. They suggested fairly well the sort of stuff that Crichton's household might have woven and dyed to cover the rough walls of their improvised home. They had the advantage over screens or flats in that they were very quickly set in place and quite as quickly removed.

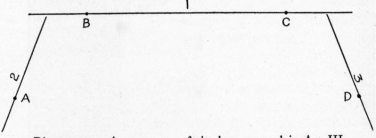

Diagram 2. — Arrangement of the battens used in Act III,
The Admirable Crichton.

The curtains were hung from three wooden battens (1, 2, 3). The two smaller battens (2 and 3) were hinged to the longer batten (1) by ropes. When the scene was in use or set, the battens were suspended from the gridiron or stage ceiling on four ropes (A, B, C, D). To strike the scene (or clear the stage) the battens were lowered, and ropes A and D were detached. The smaller battens (2 and 3) were then folded back against the longer batten (1) and drawn up out of sight of the audience.

The many courses of food placed before Crichton were served in sea shells, gourds, and rude clay dishes fashioned

[1] See illustration on page 244.

by children of the lower grades. Slices of fresh bread or pieces of banana, disguised by various sorts of greens, suggested fish, fowl, or what you will. Crichton's ingenious signs were easily managed by means of tiny wires that could be released at the proper moment and caused the signs to drop down into place with their warning words in full view. The whir of the machinery, supposed to operate them, was suggested by twirling, off stage, one of the wooden rattles so frequently used in jazz orchestras.

MASTER PIERRE PATELIN

Now and then it is good pedagogy and good fun to act one of the plays written during the Middle Ages: *Everyman*, *The Sacrifice of Isaac*, *Gammer Gurton's Needle* (arranged by Stuart Walker), or the old French farce, *Master Pierre Patelin*, translated and arranged by R. T. Holbrook. A brief description of a setting used for a production of this last may be suggestive and helpful.

It should always be borne in mind that a farce is a difficult type of play for amateurs to get across the footlights. It must go with sure and certain teamwork and must gain steadily in force and interest until the climax is reached. Cues therefore must be picked up quickly, speech piled upon speech, and pitch and tempo unerringly and unflaggingly maintained. The effect must be cumulative. This requires a skill and a knowledge of dramatic technique not ordinarily possessed by the novice. Actors in playing farce and comedy must take their parts most seriously and not let the audience see that they are enjoying them. The audience likes to feel that it gets the humor through its own cleverness.

The first problem that presented itself was the choice of a translation. The arrangement made by R. T. Holbrook seemed to preserve the spirit of the original, both in language

A setting for *Master Pierre Patelin.*

and in content, far better than any other text that came
into our hands for consideration. Some of the plays that
have grown out of the original French farce have been
changed and amended quite out of harmony with the spirit
and character of the day. The introduction of sentiment,
for example, is quite alien to this "epic of an age of rogues."
It was found advisable to cut not a few speeches in order to
avoid tediousness and repetition, but in the main the Holbrook text was followed rather faithfully. Believing that
the play would gain thereby in speed and cumulative effect,
the class decided to act it without change of scene and without dropping the curtain. The stage of the Middle Ages —
as one will see by the illustration in Brander Matthews' book,
A Study of the Drama, page 292 — permitted several localities to be presented, and a divided stage, as shown in the
following plan, was utilized with most satisfactory results.

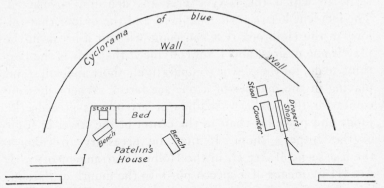

Diagram 3. — Stage arrangement for *Master Pierre Patelin.*

The right half of the stage represented the interior of
Pierre Patelin's house, with its curtained bed, two benches,
and a stool. The left half represented the street in front of
the draper's store. With this arrangement, scene succeeded

scene without interruption or break. The draper could display his goods on the counter in front of his shop, and the judge could hold court in the public square, as was the custom of the times. The action begins in the home of Patelin, and when this is completed it is easy to shift interest and attention to the left half of the stage. The draper comes from his shop and after a look at the sky to ascertain the weather prospects, he brings out several rolls of cloth, which he places on the counter close beside his window. Probably he draws the counter out a little way from the wall to facilitate the examination of his goods. When the lawyer, Patelin, has completed his purchase, the draper gathers up his cloth, replaces the stool and the counter, and retires to his shop to prepare for going to Patelin's for dinner. Action is now resumed at stage right, and Patelin and his wife plan their trick. The draper arrives, and the wild scene in which the lawyer pretends delirium is enacted. The incident between the shepherd and the draper that follows in the Holbrook text can come without a break in the play if one desires, and I am convinced that this is the best thing to do, for the play is comparatively short and will stand playing in the manner of a one-act farce. When the time comes for the trial, two bailiffs or attendants precede the judge and place his chair in the center of the street in front of the draper's shop. It may be necessary to connect the last scene of Act II, in the Holbrook arrangement, with Act III by means of a speech put into the mouth of Patelin. Save for a few minor changes in dialogue and slight planning of stage business, it is surprising how well the play lends itself to the divided stage setting used without drop of the curtain.

CHAPTER XIX

PRESENTATION OF SHAKESPEARE'S PLAYS

Stylization

Every high school will, of course, at one time or another act one of the Shakespeare plays. Let us, then, consider next how a play of the great English master can best be presented. The actual style — and to-day we are hearing a great deal about "stylization" in drama production [1] — of presentation of any play is determined by the inherent nature of the play under consideration and by the place where the performance is to be made. Shakespeare's plays, as everyone knows, were written to be acted in his own theater, on a large, uncurtained platform-stage, under the open sky, in a crude and badly lighted building. If it is intended to give the play out-of-doors, then the problem is comparatively simple. Unhampered by stage settings, the entire play can be given with the speed and continuity of interest that was possible in the Elizabethan theater.

Hamlet

Suppose one has merely a stageless gymnasium to serve as his theater. With very little expense and trouble a most delightful presentation can be given in just such a place. The production can be stylized historically. The Elizabethan stage can be suggested, or even fairly accurately

[1] For a discussion of stylization, see Moderwell's *The Theatre of Today*, Chapter VII.

reproduced. In the celebration of the three-hundredth anniversary of Shakespeare's death, such a production of

The Closet Scene from *Hamlet*. The person playing Hamlet is Ian Keith, now well-known for his work on the professional stage and in the cinema.

the folio text of *Hamlet* was done by the senior high-school class at the Francis W. Parker School.

The following extract is from the explanatory paragraphs included in the program and prepared by one of the students who participated in the performance. It will elucidate several facts regarding this particular project in play production.

In undertaking to give *Hamlet* the senior class knows that it has chosen something exceedingly difficult to present — a play requiring the best that it can give of intellectuality, emotion, and dramatic ability, and it is ready to do its utmost.

A Shakespearean play was chosen because this year is the three-hundredth anniversary of the great artist's death, and it is fit and proper that those who are fond of his works should honor him. Several of Shakespeare's plays were considered, and the majority of the class preferred to give a tragedy. It is the custom of the school to have each member of the graduating class take part in the final play, and since the *dramatis personæ* of none of Shakespeare's plays contains a sufficiently large number of female parts, it was necessary to choose the play that would best lend itself to casting girls for men's parts. The poetic nature of *Hamlet* makes it possible to have a number of the parts played by girls without detracting from the dignity of the drama. This fact, in addition to the inherent merit of the play, decided our choice.

A study of the rise of the drama and the effect that the mode of presentation had upon the technique of a play suggested the idea of presenting *Hamlet*, as nearly as our resources would permit, in the manner in which it was done in London by Shakespeare at his own theater, the Globe. Such a production would make it possible to give nearly all the text and to keep the balance and spirit of the story as few professional performances on our modern stages have been able to do. . . .

Besides being a playwright, Shakespeare was a shareholder and actor in the theater and always had his own stage and company in mind when he wrote his plays. People have added stage directions, and the modern theater has compelled changes in the setting forth of *Hamlet*, until now the play often strikes a false note, and the true sense is submerged under innovations.

Shakespeare's playhouse was round, and only the outer circle was covered by a thatched roof. The stage was about 40 feet by 43 feet, the front half was uncovered and extended out into the audience. At the rear was a tower with an interior room and a usable balcony, a forest to the left of the stage and a street to the right. On either side of the stage to right and left on an oblique line were proscenium doors, which represent the localities of Polonius' house and the King's chapel.

For the presentation of a play written in the manner of Shakespeare's plays this platform stage with no curtain and fixed scenery has many advantages. The blast of a bugle from the tower of the castle at the back of a vast, empty stage gives a greater sense of expectancy and excitement to start the play than does the mechanical rising of a curtain. Even dimmed lighting cannot represent night on the stage as did the darkness broken only by the flickering cresset lamps of Shakespeare's time. The frequent change of scene and breaks at the end of an act make the movement of *Hamlet* slower than it should be and often spoil the continuity. Shakespeare did not divide his play into acts: that has been done on account of the need for change of scene on the modern stage. It often interferes with the movement. For instance, when the ghost tells Hamlet to follow him from the tower, the curtain drops; and when we next see the two, the scene has been changed to a place outside the castle. On Shakespeare's stage there was no break here, but the ghost and Hamlet descended the stairway at the back of the castle and were soon seen at the right of the castle on the ground. There was no long pause to ruin the atmosphere of excitement and emotion reached by Hamlet and the spirit.

The extreme width of Shakespeare's stage and the fact that it extended out into the audience gave the spectators the impression of Hamlet's isolation and safety from listening ears when he gave his soliloquies at the front of the stage, and made asides seem natural.

A scene in the castle throne room was given partly inside and partly in front of the tower room door. In the same manner, the spectators would know that if two people were playing in front of the forest, they were supposed to be in the forest. The scene

An Elizabethan setting for *Hamlet*. In this performance the part of Hamlet was taken by Geneva Harrison, now a writer and actress of promise, and that of King Claudius by Arnold Horween, at present the head football coach of Harvard University.

was really only suggested in the background, and the audience used its imagination for the rest. The fore stage was used to suggest indefinite places.

The forest was made of real trees, and the houses were not merely painted scenery, so the whole setting was natural. The orchard plays a peculiar part in the march of events. It has a mysterious and awful significance, inasmuch as it is there, where the first King was killed, that the ghost leads Hamlet and tells him of the murder. Here the strolling players in dumb show disclose the method of the poisoning.

On the modern stage, the dumb show is presented in the throne room and after the call for "Lights! Lights! Lights!" the King rushes out into the darkness. It is much more sensible to have the performance outside and have men rush in with torches at the King's demand for lights.

The stage which the Seniors will use will be as nearly like that of Shakespeare as possible, but of necessity the stage must be smaller (a little more than half as large as the Globe stage), the tower lower, and modern lighting substituted for torches and cresset lamps. With this setting we hope to make the performance just as natural, swift-moving, and stirring as those which the great dramatist himself staged. — Helen Brecher, '16

As You Like It

A realistic presentation of Shakespeare's plays is a mistaken undertaking for any high school — indeed for any group of players, professional or non-professional. Right settings cannot be obtained and frequent change of scene makes a performance choppy and tedious. Professional artists, such as Rollo Peters, Walter Hampden, and John Barrymore have seen the futility of so-called realistic settings and have discarded them for simple, decorative backgrounds, which help to give atmosphere and beauty, and which permit scene to follow scene with little or no loss of time.

As You Like It was produced at the University of Chicago, by members of the high school in a very simple but most effective manner. Speed of action and concentration of attention were gained by having but one intermission. All the scenes that take place out of the forest were acted as a group. Very brief pauses indicated lapses of time, without the dropping of the curtain. For the first setting the stage was hung with a soft burlap curtain of natural color; the floor was covered with a blue-green cloth; in the center of the stage, at the back, was placed a tall piece of statuary, with a group of real box and bay trees for a background; at the right and left of the stage were two quaint iron lawn seats, backed by bay trees. The stage was effectively lighted; the result was a scene that was both suggestive and exceedingly lovely. This non-realistic setting was meant to suggest Duke Frederick's garden. Members of the duke's household made their entrance from the left, thus indicating that his palace lay in that direction. The members of Oliver's household entered from the right, where his home was presumably located. The second group of scenes comprised all those which take place in the forest. Again a lapse of time was indicated without dropping the curtain. For them the same burlap background was used — had it not been necessary to practice strict economy, a curtain of blue would have been selected — and the stage was provided with real evergreen trees and with an old log or two in the foreground. These two settings, framed by the pleasing proscenium and the gracefully draped crimson curtain of the hall, made effective and unobtrusive backgrounds that lent atmosphere to the whole play and served to bring into relief the carefully costumed players.

At a more recent production, Oliver's garden or orchard and the castle grounds of Duke Frederick were definitely

indicated.   Three stage settings were used: the garden, the
castle grounds, and the forest of Arden.   A blue cyclorama
formed the background for all.   The settings were so simple,
and so easily and quickly placed, that the waits were very
short.[1]   Oliver's garden and the castle grounds of Duke
Frederick were composed of the same units differently arranged.   Six artificial bay trees and a circular bench comprised the units of both.   The bay trees were made by the
class presenting the play.   The trees were hollow wooden
pyramids — the fourth side was omitted because unseen by
the audience — painted a dark, dead-finish green and covered with sprays of natural, prepared foliage which were
held securely in place by means of double-pointed tacks.
These trees were set in great wooden tubs.   For the scene in
Duke Frederick's garden, four of the trees were placed back
stage center — the two tall trees in the middle.   A circular
bench painted a dull gray to suggest stone was placed in
front of them.   Down stage left and right were two more
trees.[2]   To represent Oliver's garden, the trees were grouped
part way down stage right and left, — the large tree behind
the two smaller trees.[3]   This time the bench was not used.
The forest of Arden was quickly set by placing some natural

---

[1] The scenes and the waits were as follows:

Act I.	Scene I.	Orchard of Oliver's house. (Wait of two minutes.)
	Scene II.	Lawn before the Duke's palace. (Wait of two minutes.)
Act II.	Scene I.	Orchard of Oliver's house. (Wait of five minutes.)
	Scene II.	The forest of Arden. (No Wait.)
	Scene III.	The forest. (Wait of two minutes.)
Act III.	Scene I.	The forest. (No wait.)
	Scene II.	The forest. (Wait of two minutes.)
Act IV.	Scene I.	The forest. (Wait of two minutes.)
Act V.	Scene I.	The forest. (No wait.)
	Scene II.	The forest.

[2] See the upper illustration on page 171.
[3] See the lower illustration on page 171.

A setting for *As You Like It*: the lawn before the Duke's palace.

A setting for *As You Like It*: Oliver's garden.

logs at desired spots, and by dropping from above masses of unbleached cotton cloth which had been dyed to suggest the color of tree trunks. The cotton cloth was hung on hoops of various sizes and suspended at judiciously chosen intervals. A carefully planned lighting scheme bound the scene together and gave a sense of dramatic fitness and of decorative beauty.

For an outdoor setting, painted scenery should not be used unless one is able to procure (and it is rarely possible) a back drop that is painted so beautifully that it is really a work of art. If such a panoramic drop can be obtained, then it should be used with curtains or tall screens at the sides of the stage. Ugly, inartistic, painted wings and sky borders never did and never will create an illusion of reality or in any way add to the picture. Backgrounds painted in perspective are bad for other reasons than those already stated, for as the actor moves up or down the stage, painted objects in the background appear to grow large or small, as did Alice in Wonderland. A mountain that seems to suggest a mountain when the actor plays down stage becomes, as he moves towards it, first a hill and then a mere mound. Not only is all sense of illusion lost, but a grotesque effect is produced.

THE MERCHANT OF VENICE

For the *Merchant of Venice* a semi-conventional setting was devised which remained unchanged throughout the play. Screens of various widths were put together with angle irons to serve as a false proscenium and to mark off the fore stage. These, twelve in number, were covered to suggest stone with a gray flannel — a material which was not only inexpensive, but which took the light exceedingly well. The openings at

A scene from *The Merchant of Venice*: A public place in Venice.

A setting for *The Merchant of Venice*: a room in Portia's home at Belmont.

174

the right and left were slightly recessed to give a feeling of
solidity.   Mulberry-color velours curtains were so hung that
they could be drawn to shut off the rear stage from view.
The rear stage was raised and reached by two steps that
extended all the way across the middle stage from the screen
on the right to the screen on the left.   A low wall backed
the upper stage.   A cyclorama of blue flannel made the
background and was more or less visible in all scenes except
the court room.   The full stage, with a well and a well curb
placed in the center, was used for the street scenes.   The
false proscenium at the right had a usable door that served
to indicate the house of Shylock.   (Doors on the stage usually swing outward and are hinged on the up stage side of the
side walls.   This device helps to mask the region off stage
and the solid construction of doors adds greatly to the
effectiveness of a scene.)

When the scene represented the home of Portia, the door
was removed, also the well and the well curb, and a rug and
a few necessary articles of furniture were placed on the stage.
In this scene the velours curtains were allowed to show
slightly at either side of the stage.   The court room was
suggested by drawing the velours curtains, and thus shutting
out the rear stage; the well proper was removed and the
well curb transformed into a dais for the Duke's chair by
placing a rug over it.   Portia's garden was suggested by
pushing the velours curtains out of sight, removing the dais
and placing two benches down-stage right and left, and two
box-trees up stage right and left.

The skillful use of lights did much toward making the
settings effective and toward differentiating the scenes.
(The illustrations on pages 173, 174, and 176, will suggest
how the scenes were set.)   With some such background as the
one which has been sketchily described, the many scenes of

A setting for *The Merchant of Venice*: a court of justice at Venice.

A setting for *The Merchant of Venice*: Portia's garden.

such a play as the *Merchant of Venice* can be given practically in their entirety within the time limit ordinarily allotted
to a theatrical performance, and moreover, the setting is
inexpensive and pleasing. The screens can be combined in
many ways and so used for numerous plays.

TWELFTH NIGHT

Curtains were used exclusively to form the settings for
Twelfth Night, and consequently changes of scene were
effected with celerity. Black Canton flannel made a permanent proscenium — number 3 in the diagram below.[1] To

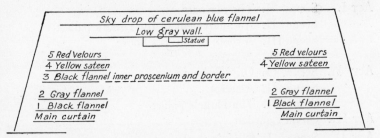

Diagram 4. — Curtain arrangement for *Twelfth Night*.

represent an apartment in the Duke's palace, the red velours
curtains, numbered 5 in the diagram, were closed.[2] For the
scenes in Olivia's house the yellow sateen curtains, numbered
4 in the diagram, were partly drawn.[3] In the scene where
Malvolio interrupts the merrymaking of Sir Toby and his
coterie, the yellow curtains were completely closed. For
the street scenes the gray curtains, numbered 2 in the diagram, formed the background.[4] These, transformed by
lighting which gave a suggestion of heavy fog, served for the
sea-coast setting. They also formed the back drop for the

[1] See the illustration on page 406.
[2] See the illustration on page 374.
[3] See the illustration on page 390.
[4] See the illustration on page 398.

place where Malvolio was imprisoned. A black wooden grating was dropped from above, and the black curtains, numbered 2 in the diagram, were drawn to meet it. When the scene of Olivia's garden was shown, all the curtains, with the exception of those forming the inner proscenium, were drawn out of sight of the audience.[1] The yellow curtains were designed and stencilled by the pupils. Members of the class took some part in designing and making the costumes, the silver screen, and the properties.

The following synopsis of the scenes is taken from the program.

Act I.   Scene   I. The seacoast
          Scene II. An apartment in the Duke's palace
          Scene III. A room in Olivia's house
          Scene IV. A street
Act II.   Scene   I. Olivia's house
          Scene II. A street
          Scene III. The Duke's palace
Act III. Olivia's garden
Act IV.   Scene   I. Olivia's garden
          Scene II. Olivia's house
Act V.   Olivia's garden

Lack of a special setting need never deter any high school from staging Shakespeare's dramas. Some of the most effective presentations made by professional actors have been done with little or no scenery. Indeed, one of Forbes Robertson's most impressive performances was given on a platform stage hung with draperies. The values and joys of having taken part in a carefully worked out performance of one of Shakespeare's plays are so great and lasting that one wonders if high-school instructors do not owe it to their students to give them at some time this rich experience.

[1] See the illustration on page 406.

CHAPTER XX

COSTUMING AND SETTING

Costuming and Setting the Child's Play

In the presentation of a play, costuming and stage setting are important matters. Their office is to give the audience the atmosphere and to help the actor to assume the character he is impersonating. It is not necessary that costume and setting be historically correct, but they should be symbolically and suggestively correct. That is, the color and line should express the feeling of the performance.

In the case of little children, imagination costumes them royally, and quickly changes a common cap or coat into a magic garment, under cover of which they easily portray the witchery and power of fairies, goblins, and the other spirits that people the old literature. The merest suggestion transforms a child into the character he wishes to assume; a feather stuck on his head makes a boy an Indian; a gun turns him into a hunter; a sword into a soldier or a knight. In playing Old King Cole anything does him for a pipe or a fiddle, and any old cloth becomes a regal robe for the king, especially if it has color. Only children and great actors are capable of such feats of the imagination.

The reader will recall from his personal remembrances of the dramatic plays of little children that the participants were always "dressing up" and taking great satisfaction in so doing. The love of costume is so deep-seated that we cannot afford to ignore it entirely, and occasionally it seems that little folk as well as high-school students should have the great delight of playing something in appropriate attire and with fitting and lovely stage background, for mere joy as well as for training in taste, simplicity of line, and harmony of colors.

Yet it would be ridiculous to try to costume many of the plays of the smaller pupils. Their efforts quickly lose their spontaneity and cease to be studies of life when we put on all these externals. Furthermore, costumes require time to make and put on and are an added expense, which is often a serious obstacle to school productions. The plays are also much better given without costume or scenery than presented in ugly material or placed in a flimsy setting. If we costume at all, let us regard simply beauty in lines, colors, and textiles. Too much dress, too elaborate or realistic a background, too much time spent on plot and language, and too high a perfection of finish destroy the simplicity and sincerity of children's plays. Under such artificial stimulation, boys and girls cease to make original contributions, because they become so absorbed in the externals of costume and stage setting that they lose the spirit of the piece.

Costume and Setting in the Upper Grades and in the High School

In the upper grades, costume and setting play a more important part than in the lower, although the essentials of acting are still dependent upon the imagination of the actor, upon his power of relating each scene to the whole play, upon his conception of character, and upon the truthfulness of his interpretation, as shown in voice, speech, and gesture.

In acting, children are, however, fundamentally dependent only on their imagination and on their power of constructive synthetic thinking. One of the most effective bits of work the author has seen was the presentation by eighth-grade boys and girls of the first scene of Act II of *Julius Cæsar*. It is a sombre scene, set in the orchard of Marcus Brutus; the time is night. A dark green cloth covered the floor; a bench and stand were the only properties; some tall dark screens were placed in the background and at the sides. All this gave a suggestion of the atmosphere, of the night, and of the trouble and the conflict going on in the mind of Brutus. The students had spent much of the year on the study of the play. At different times they had acted out the parts of Act I and the quarrel scene, and had recited the speeches of Brutus and Antony at Cæsar's funeral. In their study of the drama, they had read aloud over and over again, not formally, but in answer to questions; they had conceived vividly the relation of the first scene of Act II to the whole and had realized the dominating part played by Brutus, as well as the attitude of all the characters towards him. They always had played without costume or make-up, in broad daylight. As this manner of presenting a scene had been very little used at that time and as most of the children were acquainted with professional performances notably realistic in presentation, objections from them were to be expected, but they never came. The sincerity and earnest-ness of the actors made this informal, daylight performance thoroughly delightful and convincing.

Indeed, lack of mechanical accessories stimulates con-structive activity on the part of youthful performers and calls into action many modes of expression, for the children find intense satisfaction in constructing all kinds of scenery and stage properties, in drawing pictures of the scenes as they would like to set them, and in making sketches of the costumes. Students say this study helps them to play

This setting for *Tom Pinch* is especially interesting because the background was made of reversible screens covered on one side with cretonne, on the other side with natural-tone burlap. The screens, the bust of Pecksniff, and the architectural drawings on the walls were the handiwork of the group producing the play. All the articles in the room were called for by the stage directions.

without the scenery and the costumes, because when they have once made a model or drawing of the stage setting and characters, in imagination their play is properly set and costumed. If the play is their own, dialogue develops as the action is worked out. This is true teamwork in that each contributes; one proposes a speech; others consider and criticise. Then comes a closer, more intense study followed by another trial — and so the whole takes form. Rarely, if ever, does a child make a vain show of his play; he creates it and acts it for the joy it brings him. The so-called "shows" are not instituted by the children.

If the play is an historical or a period play (for example, a Shakespeare play), the problem of costumes takes on large proportions. To rent costumes is generally uneducative, as well as unwise. Crudely-colored, over-ornamented, ill-fitting apparel is always undesirable and frequently expensive. Moreover, the renting of costumes deprives the drama class of the opportunity of taking part in planning garments that in design, color, and arrangement have beauty and meaning, and that help to express the spirit and mood of the play.

In anticipation of the production of *The Merchant of Venice*, a note was sent to each mother in the school asking for old silks, velvets, velours, tapestries, and other materials that might be used for this purpose. The larger pieces contributed, together with the fabrics available in the costume department of the school,[1] were spread out where they could be seen easily. Selection was made then of materials suitable in color and texture for the characters who dominated the major action of the play. Next choice was made for those who must frequently play in company with the main

---

[1] Every high school should gradually build up a set of carefully selected costumes for school use and stock a chest with materials for the realizing of future hopes.

characters. In this way the stage groups were made to harmonize, and as a result the stage picture was always beautiful and appropriate. The determining factors in the selection of color and of fabric were the setting or background, the importance of the character, and the nature of the stage personality, for color was used symbolically, as well as decoratively. As soon as the materials for any costume were chosen, samples were cut and pinned on a large sheet of heavy paper opposite the name of the character and of the person who was to play the part. A second chart was kept, on which opposite the name of the character and the player, the colors of the costumes were painted in water colors. This chart showed not only the general color scheme, but the proportion of the various colors in each costume and in each group.

Then too a representation of the stage setting is made and placed on a small model stage in order that the class may gain some idea of how the play will look when given. If time permits, small figures are made and costumed to represent the characters. As a rule, stage settings should be so simple that they can be made by the pupils. The screens for *The Merchant of Venice*, seen in the pictures on pages 173, 174, and 176, were made by a group of boys in the manual training shop.

MAKE-UP

The question of make-up needs a few words of consideration. As has been stated already, make-up should be used rarely on children of the elementary school — never on very young children. In the high school it should be used only when absolutely necessary. It is the practice of many city schools to hire a professional make-up artist for the big play productions. This is an expensive and an unnecessary

This setting for *Tom Pinch* was made by using the reverse side of the screens shown in the picture on p. 182.

practice — indeed out of the question for places at a distance from a large center. The teacher of drama should have or should acquire sufficient knowledge and skill to do, or direct personally, all this work, for the instructor who has conducted the study of the play has the clearest knowledge of the characteristics of the individuals to be portrayed and is therefore the one best fitted to make up the actors for their parts. As has been affirmed more than once, all that goes to constitute a performance — acting, lighting, settings, costuming, make-up, music, and the like — must be parts of a unified whole, the *inscenierung*. This is possible only when one mind has general control and supervision.

When the footlights are not used, or are used only in moderation, and the major light comes from above, little or no make-up is needed, except for those who play character parts. Light that comes from above casts normal shadows on the face, but when the light is reversed, as is the case when powerful footlights are used, make-up must be used generously. With a dry make-up (blending powder, rouge, and a few lining pencils) a great many people can be made up in a short time. The writer prepared all the pupils for *The Merchant of Venice* in a little more than an hour. Character parts of course take the most time and skill, but even these parts (by the use of brown and gray grease paint, lining pencils to indicate wrinkles and hollows, and blending powders of various tints and shades) can be made up satisfactorily in a comparatively short time.[1] A full grease-paint make-up, such as is used by professional actors, necessitates a cold cream foundation and takes much skill and time to

[1] There has recently appeared on the market a greaseless make-up which is put on with a wet sponge. The lining colors are applied with a wet Chinese or camel's hair brush. This "Virginia Lee Make-Up," manufactured at 1715 Euclid Avenue, Cleveland, Ohio, is an excellent time saver.

apply. Artificial beards should ordinarily be shunned. With the aid of curled hair, spirit gum, and a pair of scissors, a very natural looking beard can be made. Wigs also should be avoided when possible, and when it is absolutely necessary to use one, it should be selected with the utmost care, since an ill-fitting, ugly wig does much to mar an otherwise splendid performance. By the use of liquid white mascaro the appearance of white hair can be secured without resorting to what may prove a poor substitute. In order to be sure of the effect, make-up should be put on under the same light as that in which the actor will appear when in public.

Backgrounds painted in perspective are seldom used either by the art theaters of to-day or by the more enlightened schools. The practice of buying and using second-hand scenery that has been discarded by some professional producer is stupid and baneful. With a cyclorama for the background of all exterior scenes, with screens to mask the fore stage at right and left, and with the few necessary solid units required for the play, any exterior scene, if properly lighted, can be satisfactorily and beautifully envisaged. Interiors can be set with screens or curtains. The background should always be unobtrusive, harmonious, and appropriate. More than one play has failed upon the professional stage because the designer (sometimes an artist of national reputation) has created a setting so disproportionate in its lines and masses, so insistent in color or bizarre in its pattern, that is was no longer a true background but dominated the stage and threw actor and play alike out of focus.

Every moment is precious, and the shorter the intervals between curtains, the more successful the performance. Careful planning and the aid of intelligent assistant stage managers do much to reduce the waits to a minimum. If the curtains are announced by a bell, this should have a musical sound. A plate chime of four tones is perhaps the most pleasing announcer of the acts. But a bell is not absolutely necessary, since the extinguishing of the lights in the auditorium is sufficient notice that the curtain is about to rise.

Nor should curtain calls be permitted, for the play and not the player is the important consideration. In school plays, flowers should not be handed over the footlights — indeed the presentation of bouquets should be discouraged, and everything possible should be done to make the drama rather than the personality of the player prominent. If friends will be sentimental and foolish and send flowers, these floral offerings should be brought unostentatiously to the stage by the way of the stage door.

THE PROMPT BOOK

A carefully prepared prompt book is indispensable to the prompter and to the stage director. This should clearly designate all stage business, list all properties, indicate the grouping of the characters, star the cues for off-stage effects (such as telephone rings, pistol shots, trumpet calls) and give diagrams of the lighting plots. If the printed text of the play does not offer sufficient space for the various notations needed, then a prompt book can be made by pasting the pages from two copies of the printed play in a loose-leaf note book, leaving a blank leaf opposite each page of the text.

Properties to be used should be placed on a special shelf or table, where the actors can get them when needed. If the actors are not absolutely responsible, then it is a better plan to have some reliable person in charge of the properties. It is often helpful to have posted on either side of the stage a list of the people required in each scene and of the properties necessary for each. The following lists are taken from those which were posted for the performances of *The Merchant of Venice*.

SCENE I

Venice. A public place

A. "In sooth, I know not why I am so sad." [1]

B. "Three thousand ducats —"

Well, C.	Shylock, R.[2]
Water in well	Launcelot, R.
Cup at well	Jessica, R.
Door, R. closed	Antonio, R.
Curtains out of view	Salarino, R.
	Salanio, R.
Basket for Jessica, R.	Bassanio, R.
	Lorenzo, R.
	Gratiano, R.
	Children, R.
	Tubal, L.

SCENE II

Belmont. A room in Portia's house

A. "By my troth Nerissa —"
B. "Mislike me not for my complexion —" ⎫ Morocco scenes
C. "Go draw aside the curtains —" ⎭
D. "Quick, quick, I pray thee —" Arragon scene

Remove door and well	Portia, on stage
Show curtains a little	Nerissa, on stage

[1] When performed at this time, liberties were taken in arranging the scenes. This was done because of the requirements of the modern stage and for the purpose of saving time in playing. The first few words of the scenes making the new arrangement were placed on the posted lists to help the actors to keep the new order in mind.

[2] The side of the stage on which each character was to enter was appended because the setting extended so far back that it was impossible for a person to cross the stage while a scene was in progress.

Rug
Chair, R. C.
Stool, R. of chair
Table, L. C.
Cover on table
Caskets
Scrolls in caskets
Skull in gold casket
Fool's head in silver casket
Miniature in lead casket
Cushion for ring U. R. C.

Keys for Portia
Rose for Portia
Sewing for Nerissa
Glasses for Arragon
Sword for Morocco

Balthasar, L.
Stephano, L.
Morocco, L.
Arragon, L.

SCENE V

Belmont.   A room in Portia's house]
   "I pray you, tarry — "

Remove door and well
Rug
Stool, L. of chair
Curtains show a little
Table L. C.
Cover for table
Caskets on table

Letter for Salerio
Ring for Portia
Ring for Jessica

Portia, on stage
Bassanio, on stage
Nerissa, on stage
Gratiano, on stage
Balthasar, on stage
Stephano, on stage
Lorenzo, L.
Jessica, L.
Salerio, L.
Singers and musicians, L.

Cues for music:
   Begin: "He makes a swan-like end — "
   End: at close of song.

SCENE VI

Belmont.   A room in Portia's house

A. "Madame, although I speak it in your presence — "

B. "Yes, truly, for look you — "

Remove table (no other change in setting)	Portia, on stage
	Nerissa, on stage
	Jessica, on stage
Letter for Portia	Lorenzo, on stage
	Balthasar, on stage
	Launcelot, R.

STAGE EFFECTS

Stage effects should be motivated by the story. They should not call attention to themselves at the expense of the play.   A stage effect needs always careful rehearsing because — to use the words that Hamlet addressed in warning to the First Player —

This overdone, or come tardy off, though it make the unskilful laugh, cannot but make the judicious grieve; the censure of the which one must in your allowance o'erweigh a whole theater of others.

Frequently it depends upon the skilful handling and use of a stage property.   For example, in *The Clod*, the woman, after the murder, stoops down and picks up the fragments of the cup that the unbidden guest had destroyed.   If the cup is not in a place easily accessible, the play is in danger of failing at this point of tense interest and of tragic significance. In preparing the scene it was found necessary to rehearse many times the throwing down of the cup.   It was only after many repetitions that the desired effect was secured. At first, too little force was used, so that the cup was not broken; then so much used, that the pieces flew over the footlights into the auditorium.   On another occasion the cup rolled into the footlight trough, and again it was too far up stage for the woman to make her closing pantomime and speech effective.   After many trials the actor was able to gauge his force and movements, and make sure of his result.

CHAPTER XXI

STAGE LIGHTING

IMPORTANCE OF LIGHTING

LIGHTING to-day is one of the most important factors in the production of a play. A statement in *Continental Stagecraft* by Kenneth Macgowan and Robert Edmond Jones puts the truth clearly: "Light itself seems destined to assume a larger and larger part in the drama. It is a playing force, quite as much as the actors." And Irving Pichel's statement in his excellent little book, *On Building a Theatre*, is worth attention. He writes:

If the little playhouse is without any mechanical convenience, if the stage is cramped and mean, it can still achieve visual beauty through light. This force brings into the playhouse the most vibrant, subtle, and affecting gift of the physical world, barring only the human presence.

Since the part played by light is so important, one must consider with great care the electrical equipment. Methods of illumination and machinery for stage lighting have made and are still making such rapid strides and changes that one cannot expect or hope to give very detailed advice. Before equipping a stage even for amateur purposes one should read the chapters on lighting in *The Theatre of To-day*, by Hiram K. Moderwell; *The Theatre of Tomorrow*, by Kenneth Macgowan; *Continental Stagecraft*, by Kenneth Macgowan and Robert Edmond Jones; *Play Production in America*, by

Arthur Edwin Krows; *On Building a Theatre*, by Irving Pichel, and other writers of equal authority and vision.[1]

EQUIPMENT

Ordinarily the illumination of a room does not come equally from all points, but from sunlight flooding through

A setting for *Lucky Pehr* which most pleasingly suggested a room in a church tower. The sky was a deep midnight blue. A purplish light behind the wall back stage left suggested the city below. Moonlight streaming in from off stage left accentuated the three dimensions of the columns and cast natural shadows. Illustrations showing the settings for other scenes in this play will be found elsewhere in this book.

a particular window or door. Therefore the light is not uniform in all parts of the room, nor does it come from the same direction at all times of the day, nor is it equally intense at all hours and seasons. At night the room receives its illum-

[1] Any school planning to install new stage lighting equipment will do well to seek the advice of some such expert lighting engineers as the Pevear Color Specialty Co., 71 Brimmer Street, Boston, Mass.

ination from one or more central points which light some areas more than others and which cast shadows of various shapes and shades. Out-of-doors the light is influenced, among other things, by the position of the luminary force in the sky, by the season of the year, and by the condition of the atmosphere.

It is impossible and undesirable with artificial light and artificial settings to reproduce natural light. But stage lighting should do more than merely illumine the stage and make the movements and the expressions of the actors visible, as did the old style lighting. It should contribute the charm, the sense of plasticity and of loveliness, that come from variations in the intensity and direction of light and shade and from the artistic and intelligent use of color. A concentrated high light in any spot or area of the stage desired and a moderate flood of light in other areas can be secured at will if the stage possesses a wisely chosen lighting equipment.

The fixed units of the older style of equipment were the footlights and the hanging strips or borders, which contained a large number of low-power lamps of various colors. The only absolutely indispensable fixed unit for the modern art stage (if one can say indeed that there is such a thing as an indispensable fixed unit) is the first border, which is placed down stage, or in other words as close to the proscenium arch as possible. This border — and other borders and the foots, if used — should carry high-power, colored lamps of pure blue, red, and green. This light can be blended by the use of dimming controls and any color in the spectrum can be secured. When the lamps are rightly proportioned, a light comparable to sunlight is obtained. Because the colored glass of which they are made is not as translucent as clear glass, it is advisable to have white and amber lights to supplement the blue, red, and green.   Each of these lamps should be backed with an X-ray reflector.   The front border, or an iron batten close to the first border, should be supplied with one or more aërial floodlights that can be turned to illuminate any desired area of the stage, and with adjustable hanging spotlights that will provide a concentrated high light wherever desired.

One of the greatest objections to using lamps dipped in lacquer or lamp coloring — even when lacquer of the right color can be found, which is rare — is the tremendous labor of dipping the lamps.   If high-power lamps could be used the task would not be so great, but unfortunately these cannot be dipped, for the intense heat causes the lacquer to burn off.   To obtain the beautiful effect described in the notes on the staging of *The Maid of France*, it was absolutely necessary that the blue lamps should be freshly dipped, as the play was done before the invention of the pure-color-glass lamps.   Lacquered lamps that have been used a little time become dead in hue, the coloring begins to wear off, and white light streams through, or dust collects on the lamp bulbs and dims and changes the effect of the light.   High-power nitrogen white lamps, placed in separate metal compartments and supplied with gelatin color-frames, are used successfully by some producers as the equipment of the front or first border.   One objection to the gelatin color-frame, or *color medium* as it is sometimes called, is the difficulty of getting pure color.   One is fortunate if one can obtain glass of high translucency to take the place of the gelatin color-frames.

The first border is used primarily for lighting interior scenes.   A border sufficiently far up stage, or toward the back of the stage, is useful in securing a well diffused light on the cyclorama or sky dome used in exterior scenes.   It is well to have all borders supplied with counterweights in order that they may be raised or lowered at will. Four suspension type 1000-watt flood lamps make an excellent substitute for the first or front border. They should be equipped with blue, green, red, and amber frames of gelatin or glass, and each should have its own dimming control operable from the main switchboard.

Footlights

Some producers advocate doing away entirely with foot-lights, but this step seems over-radical.

Practical experience seems to prove that there are times when a certain amount of illumination from the footlights is required. In many of the newer theaters, the foots do not extend the full length of the proscenium opening. Stages can very well be made with a footlight trough that can be covered when not needed, and the stage floor increased by so much.[1] If one's stage is comparatively shallow and it is necessary to act down stage, one finds difficulty in securing adequate illumination without footlights or some light placed farther forward than the front border. With a fire curtain, a grand curtain, and a front border curtain, the front border lights in the average school auditorium are forced back several feet from the place where, because of the limited depth of the stage, action down stage must take place, and consequently footlights are needed to augment the light from above.

Portable Lamps

Next to an excellent first border equipment, the most im-portant unit necessary to the securing of artistic effects, both

[1] Excellent disappearing footlights with natural-color heat-resisting glass fronts are manufactured by the Major Equipment Company, 4603–19 Fullerton Avenue, Chicago.

in so-called realistic plays and in dramas of the more fanciful type, is a wisely chosen group of portable lamps. These should comprise large and small spots for the securing of concentrated light, bunches or, preferably, floods for power-ful diffused light, and strips which are useful to secure a special note of color back of walls, rocks, and other places of a similar character. The spots, bunches, and floods should be equipped with gelatin color-frames, or pure-color glass frames, if they can be secured. Care must be exercised to secure numerous places where the portable lamps can be placed to advantage. Easily movable telescoping iron frames or standards, on which floods and spots can be attached, are essential. A narrow gallery just back of the proscenium arch is an acquisition to any stage, because it serves as an excellent place from which to project light upon the stage.

DIMMERS

In addition, adequate dimming devices are necessary to the flexibility which is essential if one is to secure artistic results. Each color unit and each location unit should have a separate dimming control. For example, it should be pos-sible to dim all the red lights in the first border, or all the red lights in the foots, and it should be possible to dim each border separately. Groups of similar units should be subject to a common control separate from other groups. For ex-ample, all the green lights should be controlled by a single dimmer. Every portable unit should have its own dimming control and should be operable at the main switchboard. A master dimmer should control all the lights on the stage. The switchboard should be placed so that the operator can see the whole stage and watch the registration of his lights. Around the switchboard, on a school stage, it is advisable to place an iron grille or cage to keep off curious individuals. It is well to have also a number of well chosen places about the stage where plugs can be inserted for table or for fireplace lights.

The auditorium lights should in their turn have a dimmer control and should be operated from the main switchboard on the stage. For many plays it is an excellent idea to dim the house lights slowly, and when the lights are low, to part the curtain and reveal a dimly lighted stage. Then the lights on the stage can be increased to the desired pitch, and action begun. This operation of the lights has a double result. It gives the audience a few moments to come to attention, and it allows them a brief interval to orient themselves to the scene before the acting of the fable commences. It is difficult to attend to setting and to dialogue at the same time. If the spectators are given a brief interval in which to become accustomed to the stage picture, they will be ready to give undivided attention to the actors and to the story they have to present. Certain acts can be closed effectively by an inverse manipulation of the lights. Thus abruptness is done away with, and a sense of fancy created and sustained.

Requisites of Satisfactory Equipment

In all this, an elaborate or expensive electrical equipment is not necessary, but the right sort is highly essential. The prime requisites are an excellent first border, a sufficient number of movable standard lamps, well-placed stage sockets , where the portable lamps can be attached, colored lamps and color mediums that are pure color, and adequate dimming devices.

The lighting equipment of the Francis W. Parker School, Chicago, although somewhat old style and limited in its number of units, has proved most satisfactory.   It comprises a first border, supplied with pure-color mazda

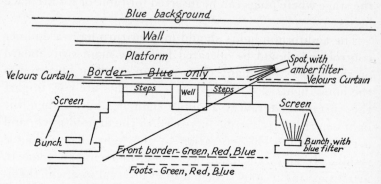

Diagram 5. — Light plot for *The Merchant of Venice*, Scene I, a public place.

lamps of red, green, and blue.   Directly over the center of the first border is a 1000-watt flood lamp so hung from an

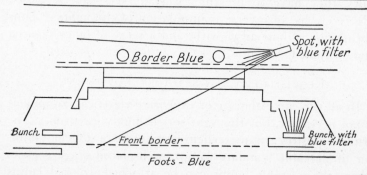

Diagram 6. — Light plot for *The Merchant of Venice*, Scene VIII, Portia's garden.

iron batten that it illumines the entire stage floor, but does not directly light the background.   At the side of the flood light there is an adjustable baby spot that can be focused on any desired area of the stage.   Both the flood and the spot have gelatin color-frames.   (The main objection to a single flood and a single spot is the necessity of using a step-ladder when it is desirable to change the color-frame.   However, even in the staging of a fanciful play with many scenes, such as Strindberg's *Lucky Pehr*, they were found to be no serious drawback.)   The Francis W. Parker school stage has a back border fitted, like the front border, with pure-color glass lamps.   (This is used almost exclusively in exterior scenes and for lighting the cyclorama.)   The footlights — always used in moderation when utilized at all — are equipped with red, green, and blue pure-color lamps.   Among the portable units are two bunch-lights of twelve lamps each — two 1000-watt standing flood lights would be an improvement — one 1000-watt portable spotlight, three portable baby spots, and two footlight baby spots.   An excellent equipment of dimmers gives a most satisfactory flexibility to this comparatively inexpensive outfit.

Notation of Lighting Scheme

Since light is an important factor in a stage presentation, it needs careful planning and intelligent rehearsals.   When at last the proper lighting for a scene has been determined, it should be carefully charted in order that it can be reproduced at will.   The diagrams on the opposite page show how the lighting for the street scene and the garden scene in *The Merchant of Venice* was noted in the stage director's prompt book.

CHAPTER XXII

THE SCHOOL THEATER

The Stage

The stage should be spacious. The proscenium opening in the school auditorium can advantageously be larger than is ordinarily considered necessary, as it can be masked and narrowed by means of screens or a false proscenium whenever desirable. In the economy of things naturally the auditorium must serve many purposes. If the proscenium opening is at least thirty-five feet, a large chorus, such as may be needed at Christmas or at commencement, can be placed upon the stage, and the voices will not be shut off from the audience by lack of ample opening.

The stage should be approached by steps extending the full length of the proscenium opening. These serve several good purposes: they make the stage seem a part of the auditorium; when a play is in performance, they give a sense of intimacy; in case of a pageant, they are indispensable as a means of ready access to the stage; at the daily assembly they offer standing room for a number of speakers (and when the younger members of the school are presenting an exercise, it is often most desirable to have several children ready at the same time to take part); when the entire student body is gathered together for chorus work, these steps, if they are thirty inches wide, offer a place for a single row of chairs on each. The footlight trough should have a removable panel or cover, in order that it can be closed when not in use.

The stage should be at least twenty-five feet deep —
deeper if possible — in order that when a play is staged some
sense of distance can be obtained. The back wall should
be without windows and curved to make a permanent
Rund-horizont or cyclorama for exterior settings. If for
any reason this is not practicable, it will be found useful
to have the back wall a plain surface that can be painted blue
or stippled with the primary colors, so that any desired color
can be brought out when the proper colored light is thrown
upon it. The wall may be left white, and the effect of sky
obtained by throwing a blue light upon it.

There should be ample space at the right and left of the
stage for the stacking of properties, furniture, and scenery
used in the play. One not experienced in play production
will be astonished to find out how much more space is
necessary than is at first apparent.

Stage experts declare that a stage should be about forty-
five inches above the floor level of the first row of seats. The
old-fashioned idea of having the stage floor slant is poor, since
a level stage is essential for the proper placing of scenes composed of rectangular screens. The stage floor should be made
of soft wood in order that the braces which help to support
the scenery can be screwed into the floor easily and quickly.

It is essential to have space over the stage so that curtains,
screens, and other parts of the setting can be drawn up out
of sight. The battens to which curtains are attached should
be counterweighted to facilitate the setting and the "striking" of scenes. There must be also some ready means for
suspending things from the stage ceiling at any point desired.
The writer has found it convenient—in the absence of a
gridiron[1] — to have the ceiling studded at fixed intervals

[1] An excellent description of a stage gridiron and its uses is to be found in Irving
Pichel's *On Building a Theatre*, page 53.

with large screw eyes.   From these, battens, screens, border
lights, or what you will, can be suspended.   A boomerang (a
high, narrow, movable platform) is essential for the purpose
of reaching these ceiling hooks, for ladders are not adapted
to this use.

It should be possible to get from one side of the stage to
the other by means of a passage below stage.   This under
passage is advisable because the setting often occupies the
entire depth of the stage and makes it impossible to pass behind it.   This plan necessitates also a stairway on either side
of the stage.

It will be found advisable to have an outside door leading
from the stage that can be used during the performance
when performers wish to leave and do not desire to go by
way of the auditorium and so attract attention.   Every
stage should be provided with one or more trap doors.   Such
an opening is necessary in many plays — in the staging of
Snow White, for example, where the dwarfs must go down
into the bowels of the earth.

Costume Room, Paint Shop, and Dressing Rooms

Provision should always be made for a room where classes
in the making of costumes can be held and where the materials in use can be spread out and left.   There should be ample
storage room for costumes and properties.   Closets and
bins are serviceable for this purpose.   There should also be
a special shop sufficiently large for the making and painting
of scenery — a place where the work can be left undisturbed
until completed.

There must be an ample number of dressing rooms provided with adequate lavatory and toilet accommodations.
They should be located sufficiently far away from the stage
so that no sounds of conversation will reach the ears of the

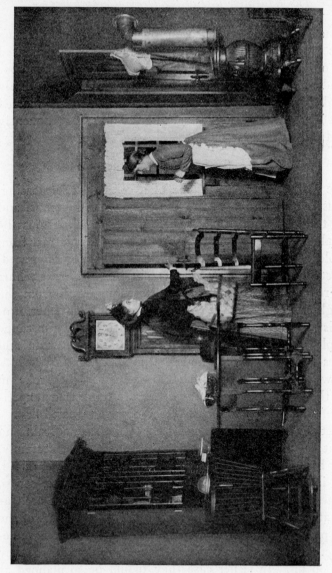

A scene from *Mr. Sampson.*

audience. Another good reason for not having the dressing rooms on the stage proper is the danger of an undesired burst of light reaching the stage from a dressing room door opened thoughtlessly during a scene when the stage is dimly lighted. Such an inadvertance has more than once marred a carefully rehearsed lighting effect. These are frequently placed to advantage below the stage.

Stage Curtain

The main curtain should be of a color that is pleasing. It must be attractive to the eye during intermissions, and when the play is in progress, if it shows at all, it must be neutral in tint, in order not to catch the eye or detract from the color scheme of the play. Experience has demonstrated, for instance, that a really lovely setting can be greatly hurt by a red front curtain that catches enough rays from the footlights to be noticeable to the onlooker while the performance is in progress. A neutral gray-green or a warm taupe is a pleasing color for the main or "grand" curtain and always blends well with the stage picture.

How shall a main stage curtain be hung? If it rolls up from the bottom, the spectator has the unpleasant experience of having the lower part of the picture revealed first — the actors' feet showing first at the rise of the curtain and last at its fall. There is one great advantage, certainly, about having the curtain roll or lift up. When it is raised, there is nothing to obstruct the light from spots, strips, bunches, or floods placed back of the proscenium arch at right and left of the stage. Yet for the effectiveness of the stage picture, curtains that part in the middle are more desirable. These can either draw aside to right and left, or they can loop up. In either case they should be so planned as to leave a place for spotlights just back of the proscenium arch. If they draw together in the middle, they should run on separate rods and overlap sufficiently to avoid gaping in the center. It is essential that they should be equipped with appliances that will ensure silence when in operation.[1] If it is planned to have the curtain loop up, then the work must be done by an expert; otherwise, one will be confronted with the all too common trouble of curtains not closing. The question of running the stage curtain is of importance, because the stage effect frequently depends greatly upon a slow, quiet curtain.

The Auditorium

Because of its importance in the educative scheme, the character, size, and equipment of a school auditorium should be carefully considered. The hall should be no larger than young people can easily fill without straining their voices; since if the speaker must keep his attention primarily upon the task of making himself heard, he has little time to consider what he is saying. Many school assembly rooms are so large that few people without mature physiques and well trained voices can make themselves heard. Therefore they are of little value in the education of young people, many of whom are immature in physical development and lack carefully trained speech. Particularly true is this of most girls of high school age. Likewise a large audience is objectionable because it does away with the sense of intimacy essential to an easy and helpful interchange of thought. Morever, it tends to over-stimulation, and creates a mob spirit that is antagonistic to the best good of all. If the school is large and the auditorium must seat the entire school body, then it is unquestionably too large for educative

---

[1] Peter Clark, Inc., 534–550 West 30th Street, New York City, is one of the firms which makes a ball-bearing rod which operates noiselessly and satisfactorily.

daily assemblies and certainly far too large for student recit-
als and plays.

Seating, Acoustics, and Ventilation

It is not our purpose to lay down any rules for the building of a hall.   All we shall hope to do is to note some observations that have been gleaned through experience.   Winthrop Ames, when he built his Little Theatre in New York
City, planned to have an ideal auditorium for intimate plays,
where everyone could see and hear.   It was built to seat
slightly less than three hundred people.   Many school auditoriums foolishly attempt to seat from one thousand to
fifteen hundred people.   For high school uses an auditorium
seating four hundred people seems to the author to be about
right, all things considered.

Many experiments have been made, both in Europe and
in this country and many data are available and should be
consulted before one builds assembly hall or theater.   It
has been stated on good authority that the acoustics are
best in those theaters whose interiors are all of wood —
pilasters of wood at intervals supporting ceiling beams.   No
cloth other than that absolutely demanded by necessity
should be used.   Overhanging balconies likewise shut off
the sound and are to be avoided.   In a few of the newer
Continental theaters the architects, as a concession, have
permitted a narrow balcony at the rear.[1]   This is generally
back of the main floor proper; when it is necessary to build
a balcony over the main floor it is very narrow, accommo-
dating not more than four or five rows of seats.   It is possible now to get expert advice on acoustics.   This necessity
of a building can be predetermined from a study of the arch-

---

[1] The Kenneth Sawyer Goodman Memorial Theater in Chicago, designed by
Howard Doren Shaw, has such a balcony.

itect's plans and mistakes prevented before it is too late to correct them. Dean Sabine of Harvard College made an extensive study of the subject, and the result of his investigation is available for practical application. The perfect acoustical properties of Winthrop Ames' Little Theatre in New York City are due to his work.[1]

The satisfactory auditorium, besides giving careful attention to acoustics, also considers well the ventilating system. The auditory properties of the hall may be spoiled because the running of the machinery that controls the ventilating system is noisy, or because the architect has planned to have the air pass from the rear of the auditorium to the front, to be taken off by vents under the stage, thus making the waves of air go in an opposite direction to the sound waves made by the speaker's voice.

The seats should be so placed that everyone will command an unobstructed view of the stage, and therefore each row should be eye distance above the row in front. This means a pronounced rake. These rows should also be nearly straight, in order that the auditor may face the stage directly. No row should be higher than the top of the proscenium.

[1] See chapter "Acoustics" in *Play Production in America,* by Arthur Edwin Krows, published by Henry Holt and Company.

PART III

NOTES ON AND ILLUSTRATIONS OF ORIGINAL PLAY–MAKING

This setting for Act I of *Tilly of Bloomsbury*, occupied full stage and remained in place throughout the performance. The scene for Act II was placed inside this setting.

CHAPTER XXIII

THE HARVEST FEASTS

THE conception of the harvest feast entertained by different peoples at different periods of history and the various manners of celebrating it are fruitful sources of study. These feasts grew out of some exalted emotional state, which, concentrated in this social function, lifted life for the time being to an ideal plane. All peoples, savage, barbarous, and civilized, have recognized some supreme being who ripens the grain and purples the grape, and so gives meat and drink to them and their children. In honor of this deity they have, with common interest and unity of thought, held periodical celebrations, holy convocations, and feasts of rejoicing.

An inquiry into the harvest feast is a logical outgrowth of the activities which are going on in the school, on the farms, and in the homes in the autumn. The thought is running through all the grades; each one is studying fruits and seeds, their habitat, preservation, and uses. The Thanksgiving celebration is the climax of this work. In our country, this holiday is an organic part of the life of the children outside the school. It is a feature of our home life, celebrated, moreover, by church and state, and must, therefore, be an integral part of the curriculum. The school, then, cannot afford to lose, for the sake of carrying out a regular fixed program, the opportunity of directing this common sentiment into artistic form and altruistic action. This translation of feeling into expression is really the broadest, deepest examination into any subject.

The following is an outline of a Thanksgiving exercise prepared by children. It is inserted because of its possible suggestive value to teachers. It should not be taken as a model for *one* program because it contains altogether too much for a single program, but it should be taken as matter which may suggest further consideration and elaboration into many schemes.

The preparation for a celebration is quite as important as the result. In this planning all the grades work together with one common purpose, helping in this way to coördinate the entire work of the school, as the different departments contribute their share to the festival.

Early in October, a committee in charge of plans was selected from the faculty; naturally, the music, the English, and the public speaking departments were represented. This committee carefully considered the history, science, and literature in each grade, in order that any essentially dramatic material closely related to Thanksgiving might be used. It decided to have the children study the Thanksgiving festivals of different peoples at different periods of history. The following topics were suggested and assigned to the different grades. The First Thanksgiving in America; The Indian Feasts as Observed by the Iroquois Indians; The Oriental Feasts; The Feast of Dionysus; The Feast of the Tabernacles; The Old English Harvest Home; The Vintage Feasts of France, Germany, and Southern Europe. Where possible these subjects were fitted to some work being done in the grade at the time; for example, the fifth grade was studying the early colonies of New England; therefore, the First Thanksgiving in America was assigned to this group. The seventh was studying the history of Babylon and the Orient and so was asked to look into the celebrations of these peoples.

Very little data could be found concerning some of the festivals. Naturally the agricultural peoples were richest in material and in dramatic forms of presentation. After a month's study, however, the committee decided to represent certain features of the Festival of the Iroquois Indians, the Finding of the Grape by Dionysus, The Greek Festival, the English Harvest Home, A Bavarian Harvest Custom, A Vintage Celebration in France, and the First Thanksgiving in America.

The children then made observations and read stories and poems on these subjects until they had absorbed not a little of the spirit of the people and the times that they were to represent. Then followed discussions and suggestions. Many of their plans the children found impossible to carry out with their limited space and meager appointments. Where dialogue was necessary, they wrote it. They also discussed the staging of their work and helped to costume the characters.

Each grade teacher presented her own subject, directed the study of her class, and coöperated with its members in making their plans. Together they selected from all the material collected that which seemed best suited for public performance. They also decided what modes of expression would best convey the idea and significance of the festival; whether it should be pageant, dance, drama, or story. The committee and the special teachers fitted the various parts into a unified program.

Early in the season there were brought from the woods and placed in cold storage, branches of oak, sumac, bittersweet, wild grapevines, branches of mountain ash, berries, and grapes for the decoration of the hall. These made an autumn background which, by a few changes could be used as a setting for each of the various units of the program.

The entertainment opened with music by the school: *I Will Praise Thee* and *Come Thou, Almighty King*. Then the account of the Feast of the Tabernacles from Leviticus XXIII, 39–43 was read. The singing of *We Plow the Fields* followed. Immediately came the festivals of the different peoples in the order given here. As a suggestion of their character, the details of each are briefly sketched.

In the Iroquois Feast, on the stage (covered to resemble green grass) a fire is burning. The priest comes forward to it, thanks the Great Spirit for the plentiful harvest of fruits, for the fish in the water, and the game in the forests. He then throws tobacco on the flames, praying that his words may ascend as does the smoke. The squaws enter, seat themselves on the ground, beat time; the men come in, dance to weird music, and circle about the blaze. During this dance one squaw after another rises, offers a short prayer to the Great Spirit, and then returns to her seat.

To illustrate the finding of the grape, Dionysus on entering moves gracefully through the trees set in the background, and speaks of the autumn and its beauty. One of the trees is covered by a grapevine on which the purple clusters are hanging. He stops to rest by this. As he leans against it, he presses one of the bunches with his shoulder, and the juice of the fruit stains his arm. He turns, touches the crushed fruit with his finger, and tastes, cautiously at first, and then again and again, for he finds that it is sweet and apparently wholesome. He looks at the tree and sees that it is covered with this vine and its fruit. Next he picks a bunch of grapes and begins to eat.

Silenus is now heard calling to Dionysus, and soon appears in the background. The pupil goes to his master, points out to him the grapes and the tree, then plucks a bunch and offers it to him. During this time they talk together about the fruit. Now they call the nymphs, who come running on; Dionysus holds a cluster of grapes high above their grasp, and they strive to reach it. Meanwhile, the satyrs have appeared in the background, and, observing the nymphs catching in their mouths the drops of juice which fall from the hands of Dionysus, they scramble up and rudely jostle one another in an effort to get a taste of the juice.

Here Dionysus finds in surprise that the bunch is squeezed dry. He shows it to them, and then runs to the tree for more, while the nymphs and satyrs look on. At this point, Dionysus gives each one some of the grapes; all eat with great enjoyment, the satyrs in the meantime playing tricks on one another. The nymphs now propose to take some of them home; one runs for a basket, while the others continue to eat and watch. Dionysus fills the basket which one of the nymphs holds. As she does so, she speaks in praise to Dionysus. He afterwards moves off the stage with the nymphs dancing after him, chanting a song of praise. The satyrs, still munching grapes, move off clumsily.

For the Greek Festival, in the center of the stage is placed a mound of sod which two men are piling up into an altar. As they work they speak of the abundant harvest and of the ceremonies of the day. When their task is completed, two young women advance, carrying wreaths, vines, and flowers, with which they decorate the altar. The men lay their presents of fruit and wine thereon. Soon they hear the approaching procession and all move off to join it. This is led by young women dancing to the sound of cymbals and flute. They are followed by children, men, and women, each of whom carries an offering and bears a torch or a staff tipped with a pine cone. As they advance about the altar they all lay upon it their gifts, and then the priest, attended by little children, comes slowly from the background, arranges upon the altar the contributions, pours a libation of wine, kindles the sacred fire, and then offers up a prayer of thanksgiving. All the people raise their hands and express in movement and attitude their thanks to the gods.

In the English Harvest Home, before the curtain rises, the voices of the merrymakers are heard singing, *Jog On, Jog On.* The scene opens on a field full of people gaily dressed in the country costume of the sixteenth century. At one side of the stage is a cart of which the back part only is visible. It is being piled high with grain. Two men are tossing bundles of grain up to a third on the cart, who is building the load; others are scattered about the field, tying the bundles and carrying them to the wagon. Women are raking scattered straw and grain together, and near them children fashion wreaths. All work on in this way until the song is finished, when one suddenly darts across the stage, picks up a bundle, holds it high over his head, and cries: "The last sheaf! The last sheaf!" All cheer as it is set in the middle of the field. The harvesters then arrange themselves on one side of the stage and begin to throw rocks and sticks at it until the one who knocks it over is proclaimed leader of the games. The queen of the harvest is then chosen by acclamation. She is led out, crowned, carried by the boys to the cart, and placed upon it. Around her they pile their fruits and flowers, and then games begin. She watches and finally rises to cheer the players. These sports are followed by an old English dance, led by the leader of the games and by the queen.

In the portrayal of the French Vintage Customs, the scene is laid in a vineyard. First, a boyish face appears in the background, peering cautiously around. As he comes in and looks about through the vines, finding no one, he calls in

French to his comrades to enter. A troop of children now runs upon the stage, peering about and in among the grape-vines. At last one cries joyously *Sur le pont d'Avignon.* Immediately the children begin to sing this song, acting it out as they do so. Just as they finish, the song of the vin-tagers rises in the distance and comes nearer and nearer. The little folk scamper quietly away, and youths and maidens enter. First the girls appear with trays, each one gathering one row of grapes, and singing as she works. The men now follow, with large baskets on their backs. Each girl empties her contribution into one of these, and all are carried to a vat placed at one side of the vineyard. When this work is finished, the men search the vines to see whether any grapes have been left. The maidens look on anxiously, for, should a bunch be discovered, the forfeit is a kiss taken by the finder from the one who missed the grapes. Suddenly a youth holds up a cluster, and there is a shout of delight. The detector attempts to discover which girl has left the bunch, but all deny and repulse him with laughs and screams. His embarrassment quickly changes to merriment and he eats the grapes as the curtain falls.

In showing the Bavarian Harvest Custom, the scene opens upon a stage, in the center of which one sheaf of grain is standing. A priest enters, reading, moves slowly across the stage, pauses in front of the wheat, lifts his hand in bless-ing, walks on, and seats himself on the opposite side. A woman, sister of the priest, now comes in. She has come to visit her brother and is looking for him. She almost stum-bles over the solitary sheaf which seems to surprise her. The priest noting her wonder goes to her and explains that it is the custom of the people to leave one bundle of grain in each field for the poor. As they talk, the farmer ap-proaches and tells her more fully about his offering. (All the conversation is carried on in German because this scene was worked out in the German class.) The farmer soon leaves to prepare, as he says, the food and drink for the feast that is held here at the close of the harvest. Next the peasants enter chanting *Wir Pflugen und wir Struren*. After the song is finished, the farmer makes a speech, thanking the

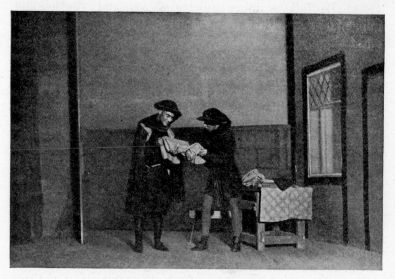

A scene from *Master Pierre Patelin.*

laborers for their faithful work and promising to dedicate a candle to the holy saint who has helped them to gather the grain. He invites them to be merry, to dance, to sing, and to feast about the sheaf that is to be left for the poor. After the dance they all seat themselves, and when the curtain drops the farmer is passing about bread, sausage, and drink.

The program closed with the presentation of gifts. These were offerings of fruits, vegetables, and other foods which the children had been asked to bring to school the day before

Thanksgiving. The little folk of the kindergarten and the first and second grades, costumed in gowns of autumn colors—green, gold, bronze, and red — crowned and decorated with autumn leaves, approached from the back of the room carrying their donations in dishes of gold, silver, and pewter. They were led by two young girls, each bearing a sheaf of wheat. A figure, dressed to suggest the Spirit of Abundance, received these gifts and piled them up artistically on the stage. The foundation of the gown Abundance wore was old-gold silk with an overdress of gray-green silk. A panel of rich tapestry in autumn colors hung straight from the neck to the hem in front and back. The whole was rich, beautiful and suggestive of Autumn.

After the presentation the children grouped themselves about the Spirit of Abundance in the middle of the stage, and sang together *Come, Children, Lift Your Voices.* After the exercise the gifts were assembled for distribution among needy families. The children wrapped them up, tied the packages, and carried them downstairs to the conveyances that had been provided.

CHAPTER XXIV

DRAMATIC PRESENTATION OF A CORN HUSKING IN THE MIDDLE WEST

CHARACTERS

UNCLE SILAS	AUNT LIZZIE
FIRST FARMER	SALLIE
SECOND FARMER	MARY
THIRD FARMER	MARTHY
JONATHAN	

[*The interior of a barn. Corn and pumpkins are used for decorations. Lanterns hang from ceiling and sides of barn. Benches and seats made of boxes are placed for the accommodation of the older guests. Numerous piles of the corn which is to be husked are placed at convenient intervals. Enter* UNCLE SILAS, *the farmer host, followed by* AUNT LIZZIE *and* SALLIE.]

SILAS. My rheumatism is so powerful bad these days, I can't git around like I us't to. [*Sits down on box.* SALLIE *hangs a lantern.*] Sit down, Aunt Lizzie. Sit down!

AUNT LIZZIE [*sitting down and speaking to* SALLIE]. There now, when you get that lantern hung, the last thing's done. [*Fanning herself with her apron.*] How warm you do get, when you are dusting around.

SILAS. Everything all right? Reckon you've got enough wood to last you?

AUNT LIZZIE. Oh, I reckon so.

SILAS. That's a right smart lot of corn for the youngsters to husk in one evening, but maybe they can. Leastways I hope they can.

SALLIE. How many will there be, Uncle, do you think?

SILAS. Wall, about thirty or forty maybe. [*Hearing people whistling and singing "Yankee Doodle," SILAS rises and leans on stick. SALLIE goes and listens.*]

SALLIE. Oh, I hear them coming. [*A crowd of people enter for the husking.*]

AUNT LIZZIE [*to one of the farmer girls, shaking hands*]. I'm powerful glad to see you. How's your ma?

MARY. She's mighty tired — been making sausages all week. [*AUNT LIZZIE shakes hands with the others. JONATHAN comes in carrying a violin wrapped in a big comforter.*]

FIRST FARMER. Here now folks, give Jonathan some room; he wants to get his muffler off.

SECOND FARMER. Come boys, we'll help him. [*One boy takes hold of an end of the muffler, and others turn JONATHAN round and round. He becomes tangled up in the comforter as the movement grows more and more rapid.*]

AUNT LIZZIE. Now, boys!

SILAS. Never mind, Aunt Lizzie, boys will be boys! It's cold to-night. You'd better git to work on that corn; and you'll have to work hard to keep warm.

[*The huskers move toward the corn.*]

A FARMER. What's it all piled up this way for?

SILAS. There's going to be a prize for the fastest husker. [*All clap their hands and cheer. SILAS raps on floor.*] Git your places.

[*Singers for the rounds and speakers for the ballads group themselves around piles to be near together. Others scatter to the different groups. All sit.*] Now, girls, speak a piece about the corn before we begin. [*A girl stands and recites Whittier's "The Corn Song," another Spenser's "Autumn," and another Riley's "When the Frost is on the Pumpkin."*]

[*The huskers begin to pick up ears.*]

SILAS [*rapping on the floor*]. There! There! now put them down. When I say "Ready! Go!" begin. As soon as you git your piles done, holler. Now see who is the best husker. Ready! Go! [*All are busy husking. Suddenly a girl squeals and jumps up gathering her skirts about her.*]

BOYS. What is it? What is it?

GIRL. A mouse! A mouse!

[*The boys laugh and go on husking. The other girls scream, jump up, and gather their skirts around them. Finding that the alarm is over they return to their work. The girls around one of the piles start singing, "Three Blind Mice."*]

[*When they finish, others answer with "Scotland's Burning."*]

[*The boys applaud each time.*]

A HUSKER. I'm through! I'm through!

SILAS [*going over and looking*]. That's fair, Hiram has earned the first prize. Sallie, bring it over.

[SALLIE *tosses him a bright red mitten.* HIRAM *holds it up and all laugh.*]

ANOTHER HUSKER. I'm done, too. What will I get?

SILAS. Git Marthy to sing a song for you. Come on, Marthy.

[MARTHY *sings* "Flow Gently, Sweet Afton."]

SILAS. Are you all through? [*He goes about and looks at the piles.*] Now clear up the floor and we will have a dance. Jonathan, come, tune up your fiddle and let's all have a dance.

[JONATHAN *tunes his fiddle and the huskers dance a jolly barn dance.*]

AUNT LIZZIE [*coming in and speaking to* UNCLE SILAS]. Uncle Silas, supper is ready!

SILAS. Supper's ready. Aunt Lizzie's waiting for us. Come on, boys and girls. [*All walk out to supper.*]

CURTAIN

NOTE: This dramatic presentation was made and played by a group of seventh and eighth graders. In connection with the project the following books were used as supplementary reading: *The Winning of the West* (Roosevelt), *A Son of the Middle Border* (Garland) and *One of Ours* (Cather).

CHAPTER XXV

A THANKSGIVING EXERCISE IN PAGEANT FORM

NOTES ON THE PREPARATION

THE Thanksgiving festival can be observed appropriately in a number of ways. The following simple pageant, all the speeches of which are taken from the Bible, was given by children of the first four grades.

As the Thanksgiving season drew near, the holiday became the natural subject of conversation in the various classes. After some preliminary talk on the part of the class, the children were asked what they were most grateful for. When they had had a few moments to think the matter over, their replies were invited. The answers came promptly and with assurance. Those of the first grade were most grateful for wheat and corn; the second grade expressed the same thought, adding fruits and flowers. The third and fourth grades were not only grateful for all these, but for forests, animals, sun, and rain. More than this, they were deeply grateful for their parents, for health, for country, and for the fact that the United States was free from war. The hope was expressed that soon all countries should keep peace.

The teacher, before the next metting of the class, selected passages from the Bible that expressed thanksgiving for those gifts which the children had named. The charm of the language and the beauty of its images pleased the children, and soon they had made the Bible words their own. The citations that expressed joy for wheat and corn were given to the first grade. The second grade was given lines about fruits and flowers, and in like manner appropriate verses were distributed among all four grades.

Knowing that the processional is a primitive form of dramatic expression, the teacher of literature arranged a simple pageant for this Thanksgiving exercise. To give a sense of unity and comradeship with the older pupils, a girl from one of the high-school classes was chosen to act as the Spirit of Autumn. A boy and a girl from the seventh and eighth grades were asked to assist in receiving the gifts that the younger children brought to the Spirit of Autumn.

A few days before Thanksgiving, ten children from each grade were selected to participate in the pageant. Those who were to say the Bible verses were not chosen until the day before the exercise, in order that there should be no feeling of special preparation or of recitation. The desire to keep the exercise simple and dignified, with thought centered on the things for which gratitude was fitting, led to the rejection of the idea of dressing up in costumes suggestive of autumn. There was one exception, however, for the girl representing the Spirit of Autumn was robed in a beautiful symbolic costume which had been designed by an artist in the school and which had been made out of really lovely material. In the procession, the members of the first grade carried sheaves of wheat and other grains, and also ears of corn. The second grade bore flowers and small trays of fruit. The third had branches of autumn leaves. One child from the fourth grade led his young brother, another bore the national emblem, and yet another carried a peace flag.

The exercise opened with the singing of *Come, Ye Thankful People, Come*. After the Bible quotations had been given all the participants joined in singing *To Thee, O Lord, Our Hearts We Raise*. The climax was reached when the

entire audience united in reading the Litany and in singing the hymn *The Earth is the Lord's.*   While the children
who took part in the pageant marched out, *We Plow the
Fields* was sung as a recessional.

The stage was hung with green curtains for a background.
At the center a small dais with a sort of throne was placed
for the Spirit of Autumn.   To the left was a large Greek
bench on which was a shallow but spacious brown basket,
in which the gifts of fruits were placed.   At the right was
a large basket such as the Indians use for carrying grain.
This was filled with vegetables and fruits, and some of the
contents were strewn upon the floor.   Stacks of corn were
placed where they would be most decorative.   Music was
played softly as the processions were taking place.

A THANKSGIVING PAGEANT

[*The leader, representing the Spirit of Autumn, is seated on
a dais at the center of the stage.   A helper stands on either side
of her.   The entire school unites in singing* "Come, Ye Thankful People, Come."   *The leader rises.*]

LEADER.   Know ye that the Lord he is God: it is he that
hath made us, and not we ourselves: we are his people and
the sheep of his pasture.

Enter into his gates with thanksgiving; and into his courts
with praise: be thankful unto him, and bless his name; for
the Lord is good; his mercy endureth to all generations.

[*Enter by the center door at the back of the auditorium, in
double file, ten or more children of the first grade bearing wheat
and corn.   They pass down the center aisle and go up the steps
at the right and left of the stage.*]

LEADER OF THE FIRST GRADE [*carrying wheat*].   He
causeth the grass to grow for the cattle, and herb for the

The setting for a *Thanksgiving Exercise.*

service of man, that he may bring forth food out of the
earth.

SECOND LEADER OF THE FIRST GRADE [*carrying corn*].
The pastures are clothed with flocks, the valleys are covered
over with corn; they shout for joy, they also sing.

[*They give their gifts to the two who attend the Spirit of Autumn,
and they place them on the bench at the left of the stage. The
children then go right and left of the dais at the back of the stage
and there remain. As the gifts are being placed, there is soft
music from the piano. Enter from the center door at the back
of the auditorium ten children from the second grade each carrying a basket of fruit or a spray of autumn flowers; beside each
member of the second grade is a child from the kindergarten carrying a large orange, a grapefruit, an apple, a pomegranate, or a
chrysanthemum. They go to the stage.*]

LEADER OF THE SECOND GRADE [*carrying fruit*]. Be
glad, then, ye children and rejoice; give unto the Lord; for
the tree beareth her fruit, the fig tree and vine do yield their
strength.

SECOND LEADER OF THE SECOND GRADE [*bearing flowers*].
The desert shall rejoice and blossom as the rose; it shall
blossom abundantly, even with joy and singing.

[*They give their gifts and join the children of the first grade
about the dais. Enter ten children of the third grade bearing
autumn leaves.*]

FIRST LEADER OF THE THIRD GRADE. Thou crownest the
year with thy goodness, and thy paths drop fatness.

SECOND LEADER OF THE THIRD GRADE. They drop upon
the pastures and the wilderness, and the hills are girded
with joy.

ANOTHER MEMBER OF THE THIRD GRADE. He sendeth the
springs into the valleys, which run among the hills. They

give drink to every beast of the field; by them shall the fowls of the heaven have their habitation, which sing among the branches.

FOURTH MEMBER OF THE THIRD GRADE. He watereth the hills from his chambers; the earth is satisfied with the fruit of thy works.

[*They deposit their gifts and join the others. Four children from the fourth grade take their places on the stage.*]

FIRST MEMBER OF THE FOURTH GRADE [*leading by the hand a young brother or sister*]. I will bless the Lord at all times; his praise shall continually be in my mouth, for I was my father's son, tender and only beloved of my mother.

SECOND MEMBER OF THE FOURTH GRADE. The Lord will command his lovingkindness in the daytime, and in the night his song shall be with me. I shall praise him who is the health of my countenance, and my God.

THIRD MEMBER OF THE FOURTH GRADE [*bearing the national emblem*]. Bless the Lord, O my soul, and forget not all his benefits, for this nation is his people, and blessed is the nation whose God is the Lord.

FOURTH MEMBER OF THE FOURTH GRADE [*bearing a peace flag*]. The Lord will bless his people with peace. They shall beat their swords into plowshares, and their spears into pruning hooks; nation shall not lift up sword against nation, neither shall they learn war any more. The Lord shall give his people the blessing of peace.

[*They join the rest of the children about the dais.*]

THE SPIRIT OF AUTUMN. O Lord, how manifold are thy works! in wisdom hast thou made them all: the earth is full of thy riches. O come, let us sing unto the Lord; let us come before his presence with thanksgiving; for his name alone is exalted; his glory is above the heaven.

[*All the children in the grades giving the exercise unite in singing* "To Thee, O Lord, Our Hearts We Raise."

The Spirit of Autumn, or one of the teachers, leads the following "Litany of Thankfulness." *All present unite in the responses.*]

For days of health,
For nights of quiet sleep,
For seasons of bounty and of beauty,
For all earth's contribution to our need,
ALL.   Father, we thank Thee!
For our country's shelter,
For our homes,
For the joy of faces and the joy of hearts that love,
ALL.   Father, we thank Thee!
For our power of growth,
For longings to be better and do more,
For ideals that ever rise above our real,
ALL.   Father, we thank Thee!
For opportunities well used,
For the blessedness of service,
For the power to fit ourselves to others' needs,
ALL.   Father, we thank Thee!
For all that brings us nearer to one another, nearer to ourselves, nearer to Thee,
For life,
ALL.   We thank Thee, O our Father!

[*The entire audience joins in the closing hymn,* "The Earth Is the Lord's." *The audience remains seated while the children who have taken part in the pageant march out of the auditorium by way of the center aisle.* "We Plow the Fields" *is sung as a recessional.*]

CHAPTER XXVI

THE PINE-TREE SHILLINGS

PREPARATION

A SECOND grade, in striving to give to a group of high-school pupils an idea of life in America during the early days of the Colonists, received intensive training in the acquirement of knowledge and got it under the best of educative motives, that of making their information serve a worthy end; they had a legitimate reason for self-expression, which is the most favorable condition for making any body of knowledge a permanent possession.

These young students became interested in the life of the Colonists. One aspect of the subject led to another, until the children had attained considerable insight into the history of the period and some understanding of the problems, the manners, and the customs of those days. They brought to school many pictures and articles belonging to the times. They made many things in wood, clay, and textiles, as the occasions arose that prompted such activities. In following out their interest in Colonial days and people, they learned many stories, both those told them at home by people who had heard them from parents and grandparents, those told at school, and those gleaned from history, literature and reading. Each pupil had a Colonial costume which he or she wore whenever the spirit moved — and it frequently did move. The children found much joy in being early settlers in imagination, if not in fact.

The time came when it was customary for each of the grades of this elementary department to plan a "happy hour" for the senior class of the high school. This particular grade naturally desired to use that which was closest to its heart and suggested that it should give a Colonial party to

A scene from the school production of *The Servant in the House*, in which Albert Carroll, now well-known as a professional actor, played Manson (the character with the uplifted hand).

the graduating class. Its members talked the matter over carefully and seriously. After much consideration of the problem and a survey of what they had which would be valuable as well as interesting to their guests, they decided that they would act in their Colonial costumes Hawthorne's story of the mintmaster who gave to his daughter, as a dowry, her weight in silver coins. They thought that Washington's Birthday would be a most appropriate time. The adoption of this date led to the idea of having George Washington and his wife act as host and hostess and of having the little play come as a portion of an entertainment given at the home of the First President. Each of the children who made the play was familiar with the whole affair and was ready to take any part and serve in any capacity that would contribute most to its success.

The text, as suggested by the members of the class, was carefully noted by the teacher, but it was left fluid and was changed somewhat from day to day. It was agreed that it was not necessary to follow slavishly the dialogue as it had been recorded on the board for general reference; the one object was to make the story clear, but it was found that this was most easily done when the play as planned was rather carefully adhered to. In the rehearsals great latitude was always allowed. For instance, the speeches of the guests in the play proper were not given absolutely as printed here, but came as the actors felt prompted to speak.

As has been stated, the pupils brought to school numerous Colonial articles of value and of interest. Many of the children thought that the seniors would like to see these treasures, and it was suggested that they be put on exhibition. One wise child conceived the idea of having them presented as bridal gifts to the mintmaster's daughter, thus making them conspicuous by using them as a part of the play. To satisfy the desire of the children to know what the pine-tree shillings were like, the class was allowed to make the coins by pouring molten lead into molds which they had constructed. It was next suggested that they make enough of these pine-tree shillings to give each guest one to keep as a souvenir of the party. The suggestion met with instant approval.

A Colonial party would not be complete without dancing. Some of the dances that they had learned in their gymnasium classes the children thought would do admirably. In order that these should be done with the ease and grace that the occasion merited, the pupils asked to be allowed to spend some extra time in acquiring the desired perfection. The selection of suitable refreshments, too, demanded many conferences and wise choice. Old rules for the making of such Colonial good things as baked Indian pudding were brought to class and read for the consideration of all.

Suggestion followed suggestion. After due consideration some were accepted and others were discarded. A great deal of arduous work was necessary in the preparation of the entertainment, and this work was done with a will and with great joy. There was the planning and making of the scales, a task which called for not a little manual cunning. The needed skill, under the impelling motive that stimulated the children, was developed far more rapidly than would have been possible under less strongly motivated work. There were problems in number which had to be done and which it was no drudgery to perform. Reading, writing, and spelling each came in for its share of attention. In fact, the pupils, in carrying out their delightful project, learned many valuable things in a natural and happy manner and with a minimum of labor and a maximum of interest and of permanency. Every child had an active part in making ready and giving the party. After the dancing of the minuet, the members of the senior class were invited to join the second grade in dancing old reels and rounds. Simple refreshments that had been prepared by a part of the class as their contribution to the party were served. The affair was given in a small gymnasium. Children dressed as pages showed the seniors to seats arranged in a large semicircle. As soon as they were seated, George Washington, his wife, and their friends entered, and when it was time, *The Pine-Tree Shillings* took place on the small stage where all could see the performance.

The Play

[*Two Pages show the guests to their seats in front of the stage.*]

A PAGE. George Washington and his wife welcome you to their home to-day.

A MEMBER OF THE WASHINGTON HOUSEHOLD [*entering from an adjoining room*]. They are here to receive you now.

[*The* PAGES *open the door, and* WASHINGTON *and his* WIFE *and* FRIENDS *enter.*]

WASHINGTON [*addressing the members of the senior class*]. You are most welcome to our home to-day.

MARTHA WASHINGTON. We are indeed glad that you have come to our party.

WASHINGTON [*turning to a member of his own group*]. I hear that some of you have a surprise for us.

A FRIEND. Yes, a little play.

MARTHA WASHINGTON. A play! That is indeed good news.

FRIEND. A true story about something that happened in Massachusetts many years ago.

WASHINGTON. And what is the title of this play?

FRIEND. It is called *The Pine-Tree Shillings*.

WASHINGTON. Let us sit where we can see this play of *The Pine-Tree Shillings*. [*They sit where they can get a view of the stage. The play of* The Pine-Tree Shillings[1] *is now performed.*]

[1] Arranged from Hawthorne's *True Stories from History and Biography.*

SCENE: CAPTAIN HULL'S *best room.*

[*Some one knocks at the door.* HODGE, *the servant, opens it.*]

MR. CLIFTON [*entering*]. Is Captain Hull at home, my fine fellow?

HODGE [*with surprise*]. The captain?

MR. CLIFTON. Is not this the mintmaster's house?

HODGE. Aye, to be sure, and a good mintmaster he is.

MR. CLIFTON. Reason enough he has. Who would not work for such a share of silver shillings?

HODGE. One out of twenty is only a reasonable share for the trouble of coining them.

MR. CLIFTON. Reasonable share indeed! I wager that there is not a chest or cupboard in this house that is not filled with pine-tree shillings.

HODGE [*winking*]. That is true enough. They will come in handy for the wedding.

MR. CLIFTON. What, a wedding! Whose wedding? Is the captain himself getting married?

HODGE. Most certainly not! But what do you want with Captain John Hull?

MR. CLIFTON. I want to have this silver tankard, these old spoons, and these old buckles melted into pine-tree shillings. We want to pay our pastor in coin. Last quarter he had to take two quintals of fish, six bushels of corn, and three cords of wood for his labor among us. But tell me more about the wedding. One doesn't hear the news when one lives ten miles away, as I do. Tell me, who is to be married.

HODGE. Miss Betsy.

MR. CLIFTON. Dear! dear! Is that so? Betsy Hull! Little Betsy Hull!

HODGE. And not so little, either. She is like her father, round and plump as a pudding.

Mr. CLIFTON. That comes from their hearty feeding on rich food — Indian pudding, doughnuts, and pumpkin pies.

HODGE. The ceremony is going on at the church even now. It is time that the wedding party was returning. [*He goes to the window.*] Here they come.

MR. CLIFTON. Dear, dear! I must get out of this place. I can't go out of the front door, because they will see me.

HODGE. Why all this haste and excitement?

MR. CLIFTON. My good fellow, they, with all their finery, must not see me like this. You will have to show me the back door. I will bring the silver back another time.

HODGE. All right. Come this way. [*They go out. Then the wedding guests enter.*]

A GUEST. Such a lovely wedding!

A GUEST. Such a sweet bride, and so plump!

A GUEST. How splendid her father looked!

A GUEST. Did you see that his buttons were all made of shillings and sixpences?

A GUEST. How handsome the bridegroom, Samuel Sewall, is in his gold-lace waistcoat.

A GUEST. The captain seems very fond of his new son-in-law.

A GUEST. That is not surprising, for he is a young man of character.

A GUEST. And industrious in business.

A GUEST. They say that Samuel Sewall did not ask for any marriage portion.

A GUEST. None at all. I should think that the mint-master *would* like him.

A GUEST. Here they come.

A GUEST. How round and rosy she is! Just like a great red apple!

A GUEST. She is like one of the full-blown peonies in

her own garden. [*Enter* CAPTAIN HULL *and the* BRIDE *and* BRIDEGROOM.]

CAPTAIN HULL. Well, son Sewall, you will find that Betsy is a heavy burden, [*All laugh.*]

BETSY. Father, cannot you give up your jokes for one day?

SAMUEL SEWALL. I am sure that your daughter will never be a burden to me, but always a great blessing.

CAPTAIN HULL. Hodge, bring the scales.

HODGE. The scales did you say?

CAPTAIN HULL. Yes, the large ones.

A GUEST. Now what is the captain going to do with scales? [*The scales are brought in.*]

A GUEST. They are the sort of scales that merchants use to weigh bulky articles.

CAPTAIN HULL. Now, daughter Betsy, get into one side of the scales.

BETSY. Is this another of your jokes, father? [*She gets into one side of the scales.*]

A GUEST. Perhaps he is going to make her husband pay for her by the pound.

CAPTAIN HULL [*to one of the servants*]. Now bring me that chest. [*The* SERVANTS *tug and pull and finally get the chest across the room.* CAPTAIN HULL *takes a large key and opens it. The chest is filled with pine-tree shillings. The* GUESTS *all cry,* "Oh!"]

SAMUEL SEWALL. What is this, the whole Massachusetts treasury?

CAPTAIN HULL. No, indeed. This is my honest share of the shillings which I have coined. [*To the* SERVANTS.] Fill the other side of the scales with the silver coins.

A GUEST. I wonder how much it will take to weigh her down? [BETSY *giggles.*]

A GUEST. In this case she certainly is worth more than you. [*All laugh. The* SERVANTS *continue to pile bags of coins on the scales until the side on which* BETSY *sits is lifted from the floor.*]

BETSY [*with a little squeal*]. Oh, I am being raised off the floor!

CAPTAIN HULL. There, son Sewall, take these shillings for my daughter's marriage portion. Use her kindly, and thank heaven for her. It is not every wife who is worth her weight in silver!

SAMUEL SEWALL [*helping* BETSY *out of the scales*]. Thank you for your silver pine-tree shillings, father. You have been most generous, but of the two gifts Betsy is the more precious to me.

A GUEST. Let us show our humble gifts to the bride and the bridegroom. [*The* GUESTS *present their wedding gifts.*]

CAPTAIN HULL. Now for the dance!

[*The play now merges into a sort of epilogue.*]

BETSY. Father, before we begin to dance, I wish to have a word with my husband. [*She turns to* SAMUEL.] Samuel, father has given you many bags of silver pine-tree shillings. Will you give me one bag to use as I wish?

SAMUEL. Certainly. [*He gives her one of the bags.*]

BETSY [*turning to the audience*]. I wish each of you to have one of our silver shillings to keep in memory of this day. [*She turns to the* PAGES.] Will you help me to give these to our guests?

WASHINGTON. And while that is being done, we can have the floor cleared for the minuet. [*The pine-tree shillings are distributed, and the chairs are pushed back, leaving the center of the room free for the dancing.*]

CAPTAIN HULL. And now for the dance!

SAMUEL SEWALL. President Washington and his good wife will lead the minuet. [*The players dance.*]

WASHINGTON [*turning to the seniors*]. We invite all our friends to join us. [*Dances follow.*]

CAPTAIN HULL [*at the conclusion of the dances*]. We now invite you all to partake of refreshments. [*Refreshments are served, and the party breaks up.*]

CHAPTER XXVII

THE WOODMAN AND THE GOBLINS

The Story

Once upon a time a woodman lived in the heart of a very thick wood. I don't know where the wood was — Scotland, maybe, or perhaps Germany, for there are not many thick woods left in Scotland. And this woodman lived all by himself. He did not have any children to look after nor any wife to look after him. But he was a clever old fellow and managed things somehow. He built his own house and did his own cooking and mended his clothes and did all the washing that he considered quite necessary. It wasn't a very nice house: not very clean and not very tidy. He thought that things were tidy enough when they were around where they would be handy, and he had sometimes to look about a long while when he wanted a new dishrag. But when anything got lost, he had nobody to blame but himself.

Shall I tell you what he was like? He was a little stumpy fellow, rather fat, like Santa Claus, and rather good-natured, though not altogether so good-natured as Santa Claus. And he didn't have bright red clothes and white fur and white hair and a red face. His hair was gray; his face was the color of old furniture; and his clothes were made of brown leather. It is a hard thing to sew buttons on leather, and here and there a bit of string does about as well.

Well, one afternoon he suddenly remembered that he had

243

The Admirable Crichton, Act III.

244

to go to the village, which was miles and miles away, to get a new ax. His old one was of no use; he had sharpened it so often that there was very little of it left, and he had work to do the next day and needed the ax badly. So, although it was getting late and it would be dark before he could get back, he started off. The wood was dark early — you know woods are always dark early, and where the trees grow thick it is sometimes dark all the time.

He found his way to the village all right, got the ax, and set out on his way home again. He didn't bother about the darkness; at any rate, he didn't bother much. He knew the way well enough and would have told you that he could find his way home with his eyes shut. He didn't think much about it; he was thinking about something quite different. He was thinking about some bogy stories that silly folks up at the village were telling. Then he remembered that it was Halloween and that all the witches and fairies and goblins were out that night. Looking up suddenly, he discovered that he didn't know where he was. The road looked different somehow. He couldn't remember ever having been there before. It was the thickest part of the wood he had ever been in. The trees grew very, very close together — so close that he could hardly squeeze between them.

When he was looking about to try to find the path — it was so dark he could hardly see at all, he had to feel about with his hands — in a hollow place in the roots of a huge beech tree he came upon six — I think it was six — big eggs.

Now, he was not hunting for eggs, but these were so big and so queer looking, that he began to wonder about them. He thought: "I'll take them home and hatch them out and see what queer fowl will come out of them. If I can get hens that lay thumping big eggs like that every day, I won't have far to look for a breakfast." So he took them up and started to look for the road again. He found it after a bit of trouble and got home safe and sound without meeting any other adventure.

When he got into the house, he looked at the eggs again and thought what a splendid omelet they would make. He was very hungry after being in the woods so long. Then he thought it would be a pity not to hatch one of the eggs and get a hen that would lay more eggs like these. He was afraid, however, that the one he saved might be bad and not hatch at all. He talked the matter over with himself and decided reluctantly (he was very hungry) to hatch them all out, just to be on the safe side.

How was he to hatch them? He couldn't stay in bed for three weeks; that was out of the question. He was afraid to trust the cat, and moreover she wouldn't do it if he asked her; and besides she was not big enough to keep them all warm, and she wouldn't keep still long enough.

He thought of a piece of red flannel that he had bought to make shirts of. He cut it up and wrapped each egg in a piece. Then he set the eggs around the fire; and for three weeks he kept the fire going at not too fierce a heat, never letting it go out either day or night. It was a great responsibility, but if one wants something one must work for it, and he wanted hens.

The day came at last when the eggs showed signs of life. They moved a little — just a teeny, teeny little bit; he had to look very close to be quite sure. And at last one began to chip, and then another began to chip. One of the cracks opened, and out came — not a chicken's head, as he had expected — but a little fist, a little squirming hand, something like a baby's hand, only smaller and dark in color. And soon there was a cracking and a squealing and a squirming, and out of one egg bobbed a head, and out of another a foot; and after the hands and heads and legs, the bodies came wiggling, and six of the queerest looking imps that you could imagine were soon sprawling on the floor. Did you ever see little doggies or little puppies, when they are just newly born? You know the funny way they stretch their necks about and tumble over one another. Well, these little goblins behaved like that!

The poor man didn't know what to think or say or do. He stood scratching his head and staring. He had never had any family before, and he didn't have any neighbors to give him advice about what to do now.

The poor things looked cold. Do you know what he did? He just snipped a little round hole out of each of the pieces of flannel that the eggs had been wrapped in. Then he put the flannel over the little shivering bodies, with their heads sticking out of the holes. It was funny, but he didn't laugh. It is a serious matter to get a big family like that so suddenly, and especially when you don't expect it!

Then he had to feed them. I don't know how he did it. I know he didn't have any feeding bottles, so I suppose he dipped bits of flannel into milk and then let the little goblins suck the flannel. They weren't old enough to manage to suck it through straws; but that's what they did later on, when they could help themselves.

I can't tell you all the trouble he had with them or what he did when they were sick — they were often sick, because they ate and ate all day and every day and didn't know when to stop. All this kept the poor man very busy, and the goblin babies were a great anxiety to him. Sometimes he was so tired of it all that he thought of running away and leaving them altogether, but he could not do that, for he knew they would die of cold and hunger if he did. But he always comforted himself with one thought: "When they grow up, they can work for me.   If I work for them so hard now, they will surely do things for me by and by." He imagined them running his errands to the village, cooking the food, tidying up the house, chopping the firewood, and going down to the spring for drinking water.

But as they got older, instead of helping him, they hindered him more and more. "Nothing to help and everything to hinder" seemed to be the rule of their life. They were terribly full of mischief. They didn't laugh or talk much, but they were always busy doing something they ought not to do. They were goblins, you see. The poor man was often nearly out of his wits with their wickedness, and when they did something especially atrocious he could almost have turned them out of doors. At last he could bear it no longer and decided that he must do something to get finally rid of them.

Now, though they were so lively and full of sin all day long, whenever the candle was lit in the evening a strange change came over them. They all became quiet at once. They stopped putting walnut shells on the cat's feet or spreading sticky stuff in the old man's books — whatever they were doing, indeed. They gathered around the table, leaned their elbows on it, their chins in their hands, and stood staring at the candle with eyes like the letter *O* with a dot in the middle.

One night, when the candle was lit, an idea came into the woodman's head. He thought: "I know what I will do. I'll take them back to the place where I got the eggs. If I put the candle in the lantern, they will follow the light, and I will take them to the beech tree and leave them there. Some of their own people will be sure to find them."

He took the candle and put it into the lantern. All the goblins crowded around to see him do it; and they chatted among themselves, without taking their eyes off the candle long enough to wink. They didn't move an eyelash; they just stared and stared and stared, till the old woodman felt himself staring too in sympathy. But he made for the door and passed out into the night.

The goblins all came stumbling after, without looking at their feet or watching where they were going, their eyes glued to the light. Sometimes one fell, but got up again in a moment and went on, bumping into his neighbor as before.

On the queer procession moved through the dark woods, and the maddest shadows and the wildest lights danced around their path. If they hadn't been goblins, they would have been scared out of their five wits. There was no sound but the crackling of twigs under their feet or a dull thud when one of the goblins stumbled over a root or a stone.

The woodman found the beech tree — he knew it by its odd shape. He hung the lantern on a broken branch; and after seeing that it was secure, he turned to go home.

But it was one thing to come through the woods with a lantern and another to go through these tangled paths in the dark. When he turned he could see nothing. All about him was total darkness. He looked back at the light. The goblins had squatted down on the ground in a circle and sat staring up at the lantern. He turned away again and went groping forward like a blind man. Branches struck him sharply in the face; he hurt his hand on a branch that broke as he thrust it aside. He slipped on a bit of wet ground and fell to the earth. He got up on his knees and crawled forward a little farther, and something clutched him by the belt. He got a terrible fright, thinking it was some monster; but when he felt it over, he found it was only a big fallen branch that had caught on his belt.

Then he sat up and turned to the light again. It had a homelike look about it. His anger against the goblins had given place to his terror of the woods. The little homely faces, all so quiet now, attracted him in spite of himself.

The light attracted him more and more, and although he struggled for a time against the magic of it, he gave up at last, and crept back to the little group he had left. He took a place in the circle, forgetting everything, and filled with a great still hunger for the light of the lantern. The spell had come upon him too.

How the Play Was Made

The story of *The Woodman and the Goblins* was told to a third grade just before Halloween by John Duncan, the noted artist. It embodies the spirit of the Halloween festival, in which children are always intensely interested. Morever, the Goblins, the Cat, the light, and the action made such a strong appeal to the children that they begged to be allowed to act out the tale.

The story was told over many times, and the children discussed ways and means of turning it into a play. Each was free to contribute his part to this discussion; each judged as to the value of the suggestions made and helped decide upon the final results. The outline of the speeches developed in the effort to act out the story, and thus they were the result of necessity. Things had to be made clear in some way, and since the Woodman had no one to talk to but himself, the play took on a monologue form. It seemed possible that the Woodman might talk to the Cat, but this idea was given up because the Cat did not seem to be a friendly one. The play, however, was never a monologue in spirit, and the action involved many persons and much pantomime.

The speeches were changed at every rehearsal and were left more or less to the will of the Woodman, even at the last. Many different children had an opportunity to play this part, so there was a great deal of practice in oral composition and much consideration of the speeches. Soon it became evident that, if the play was to run smoothly, each child must know the final words (or action) preceding his own speech — the so-called "cue." This necessity tended to give the speeches and action more or less fixity; gradually and unconsciously the form was evolved about as printed here, and each one of the children set it down from his memory of the classroom performances. Thus the lines were actually not written out until after the play had been given several times.

While working with the dialogue, the pupils decided that the inconclusive ending of the story was not satisfactory. They felt content about the Goblins when they were taken back to their own home at the beech tree, for they thought that surely their own people would find them and care for them. But they did not like to leave the Woodman under the spell of the light. Many plans for releasing him were therefore proposed, and discussed, and rejected. Finally it was suggested that in the morning the daylight would dim the candlelight and so break the spell, leaving him free to go home. This termination satisfied the children.

In making this play, the initiative was the children's and the product was theirs; it was arrived at by free and independent thinking. The teacher worked with them, doing his part as judge and critic and holding them steadily to the business in hand, but leaving them free to initiate, judge, and determine what to do.

The young playwrights found their complete satisfaction in acting their production to the school on Halloween morning. At one of the presentations, the child playing the part of the Woodman added a bit of business in Act IV which made the instructor think at first that he had forgotten the action. It was a trying but interesting moment. The Woodman put the candle in the lantern, moved about the room with the Goblins following, and then, contrary to what had been done on previous occasions, suddenly turned from the door and went towards the table. There he set the lantern down, exclaiming: "I can't do it! I can't do it! Some harm might come to them." He looked at the Goblins, once more grouped about the light; then he took the lantern up again saying, "The beech tree is their home, and their people will find them there." Then he moved out as agreed upon in the play. So thoroughly were the children in the spirit of the play, that the Goblins followed the light during this unexpected movement without showing the least confusion at the change.

The Play

Characters

Woodman	Ghosts
Goblins	Witches
Cat	

Costumes and Properties

Woodman: *Breeches and jacket of brown leather, or any cloth that resembles leather.*

Goblins: *Close-fitting one-piece suits of gray or dull brown, covering head, hands, and feet; the eyes, mouth, and nose showing. Union suits can be used.*

Cat: *Black hood drawn around the face, showing eyes, mouth, and nose. Black cape falling straight from hood all around with only slight indentation at neck. Cloth ears are attached* *to hood and braced with wire so as to stand up. Tail is made of heavy pliable wire without spring in it, so that it will remain in any position into which it is bent. Base of tail is bound to the back of child's body underneath suit.*

Cat costume for *The Woodman and the Goblins.*

Tail is suitably wrapped in black cloth. One-piece suit of soft black, covering hands and feet. Mittens will do for hands, and stockings or socks for feet. A small bell hung about the cat's neck on a ribbon. Cat's whiskers made of wire or broom-straws, attached to sides of hood around lower part of face.

GHOSTS *and* WITCHES: *Long robes, or cloaks with flowing sleeves, dark gray, brown, black, or white.*

EGGS: *Half ovals, made of wire, covered with white or gray paper.*

ACT I

SCENE: *Interior of Woodman's hut; fireplace, cupboard, bed, table, stool. Things in disorder.*

WOODMAN [*seated at table*]. Oh dear! I am so tired of getting my own meals. I wish I had some one to help me. I sometimes go without eating, because I hate to cook so. Now I'll get the partridge. [*Goes after it.*]

Why! Where is it? [*Hunts for it.*] I'll warrant the Cat has it! [*Looks for Cat.*] Ah, there she goes! She has it in her mouth! [*Chases* CAT. *She runs out of the room. He throws wood at her.* CAT *meows. He peers after her.*] My, her eyes blaze like a witch's! [*He turns back into the room.*]

Well, I have some bacon, anyway. [*Hunts for bacon, slices it, and puts it over the fire. Burns finger. Puts food on table. Hunts for knife and spoon. Sits down and begins to eat.*]

[*Suddenly in alarm.*] My, this is Halloween and I have to go to town to-night to get a new ax! I hate to go through the woods. The witches and goblins and fairies and ghosts are all out tonight. Last Halloween, a man saw a light far off in the wood. He couldn't take his eyes off it. He followed it and suddenly it vanished and left him alone in the field.

[*Looks around and sees a goblin at the window.*] What's that at the window? [*Looks around again.*] But I have to go, and I might as well start at once. [*Puts on coat and hat and slowly leaves hut.*]

CURTAIN

ACT II

SCENE: *Dark woods; large tree in center. Six large eggs are lying about large tree.*

[*Enter Woodman, feeling about. He carries a new ax over his shoulder.*]

WOODMAN. My, those were queer creepy stories they were telling in the village — of bogies and ghosts and goblins. I can fairly see them now.

[*Stares about.*] Why, where am I? I thought I could find the way home with my eyes shut, but this road looks strange! I don't believe I have ever been here before! The trees are so close together!

[*Drops on his knees and begins to feel around for a path. Comes up to the tree, where he finds the six eggs.*] Eggs! Big eggs! [*Tries to see, feels them over, counts them.*] I'll take them home and hatch them out and see what queer fowl will come out of them. If I can get hens that will lay thumping big eggs like these every day, I won't have far to look for a breakfast. But how can I hatch them? I can't stay in bed with them three weeks, and I can't trust the Cat. Even if she were big enough, she would not sit still anyway. [*Puzzled and distressed.*] Ah, I know. I'll wrap them in that red flannel I bought for a shirt and set them about the fire. [*Takes off his jacket and spreads it out to carry eggs. Begins to gather them together and place them in the jacket.*]

CURTAIN

ACT III

SCENE: *Interior of* WOODMAN'S *hut.   Eggs before the fire-place, covered over with pieces of red flannel to keep them warm.   Goblins are inside the eggs.*

WOODMAN [*standing in front of fireplace, looking at eggs*]. What queer eggs these are!   They have been here by the fire for three weeks now.   Something ought to be coming out pretty soon.

[*Sees a little movement.   First one and then another begins to chip.   Hears a crackling noise.*]   They are beginning to hatch now.   [*Then one of the cracks opens, and a hand comes out, then a leg, then a head, and soon all the* GOBLINS *are squirming and wiggling and stretching themselves on the floor.* WOODMAN *is both astonished and frightened. Watches them.*]   What shall I ever do with these things? They need clothes, food, and everything; but first they need clothes.   Ah, I know!   The pieces of flannel!   [*Cuts holes in red flannel squares that have been over eggs and puts them on* GOBLINS, *pulling them over their heads.*]

Now something to eat!   [*Gets some milk and dips a rag in it; gives it to* GOBLINS *to suck.*]   These goblin babies are going to be a lot of trouble!   Well, if I have to take care of *you*, you will have to work for me by and by.   I know what you'll have to do: you'll have to cook my food and wash my dishes; you'll have to carry water and go on errands for me — I hate to do these things myself, anyway!

CURTAIN

ACT IV

SCENE: *Interior of* WOODMAN'S *hut.*

[GOBLINS *around a dish, all eating together, gobbling down the food.* WOODMAN *watches them.*]

WOODMAN. Oh dear! They are eating so much and so fast, they will make themselves sick again and keep me awake all night with their cries. [*One* GOBLIN *claps his hands to his stomach and begins to howl and dance with pain; he runs and lies down in corner of room.*] I am tired of living! I believe I'll run away and leave them altogether. But no! They would die of cold and hunger. I can't do that.

[GOBLINS *gradually scatter about room, playing tricks on one another and on the* CAT. *They push and pull one another. They put nut shells on the* CAT'S *feet while he sleeps, and they put sticky stuff on the leaves of the* WOODMAN'S *book, etc.* WOODMAN *sits down to read.* GOBLINS *continue to play around room. They tease* WOODMAN; *pull his hair, and tickle his toes. Finally he spanks one. This frightens them, and they huddle together and begin to cry.*] Oh, I'm almost crazy!

I know what I'll do! I'll light the candle. That will quiet them. It is the only thing that ever quiets them. [*Lights candle. Light fascinates* GOBLINS, *who instantly stop crying and, softly creeping nearer, sit perfectly spellbound, their chins in their hands, never taking their eyes from light.*] Well, I'm glad something will keep those pests still! [*Reads on. Suddenly puts down book.*]

How in the world shall I ever get rid of them? I've had them for a year now. I thought they would be of some use, but they grow more and more mischievous every day.

They never help me, but hinder me in every way. They pester the life out of me; and the Cat is as bad as they are. They have bewitched her too! [*Thinks.*]

Ah, I have it! This is Halloween again. I'll put that candle into my lantern, and see if they will follow the light. If they will go, I'll take them back into the woods, to the beech tree where I found the eggs, hang my lantern there, and leave them to their own people. Then I'll go home. [WOODMAN *puts the candle into the lantern and moves about the room to see if his plan will work.* GOBLINS *watch, and follow lantern about room.*] WOODMAN *goes out the door, shouting delightedly*]. It works! It works! It works! [GOBLINS *all stumble out after him, eyes glued on light.*]

CURTAIN

ACT V

SCENE: *Woods. Shadowy figures flitting about in the dark.*

[WOODMAN *comes through forest, followed by* GOBLINS, *stumbling over one another, eyes still fixed on the light. He moves about until he finds the tree.*]

WOODMAN. The beech tree at last! [*He hangs up his lantern. The* GOBLINS *form a circle around it, never turning their eyes away.* WOODMAN *looks at the* GOBLINS *and at the light.*]

Ugh! I mustn't look at it myself. It will bewitch me too! [*Covers his eyes, and starts to leave. Shadowy figures meet him at every turn he makes and frighten him. He falls over a tree or stump and is in terror. He rises and stumbles on. A branch catches his belt; he cries out in fear, thinking that he has been seized by some monster.*]

Oh! I am afraid to go on! [*He turns back to the lantern, glad to see it and the* GOBLINS. *Slowly sinks on his knees, and takes his place among the* GOBLINS *with eyes fastened on the light. The shadowy figures flit about in glee. Then there is a glimmer of light in the east, and suddenly the shadowy figures are still. The day dawns in the east; terror seizes the shadows; they shrink and flee away. Great* GOBLINS *hurrying to escape the approaching daylight enter. As they scurry across the stage, they see the little* GOBLINS *and take the latter with them as they disappear into the woods. Gradually the daylight increases, and the candle in the lantern grows more and more dim. The spell is broken. The* WOODMAN *stirs, rubs his eyes, and sees the light in the east. He rises.*]

The daylight! The daylight! The spell is broken! [*He looks about and sees that the* GOBLINS *are gone.*] The Goblins are safe at home — safe at home! [*Then he turns to leave the tree and the woods, going towards the light.*] I am free again! I am free again!

CURTAIN

CHAPTER XXVIII

MR. WOLF MAKES A FAILURE

Notes on Making and Playing

The adaptation of Joel Chandler Harris' story was the common effort of a third grade. Several tales from *Uncle Remus, His Songs and His Sayings* had been read to the class, and these had been acted by the members in a purely informal way.[1] A truly social motive actuated the more careful work in *Mr. Wolf Makes a Failure*. The children wished to play it for the second grade. The idea of having it typed grew out of a wish to preserve the play so that the next year's class might have it to read. The dramatization is the composite whole which the children achieved, guided, but in no way dictated, by the teacher. It is interesting to note that in dramatizing as well as in telling *Uncle Remus*, these pupils never attempted to use the Negro dialect, but always put the stories into idiomatic English. The play was acted finally on the stage. There were, however, neither costumes, settings, nor stage lights. The center represented the road; the right was supposed to be the location of Brother Rabbit's house; the left, Brother Fox's. There were no curtains to mark the scenes, and the action was continuous.

[1] Among those which lend themselves to dramatization are: *Uncle Remus Initiates the Little Boy, Mr. Terrapin Appears Upon the Scene, The Awful Fate of Mr. Wolf, Mr. Fox Goes A-Hunting, but Mr. Rabbit Bags the Game, Mr. Rabbit Finds His Match at Last, How Mr. Rabbit Saved His Meat,* and *How Mr. Rabbit Succeeded in Raising a Dust.*

The Play [1]

Characters

BROTHER FOX
BROTHER WOLF
BROTHER RABBIT

ACT I

SCENE: *The big road.*

[BROTHER FOX *is walking down the road. He is mighty downhearted, for he is thinking how* BROTHER RABBIT *has several times of late got the better of him. He sees* BROTHER WOLF *coming up the road and starts to slink away into the woods, but* BROTHER WOLF *sees him and calls to him.*]

BROTHER WOLF. Good morning, Brother Fox.

BROTHER FOX. Good morning, Brother Wolf.

BROTHER WOLF. How are you this morning? You are not looking quite well.

BROTHER FOX. Oh, yes, I am well.

BROTHER WOLF. How is your family?

BROTHER FOX. They are all so-so. How is your family?

BROTHER WOLF. They never were better, thank you. [BROTHER FOX *still looks downhearted.*] But, Brother Fox, you certainly look as if something were troubling you.

BROTHER FOX [*trying to laugh*]. Oh no, there is nothing troubling me.

BROTHER WOLF. Have you seen Brother Rabbit around here lately?

BROTHER FOX. No, I have not seen him for some time.

---

[1] The play is adapted from *Uncle Remus, His Songs and His Sayings*, by Joel Chandler Harris and is used here with the special permission of D. Appleton & Co., New York, publishers of Mr. Harris's books.

BROTHER WOLF. Brother Rabbit has played some mean tricks on me. I am trying to fix up a plan to catch him.

BROTHER FOX. Well, I hope you will succeed. Brother Rabbit is a nuisance around here.

BROTHER WOLF. I am sure I can catch him if you will help me.

BROTHER FOX. Tell me your plan, and if it is a good one, perhaps I will help you. I am no friend of his.

BROTHER WOLF. We must get him into your house.

BROTHER FOX. Oh, that old trick is worn to a frazzle.

[BROTHER FOX *starts to walk away*.]

BROTHER WOLF. Come back here, Brother Fox, and let me explain my plan. I have a sure way to get him into your house.

BROTHER FOX [*coming back again*]. How are you going to do it?

BROTHER WOLF. Fool him there.

BROTHER FOX. Who will do the fooling?

BROTHER WOLF. I'll do the fooling if you will do the gaming.

BROTHER FOX. How are you going to do it?

BROTHER WOLF. You run along home, get on the bed and pretend that you are dead. Don't say anything until Brother Rabbit comes and puts his hands upon you. Then, if we don't get him for supper, Joe's dead and Sal's a widow.

BROTHER FOX [*pleased with the plan*]. That looks like a mighty good game. I will hurry home and stretch out on the bed while you go over to Brother Rabbit's house.

BROTHER WOLF. Good! I will go over to Brother Rabbit's now. Remember do not say anything or move until Brother Rabbit puts his hands on you.

Brother Fox. I understand. We shall surely get him this time. [Brother Fox *hurries off home, while* Brother Wolf *goes to the house of* Brother Rabbit.]

ACT II

Scene: Brother Rabbit's *house.*

[Brother Rabbit *is seated in a rocking chair reading the paper.* Brother Wolf *raps at the door. No answer.* Brother Wolf *raps again.*]

Brother Rabbit [*in a sickly voice*]. Who is there?

Brother Wolf. Friend.

Brother Rabbit. Too many friends spoil the dinner. Which one is this?

Brother Wolf. I bring bad news, Brother Rabbit.

Brother Rabbit. Bad news is soon told. [Brother Rabbit, *with his head tied up in a red handkerchief, goes to the door.*]

Brother Wolf. Brother Fox died this morning.

Brother Rabbit. You say Brother Fox died this morning?

Brother Wolf. Yes, it was very sudden.

Brother Rabbit. Where is your mourning gown?

Brother Wolf. I am going after it now. I just called to bring you the sad news. I went down to Brother Fox's house and found him stiff. [Brother Wolf *goes off.*]

Brother Rabbit. I wonder if Brother Fox really is dead. [Brother Rabbit *sits down and scratches his head and thinks.*] Perhaps it is true that Brother Fox is dead. Anyway, I believe I will drop around by Brother Fox's house and see how the land lies. [Brother Rabbit *goes out.*]

ACT III

SCENE: BROTHER FOX'S *house.*

[BROTHER FOX *is on the bed.*]

BROTHER FOX.   I wonder if Brother Rabbit will come.
If he does I will surely catch him this time.   He shall
never leave this house alive.   I hear someone coming now.
I must pretend to be dead.   [*He stretches out and folds his
paws on his stomach.*]

BROTHER RABBIT [*peeping cautiously in at the door*].
Nobody is stirring.   [*He sees* BROTHER FOX.]   There is
poor Brother Fox.   Nobody around to look after Brother
Fox — not even Brother Turkey Buzzard has come to the
funeral.   I hope Brother Fox is not dead, but I suspect he
is.   Everyone down to Brother Wolf has left him.   It is
the busy season with me, but I will sit up with him.   He
seems as if he were dead; yet he may not be.   When a man
goes to see dead folks, dead folks always raise up their
behind leg and holler "Wahoo!"   [BROTHER FOX *keeps
perfectly still.*   BROTHER RABBIT *speaks louder.*]   Mighty
funny!   Brother Fox looks as if he were dead, yet he does
not do as if he were dead.   Dead folks hist up their behind
leg and holler "Wahoo!" when a man comes to see them.
[BROTHER FOX *lifts up his foot and cries* "Wahoo!" *and*
BROTHER RABBIT *tears out of the house as if the dogs were
after him.*]

BROTHER FOX [*very much surprised, slowly sits up and looks
about for* BROTHER RABBIT].   Now, I wonder what Brother
Rabbit ran away for!   I wonder!

THE END

CHAPTER XXIX

THE MAGIC GIFTS

MAKING AND STAGING THE PLAY

THIS dramatization resulted from the reading of Grimm's fairy tale, "The Nose Tree," in *The Heart of Oak Books*, Book III, edited by Charles Eliot Norton. The interest in the "The Nose Tree" was so great that the children of the fourth grade wished to make it into a play that they could act before the whole school.

As the class was unusually mature and had had considerable experience in such work, its members were allowed to try to carry out their wishes. A rereading of the story with this purpose in mind revealed the fact that the task of making an effective play would involve the solving of some difficult problems. Many things entirely reasonable in the story were apparently physically impossible to accomplish on the stage; and the many changes of place and action used in the story would be objectionable in dramatic presentation. Yet the difficulties seemed only to increase the eagerness with which the problem was attacked. The children were confident that by making certain alterations a thoroughly interesting and actable play could be made.

To begin with, the young playwrights prepared an outline of the incidents that they thought should make up the drama. This outline, they found, contained a very large number of scenes. They concluded that this would never do, because a multiplicity of acts breaks the continuity of

Black Canton flannel curtains formed the background for all the scenes of this production of *Androcles and the Lion*. In the Prologue, spot lights illuminated the limited area in which Androcles, his wife, and the Lion acted. A suggestion of the jungle from which the Lion emerged was secured by means of a single painted flat.

the story and causes the audience to lose interest. As some-one remarked, "The audience does not want to look at the curtain all the time, while we are running about changing things for the new scene." By taking liberties with the text and by combining incidents, an outline which promised to make an effective and organic play, true to the spirit if not to the letter of Grimm, was evolved. Much care was spent upon this part of the work because the teacher realized that a well-balanced, coherent play depends upon a well-planned and carefully stated enumeration of the incidents. That the children intuitively obeyed the laws of play structure can be seen from their outline which follows:

ACT I. A wood. The three discharged soldiers receive the three magic gifts from the Little Man of the Forest.

ACT II. In front of the King's palace. The three soldiers, now dressed like princes, visit the King and the Princess. She gets possession of the magic purse.

ACT III. A road. The soldiers discover the loss of the magic purse and determine to go back to the palace in search of it.

ACT IV. Same place as Act II. They discover that the Princess is the thief. In trying to get back the purse they lose the magic cloak and the magic horn. The soldiers separate, to begin life over again.

ACT V. The Third Soldier eats the magic apple, and his nose grows longer. The Little Man of the Forest comes and gives him a magic pear, and he is cured. The Little Man of the Forest suggests the magic fruits as means of getting the Princess to surrender the magic gifts.

ACT VI. The three soldiers disguised play their trick on the Princess and succeed in recovering the three magic gifts.

Analysis on the part of the reader will reveal the excellence of the technique of the play as an organic whole. Act I introduces the main characters and gives the exposition of the situation; it also supplies the exciting force in the gift of the three magic articles. Act II continues the exposition and develops the plot by the introduction of the Princess, who is the opposing force of the play. The loss of the purse leads to the dramatic clash. Act III gives rising action. Act IV gives an apparent check to the opposing force, through the discovery of the thief. Then follows continued rising action, or complexity, and the crisis of the play in the loss of all of the gifts and the separation of the impoverished soldiers. Act V reveals the discovery of the power of the magic apples and pears, and the unraveling of the plot — the descending action. Act VI gives the dénouement, the punishment of evil and the reward of perseverance.

After the choosing of the incidents and their arrangement into acts, the class played the first act, using whatever dialogue the actors thought necessary. The members criticized freely and gave constructive suggestions as to how the dialogue could be made clearer and more adequate. The act was played several times, until, under the motive of making the situation more vivid, the children developed terse and effective dialogue as the natural accompaniment of action and incident. The class wished to preserve the play in written form, so that the results of their work might be kept both for their own use and for any future class that might like to have the story of "The Nose Tree" in play form.

The speeches were suggested in order and were written on the board by either the teacher or one of the pupils. They were freely criticized and changed until the majority of the pupils were satisfied. The text, in truth, was never absolutely fixed in form as long as the class worked upon it. Even up to the last rehearsal, there were slight changes in the wording of the dialogue, as the deepening emotions of the actors found freer expression and more natural speech.

Of course difficulties of all sorts arose. The lapses of time in Act I were difficult to manage. The appearance of the Little Man of the Forest during intervals of the night is most reasonable in the story, but to give the three gifts within the playing time of one act and at the same time make the soldiers' naps seem plausible, was a grave problem. The pupils spent much time studying the text, and did much deep thinking. They succeeded in finding ways out of most of their perplexities and when they found themselves unable to solve a problem, the teacher assisted.

The intensive study of a story which such dramatization requires gives splendid exercise to the critical faculties of the young students. The children discovered that Grimm has the Little Man of the Forest say, when he gives the horn to the soldiers, that its notes have the power to draw after them the crowds of the streets and "set them to dancing." Now when the trumpet is really used by the soldiers, the crowd that collects is made up of soldiers. Dancing would be quite out of harmony with the situation; so they changed the words to read, "and make them do whatever you may desire." The story as told by the brothers Grimm states that the Princess "was a fairy and knew all the wonderful things that the three soldiers brought." Some member of the class said, "Well, if it is true that she was a fairy and knew everything, why didn't she know what caused her nose to grow long and where she could find a cure?" Here was an important problem to solve. Again they searched the text and concluded that Grimm had not been consistent. They finally decided that, since the development of the plot depended upon the ignorance of the Princess as to the soldiers' trick, in the play she must be made, not a fairy, but a plain princess. Acting the story revealed also the fact that the Second Soldier in the tale has a larger share of adventures than his brothers. To make the distribution more equal, it was suggested that the First Soldier should disguise himself as the gardener's boy, while the Third Soldier should act as the doctor.

The children found that some of the episodes, effective in the story, would have to be changed or left out to fit the dramatic telling, and that other incidents would have to be invented to make the drama complete. It would be necessary, for example, to show the soldiers' discovery of the loss of their magic purse. To meet this need the incident of the buying of the strawberries was invented.

How to make the nose actually grow long was a puzzle. Many ingenious but impracticable schemes were suggested before someone thought of the artificial noses often used as favors at parties. This idea solved the difficulty; but the artificial nose would have to be put on behind the scenes. Conversation and action were therefore invented with this necessity in mind. The soldier, after feeling the pain, goes to the near-by brook to bathe his nose, in hope that the water will allay the pain. This action gives time for the adjustment of the artificial nose. An equally good excuse was found for getting him off the scene when his nose was cured. The coming and going of the Princess's nose was likewise successfully planned. These and similar problems furnished splendid motives for the exercise of creative imagination and made the class appreciate the difference between the two forms of story-telling — the tale and the drama — and gave them practice in careful analysis, criticism, and terse expression. The children did everything that they could in the making of the dramatization, but when a problem arose too difficult for them to solve fully, or when they had worked as long as they could with profit to themselves and were in danger of reaching the point of fatigue, the teacher came to their aid and offered suggestions, which they were free to accept or reject as their judgment prompted.

While the dialogue was being planned, the director kept in mind the advisability of as general a distribution of the speeches among the various characters as the exigencies of the story permitted.

According to the story, the Princess sang a ballad, but what were the words and the tune? The brothers Grimm do not inform us; so members of the group went to work to invent a ballad. This step meant the writing of verse. When a satisfactory ballad was selected from the large number of verses voluntarily and eagerly written, the class went to work to set it to music.

All the acts were played several times before any dialogue was written. The making in the classroom of the text for all six acts proved to be too slow a process. It was decided, therefore, to let each person select an act or a portion of an act and write it at home. To facilitate this work, the students, with the help of the teacher, carefully worked out and placed on the board a scenario of each act. Each pupil copied the part of this which referred to the particular act on which he chose to work and used it as a guide while making his composition. To illustrate what we term a scenario, that used in Act V will serve.

ACT V. A wood. The Second Soldier, stretched out under a tree, awakes and recalls what has happened. He is hungry; he finds an apple that has fallen from the tree and eats it. His nose begins to pain him. He goes to a near-by brook to bathe it. His brothers, worn with travel, enter. The Second Soldier returns. His nose has grown long. His brothers ask what has happened. He tells them. All are in despair. The Little Man of the Forest appears. The Little Man tells them to gather some pears. The Second Soldier eats a pear. He goes to bathe his nose again. He returns with his nose its natural size. The Little Man tells them that they can use the magic apples and pears on the Princess and so get back the gifts she has stolen. They thank the Little Man. He goes. The three soldiers make their plans. The First Soldier says he will disguise himself as a gardener's boy. The Third Soldier says he will disguise himself as a doctor. They begin to gather the apples and pears.

The children, after they had worked at home on the dialogue of the act they had chosen, then read to the class what they had written. A free discussion followed as to the merits or demerits of each contribution, and when this had gone as far as seemed profitable to the class, the instructor took the work of the individual children and made a composite piece of writing. Whatever changes or additions were made by the teacher, for the purpose of clarifying or vivifying the telling of the story, were submitted to the class for approval.

The play grew like a mushroom in size and scope and proved a bigger piece of work than had been anticipated; but at no time did anyone suggest that it was too difficult to finish. The class, nevertheless, was unable to complete the play before the close of the year. The work was continued when school was resumed, and when the text was completed it was mimeographed and rehearsals were begun in earnest.

Never was the text slavishly adhered to. The teacher strove to stimulate, direct, and deepen the thinking and feeling of the children. Under the stimulus of the rehearsals the actors grew in characterization, and the dialogue changed and became more forceful and clear.

As the production of the play advanced, certain details too subtle to be explained to the children were incorporated into the play by the teacher. For example, he planned to have the two guards at the beginning of Act II enter, rather than to have them discovered on the stage at the rise of the curtain. It is easier for children to make their speeches as they move. If they were on the stage at the rise of the curtain, in order to be heard distinctly they would have to wait until the curtain was well up before they could speak. This pause would be likely to cause self-consciousness on the part of the actors.

The play was rehearsed for a long period without assigning the parts permanently. Finally the class was divided into three casts, in order to give everyone an opportunity. The parts were assigned with the needs of the particular children in mind, rather than with regard to their acting ability. The cast ready first was allowed first performance.

The children made many sketches of the settings and of the costumes, both in black and white and in water color, but they were too young and too busy with the presentation of the play to do much actual work in the execution of costumes and settings. The idea of simplicity and of beauty in line, color, and arrangement actuated the working out of the staging. The platform on which *The Magic Gifts* was done was not an ideal one; and its limitations had to be borne in mind constantly. It was very small, with permanent doors at right and left. (Stage right and left are the right and left of the actor as he faces the audience, as is indicated in the diagram on page 274.) The size of the stage helped to determine the character of the setting. That there should be no long waits, arrangements were so planned that the labor of setting was reduced to the minimum.

The names given the various positions on the stage are customarily abbreviated; for example, R. C. equals *right center*.[1]

---

[1] For the sake of clarity the author has found it simpler in working with children to keep to the older stage terminology.

At the back of the stage there was hung, without any fullness, a curtain of Canton flannel that had been dyed a cerulean blue. In front of this, stood a wall some five and a half feet high. The framework of this wall was made of wood and covered with gray building paper. The paper was lined with crayons to suggest stone. At the back, stage right, stood a poplar tree (a silhouette cut out of beaver board and painted with a flat-toned green paint). A

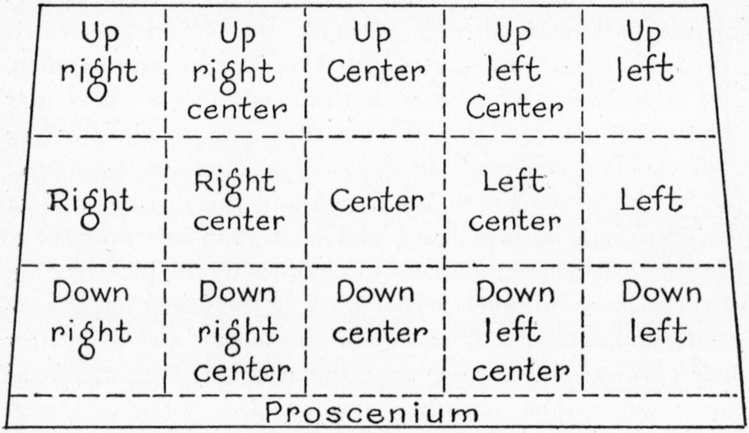

Up right	Up right center	Up Center	Up left Center	Up left
Right	Right center	Center	Left center	Left
Down right	Down right center	Down center	Down left center	Down left
		Proscenium		

Diagram 7. — Plot of the various positions on the stage.

few feet in front of the back wall, at stage left, stood a shorter wall with a gate at the right end. Behind it stood another silhouetted tree, which served to hide the doorway at upper stage left. Diagram 8 will aid the reader to understand the arrangement.

Act I was next arranged by hanging (in front of the wall at the back) without folds, a Canton flannel curtain similar in color to the one used back of the rear wall. Green curtains, as indicated in Diagram 9, were hung in front of the shorter wall and also down stage right and left. These were

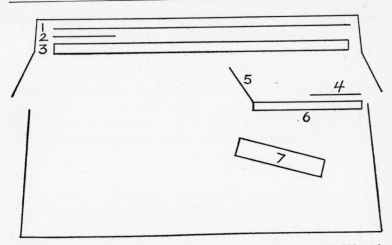

Diagram 8. — Stage arrangement for *The Magic Gifts*. Acts II, IV, and VI, the terrace in front of the King's palace: *1.* blue curtain; *2.* poplar tree; *3.* wall; *4.* poplar tree; *5.* gate; *6.* short wall; *7.* bench.

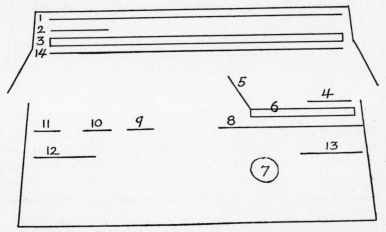

Diagram 9. — Stage arrangement for *The Magic Gifts*. Act I, a forest: *1.* blue curtain; *2.* poplar tree; *3.* wall; *4.* poplar tree; *5.* gate; *6.* short wall; *7.* fire; *8, 9, 10, 11, 12, 13.* green curtains; *14.* blue curtain.

specially dyed and were hung full, so that in the light which came from the green bulbs in the first border and from the one red light in the brush fire, the spectator got the suggestion of a mysterious forest. The fire was made by putting a red electric light into an iron pan some three inches deep, and covering it with brush and branches.

At the end of Act I all that was necessary to prepare the stage for Act II was to remove the fire and the blue curtain

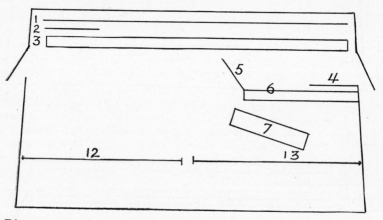

Diagram 10. — Stage arrangement for *The Magic Gifts*. Act III, a highroad: *1.* blue curtain; *2.* poplar tree; *3.* wall; *4.* poplar tree; *5.* gate; *6.* short wall; *7.* bench; *12, 13.* green curtains.

in front of the wall, lift the green curtains out of sight, turn on the amber lights, and place a bench at the left center of the stage. (See Diagram 8.) The seat, especially designed, was made and stained by a group of pupils in one of the highschool classes. Act III was made ready by using the green curtains that were down stage right and left in Act I. When drawn together they hid the rest of the stage, as indicated in Diagram 10. Act V was set by using the green curtains, which hung in front of the shorter wall in Act I, to shut off the rear of the stage. The green curtains at the front right and left were pushed back to add to the effectiveness of the scene. (See Diagram 11.) The light in this act was kept as subdued as possible.

The following notes may give additional help to anyone who wishes to stage *The Magic Gifts*. False noses can be obtained at almost any store where favors for parties are kept. The application of a little flesh-colored grease paint

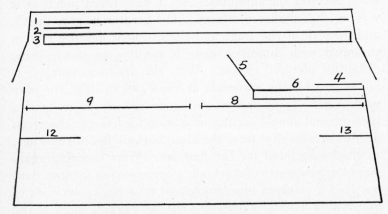

Diagram 11. — Stage arrangement for *The Magic Gifts*. Act V, a wood: *1*. blue curtain; *2*. poplar tree; *3*. wall; *4*. poplar tree; *5*. gate; *6*. short wall; *8, 9, 12, 13*. green curtains.

to the surface of the false nose helps to make it look more natural and makes it blend better with the human flesh. These false noses are expected to hold to the human nose by their natural pressure, but it is much wiser to have a fine flesh-colored elastic cord go round the head. The chopped apple and pear are well suggested by using puffed rice. A white bottle for the apple and a blue one for the pear are used in order that the color may help the audience to follow the actions of the supposed doctor. The detachment of soldiers in the fourth act is not necessary. If, however, the class is large, the army serves to give every member of the group a chance to appear in the play. The magic cloak is red in color in order that the audience can readily distinguish it from the other cloaks in the play.

A presentation of *The Magic Gifts*, given a few years after the performance just described, was done on a much larger stage that permitted a simpler arrangement of scenes and more effective backgrounds. Act I was staged much as it was on the smaller platform. The greater height, depth, and breadth of the stage and the excellent lighting system equipped with dimmers made it possible to secure some delightful pictorial effects. With the desire to employ as far as possible the materials at hand and to stage the play with as little labor as was consistent with the securing of a pleasing and simple setting, it was decided to use the green denim curtains that form the usual background of the stage, as the background for the first act. Were the play again staged in this particular school, a cyclorama of Canton flannel dyed a cerulean blue, hung taut on semicircular rods of iron, would doubtless represent the sky backing in all of the scenes that require the full stage. A very good and easily managed suggestion of clumps of trees was again secured by the use of Canton flannel dyed a dark greenish-brown, hung closely bunched about halfway down the stage, as shown in Diagram 12. At the beginning of the first act, the stage was rather dimly lighted. As the act progressed, the waning day was easily indicated by the use of the dimmers. Throughout the play, no footlights were used. The major part of the scene was played with a blue light, the red glow of the fire casting great shadows from the tree trunks and the figures moving about behind the fire. The back curtain was hung in great folds, which in the dim blue light gave an effect of a forest of tree trunks. Members of high-school classes that had studied drama and stagecraft were eager to assist in the working out of the lighting.

For the rest of the play two screens, each having three folds, were placed down stage at the right and the left. These prove invaluable in the staging of all types of drama. They divide the stage conveniently into a fore and a back stage. Thus by drawing curtains, the fore stage can be shut off from the back, as shown in Diagram 14. The back stage

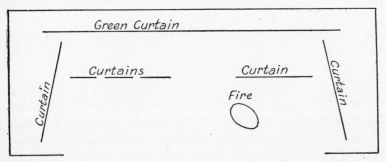

Diagram 12. — Stage arrangement for Act I (a forest) in a recent production of *The Magic Gifts*.

is most convenient to use as an out-door setting, while the fore stage can be used for almost any locality. The middle fold of these screens has an opening about the size of a small door. A curtain made of the same material as the screen is used to cover the opening when it seems desirable to do so. For this specific occasion a curtain of cerulean blue Canton flannel was lowered at the back to suggest the sky. A wall made of a light framework of wood, covered with gray building paper, and decorated with crayons to give the effect of stone, ran all the way across the stage, as indicated in Diagram 13. The gate in the wall was imagined to be just out of sight at the left of the stage. A garden bench and a small table completed the setting. The castle entrance was the opening in the screen on the right. The garden was supposed to be off stage upper right.

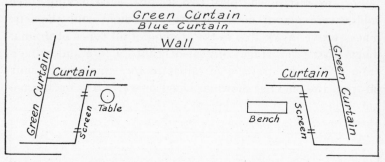

Diagram 13. — Stage arrangement for Acts II, IV, and VI (the terrace in front of the king's palace) in a recent production of *The Magic Gifts*.

As a background for Acts III and V, the green curtains used in Act I as the clump of trees were drawn across the center of the stage to fill the space between the two screens.

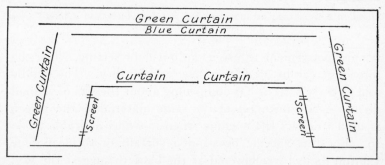

Diagram 14. — Stage arrangement for Acts III and V in a recent production of *The Magic Gifts*.

(See Diagram 14.) It was found that, with the settings described, the six acts of the play could be run with very little waiting.

In order to make a little introduction[1] to the play and at the same time to create a spirit of expectancy and intimacy, the Little Man of the Forest came before the grand curtain (as the main curtain is called by professionals) and, after looking about as if bewildered to find himself in a strange place, said, "I am the Little Man of the Forest. I have magic gifts for those who deserve them and who know how to use them well. Come with me, and if the eyes of your imagination are not too dim you will see a deep forest and — but I hear three old soldiers approaching. Hasten (*beckoning to the audience*) for they must not see us here."

At that, the Little Man of the Forest stealthily and silently made his way through the opening of the grand curtain, which promptly rose on the first act.

THE PLAY

CHARACTERS

THE FIRST SOLDIER
THE SECOND SOLDIER
THE THIRD SOLDIER
THE LITTLE MAN OF THE FOREST
THE KING
THE PRINCESS
A MAID
TWO GUARDS
A WOMAN WHO SELLS STRAWBERRIES
THE LEADER OF THE ARMY
SOLDIERS

[1] The making of an original prologue furnishes members of the class excellent work in composition; moreover it frequently provides another part which is often most desirable when one has a large number of pupils who must be given an opportunity to share in the performance.

ACT I

[*The last rays of the setting sun cast long shadows through a dense wood.   Three old* SOLDIERS *enter wearily.*[1]]

FIRST SOLDIER.   Oh, I am weary.

SECOND SOLDIER.   So am I.

THIRD SOLDIER.   We have walked since early morning and are still a long way from home.

FIRST SOLDIER.   I am hungry as well as tired.   The blackberries that we found by the roadside were good, but not very filling.   [*He seats himself on the ground.*]   It is hard on old fellows like ourselves to be turned out of the army penniless.

SECOND SOLDIER.   Yes, after we have served our country faithfully for many years.

THIRD SOLDIER.   I am glad the wars are over, but it will be hard to earn a living.

FIRST SOLDIER.   Especially when there will be so many soldiers looking for work.   [*It has been getting dark gradually.*]

SECOND SOLDIER [*sighing*].   Well, I suppose we should start on our way.   [*The* FIRST SOLDIER *rises.*]

THIRD SOLDIER.   See how dark it is getting.

SECOND SOLDIER.   I am afraid we shall not be able to reach any village to-night.

THIRD SOLDIER.   We shall have to sleep here in the woods.

FIRST SOLDIER.   I don't like the idea of sleeping in this gloomy forest.   But I think you are right when you say that we shall have to spend the night here.

SECOND SOLDIER.   As long as we have no food, we may as well lie down and get some sleep.

---

[1] The stage directions in this text refer to the presentation described on pages 278–81.

THIRD SOLDIER. I think so, too. I am terribly weary. Sleep will make us forget how hungry we are.

[*They spread out their cloaks on the ground.*]

FIRST SOLDIER. I wonder if there are not wild beasts in these woods?

THIRD SOLDIER. It looks as if there might be.

SECOND SOLDIER. It will not be safe to sleep here.

THIRD SOLDIER. One of us can sit up and watch while the others sleep. Then we shall feel more safe.

SECOND SOLDIER. We can take turns watching.

FIRST SOLDIER. Yes, a good idea. I will take the first turn.

SECOND SOLDIER. Very well. Call me when you are tired.

[*The* SECOND *and* THIRD SOLDIERS *lie down. The* FIRST SOLDIER *makes a fire.*]

FIRST SOLDIER. It is damp and chilly in the forest when the sun goes down. This fire will keep us warm and at the same time help to keep the wild beasts away. [*He leans against a tree, yawns, and looks anxiously into the gloom.*] It is lonely and dark. [*The* LITTLE MAN OF THE FOREST, *in a red jacket, appears in the distance, moving in and out among the trees. The* FIRST SOLDIER *starts; rubs his eyes.*] What is that red thing moving among the shadows? [*In fear.*] Who's there?

LITTLE MAN. The Little Man of the Forest. Who are you?

FIRST SOLDIER. A friend.

LITTLE MAN [*coming down toward the old* SOLDIER]. What sort of friend?

FIRST SOLDIER. An old broken soldier with his two comrades who has nothing left to live on. [*He looks the* LITTLE

MAN *over curiously and says cautiously.*] But come, sit down and warm yourself.

LITTLE MAN. Well, my worthy fellow, I am sorry you have been so unfortunate. I will do what I can for you. Take this cloak and show it to your comrades when they wake. [*He offers the* SOLDIER *an old red cloak.*]

FIRST SOLDIER. Thank you kindly, but you will need your cloak. The nights are chilly.

LITTLE MAN. But I want you to have it. I shall not miss it, for my red jacket keeps me warm. Please accept it. [*The* SOLDIER *takes the cloak reluctantly.*] Whenever you desire anything, put this cloak over your shoulders, wish, and your wish will immediately come true.

FIRST SOLDIER. Thank you, my good friend. If that be so, you have made an old soldier happy. May heaven reward you for your kindness. [*The* LITTLE MAN *bows and moves slowly away. Every now and then his red jacket is seen as he glides hither and thither among the forest shadows.*] I will wake the others and tell them of our good fortune. [*He starts to awaken them, then pauses.*] No. I will wait and show it to them in the morning.

SECOND SOLDIER [*turns uneasily, shivers, and awakes*]. I am so cold I cannot sleep. [*He rises, goes over, and sits by the fire.*] The fire feels good! I will sit here for a while. [*Addressing the* FIRST SOLDIER.] If you would like to get a nap, I will watch in your place for I am no longer at all sleepy.

FIRST SOLDIER. My eyes are heavy. There is no need of two people to keep guard, so I will take your offer and catch a wink of sleep. [*He lies down and takes a nap.*]

SECOND SOLDIER. This is a chilly and gloomy spot in which to spend a night. I shall be glad when morning comes. [*He puts wood on the fire, sits down again, and then catches sight of the red jacket of the* LITTLE MAN *moving quietly among the trees*.] Do I see something moving there in the shadow of that oak tree? [*He rubs his eyes*.] My eyes are still heavy with sleep. I certainly see something moving. Who are you?

LITTLE MAN [*coming closer*]. The Little Man of the Forest. At your service.

SECOND SOLDIER [*to himself*]. He evidently means no harm to us. [*To the* LITTLE MAN.] Come to the fire and warm yourself. I wish we had something to offer you to eat, but alas, we have nothing, for we are only poor discharged soldiers.

LITTLE MAN [*going to the fire*]. I am sorry to hear that. You shall not go on your way empty-handed to-morrow. Pray take this purse. [*He gives the* SECOND SOLDIER *a purse*.] Guard it well, for it is a magic purse and will always contain gold. I may not tarry now, so farewell. [*He moves away*.]

SECOND SOLDIER [*who has been too astonished to thank the* LITTLE MAN]. Am I dreaming? Surely this purse is real.

THIRD SOLDIER [*yawns — awakens, and sits up*]. My nap has refreshed me, so I will take my turn now.

SECOND SOLDIER. Very well, if you so wish.

THIRD SOLDIER. Have you had a safe watch?

SECOND SOLDIER. Quite safe, thank you. [*To himself*.] I will save the good news until morning. [*To the* THIRD SOLDIER.] Call me if you need me. [*The* SECOND SOLDIER *prepares to go to sleep. After an interval, a faint horn is heard in the distance*.]

THIRD SOLDIER. What is that sound? Listen! [*The sound comes nearer*.] Who is there?

LITTLE MAN [*coming from out the shadows of the forest*]. Do not be alarmed. I am only the Little Man of the Forest.

THIRD SOLDIER.   What can I do for you, Little Man of the Forest?   I have no food to share with you, but enjoy our poor fire with me, if you will.

LITTLE MAN.   I cannot tarry here, but before I go I wish to give you this horn.   Play upon it, and it will always draw a crowd and make everyone forget his business and do whatever you may desire.

THIRD SOLDIER.   And you give this wonderful horn to me? Little Man, I wish I could repay you, but alas, I have nothing to give but my gratitude.

LITTLE MAN.   Use the horn wisely, and I am well repaid. And now farewell.   [*The* LITTLE MAN *goes.*]

THIRD SOLDIER.   I must awake my comrades and share with them my good fortune.   [*He arouses them.*]   Awake, comrades, awake, and hear what has chanced.   [*They awake.*]   Here I have a magic horn which gives forth lovely music.   But that is not all.   Its notes have power to draw after them the crowds of the street and make them do whatever we wish.

FIRST SOLDIER.   Where did you get it?

THIRD SOLDIER.   Just now, from a jolly little man in red.

SECOND SOLDIER.   The Little Man of the Forest!   He visited me while I watched and gave me a purse which will never lack gold.

FIRST SOLDIER.   The same little man visited me and gave me a cloak.   One needs only to put it over his shoulder and wish for anything his heart may desire, and directly the wish will come true — at least so the Little Man of the Forest says.

THIRD SOLDIER.   If his words are true, and I believe they are, this is a fortunate night for us, surely.   To-morrow we will try our gifts and share our good fortunes.

SECOND SOLDIER. Let us travel together and see the world and make use of only the magic purse for a while.

FIRST SOLDIER. Then when we find a spot that suits us and we are tired of roving, we will try the magic cloak and wish for a home of our own. Now, comrades, go back to your slumbers, and I will act as guard for an hour and then call one of you to take my place.

SECOND SOLDIER. Well, so be it. Once more, good night.

THIRD SOLDIER. In truth, it has been a *good* night for three old soldiers. [*The* SECOND *and* THIRD SOLDIERS *go to sleep. The* FIRST SOLDIER *sits silently on guard as the curtain slowly closes.*]

CURTAIN

ACT II

[*The terrace in front of the* KING'S *palace. At the right is a door leading into the palace. A wall runs along the back of the terrace, and in the center is a gate. To the left is an entrance to the garden. Two* GUARDS *enter from the garden and come down the stage as the curtain rises.*]

FIRST GUARD. The King's garden never looked more beautiful than it does this summer.

SECOND GUARD. The June flowers are now at their best. The rare rosebush that was sent to the Princess by the King of France is in bloom.

FIRST GUARD. That will please the King. [*The* KING *enters. The* GUARDS *salute.*]

SECOND GUARD. The King!

KING. I have just seen from my tower a strange coach, drawn by three dappled gray horses coming along the road. Only kings' sons travel in such grand style. The coach seems to be coming this way. Find the Princess, and tell her to be ready to receive unexpected visitors.

In this production of *Androcles and the Lion*, the introduction of two Roman banners and two benches set the stage for Act I.

FIRST GUARD. Yes, Your Majesty, I will find her at once. [*The* FIRST GUARD *goes out.*]

KING [*to the* SECOND GUARD]. Go to the gates, and if the coach brings guests, admit them most cordially. Then summon the Princess and me. It is such a warm day, that we will receive them here in the garden where there is a delightful breeze from the lake. I must make myself ready to meet these distinguished visitors.

SECOND GUARD. Your will, O King, shall be fully obeyed. [*The* KING *goes out.*] I hear the sound of horses' hoofs on the road. [*He looks off the stage.*] The coach is drawing to a stop. [*There is a rapping at the gate. The* GUARD *hastens off to answer it. Presently the three* SOLDIERS *enter. They are now dressed in beautiful clothes and look young and handsome. A* SERVANT *bearing gifts follows them.*]

FIRST SOLDIER. We have come to pay our respects to the King and the Princess.

SECOND SOLDIER. We hope it will be the King's pleasure to receive us this morning.

SECOND GUARD. The King and the Princess are both in the castle and will be glad to receive you. Will you be seated on this bench in the shadow of these trees? [*The* SOLDIERS *sit and the* SECOND GUARD *goes out.*]

THIRD SOLDIER. Well, things have changed since we were discharged from the war.

SECOND SOLDIER. It was a fortunate night for us when the little dwarf in the red jacket visited us and gave us the three magic gifts.

FIRST SOLDIER. What a wonderful year of travel we have had! It has made us all younger to see the splendid things the world contains.

THIRD SOLDIER. I greatly enjoyed it all, but I am glad we have settled down in our castle.

FIRST SOLDIER. How easily we got our castle! I put on this magic cloak, wished, and there it stood!

SECOND SOLDIER. A splendid castle furnished with everything heart can desire!

THIRD SOLDIER. Yes, I love the green lawns that spread around it, and the flocks of sheep that graze about!

FIRST SOLDIER. And now we shall see what our neighbors in this castle are like. [*Enter* KING *and* PRINCESS. *The* SOLDIERS *bow to them.*]

KING. I bid you welcome to my palace.

PRINCESS. Yes, you are indeed welcome.

FIRST SOLDIER. We have recently come to live at our new castle, not many leagues from here, and our first pleasure has been to come to-day to pay our respects to you, King, and to your beautiful daughter, the Princess.

SECOND SOLDIER. Pray, accept these gifts as tokens of our friendship. [*The* GUARD *gives one package to the* KING *and another to the* PRINCESS.]

THIRD SOLDIER. These gifts are unworthy the possession of a King and a Princess, but we hope you will enjoy them because we have brought them from a far-away land.

PRINCESS. So you have traveled?

SECOND SOLDIER. Oh, yes, we have spent a year visiting many distant countries.

FIRST SOLDIER. But nowhere have we found a lovelier place than this beautiful country of yours, so we decided to build ourselves a castle and spend the rest of our days here.

KING. I am delighted to hear that you like our country so well. Come into the palace and have some refreshments.

FIRST SOLDIER. We shall not have time now, for we can stop only for a few minutes.

KING. But you must have just one glass of a cooling

drink. I will have it served here. [*To the* FIRST GUARD.] Order refreshments. [*The* SECOND SOLDIER *is talking with the* PRINCESS, *who is looking at her gift. The* KING *speaks to the* FIRST *and* THIRD SOLDIERS.] While we wait, you must come into the garden and look at our rare rosebush that is in bloom for the first time. It will take but a few minutes. [*The* KING *and the* FIRST *and* THIRD SOLDIERS *go out.*]

PRINCESS [*looking at the gift*]. This necklace is most beautiful. Never have I seen stones of a richer color.

SECOND SOLDIER. I am glad it pleases you. We found it in Italy.

PRINCESS. The lovely purse that you carry in your hand — did you get that, too, in Italy?

SECOND SOLDIER. Oh, no. I had the purse before I went abroad.

PRINCESS. It is certainly a very odd purse. May I look at it?

SECOND SOLDIER. Indeed you may, Princess. [*He lets her take the purse.*]

PRINCESS [*carefully examining it*]. It is most quaint. I am sure it must have an interesting history.

SECOND SOLDIER. Indeed, it has a strange history. Moreover it possesses marvelous qualities. It is one of three priceless gifts that a generous friend gave us. I would not lose it or part with it for the rarest jewel in your father's beautiful crown. [*A* SERVANT *enters with refreshments, which he places on a small table and then goes out.*] It is time my brothers were returning. If you will excuse me, I will try and find them.

PRINCESS. Certainly. [*She returns the purse.*] You will find them in the garden, just beyond the quince hedge. [*The* SECOND SOLDIER *bows and goes off, leaving the* PRINCESS *alone.*] A purse with magic power! How I wish it were mine! If I could only find some scheme for getting it away from him. [*She thinks. Her face suddenly lights with joy.*] I have a scheme, and, if I can only get him alone for a few minutes, I am sure it will work. I have a sleeping potion that I will put into his glass. After he drinks, the potion will cause him to doze for a few moments. While he sleeps, I will take his purse and put in its place one that I have. The purses are much alike in appearance. I shall get it now. [*Exit* PRINCESS. *The* SECOND SOLDIER *enters directly.*]

SECOND SOLDIER. I could not find them in the rose garden; and I did not go farther for fear of getting lost among the hedges and arbors. [*Looking about.*] Where is the Princess?

PRINCESS [*entering*]. Did you find your brothers?

SECOND SOLDIER. No, I couldn't find them anywhere.

PRINCESS. Then we will not wait for them before having just one glass of this cold punch. [*As she talks, she fills two glasses. When he is not looking, she puts a drug into his glass.*] It is a fruit punch made after a famous old recipe. The King is very fond of it. I hope you will like it. [*She passes him the glass.*]

SECOND SOLDIER. I drink to your health, Princess. [*She watches him eagerly as he drinks.*] It has a curious flavor, but it is very pleasant to the taste. I really like it very much. [*The drug begins to take effect.*] I wish I knew how it was — [*He falls asleep before he can finish his sentence.*]

PRINCESS. He is fast asleep. Now for the purse. [*She quickly puts her purse in place of his. She looks with delight at the magic purse for a minute, and then hides it in her pocket. He soon awakens. She continues to talk as if nothing had happened.*] I shall be glad to send you a list of the fruits that the punch contains and also their amounts.

SECOND SOLDIER [*much amazed*]. Why, I believe I must have dozed for a moment. Pray forgive me, Princess.

PRINCESS. Oh, do not mention it. The heat of the day and the long journey in your coach have been enough to make anyone sleepy. [*Enter* KING, *with the* FIRST *and* THIRD SOLDIERS.]

THIRD SOLDIER. A most wonderful garden!

FIRST SOLDIER. Filled with the rarest of plants! [*The* PRINCESS *has poured drink for them.*]

PRINCESS. Your little walk through the garden must have served to increase your thirst. [*She passes them the glasses and they drink.*]

FIRST SOLDIER. Most refreshing!

SECOND SOLDIER. The Princess has promised to let us have the rule for making the punch.

FIRST SOLDIER. That is indeed good of her. Now we must say good-by. We hope we may soon have the great honor of a visit at our castle from your royal self and the Princess.

KING. We thank you for your cordial invitation.

[SOLDIERS *say good-by to the* KING *and* PRINCESS.]

CURTAIN

ACT III

[*A highroad.*]

THIRD SOLDIER. The King's garden is certainly very beautiful.

FIRST SOLDIER. I think ours will be just as lovely when our plants have had a few years to grow.

SECOND SOLDIER. I am glad that you suggested that we leave the carriage and walk a way.

THIRD SOLDIER.   Yes, I am happy to get a little exercise.
[*A woman's voice is heard off the stage.*]

WOMAN.   Fresh strawberries for sale! Fresh strawberries! Strawberries picked fresh this morning! Large sweet strawberries!

FIRST SOLDIER.   Shall we purchase some if they are good?

THIRD SOLDIER.   Yes, I should enjoy some strawberries for luncheon.   [*Enter* WOMAN *with basket of strawberries.*]

WOMAN.   Strawberries, fresh strawberries! None better to be had even in the King's garden.

FIRST SOLDIER.   Let us look at the berries.

WOMAN.   A shilling a box, absolutely fresh, and extra sweet and large.

FIRST SOLDIER.   Well, we will take three baskets. [*To the* SECOND SOLDIER.] You have the purse. You can pay the bill. [*The* SECOND SOLDIER *gives her the money.*] You can give them to our servant, who is just behind us there on the road. He will put them in our coach.

WOMAN.   Yes, my lord. Thank you for buying some of my berries. [*She goes off, still calling.*] Strawberries, fresh strawberries!

[*The* SECOND SOLDIER *is looking perplexedly into his empty purse.*]

THIRD SOLDIER.   What is the matter?

SECOND SOLDIER.   Brothers, look! There is no more money in the purse!

FIRST SOLDIER.   That is very strange.

THIRD SOLDIER.   Never before has the magic purse been empty, no matter how much we took out of it!

FIRST SOLDIER.   Let me look at it. [*He examines it.*] Why, this is not our purse.

SECOND SOLDIER [*examining it*].   You are right.   This is

certainly not the purse the Little Man of the Forest gave me. Mine has gold around the edge, and this has leather.

FIRST SOLDIER. But where is our purse?

SECOND SOLDIER. I am sure I don't know.

THIRD SOLDIER. You must have lost it! But how could you have lost it? [*The* SECOND SOLDIER *shakes his head.*]

FIRST SOLDIER. And where did this one come from? [*The* SECOND SOLDIER *again shakes his head.*]

THIRD SOLDIER. You had the magic purse this morning when we paid the servants.

SECOND SOLDIER. Yes, and I thought I had had my purse with me ever since.

FIRST SOLDIER. Are you sure you have not let anyone have it?

SECOND SOLDIER [*thinking*]. No one has had it but myself. But stay! While you were in the garden the Princess asked to look at it. But she had it in her hand only a moment, and I watched her all the time.

FIRST SOLDIER. You did not leave it when you came to search for us?

SECOND SOLDIER. No, I had it with me.

FIRST SOLDIER. Well, this is strange.

SECOND SOLDIER [*suddenly remembering*]. Brothers, I do remember a time when some one could have stolen our magic purse and put this in its place.

FIRST SOLDIER. When?

THIRD SOLDIER. When?

SECOND SOLDIER. While you were in the garden, the Princess gave me a glass of the punch. Either the drink or the heat of the day made me sleepy, and I dozed for a few seconds.

FIRST SOLDIER [*amazed*]. You say that after the Princess gave you a cooling drink you really fell asleep?

SECOND SOLDIER. Yes, but only for a few moments.

THIRD SOLDIER. She must have put a sleeping potion into the glass.

FIRST SOLDIER. Perhaps that is true. Yet we must not be hasty in suspecting anyone.

SECOND SOLDIER. What shall we do?

FIRST SOLDIER. We will go back to the King's palace and find out, if possible, who has taken the purse.

SECOND SOLDIER. Let us turn back at once.

FIRST SOLDIER. It will be easier for one person to search for the thief. I will use the magic cloak to get me secretly over the wall and I will do my best to find out what has become of the purse.

THIRD SOLDIER. That is a good plan. We will wait outside the wall to come to your aid if you need us.

SECOND SOLDIER. Take good care of yourself, or harm may come to you.

THIRD SOLDIER. And guard well the magic cloak! Let us make haste! [*They hurry back toward the palace.*]

CURTAIN

ACT IV

[SCENE: *Same as Act II.*]

[*The* PRINCESS *is seated on the bench, emptying money from the magic purse. She has obtained a considerable pile of coin.*]

PRINCESS. There is no end to the money that one can get from this magic purse. [*She begins to pile up the money.*] I believe that I am the richest princess in the world. Just think of all the beautiful things that I can buy! [*She continues to pile up her money.*] The castle gate is locked, so no stranger can get in, but I think I had better hide my money,

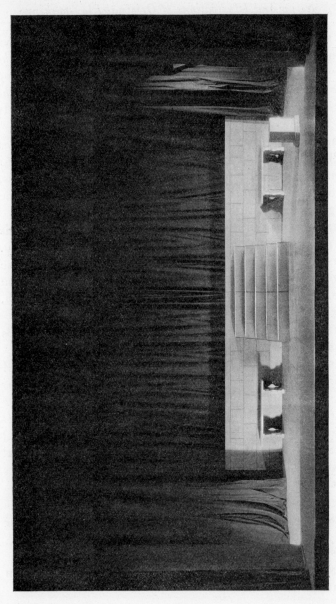

In this production of *Androcles and the Lion*, the black curtains in front of the platform were drawn aside for the first scene of Act II.

for I should not like even the servants to know that I have so much gold. [*She puts the money into a little bag that she carries at her waist. The* First Soldier *appears at the top of the wall. She does not see him, for she is looking in the purse again.*] There is still more gold in the purse. It truly has no end.

First Soldier [*to himself*]. The magic purse! So it *was* the Princess who stole it. [*He puts his magic cloak over his arm and comes down from the wall.*] Pardon me, Princess, but you have my brother's purse. He lost it here some time during our recent call.

Princess [*startled*]. You are very much mistaken. This is the purse that the King of France gave me for my birthday.

First Soldier. There can be no mistake, for I recognize the gold trimmings. I will take my brother's purse, if you please. [*He reaches for the purse, but she runs from him, crying loudly.*]

Princess. Help! Help! Thieves! Oh, help! [Guards *are heard coming.*]

First Soldier. Too late! I must hasten to escape! [*In his excitement, he forgets to use the magic cloak which is olded on his arm. He climbs the wall hurriedly. His cloak catches on a projecting stone. The* Guards *rush in. He does not have time to regain his cloak, but has to jump to save his life.*]

Princess [*to the* Guards]. Oh, thank you! thank you! It was some prowling stranger, perhaps come to steal flowers from the garden.

Second Guard. He has left his cloak.

Princess. Give it to me. [*The* Guard *gives her the cloak.*] I will look after it.

First Guard. I will hasten after the thief.

Princess. Oh, no. Do not do that. He has stolen nothing.

FIRST GUARD [*reluctantly*].   Be it as Your Highness commands.   [*The* GUARDS *go into the palace.*]

PRINCESS.   This is a strange cloak.   I wonder if it has not some magic qualities as well as the purse.   It seemed to help him over the wall.   Well, for safety, I think I had better lock up both the purse and the cloak in my room. [*She goes into the castle.   After a short time, the* FIRST SOLDIER *is seen looking over the wall.*]

FIRST SOLDIER [*to his brothers, who are unseen as yet*]. Brothers, there is no one about.   I will climb down and open the gate for you.   [*He climbs over the wall and unlocks the gate.   His brothers enter.   They look about for the purse.*]

SECOND SOLDIER.   There is no purse here.

FIRST SOLDIER.   And my cloak has gone too.

THIRD SOLDIER.   Misfortune after misfortune!   Tell us again how you lost the magic cloak.

FIRST SOLDIER.   Well, you see, the Princess refused to give up the purse, and just as I was about to take it from her by force, she shouted "Help!   Help!   Thieves!"   Before I could get the purse, two guards rushed out of the castle.

THIRD SOLDIER.   Why didn't you use your magic cloak and make your escape?

FIRST SOLDIER.   In my excitement, I forgot its magic power, and began to climb the wall.   My cloak caught, and I did not have time to save it.

SECOND SOLDIER.   What are we to do next?   Two of our precious treasures are gone.   How shall we get them back? [*They ponder over the problem.*]

FIRST SOLDIER.   It will do no good to ask the Princess to give them up.   She will only refuse.

THIRD SOLDIER.   We must force her to give them up.

SECOND SOLDIER.   But how?

FIRST SOLDIER. We might be able to force the King and Princess to give up our treasures if we had an army.

THIRD SOLDIER. Let us raise an army.

SECOND SOLDIER. How could we raise an army?

THIRD SOLDIER [*suddenly thinking of their as yet unused gift*]. The magic horn! We have forgotten the magic horn!

FIRST SOLDIER. The magic horn! I *had* forgotten it!

THIRD SOLDIER. The Little Man of the Forest told me that whenever we blew upon it people would flock to us.

SECOND SOLDIER. Let us put it to the test. [*The* THIRD SOLDIER *blows upon his horn. The sound of approaching feet is heard. The* FIRST *and* SECOND SOLDIERS *look out through the gateway.*]

FIRST SOLDIER. The horn works!

SECOND SOLDIER. Keep on blowing, brother! A huge army is gathering. [*The* THIRD SOLDIER *continues to blow. The sound of the approaching army grows in volume and men begin to pour into the courtyard.*] Here comes the leader now.

LEADER OF ARMY [*to the three* SOLDIERS]. What are your wishes?

FIRST SOLDIER. We want to force the King of this palace to surrender the valuables that his daughter has stolen from us.

LEADER OF ARMY. He shall do so. [*He goes to the door and knocks loudly. It is soon opened by one of the* GUARDS.] We command the King to surrender immediately the treasure that his daughter has stolen from these three soldiers.

GUARD. I will give His Majesty your message. [*He goes into the palace.*]

LEADER OF ARMY [*to the three* SOLDIERS]. If the King refuses to do as you wish, my army will soon bring him to terms.

SECOND SOLDIER. Is your army strong enough to force him to do so?

THIRD SOLDIER. If you need more soldiers, we can get them by blowing on this horn.

LEADER OF ARMY. I am sure I have enough men now. [*The* GUARD *re-enters.*]

GUARD. The King refuses to consider your commands.

LEADER OF ARMY. Then we shall have to force him to do so. He may expect an immediate attack on the castle. [*The* GUARD *bows.*]

GUARD. I will tell the King what you say. [*The* GUARD *goes into the castle.*]

LEADER OF ARMY. The castle can be taken most easily from the rear. We will make the attack there. [*Turning to his men.*] Right about face! March! [*They go out, followed by the three* SOLDIERS. *When all have gone, the* KING *and the* PRINCESS *look anxiously out of the castle door, and then come cautiously out.*]

KING [*to the* PRINCESS]. You have certainly got us into terrible trouble. You must give up the purse and the cloak immediately.

PRINCESS. Oh, no, father, I cannot give them up. I cannot part with them. They are the most precious treasures in the world.

KING. But I am afraid their great army will defeat our soldiers and force us to surrender not only those treasures but even the palace itself.

PRINCESS. Our army can drive them back.

KING. I am not so sure of that. I wonder where they got so many followers?

PRINCESS. I think I know. I was watching through a tower window, and I saw one of them take a curious horn and blow upon it. As he blew, an army suddenly sprang up and came to his help. I believe it is a magic horn, and if we can get it away from them, their power will be gone.

KING. But doubtless they have other magic gifts that they can use against us.

PRINCESS. No, I am sure the horn is the last. When they visited us this morning, the one who had the purse said that they had three priceless treasures. I am sure he meant the purse, the cloak, and the horn.

KING. Well, I do not like this meddling with magic. Daughter, I beseech you to give up the purse and the cloak, or we shall get into more trouble.

PRINCESS. Oh, father, wait just one hour. I have a plan for getting the horn. My maid and I will dress up as poor girls. We will go among the soldiers singing and selling trinkets. We will watch for a moment when they are not looking and then take the horn.

KING. I do not like these tricks.

PRINCESS. Oh, but think how rich and powerful we shall be with these three priceless things.

KING [*reluctantly*]. Well, I will give you one hour.

PRINCESS. Thank you, father, thank you!

KING. But come, daughter, we are not safe here, and I must direct the defense of the palace. [*They go in, and directly the three* SOLDIERS *enter.*]

FIRST SOLDIER. Everything goes well.

THIRD SOLDIER. The palace is strongly built, but as soon as we can get the army in place, we shall gain the mastery and bring the King and the Princess to terms.

SECOND SOLDIER. Here comes a small detachment of soldiers to guard this entrance to the castle. [*Enter a group of armed men under a commander.*]

FIRST SOLDIER. The Princess will soon regret the hour she stole our purse.

SECOND SOLDIER. Well, brothers, I for one am weary. [*He spreads out his cloak and sits upon it.*]

THIRD SOLDIER. So am I. While we wait for the army to get in place, I am going to get a little rest too. [*He doubles up his cloak for a pillow and lies down. The horn at his side is in his way as he lies upon the ground. He sits up and unfastens it.*] This horn has surely saved the day for us. Nevertheless, it is not a very soft thing on which to lie. [*He puts it under his pillow.*]

FIRST SOLDIER. Guard it well! [*The* PRINCESS, *singing, is heard outside the gate. Her* MAID *and she, disguised as poor girls, enter. The* PRINCESS *carries a basket filled with trinkets. Soldiers follow her.*]

PRINCESS [*singing*].

> Come, buy my pretty trinkets.
> They come from far-off lands.
> Come buy the pretty trinkets
> I hold here in my hands.

[*She shows the soldiers who follow her the trinkets.*]

> Come buy my pretty trinkets,
> I have them here to sell.
> Come buy the pretty trinkets,
> For they will please you well.

[*To the three soldiers.*] Won't you look at my trinkets?

FIRST SOLDIER. Let us see what the girl has.

SECOND SOLDIER. We are too poor to buy much, but looking costs nothing. [*The* FIRST *and* SECOND SOLDIERS *look at the trinkets.*]

PRINCESS. Choice trinkets from all parts of the world, and the prices are very reasonable. [*To the* THIRD SOLDIER.] Won't you look at these pretty things?

SECOND SOLDIER [*to the* THIRD SOLDIER, *who is still resting on the ground*]. Come and see them. They are really very beautiful. [*The* THIRD SOLDIER *rises and goes over to look at the things in the basket.*]

A SOLDIER. Sing us your ballad again. [*The* PRINCESS *makes a sign to her* MAID. *Then she sings her song again. While she is singing, the* MAID *watches her chance, and when no one is looking she steals the horn from the* THIRD SOLDIER'S *cloak.*]

PRINCESS. Won't you help a poor girl by buying some trinkets?

FIRST SOLDIER. I am sorry to say I am too poor to buy anything to-day.

SECOND SOLDIER [*looking through gateway*]. Brothers, something is wrong! The army is marching away from the castle. [*All except the* PRINCESS *and her* MAID *hurry to look.*]

MAID [*aside to* PRINCESS]. I have the horn.

PRINCESS [*taking the horn*]. Good. Now their power is gone, and we can laugh at them, for they are helpless.

KING [*opening the palace door*]. Hurry in this way. Hurry! [*They hurry in, and the* KING *quickly closes the palace door. The three* SOLDIERS *at the gate have not seen what the* PRINCESS *and her* MAID *have done.*]

FIRST SOLDIER. The army is certainly retreating. What can it mean!

THIRD SOLDIER. I don't know. I will blow on the horn, and we shall soon have them back. [*He goes to get the horn and discovers his loss.*] My horn! Where, oh where is it?

FIRST SOLDIER. Why, you had it a few minutes ago.

SECOND SOLDIER. You put it in your cloak. [*He searches.*]

THIRD SOLDIER. It is gone! Stolen!

FIRST and SECOND SOLDIERS [*in horror*]. Gone!

FIRST SOLDIER. Who could have been the thief?

SECOND SOLDIER. The two girls!

FIRST SOLDIER. Yes, the girls. Where are they?

THIRD SOLDIER. They have disappeared.

SECOND SOLDIER. They did not go through the gate.

FIRST SOLDIER [*looking toward the palace and suddenly realizing what has happened*]. I understand it all! They were not poor girls, but the Princess and her maid, and they are now safe in the palace. All our treasures are gone forever. [*They are forlorn and disheartened.*]

SECOND SOLDIER. You are right. We are penniless again, and there is no way in which we can get back our magic gifts.

FIRST SOLDIER. We shall have to start life over again.

SECOND SOLDIER. True, but what can we find to do?

FIRST SOLDIER [*shaking his head*]. I am sure I don't know.

THIRD SOLDIER. Each will have to seek his bread and shelter as well as he can.

FIRST SOLDIER. Let us keep together and share our ill fortune as we have shared our good fortune.

SECOND SOLDIER. Yes, let us not separate.

THIRD SOLDIER. But we must separate. It will be much easier for us to find work and food if each goes his own way. I shall take the highway that leads east. If I meet with success, I will try to get word to you.

FIRST SOLDIER. Well, if you insist. Do as you think best. Nevertheless [*turning to the* SECOND SOLDIER], we will travel together.

SECOND SOLDIER. Indeed we will. If we are successful in finding work, we will try to let you know.

THIRD SOLDIER. Good-by!

SECOND SOLDIER. Good-by! Heaven send that we shall soon meet again! [*After their good-bys the* THIRD SOLDIER *goes off to the right. The others look after him sadly, and then go off to the left.*]

CURTAIN

ACT V

[A wood.]

[The THIRD SOLDIER *is asleep on the ground under a tree.]*

THIRD SOLDIER *[waking].* Where am I? *[He looks about him.]* Oh, in the wood. *[He sits up.]* Now I remember all that happened yesterday. The loss of our precious treasures, our separation, and my weary walk trying to find work and shelter. *[He rubs his back.]* How weary and stiff I feel. The damp earth does not make a very comfortable bed. And, oh, how hungry I am! *[He looks about and finds an apple.]* Good luck! Here is an apple! It has fallen from this tree, which is laden with fruit! *[He begins to eat it.]* I wonder where my brothers are this morning? I hope they have met with better success than I have. *[He continues eating. Suddenly he feels a terrible pain in his nose.]* Oh, my nose! What sharp pains! This must come from sleeping on the damp earth! *[He feels another twinge of pain.]* My nose pains terribly! *[The pains increase.]* Oh! Oh! what shall I do? *[He walks up and down. He stops suddenly.]* There is a brook close by. Perhaps if I bathe my nose it will feel better. *[He hurries off right. Soon the* FIRST *and* SECOND SOLDIERS *enter from the left.]*

FIRST SOLDIER. I wonder if we shall be able to find work to-day?

SECOND SOLDIER. I certainly hope we shall, for we must have money and food.

FIRST SOLDIER. And a place to sleep. *[With a sigh.]* How I miss our comfortable home.

SECOND SOLDIER. I wonder where our brother is this morning. Let us hope that he is safe and has found work.

[*The* THIRD SOLDIER *enters. His nose has grown several inches long.*]

THIRD SOLDIER [*recognizing his friends*]. Oh, comrades, are you here? [*The* SOLDIERS *look at him in amazement.*]

SECOND SOLDIER. It can't be that you are our old comrade.

THIRD SOLDIER. To be sure I am. [*They still stare at him, uncertain.*]

THIRD SOLDIER. Why certainly you know your own comrade!

FIRST SOLDIER. But what has happened to you?

SECOND SOLDIER. Your nose, what ails it?

THIRD SOLDIER. I'm sure I don't know. But it pains me greatly. It must have come from sleeping on the damp ground. When I awoke just now, I felt stiff and sore all over, but I didn't notice any trouble with my nose until just as I was eating an apple that I found here on the ground. Then the pain came suddenly.

FIRST AND SECOND SOLDIERS. Yes! How strange!

THIRD SOLDIER. I hurried down to the brook to bathe my nose in the cool water, for it was beginning to swell. Has it swollen much?

FIRST SOLDIER. Much! It has not only swollen, but it has grown longer!

SECOND SOLDIER. It has grown so long that we did not know you at first. [*The* THIRD SOLDIER *feels his nose.*]

THIRD SOLDIER. Oh, brothers, it has grown! What shall, what shall I do? [*They shake their heads.*]

SECOND SOLDIER. Will our misfortunes never cease?

FIRST SOLDIER. They have certainly come very rapidly during the last few hours. [*The* LITTLE MAN OF THE FOREST *appears in the distance.*] There is someone moving in those bushes.

SECOND SOLDIER. He has a red coat. [*Looking carefully.*] Brothers, I believe it is our good friend, the Little Man of the Forest.

FIRST SOLDIER [*after a moment's looking*]. It *is* he! [THE LITTLE MAN *comes toward them.*]

LITTLE MAN. Good morning, friends, good morning! How are you all to-day?

FIRST SOLDIER. We are most unhappy.

SECOND SOLDIER. Most miserable!

LITTLE MAN. Unhappy and miserable? Tell me why.

SECOND SOLDIER. We have lost the three precious gifts that you gave us.

FIRST SOLDIER. They were stolen by a princess.

LITTLE MAN. I am sorry to hear of this great misfortune. [*Turning to the* THIRD SOLDIER.] It appears to me that something is the matter with your nose. Are you in pain?

THIRD SOLDIER. Oh, I am suffering greatly. I ate an apple that I found under this tree, and soon my nose began to ache and pain me. Then it began to swell, and now it has grown terribly.

LITTLE MAN. That, too, is a great and painful misfortune. Well, I see I must find a cure for you.

THIRD SOLDIER. Oh, can you do so? And will you?

LITTLE MAN. Yes, I can, and what is better for you, I will. [*Looking off left.*] Just beyond that sumach bush do you see a pear tree?

FIRST SOLDIER. A pear tree? Yes!

SECOND SOLDIER. Indeed we do.

THIRD SOLDIER. Just there, beyond the sumach.

LITTLE MAN. Gather a pear from that tree, eat it, and your nose will come right again.

THIRD SOLDIER. I will try your cure instantly.

SECOND SOLDIER. Yes, do so. I will help you find a pear. [*The* THIRD *and* SECOND SOLDIERS *hurry off.*]

FIRST SOLDIER. How can we ever repay you for your many kindnesses?

LITTLE MAN. Oh, I wish no payment. It is always a pleasure to help people who are in trouble.

FIRST SOLDIER [*looking off to where his brothers have gone*]. He has found one and is eating it. Let us see how it works. [*He hurries off.*] Brother, how do you feel?

THIRD SOLDIER [*off stage*]. The pain is going. Yes, it is going.

SECOND SOLDIER [*off stage*]. And your nose is going, too. [*During this conversation, the* LITTLE MAN *stands quietly watching, his merry eyes twinkling with delight.*]

FIRST SOLDIER [*off stage*]. It is fast getting smaller. How do you feel now?

THIRD SOLDIER [*off stage*]. The pain is all gone.

SECOND SOLDIER [*off stage*]. Good! And your nose is its natural size again. [*They hurry back. His nose has shrunk to its natural size.*]

THIRD SOLDIER. Little Man of the Forest, I thank you! I thank you! You are our truest and best friend.

FIRST SOLDIER. Our faithful friend!

SECOND SOLDIER. We shall never forget your kindness.

LITTLE MAN. I will do something more for you yet. Take some of these pears and apples with you; you will find them useful. Whoever eats one of these apples will have his nose grow as yours did, but if you give him a pear, all will come right again.

THIRD SOLDIER. But I could not bear to have anyone suffer as I have suffered.

LITTLE MAN. Right! Very right you are. But the Princess needs a little lesson in manners. Try the apple on her. Then look sharp, and you will get what you want from her. Now I must be off. Good fortune be with you. Good-by!

First Soldier. Good-by, kind friend!

Second Soldier. We shall never cease to be grateful to you.

Third Soldier. Heaven reward you for the relief and happiness that you have brought me this day. Good-by! [*The* Little Man *disappears.*]

First Soldier. The Little Man's idea is a splendid one.

Second Soldier. And the Princess does deserve a lesson.

First Soldier. What say you to my disguising myself as a gardener's boy and going to the palace with these apples for sale?

Second Soldier. An excellent idea!

First Soldier. Everyone will wish to buy them, for they are as handsome apples as ever anyone has seen. But I will refuse to sell to anyone except the Princess.

Third Soldier. When she has eaten and her nose has grown long, I will present myself as a famous physician with a marvelous cure for long noses.

Second Soldier. And give her one of the magic pears.

Third Soldier. Yes, I will chop one of the pears and put it in a bottle, so that it will look like medicine.

Second Soldier. That's a good idea.

Third Soldier. Brothers, once I am admitted to the presence of the Princess, I will never leave the palace until the three magic gifts are in my possession.

First Soldier. Let us hasten to gather some apples and pears.

Second Soldier. The future begins to look bright again. [*They set about the task of gathering the fruit.*]

CURTAIN

ACT VI

[SCENE. *Same as Act II.*]

[*The* KING *and the* PRINCESS *enter from the garden.*]

PRINCESS. You see I was correct in saying that when we got the horn their power would be gone.

KING. Let us hope that you are right and that we shall never hear from them again.

PRINCESS. Of course we shall never hear from them again! We can enjoy the three magic treasures without any fear.

KING. Nevertheless, I wish we had never seen the magic treasures.

PRINCESS. Oh, father, think of all that we can do with them!

KING. My child, I do not believe anyone can get happiness out of things which do not rightfully belong to him. But now that our walk is ended, I will go in and rest.

PRINCESS. And I will go into the garden and get some roses. [*The* KING *goes in the palace, and the* PRINCESS *goes into the garden. Two* GUARDS *enter from the palace.*]

FIRST GUARD. It was a wonderful sight yesterday to see the enemy scatter.

SECOND GUARD. They fled so rapidly that they had to leave their weapons behind.

FIRST GUARD [*looking out through the gateway*]. You can see some of them now, just beyond the dike.

SECOND GUARD. There comes a gardener with his basket. I wonder what he has for sale. [*Enter the* FIRST SOLDIER, *dressed as a gardener's boy. He carries a basket of apples.*]

FIRST GUARD. Show me what you have in your basket.

SECOND GUARD [*looking in the basket*]. Apples!

To set the stage for the second scene of Act II in this production of *Androcles and the Lion* it was necessary merely to move the two sections of the stairs from the center of the platform, where in the first scene of Act II they had hidden the lion's den, to a place at either end of the platform.

FIRST GUARD. And wonderfully fine ones too!

SECOND GUARD. What are you charging for them to-day?

FIRST SOLDIER. I cannot sell you any of them. They are for the Princess. [*Enter the* PRINCESS.]

PRINCESS. Did I hear someone speak of me?

FIRST GUARD. Yes, the gardener says his fine apples are for you.

PRINCESS. Apples! Let me see them. [*The* FIRST SOLDIER *shows her the apples.*] What handsome apples! I certainly will take all you have. [*She takes money from her purse and gives it to the* SOLDIER.] Here, take this for your pains. You need not bother about the change.

FIRST SOLDIER. Thanks, Princess, thanks! You will find these delicious eating apples, neither too sweet nor too sour. I will call for the basket some other day. [*He goes off.*]

PRINCESS [*taking an apple*]. It does look unusually good. [*She bites it.*] He was right. It is delicious. [*To the* SECOND GUARD.] You may take them to the palace. [*He does as he is bid.*] I do enjoy a good apple. And these are — [*A twinge of pain seizes her nose.*] Oh, oh, what a horrid pain in my nose! [*Again the pain seizes her.*] Oh, there it is again.

FIRST GUARD. Can I do anything for you?

PRINCESS. No, I think not. [*The pain increases.*] It is getting worse! What can be the matter! Ouch! Ouch!

FIRST GUARD [*going to the door to summon* MAID]. Marie! Marie!

MAID [*entering, sees that something is wrong*]. Why, what is the matter, Princess?

PRINCESS. Oh, I don't know! [*The pain still increases.*] Ouch! Ouch! my poor nose, my poor nose!

MAID. Let me see. [*She examines the nose.*] It is very much swollen. Let us hurry into the palace and see if we cannot do something to relieve you.

PRINCESS. Yes, yes, let us do so. Oh, how it pains! Ouch! Ouch! [*They hurry into the palace.*]

FIRST GUARD. I wonder what the trouble can be. I hope it is nothing serious. [*Enter* SECOND GUARD.] Did you know that the Princess had just been seized with a terrible pain in her nose?

SECOND GUARD. No, I did not know anything was wrong. It must have been very sudden, for she seemed well and happy five minutes ago. [*Enter the* KING *in a great hurry.*]

KING. Hasten to the village and bring a doctor as quickly as you can. The Princess is very ill. Her nose is very much swollen and enlarged. Hurry! Hurry!

FIRST GUARD. Yes, Your Majesty.

SECOND GUARD. We will bring help as quickly as we can. [*They rush out.*]

KING. What can be the matter with the Princess? Her nose is growing longer and longer. [*Walking about uneasily.*] I hope the guards will hurry. I hope they will hurry. [*Enter* GUARDS *with* THIRD SOLDIER *disguised as doctor.*]

FIRST GUARD. Here is a physician.

THIRD SOLDIER. Yes, your men just met me as I happened to be passing by the palace wall. They tell me that your daughter is ill. What seems to be the trouble?

KING. Oh, doctor, it is her nose. It is growing larger and larger, and it pains her terribly.

THIRD SOLDIER. Bring her here where the light is good, and I will see what can be done for her.

KING [*to the* FIRST GUARD]. Tell the Princess that the doctor is here, and have her come out immediately. [*To the*

Second Guard.] Guard the gate and allow no one to enter. [*To the doctor.*] Oh, do you think you can cure her?

Third Soldier. I am sure I can help her. Treatment of the nose is my specialty.

King. Cure her, and you shall name your own reward. I will hasten to bring her to you. [*He enters the palace.*]

Third Soldier [*taking out a blue bottle*]. Here in this blue bottle is the precious chopped pear. But before I give the princess any, I shall have to punish her a little more. [*He takes out a white bottle.*] I will give her a dose of the apple which I have chopped and put in this white bottle, and give her a little more nose and pain. [*Enter* First Guard, the King, *followed by the* Princess *and her* Maid. *The nose of the* Princess *is now about three inches long.*]

Princess [*weeping*]. Oh, father, what shall I do? What shall I do?

King. Do not cry, my child. The doctor will cure you.

Third Soldier. Yes, I will soon help you. First, we must see what the trouble is. [*He examines her nose with a magnifying glass. Then, very wisely.*] Yes, yes! [*He continues his examination.*] It pains you considerably?

Princess. Oh, yes, doctor — sharp, piercing pains.

Third Soldier [*producing a white bottle containing the chopped apple*]. A spoon, please.

King [*to the* Guard]. Get a spoon. [*The* Guard *hurries out.*]

Third Soldier. This is a rare and wonderful remedy. It is called applelargissimus. [*The* Guard *returns with a spoon, which he gives to the supposed doctor. The doctor measures out a spoonful of the chopped apple.*] Now, Princess, take this applelargissimus, and I am sure you will soon feel a change. [*He gives her a spoonful. To the* King.] I will return later in the day and see how the Princess is.

KING. Oh, doctor, if you can cure my daughter, anything you may ask for you shall have.

THIRD SOLDIER. Thank you. I have no doubt the Princess will soon be well again. Good morning. [*The* THIRD SOLDIER *goes out.*]

KING. Do you feel any better, my child?

PRINCESS. Not yet, father.

KING [*to the* FIRST GUARD]. Bring the measuring stick so that we may see if the nose has grown any shorter. [*The* FIRST GUARD *goes out.* KING *to the* MAID.] How long was the nose when we last measured?

MAID. Three and one-eighth inches, Your Majesty.

KING. Yes, I remember. Three and one-eighth inches. [*Enter* FIRST GUARD *with a foot rule, which he gives to the* KING. *The* KING *measures the* PRINCESS'S *nose.*]

PRINCESS [*eagerly*]. Is it any shorter?

KING. I am afraid not.

PRINCESS. What does it measure now?

KING [*to the* MAID]. You measure it. My hand trembles.

MAID [*after measuring*]. It measures three and one-quarter inches.

PRINCESS [*weeping*]. It is growing longer. What shall I do, what shall I do?

KING [*to the* FIRST GUARD]. Hurry after the doctor and bring him back with all speed. [*The* GUARD *rushes off. The* KING *measures the nose again.*] It is — it is growing larger. [*The* PRINCESS *weeps loudly. Her* MAID *tries to console her. The* KING *paces up and down.*]

KING. Oh, why doesn't the doctor come. Why doesn't he come! [*The* THIRD SOLDIER *enters.*]

THIRD SOLDIER. What seems to be the trouble now?

KING. My daughter's nose is still growing longer. Cannot you help her?

THIRD SOLDIER. Most certainly I can. Do not be disturbed. I will change the medicine. [*He produces the blue bottle.*] This is a rare and even more powerful medicine than the first. It is called pearshortissimus. [*He measures out a spoonful of the chopped pear and gives it to the* PRINCESS.] Now, a spoonful of the wonderful pearshortissimus and all will be well. [*The* PRINCESS *takes the medicine. All watch with great anxiety. After a few minutes she gives a cry of joy.*]

PRINCESS. Oh, the pain is gone!

KING [*to the* MAID]. Measure again. [*She does as instructed.*]

MAID [*joyfully*]. Two and three-quarter inches!

PRINCESS. Oh, it is getting better.

KING. Let me measure. [*He measures.*]

THIRD SOLDIER [*aside, while* KING *is measuring*]. Now they see that I can help them. But I must not let her get well too quickly. I must frighten this cunning Princess a little more before I can get what I want from her. The chopped apple again! [*To the* PRINCESS.] I knew my medicine would help you. I will give you one more spoonful of the applelargissimus, and you will be quite well. [*He gives her a spoonful of the chopped apple.*] Now I shall have to leave you for a little time.

KING. But you will come back soon, won't you?

THIRD SOLDIER. It will be quite unnecessary, but since you desire it, I will come back.

KING. We are already deep in your debt. But do return soon.

THIRD SOLDIER. I will do as you wish. Once more, good morning. [*The* SECOND GUARD *goes out. The* THIRD SOLDIER *is just leaving when* PRINCESS *cries out with pain.*]

PRINCESS. Oh, oh, the pain again! [*The* KING *exclaims and hastens to her side. The* MAID *applies the ruler.*]

THIRD SOLDIER [*returning*]. The pain returning? Impossible!

MAID. And the nose is getting longer again!

THIRD SOLDIER [*with a pretence of great concern*]. This is indeed a strange case. Something works against my medicine and is too strong for it. Will you excuse me if I speak very plainly?

KING. Speak. Oh, tell us what the trouble is. [*He dismisses the* GUARD.]

THIRD SOLDIER. By the force of my art I know what it is. [*Speaking to the* PRINCESS *with great seriousness.*] You have stolen goods about you, I am sure. If you do not give them back, I can do nothing for you. [*The* KING *looks troubled. The* PRINCESS *is frightened.*]

PRINCESS. It is not true. I have no stolen goods.

THIRD SOLDIER. Very well, you may say what you will and do as you please, but I am right, I am sure. Remember, you will die if you do not tell the truth and restore the stolen property. Good-by. [*He starts to go, but the* KING *detains him.*]

KING. Oh, do not forsake us.

THIRD SOLDIER. I cannot help you until the stolen goods are returned. [*The* THIRD SOLDIER *goes. The* GUARD *goes with him.*]

KING. Oh, daughter! daughter! Give back the cloak and the purse and the horn that you stole.

PRINCESS. I can't. I won't.

MAID. I beg you to give them back.

PRINCESS [*seized with terrible pain*]. Oh, oh! my poor, poor nose!

KING. You'll never be well until you do as the doctor tells you.

MAID [*measuring*]. Oh, it is still growing longer!

KING [*imploringly*]. Please let Marie get the things.

PRINCESS [*caught by another sharp pain*]. Ouch! Ouch! The pain is unbearable. I cannot stand this suffering any longer. Do as you like. Give them back again. I will do anything to get rid of this pain.

MAID. I will fetch them. [*She runs off eagerly.*]

KING [*calling*]. Guard! Guard! [*The* SECOND GUARD *enters.*] Hasten after the doctor and bring him back. [*The* GUARD *exits. To the* PRINCESS.] You have done right, my child. Have patience, and the doctor will be here. He *can* and *will* cure you — as soon as we are rid of those miserable things. [*Enter* MAID *with cloak, purse, and horn.*]

PRINCESS. Give them to the King. I never want to see them again. I am going inside, for I am ashamed to meet the doctor. [*The* PRINCESS *and the* MAID *enter the palace.*]

KING [*looking at the cloak, purse, and horn*]. Who would believe that these harmless appearing things could have so much power for good or evil. [*The* THIRD SOLDIER *enters.*] Oh, doctor, you were right. My daughter has some things which are not rightfully hers. Here they are — a purse, a cloak, and a horn. They belong to three soldiers. Will you find them and return their property?

THIRD SOLDIER. I think I can find the three soldiers very easily. Your daughter has been very wise to give these things up before it is too late for me to help her. [*He gets out the blue bottle.*] Give her one spoonful of this pearshortissimus, and she will recover with marvelous quickness.

KING [*taking the bottle*]. I will give it to her myself. [*He hurries into the palace.*]

THIRD SOLDIER. Now to summon my brothers. [*He goes to the gate and waves the cloak.*] The Little Man of the Forest has again saved us! Now that we have the three magic gifts back again, we will guard them more carefully.

[*Enter the* First *and* Second Soldiers.]

First Soldier. You have succeeded?

Second Soldier. You have the precious gifts again?

Third Soldier. Yes, we have them safe once more, and we will keep them safe this time.

[*Enter the* King.]

King. Oh, doctor, the Princess is cured. See, she is entirely well again.

[*The* Princess, *attended by the* Maid, *enters very humbly. She starts to draw back when she sees the three* Soldiers.] You have found two of the soldiers already.

Third Soldier. Yes, and I am the Third Soldier. [*He throws off the doctor's cloak.*]

King. You are the Third Soldier!

Third Soldier. Yes.

King [*overwhelmed with sense of shame*]. How can we hope to be forgiven for our wicked actions?

Princess. I was to blame, father — I, and I alone. [*To the* Soldiers.] Do not think unkindly of my father, and try to forgive a silly Princess.

Third Soldier. You have our forgiveness.

Second Soldier. And now, brothers, home again.

First Soldier. Home with our treasures and magic gifts once more. [*The three* Soldiers, *each with his magic gift, start off homeward.*]

CURTAIN

CHAPTER XXX

THE BOX OF PANDORA

MAKING AND STAGING THE PLAY

THE children of the fifth grade who dramatized Nathaniel Hawthorne's *The Paradise of Children*, gave it the title *The Box of Pandora*. In making the dramatization, the class thought it wise to use Hawthorne's own language as far as possible. So after the preliminary steps of forming a general plan of the play, the story was reread, and all the passages that the children thought could be used verbatim as dialogue were underscored. Different members then suggested the stage directions and whatever additional conversation was needed to make the play complete. They wrote out on slips of paper the speeches that they themselves originated. Next they cut out from their fifteen-cent copies of *The Wonder Book* the text that they had decided to use. The written and the printed material was pasted on sheets of paper which would fit their literature notebooks, and the play was ready for use.

The literary language of Hawthorne is, of course, not the speech customarily used by children of the fifth grade; but through the close study of the text, necessary in the making of a play, the language and style were in a measure assimilated by the children and made a part of their permanent possession. Considerable increase in vocabulary was thus a noticeable and valuable result of the work.

The simplest and perhaps the most effective background

for productions of this type is secured by the use of curtains, although well-proportioned screens covered with burlap in natural color or material in the natural linen hue can be used. When the play was first presented, gray-green curtains, hung with a little fullness, were used as the background.

Throughout the seven settings for *Lucky Pehr*, screens covered with gray flannel made a permanent fore stage. A black flannel curtain, hung at the back of the stage, gave the feeling of depth; it also made an excellent background for the spirits and ghosts. The arched places at the right and left of the stage served as niches for the statues of the two saints.

Pandora's box had to be made large enough for the children impersonating the Troubles to come out of it. But since no arrangement of suitable size could hold all the Troubles, it was necessary to devise some plan whereby the actors could enter the box unseen by the audience. The play was presented on a very small stage devoid of any modern improvements. Lacking a trapdoor, the children could not enter through the bottom of the box. Finally it was decided to use a box 36 inches long, 20 inches wide, and about 28 inches high. One end was left open to permit the entrance of the Troubles and Hope. The box was then placed on the stage in the position shown in Diagram 15. The cover was hinged on the side nearest the audience, so that when the box was opened the audience was unable to see into it. When Pandora opened the lid, two Troubles secreted in the box jumped out. Others, unseen in the auditorium, crawled into the box from their hiding place

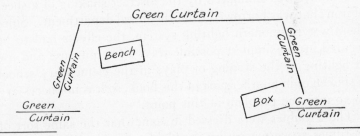

Diagram 15. — Stage arrangement for *The Box of Pandora*.

behind the wings at the left of the stage and jumped out into the room of Epimetheus. It was found that to have all the little creatures come from the box was not only unnecessary but inadvisable, because this took too long. Under cover of the darkness that came as soon as Pandora lifted the lid, the greater number of the Troubles were able to come directly from the wings.

The members of one of the upper grades had charge of the construction of the box. They used a packing case as their foundation. This foundation was covered with heavy building paper. Then a molding made of wooden strips three inches wide was put around the edge of the top and also on the side and end seen by the audience. The wood was stained and the paper was decorated with pastels, to suggest the decorations that Hawthorne describes in his story.

Other than the Pandora box, the stage demanded no furniture, but for the sake of balance a Greek bench was placed right center up stage, close to the back curtain.

The text of the play speaks of opening a door to let the mischievous visitors out, but the children soon realized that this did not need to be a material door seen by the spectators. It could be imagined just behind the wing at the right of the stage.

Thunder was simulated by the discreet shaking of a sheet of iron that was borrowed from the metal department. Since there was no modern lighting system, the effects had to be secured in the simplest possible way. The purpose and use of lighting in the staging of plays in the elementary school is spoken of in another part of this book, so it is not necessary to go into the problem at this point.

The Troubles were dressed in somewhat the same sort of costumes as were worn by the Goblins in *The Woodman and the Goblins*. The only change was the addition of tails with barbs at the end.

The Box of Pandora was played a few years later on a larger stage equipped with a more complete lighting system. The more adequate space and lights made it possible to stage the performance much more effectively. Before describing in a brief manner the second staging of the play, it may not be amiss to tell what motivated it and what led up to it.

A fourth-grade class, while studying Greek life and literature, asked to read this play about Pandora made some three or four years earlier. Their reading of the play was followed by the desire to act it. This was done in class in a most informal way. Since their interest was still keen, they asked to give the production for the whole school. They were sure that all would enjoy it, especially as it could be done on a larger stage, where there would be ample space for free action. In their Dalcroze classes, the children had been having a number of Greek games that they played with much joy. It was remarked that these games were perhaps the very games that the companions of Epimetheus played and in which (as we learn in the play) he wished Pandora to join. The suggestion followed that it would be an excellent idea to do some of these games as a sort of introduction to the play. This plan was followed with most pleasing results.

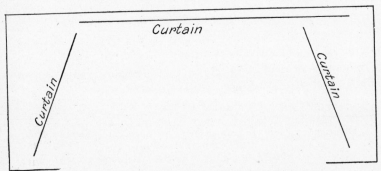

Diagram 16. — Stage arrangement for the Greek games.

For the Greek games, the stage was hung with green denim curtains, as shown in Diagram 16. The change to the setting for the play was quickly effected because of the simplicity and practicability of the units that composed it. The large curtain of green denim that formed a background for the Greek games served the same purpose for the play. Two screens covered with denim of the same color as the curtains were used at the right and left of the stage. They were in three folds and were easily moved. Two tall columns were very effectively placed, as indicated in Diagram 17. A trap in the stage down right center, made it possible to place Pandora's box in the prominent place that its importance in the story demanded. The bench stood at the left center down stage. Far up stage in the background was a pedestal, on which was placed a graceful Greek urn that a former senior class had made in the clay room and had presented to the school. The urn was filled with large ferns. From their study of Greek homes, the class had learned that

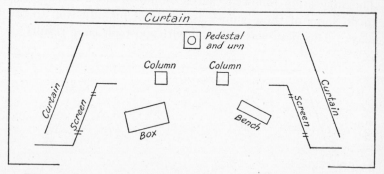

Diagram 17. — Stage arrangement for a recent presentation of *The Box of Pandora.*

beautiful cloths of rich hue were used by the Greeks in decoration. A large piece of wine-colored material was, therefore, thrown over the pedestal, and a large skin of white fur was thrown over the bench. The box was, of course, bottomless. The Troubles were ready under the stage and climbed into the box, when the time came, by means of a ladder. The columns were made of wood, covered with heavy building paper and tinted with crayons. The color scheme for the costumes was worked out during the art period, with the aid of the art teacher. Great care was taken to have the whole color scheme one of beauty and harmony, not only as a matter of good taste but also as an expression of the central thought of the play. There were, as usual, two casts, in order to give as large a number as possible a chance to participate. The play was done several times, so that each actor could have two performances. A second performance has always, we may repeat, a great educative value.

THE PLAY

CHARACTERS

HERMES[1]   PANDORA
EPIMETHEUS   TROUBLES
          HOPE

SCENE: *A room in the home of* EPIMETHEUS.

[*As the curtain rises* EPIMETHEUS *and his companions are heard singing outside.*]

HERMES [*standing beside a huge chest*]. The world is in its infancy now, but oh, what a good time in which to live! Now every one is a child, and there are no dangers or troubles, and everyone is happy throughout the livelong day. There is no quarreling, no sickness, and no one is ever thirsty or sad. The joyous children of this earth little realize that their happiness depends largely on the fact that they are still ignorant of the contents of this box. Should curiosity lead any one to lift the cover, the world would become a very different sort of place from what it now is — but soft! here comes Epimetheus. [EPIMETHEUS *enters; he notices Hermes and hesitates.*] Come in, and let me tell you why I am here. I have come from a far country, and, although you do not know me, yet I know you, and I have come to ask a great favor of you.

EPIMETHEUS. And what is that favor?

---

[1] The study of the Greeks which the class had made the previous year led the students to wish to call the messenger of the gods by his Greek name; so they discarded the title *Quicksilver* used by Hawthorne, and substituted *Hermes*.

HERMES. This precious box that I have brought with
me I wish you to keep safely for me.

EPIMETHEUS. That I will, and gladly too.

HERMES. In return for your kindness, I will send you,
very shortly, a little playmate and helper. Her name is
Pandora. Now I must go. Remember, I shall depend upon
you to care for the box until my return.

EPIMETHEUS. You can trust me fully to guard it. Many
thanks for the playmate you have promised.

HERMES. Good-by. [*He goes.*]

EPIMETHEUS. Good-by. [*Looks after* HERMES.] I wonder who the stranger can be. I have never seen him before.
And why has he brought the box to me? Well, I will take
excellent care of it until he returns. [*He looks the box over
carefully.*] It is truly a beautiful box! How dark and rich
the color of the wood is! It is so highly polished that I can
see my face in it. This side is finely carved. Here are figures of children, playing amid flowers and foliage. [*The door
opens and* PANDORA *enters.*]

PANDORA. Are you Epimetheus?

EPIMETHEUS. Yes, I am Epimetheus, and I am sure you
are Pandora, the playmate and helper who was promised me
by the stranger.

PANDORA. Yes, I am Pandora. [*She perceives the box.*]
Oh! What a lovely box! Pray, what have you in it?

EPIMETHEUS. My dear little Pandora, that is a secret,
and you must be kind enough not to ask any questions about
it. The box was left here to be kept safely. I do not myself
know what it contains.

PANDORA. But who gave it to you? And where did it
come from?

EPIMETHEUS. That is a secret, too.

PANDORA. How provoking!

EPIMETHEUS. Oh come, don't think of it any more. Let us run out of doors and have a merry time with the other children, or, if you prefer, let us go and gather some ripe figs and eat them under the trees, for our supper. And I know a vine that has the sweetest and juiciest grapes you ever tasted.

PANDORA [*unable to get the box out of her thoughts*]. I am not hungry, and I do not care to play. I think I would rather remain here. [*To herself.*] I wonder what can be inside that great chest! [*To* EPIMETHEUS.] You might open the box and then we could see for ourselves.

EPIMETHEUS. Pandora, what are you thinking of! [*His face expresses great horror.*]

PANDORA. At least you can tell me how it came here.

EPIMETHEUS. It was left, just before you came, by a person who looked very smiling and very intelligent. He was dressed in an odd kind of cloak and had on a cap that seemed to be made partly of feathers, so that it looked almost as if it had wings.

PANDORA [*guessing that it was* HERMES, *eagerly*]. What sort of a staff had he?

EPIMETHEUS. Oh, the most curious staff you ever saw! It was like two serpents twisting around a stick and was carved so naturally that at first I thought the serpents were alive.

PANDORA. I know him. Nobody else has such a staff. It was Hermes; and he brought me hither as well as the box. No doubt he intended it for me; most probably, it contains pretty dresses for me to wear, or toys for you and me to play with, or something very nice for both of us to eat!

EPIMETHEUS. Perhaps so, but until Hermes comes back and gives us permission we have neither of us any right to lift the lid of the box. But let us not talk any more about it. Come out and play. My friends are waiting for me in the garden.

PANDORA [*her thoughts still cn the box*]. No, thank you. I will stay here for a little while. [*She sits.*] But you go and join your friends.

EPIMETHEUS. Well, if you will not come, I will go and gather some ripe grapes and bring them to you; then you will see how delicious our fruit is. [*Goes out.*]

PANDORA. I do wish he had a little more enterprise. [*She goes close to the box and examines it.*] It really is a very handsome box and quaintly ornamented on this side, and here, carved on the top, is a face with the oddest mischievous expression. The box most probably contains something very valuable and lovely. I wish Epimetheus would open it. [*The voice of one of the* TROUBLES *is heard from the box.*]

THE VOICE. Pandora! Pandora!

PANDORA [*looking about eagerly*]. Who can have called me? There is no one here.

THE VOICE [*persuasively from the box*]. Do not be afraid, Pandora! What harm can there be in opening the box? Never mind that poor simple Epimetheus! You are wiser than he and have ten times as much spirit. Open the box, and see if you do not find something very pretty!

PANDORA. Where does the voice come from? I am sure I heard some one speak. Can the voice come from the box? [*She puts her ear close to the box.*] I do not hear anything stirring inside. It must have been my imagination. Oh, how I long to know what is in the box! I am afraid Epimetheus would be much provoked if I should venture to look in. I wonder if the chest is locked. [*She examines it carefully.*] It is not fastened by a lock; merely by this heavy cord which is tied here in this great knot. Why, what a curious knot it is; it has no ends! It must have been a very ingenious person who tied it, but I think I could untie it. I am resolved at least to find the two ends of the cord. [*She examines the knot.*] I really believe that I begin to see how it was done. Nay, perhaps I could tie it up again after undoing it. There would be no harm in that, surely. Even Epimetheus would not blame me for that. I need not open the box and should not, of course, without the foolish boy's consent, even if the knot were untied. [*As she works,* EPIMETHEUS *and his companions are heard singing without. She stops to listen.*] What a beautiful day it is! Perhaps it would be better if I were to let this troublesome knot alone and go out to join Epimetheus and his playfellows. [*She glances at the face on the lid of the box.*] That face looks very mischievous. It really seems to be smiling. I wonder if it smiles because I am doing wrong. I have the greatest mind in the world to run away. [*By an accidental twist the cord untwines itself and the box is without a fastening.*] This is the strangest thing I ever knew! What will Epimetheus say? And how can I possibly tie it up again? [*She attempts to restore the knot, but in vain.*] I cannot recollect the shape and appearance of the knot. It seems to have gone entirely out of my mind. I shall have to let the box remain as it is until Epimetheus comes in. But when he finds the knot untied, he will know that I have done it. How shall I make him believe that I have not looked into the box? I shall never be able to do so. [*She hesitates distressed and wondering what she will do next.*] If he is going to suspect me of having looked into the box, I might just as well do it at once. [*A murmur of voices comes from within the box.*]

VOICES [*coaxingly from the box*]. Let us out, dear Pandora; pray let us out! We will be such good playfellows for you. Only let us out!

PANDORA [*perplexed but eager to satisfy her curiosity*]. What can it be? Is there something alive in the box? [*Her curiosity gets the better of her perplexity.*] Well — yes — I am resolved to take just one peep — only one peep — and the lid shall be shut down as safe as ever! There cannot possibly be any harm in just one little peep.

[EPIMETHEUS *enters softly with some grapes. He sees* PANDORA *with her hand on the lid on the point of opening the box. He is about to step forward and stop her but hesitates.*]

EPIMETHEUS. Since she is resolved to find out the secret, I, too, should like to know what the box contains. [*As* PANDORA *raises the lid, the room becomes dark. Thunder is heard. She lifts the lid upright, and there is a sudden rush of winged creatures from the box. The* TROUBLES *fill the room, buzzing, darting about, and stinging* EPIMETHEUS *and* PANDORA.]

EPIMETHEUS. Oh, I am stung! I am stung! Naughty Pandora! Why have you opened that wicked box? [PANDORA *lets the lid fall and starts up. A* TROUBLE *stings her and she begins to cry with fright and pain. The* TROUBLES *continue to fly about until it occurs to* EPIMETHEUS *to run and open the door to let the* TROUBLES *escape. When they have all departed,* PANDORA *flings herself on the floor, and, with her head resting against the box, cries, and sobs.* EPIMETHEUS, *very angry, sits sullenly in a corner with his back to* PANDORA. *Suddenly there is a gentle tap on the inside of the lid.*]

PANDORA. What can that be? [EPIMETHEUS *does not answer.*] You are very unkind not to speak to me. [*She sobs again. The knock is repeated.*]

PANDORA. Who are you? Who are you inside this naughty box?

HOPE [*from within, sweetly*]. Only lift the lid and you shall see.

PANDORA.   No, no, I have had enough of lifting the lid! You are inside of the box, naughty creature, and there you shall stay!   There are plenty of your ugly brothers and sisters already flying about the world.   You need never think that I shall be so foolish as to let you out.   [*She looks toward* EPIMETHEUS, *expecting him to commend her for her wisdom.*]

EPIMETHEUS [*muttering*].   You are wise too late.

HOPE [*persuasively*].   Ah, you had much better let me out.   I am not like those mischievous creatures that have stings in their tails.   They are no brothers and sisters of mine, as you would see at once, if you were only to get a glimpse of me.   Come, come, my pretty Pandora!   I am sure you will let me out!   [PANDORA *is cheered by the pleasant voice.* EPIMETHEUS *turns half around, and seems to be in better spirits.*]

PANDORA.   Epimetheus, have you heard this little voice?

EPIMETHEUS.   Yes, to be sure I have, and what of it?

PANDORA.   Shall I lift the lid again.

EPIMETHEUS.   Just as you please.   [*He is really eager to have the lid lifted again but is unwilling to admit this to* PANDORA.]   You have done so much mischief already, that perhaps you may as well do a little more.   One other Trouble, in such a swarm as you have set adrift about the world, can make no very great difference.

PANDORA.   You might speak a little more kindly.   [*She wipes her eyes.*]

HOPE [*from within the box*].   Ah, disobedient boy!   He knows he is longing to see me.   Come, my dear Pandora, lift the lid.   I am in a great hurry to comfort you.   Only let me have some fresh air, and you shall soon see matters are not quite so dismal as you think them.

PANDORA.   Epimetheus, come what may, I am resolved to open the box.

EPIMETHEUS. And, as the lid seems very heavy, I will help you! [*He runs across the room and lifts the lid. The room becomes light again.* HOPE, *a sunny and smiling little personage, comes forth. She flies to* EPIMETHEUS *and lays the least touch of her finger on the inflamed spot where the* TROUBLE *had stung, and immediately the anguish of it is gone. She kisses* PANDORA *on the forehead and her hurt is cured.*]

PANDORA. Pray, who are you, beautiful creature!

HOPE. I am to be called Hope. And because I am such a cheery little body, I was packed into the box to make amends to the human race for that swarm of ugly Troubles, which was destined to be let loose among them. Your one wrong act of opening the lid of the box entrusted to your care by Hermes has brought calamity to the whole world.

PANDORA. I am very, very sorry! Indeed I am!

HOPE. Sorrows, diseases, cares, and many kinds of evil have gone forth to afflict mankind and to bring many tears and heartaches where formerly existed only joy and happiness. The flowers, which have never been known to fade, will now begin to droop and shed their petals in a day or two, and the children, who seemed immortal, will grow older and older day by day and become youths and maidens, men and women.

PANDORA [*sobbing*]. Oh, I am most unhappy! My wrong act has brought pain not only to myself but to all the world.

EPIMETHEUS. It is largely my fault, for I should have prevented you from lifting the lid. My curiosity made me false to my promise. [*He seems quite repentant.*]

HOPE. Never fear, we shall do pretty well in spite of them all.

PANDORA [*drying her tears*]. Your wings are colored like the rainbow. How very beautiful!

Hope. Yes, they are like the rainbow, because, glad as my nature is, I am partly made of tears as well as smiles.

Epimetheus. And will you stay with us forever and ever?

Hope. As long as you need me — and that will be as long as you live in the world — I promise never to desert you. There may come times and seasons now and then when you will think that I have utterly vanished. But again and again and again, when perhaps you least dream of it, you will see the glimmer of my wings on the ceiling of your cottage. Yes, my dear children, and I know something very good and beautiful that is to be given you hereafter!

Pandora. Oh tell us — tell us what it is!

Epimetheus. Yes, tell us what it is!

Hope [*putting her finger on her rosy mouth*]. Do not ask me. But do not despair, even if it should never happen while you live on this earth. Trust in my promise for it is true.

Epimetheus. We do trust you.

Pandora. For you bring us hope and joy again.

Hope. I must go now, for the world needs me. Good-by. Trust me, and all will be well.

Epimetheus and Pandora. Good-by.

[*As* Hope *goes she turns and smiles assuringly.*]

CURTAIN

CHAPTER XXXI

THE BREMEN TOWN MUSICIANS

MAKING AND STAGING THE PLAY

THE making of this play was the result of one of the first experiments in the project method. Dr. Colin Scott of the

This photograph of a setting for *Lucky Pehr* gives an idea of the simple units that comprised the scene in the woods.

Cook County Normal School believed that children should have some voice in determining their own course of study. Later on, Dean Jackman introduced the project idea into the School of Education of the University of Chicago and allowed the elementary children to divide themselves into groups for the study of special subjects, which they themselves selected. They met once a week for two hours, and they were required, by the terms of their understanding with Dean Jackman, to continue together the study of the subject they had chosen until something tangible and worth while had been accomplished.

Into the dramatic department came a few pupils from all the grades, from the first to the eighth. A number of stories were read and considered from the viewpoint of play-making. The difficulty was to find something which would be interesting to the older children and at the same time simple enough for the little folks. The class finally selected the old folk tale, *The Bremen Town Musicians.*

An eighth-grade boy was chosen as general director. Each of the older boys and girls wrote a play based on the story, and each of these plays was thoroughly discussed. From these the play given below was made. An eighth-grade boy played the Donkey; a seventh-grade boy, the Dog; a girl from the fifth grade, the Cat; and a little girl, the Cock.

The children talked over carefully the stage setting for Act II, because it was necessary to show the robbers in the room as well as the animals outside looking through the window. They finally decided to have the left portion of the stage represent the interior of the room and the right portion the space outside the house. The wall containing the open window would extend at right angles to the front of the stage.

The children first planned to have the robbers use such terms as "Ain't dem birds?" and "How's dem fer jewels?" which they had observed on the funny page of the Sunday paper. After this point had been thought over carefully, it was agreed that even the thieves in old folk tales were not guilty of such English, and the dialogue was rewritten in the present form.

The Rooster costume was made of brownish cotton material. The tail, wings, red comb and yellow beak were wired in order to keep them in shape. Yellow cloth was used to bind the legs. The costumes of the Donkey and the Dog were made of cotton flannel. The Cat's costume was very like the one described on pages 252 and 253.

The Bremen Town Musicians was first played in Scammon Gardens of the University of Chicago, on a natural stage. There were so many avenues of trees and shrubs opening from the stage that the peregrinations of the animals on their way to Bremen were easily managed. When acted indoors green denim draperies formed the background throughout. A large two-fold screen, with an opening in one fold to represent a window, was used to suggest the house in Act II.

The Play

Characters

A Donkey   Robber Chieftain

A Dog   Robber Bill

A Cat   Second Robber

A Rooster   Third Robber

Other Robbers

ACT I

Scene: *A road through the woods.*

[*Enter* Donkey, *slowly.*]

Donkey. Such is life! I have worked for my master twenty long years, and now that I am getting too old to carry heavy burdens, he turns me out on the road to starve. [Donkey *brays long and loudly and sadly. He is struck with pride at his voice.*] Listen to that voice of mine! [*Stands and tries his voice again.*] Oh, it's beautiful! [*Thoughtfully.*]

I ought to be able to do something with it! [*With determination.*] I'm not going to die! I will go to Bremen and become a musician! [*Brays, tosses his head, and walks on briskly. He meets* DOG *on the road.* DOG *barks woefully, gasps for breath, lies down.*] Good morning, Friend Rover! You're sorry-looking indeed. What are you gasping for, you big fellow?

DOG. Well, because I'm too old to hunt, master says there's no more use for me, and so my end is near!

DONKEY. Never mind, Brother. We're in the same boat, you and I. Cheer up, and come with me! I noticed your fine tenor. I'm going to Bremen, to become a musician. We two will make a charming duet. Let's try a song. [DONKEY *brays and* DOG *barks, as they walk on together, singing their song. They go off stage. Enter* CAT, *meowing.* DONKEY *and* DOG *reappear;* DOG *barks at* CAT. DONKEY *stops* DOG.] Here! Stop that! [*To* CAT.] Pussy, why so broken-hearted? You have a face like three rainy days. Now then, old shaver, what's gone askew with you?

CAT. Cruel fate! One hardly feels gay, looking forward to a watery grave. My claws and teeth are dull, and as I can catch no more mice, my mistress will have me drowned — droww-oww-owned! [CAT *meows and howls in painful anticipation.*] So I ran away. Now where am I to go and where can I get anything to eat?

DONKEY. Well, we have escaped the same fate, Rover and I. Now suppose you join us?

CAT. And pray, sir, what do you intend to do?

DOG. We found, though we were too old to work, that we could sing, so we are going to Bremen to become musicians. You know *you* have a charming voice, for who has not heard your midnight serenade? [CAT *at this becomes very dignified and affects fine manners.*]

CAT. I will join you with pleasure, for it has always been my ambition to devote myself to my Art! [*Shows off voice with fancy howling and meowing. Crow of* ROOSTER *is heard from off stage. Enter* ROOSTER *from back, head and wings hanging disconsolately.*]

DONKEY. Now what's the matter with you, Cockydoodle-doo?

ROOSTER. Oh dear! Oh dear! I've heard them say, under their breath, that they would make soup of me to-morrow for the guests. So now I'm crowing at full pitch, while I can.

CAT. Well, they must be hard up, if you are the best they can get.

DONKEY. But he can sing! And we are in need of a fine high voice to complete our musical company. Ah, Red Comb, you'd better come away with us. Are you willing to be one of us? We are on our way to Bremen, to become musicians You can find something better than death everywhere.

ROOSTER. Nothing will please me more! Let's be off!

DONKEY. You have a good voice, and if we make music together, it must have some quality. [*The four of them start on their way to Bremen.*]

DOG. Now, comrades, I for one am tired. Let us rest for the night under this tree and go on in the morning.

DONKEY. Well, I think we can do no better, though my stomach is pretty empty. [DONKEY *and* DOG *lay themselves down under the tree.* CAT *and* ROOSTER *both settle themselves in the branches,* ROOSTER *as high as he can go, to be safe.*]

ROOSTER [*looking in all four directions*]. Up, friends, up! I see a light!

ALL. Where? Where?

ROOSTER. Yonder, yonder on the hillside. [*They all start off.*]

CAT. Let's start our concerts there, and we may yet go satisfied to bed. [*They go off stage, intently on their way.*]

CURTAIN

ACT II

SCENE: *The robbers' room occupies the left portion of the stage; the open space outside the house occupies the right portion; the wall with the open window extends at right angles to the front of the stage Inside house, robbers seated around a table, eating.*

[DONKEY *looks into the window, putting his forefeet on window ledge.*]

ROOSTER [*in stage whisper*]. What do you see, my Gray Horse?

DONKEY. See? What do I see? A table covered with good things to eat and drink! And robbers, enjoying themselves! How I wish we were there. [*Animals go off stage to consult and to make their plans.*]

ROBBER CHIEFTAIN. Comrades, the time has come for dividing the booty! You, Bill! Bring it in! [BILL *enters from back, comes forward to table, carrying a bag, the contents of which he pours on the table.*]

ROBBER BILL. Aren't these great? How are these for jewels? [*They all crowd around, examining the jewels.*]

ROBBER CHIEFTAIN. Well, I'll be generous this time. [*Gathers the jewels together on the table and divides them into two piles.*]

ROBBER CHIEFTAIN. Here, you divide half among yourselves.

SECOND ROBBER [*angrily*]. That's not fair! We did the work while you were roistering around!

THIRD ROBBER [*threateningly*]. You won't cheat us! You know that, don't you?

ROBBER CHIEFTAIN [*rises in anger. Loudly*]. Am I chief, or am I not? He who raises a hand dies!

ROBBER BILL. Give me mine! Give me mine! I'll take it.

SECOND and THIRD ROBBERS. Give us our share! We'll take it. [*During this scene the animals have come on the stage. DONKEY stands with his front feet on the window ledge, DOG has climbed up on DONKEY's back, and CAT on the back of DOG. ROOSTER has perched himself on CAT's back. The animals perform their music all together, making a horrible din.*]

ROBBER [*frightened*]. Let's run! Let's run! Let's run to the woods! [*ROBBERS run out, back, to the woods. Animals burst through the window into the room and gather with speed around table.*]

ROOSTER. Well, we won't go hungry to-night!

DOG. Let's start in! My mouth is watering! [*They all eat hungrily.*]

DOG. Let's go to bed. [*DONKEY lies down front stage, legs straight out. DOG lies down under table. ROOSTER perches on beam of roof or on a limb of a tree. CAT puts out the candlelight, and then stretches out on the hearth in front of the warm ashes. Short wait.*]

ROBBER CHIEF [*from edge of woods at right of stage*]. We ought not to have let ourselves be frightened out of our wits. Bill, you go and examine the house. [*BILL sneaks slowly into house and up to table. He picks up the candle and goes to the fireplace. Taking the glistening, fiery eyes of CAT for live coals, he holds a lucifer match to them to light it. CAT flies in his face, spits at him, and scratches him. DOG jumps out from under table and bites his leg. DONKEY gives him a smart kick with his hind foot.* ROOSTER *crows loudly and excitedly from beam.*]

ROOSTER. Cock-a-Doodle-Doo! Cock-a-Doodle-Doo! [BILL *runs wildly back to comrades. The Robbers eagerly ask what he found in the house.*]

BILL [*speaking to other robbers*]. Comrades, a witch sat in the hearth and scratched me. A man jumped from under the table and stabbed me. A huge fellow had hidden behind the door, and he flew at me with a club, and I heard the awful voice of a judge, calling: "Bring the culprit back! Bring the culprit back — Do!" Don't let's ever go back there again!

ALL ROBBERS. We'll *never* go back there again! [*They rush away in great fear.*]

CURTAIN

This simple setting for *Lucky Pehr* was designed to suggest a street. The statues were in reality human beings, costumed and painted to look like old bronze. Silhouetted against the blue sky and framed by the gray walls, they made a wonderfully effective picture.

CHAPTER XXXII

RIP VAN WINKLE

THE play of *Rip Van Winkle* was made by a fifth-grade class after the children had studied the history of the early Colonies [1] and had read Irving's story of Rip Van Winkle. The little play flowered forth naturally. It utilized the children's historical and geographical knowledge, and their interest in the life of the Dutch people and in the dramatic story of Rip was the climax of this study. The making of the play added a new motive. They were obliged to review, analyze, and criticize the whole story, the incidents, the characters, the costumes, the setting, and the adaptation of the action to the possibilities of our stage.

So dramatic and objective were the situations in the story that they lent themselves readily to effective stage presentation, and there was no necessity for narration of action that had to take place off stage. As a beginning, the class made a list of the incidents of the story in the order in which Irving gives them, but they soon discovered that, while

[1] In the *"Course of Study,"* Volume I, page 864, published by the Chicago Institute, Miss Emily Rice gives an outline of a study of Colonial history for the fifth and sixth grades. Miss Rice, in speaking of giving this period to these grades, says: "For these older children the study of the life of our Colonial forefathers seems especially desirable. This period is a comparatively simple one as far as institutions are concerned. The struggles of the pioneers with the hard conditions of the new environment are such as children of this age can appreciate. The problems of the development of their industries are such as the children can work out for themselves. It is a period of adventure and heroic action. Both from the standpoint of industrial life and qualities of character, it furnishes suitable material for the middle grades."

the story was dramatic in quality, nevertheless, it was not such in form. There were long descriptions, quite appropriate to expression in story but not in drama Without conscious thought of play-making technique, they found themselves making up incidents, dialogue, pantomime, and stage settings which embodied as much of the descriptions as was necessary and effective in the telling of the story in the form of drama. The list of events was written on the blackboard. This made it possible for the class to see the entire material at once. After much discussion and many criticisms and changes, the following points were decided upon as necessary to the play.

The village in the Kaatskills
The villagers
The traveler
Reading of old newspaper
Entrance of Rip, children, and dog
Entrance of neighbor woman
Stories told to the children
Thunder and reference to Hendrick Hudson and his visit to the Kaatskills every twenty years
Entrance of Gretchen and introduction to Rip's children
Rip and dog driven off the porch by Gretchen
The start up the mountain

The children felt that the first part ended at this point and it was therefore called Act I.

Rip on the green knoll with his dog
Rip starts home
Voice calling to Rip
Appearance of short, stout old man with keg on shoulders
Pantomime of old man with Rip, asking Rip to carry keg
Climb up the mountain, carrying keg alternately
Thunder during the ascent

Arrival at the amphitheater
Other strange personages, and their mysterious silence and behavior
Peals of thunder
Opening of the keg and pouring of liquor into flagons
All drinking
Rip drinks and is gradually overcome
Rip falls into a deep sleep

The children thought that the natural end of the second part, or Act II, was at this point.

The awakening
Rip finds himself on the green knoll again
Thinks he has slept only one night
Rip's stiffness and difficulty of movement
Rip calls for his dog Wolf
Rip discovers old fowling piece instead of his own gun
Rip's slow descent to the village
Rip's fear of Gretchen
Rip's entrance into village on election day
Village orator
The voting
Recognition of Rip by his daughter Judith and old neighbors
Reception of Rip and reinstatement in village and family

This ended the outline and completed Act III. The story was then studied to find out what kind of man Rip was, because the children felt they must know him well to act him. His characteristics, as noted in the story, were written on the blackboard; every child contributed, and read aloud from the story to prove his point. They decided that Rip was

Good-natured
Loved by children and dogs
A kind neighbor
A favorite with all the good wives of the village

Good at frolics and cornhuskings
A henpecked husband
A good fisherman and a good hunter
Not a good worker — shirked and blamed "ill luck" for his troubles
Selfishly neglectful in his treatment of Gretchen and his children

Teacher and children next discussed the costumes and decided what could be done with the few materials at hand, for at that date this particular school had no accumulated stock of costumes upon which to draw; everything had to be designed and made by the children. During all the study of the history of New York, the class had been actively engaged in some of the industrial occupations of the Colonists— spinning, carding, weaving, sewing, and studying design and color — so that the children were ready for the work of planning and making the costume each was to wear.

The wide, expansive breeches featured all the men's costumes. These were not difficult to make; in fact, the complete outfitting of the characters was easily managed. The choice of colors and the differentiation of the designs in the suits of Hendrick Hudson's men, as outlined by Irving, presented the greatest problem. Gretchen and the other women wore simple Dutch apparel; full skirts, plain tight waists, caps, collars, and kerchiefs. Since Rip and young Rip were usually in rags, the children thought that their appearance would be a simple matter, but they soon realized that the rags ought to be the remains of Dutch costumes of the proper date. Because the class had a fund of information, the scene in the amphitheater was faithful to the spirit of the story.

In the original production of *Rip Van Winkle*, the school had no stage or stage equipment. A large low platform, made in sections, was placed at one end of the gymnasium. As a background, a very large, old blue curtain was hung.

The front curtain was a soft gray-green, attached to a rudely built frame that served as the proscenium opening. In the first act Rip's house was placed stage left and the inn stage right. Their fronts were constructed in the manual training shop. Before the inn were several benches and a table. Before Rip's house, on a tumble-down porch (a low platform), were a rude bench and a washtub. The main road was supposed to run across the back of the stage.

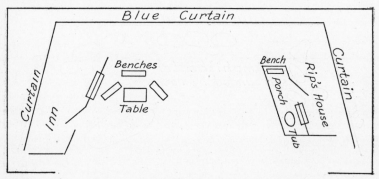

Diagram 18. — Stage arrangement for *Rip Van Winkle:* the scene in the village.

Because of the lack of available equipment, it was necessary to "make believe" concerning many things. It was not possible, for example, to show to the audience the mountain up which Rip, the old man with the keg, and the dog climbed, so the class pretended that the level stage was the steep mountain side, and made little attempt to secure a realistic representation.[1]

[1] After the various limitations were once accepted, they passed out of mind. It is a curious thing that in stage presentation, even with the most complete stage equipment and settings, the audience is constantly accepting limitations and supplying the missing elements from their imagination, without detriment to the play. For example, we all accept three sides of a room and agree with ourselves that we are looking into a room with four walls, the missing fourth wall being supplied by the imagination.

For Act II and for Scene I of Act III the stage was cleared, save for the blue curtain which formed the background throughout the play. The green knoll down stage left center was suggested by green cloth placed over a low mound and rocks surrounding the amphitheater back stage were made of piles of boxes covered with gray cloth.

In the Boucicault dramatization of *Rip Van Winkle*, which Joseph Jefferson made famous, Rip's drunkenness is the

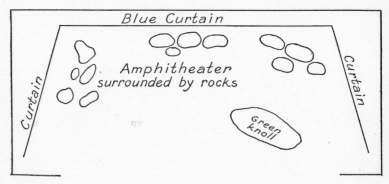

Diagram 19. — Stage arrangement for *Rip Van Winkle:* the scene in the mountains.

primary cause of all his troubles. In the story as told by Irving, Rip is shiftless, idle, and lazy, but not addicted to drink. In fact the first and only mention of liquor is made at the time when the old man with the keg appears, and Rip joins Hendrick Hudson's men in drinking. Immediately after this Rip falls into the deep sleep on the mountain. The children never talked about this aspect of the plot, but constructed their play on the facts set forth in the narrative, and accepted without comment the drinking in the amphitheater as natural under the exceptional circumstances. Rip himself was a real character to these children, a simple, good-natured soul.

Much of the expression was in pantomime; speech was used only when it was impossible fully to express the thought by gesture and movement alone. The dialogue was a community product and developed in much the same manner as in the play of *The Woodman and the Goblins* as described on pp. 250-252. The teacher served merely as a member of the class and shared in the construction, but he was not there to "make dialogue," or to show the children how to act. When an obstruction appeared in their way, he was ready to remove it by questions or suggestions; he was there to inspire the class to more truthful and clearer thinking on the material and also to make them see the right of the audience to have the play so constructed that all could be clearly comprehended.

The teacher should be as free with help in this work as in any other. To illustrate this point: the play, when finished, did not mention Rip's children until the very end, and as Judith really was one of the resolving forces, the instructor suggested that the audience might understand more fully and more sympathetically the part of Rip's children in the play if they were introduced with the other characters in the first part. "To be sure!" cried one of the young playwrights, "because young Rip and Judith lived right there in the village with their father and mother, and all the villagers knew them, so they should appear early in the play." Here was a good lesson in dramatic construction, as well as a delightful experience in original thinking and analysis.

The mysteries and complications, the working up to the climax, and the unravelment and resolution of the plot, were clearly set forth in the play and appealed in the strongest manner to youthful imaginations. The human elements of the narrative stirred their emotions and were a great intellectual and dramatic satisfaction: the solemn, silent old men,

Rip's long sleep on the mountain, the climax when Rip awakens and the plot begins to work out, the happy outcome of the situation when Rip's daughter recognizes him and takes him home to live with her.

Pupils of the intermediate grades (the fifth and sixth) have a great interest in construction and mechanics; therefore, this is a good time to teach form. These children in particular had developed some idea and appreciation of the technique of a drama and were critical of such things as character, plot, climax, and outcome. Naturally, then, they were able to utilize effectively some of the laws of dramatic technique in the construction of their dramatization and the thoroughly good play that resulted gave them distinct joy quite apart from the pleasure of making it.

THE PLAY

CHARACTERS

NICHOLAS VEDDER

DERRICK VAN BRUMMEL

BROM DEUTCHER

GRETCHEN (DAME VAN WINKLE)

TRAVELER

RIP VAN WINKLE

NEIGHBOR WOMAN

ORATOR

A MEMBER OF THE CROWD

SHERIFF

JUDITH VAN WINKLE

WAITER, CHILDREN, YOUNG RIP VAN WINKLE, WOLF, the dog, OLD MAN, HENDRICK HUDSON and HIS MEN, CROWD, JUDITH'S CHILD.

ACT I

SCENE: *A village in the Kaatskills.*

[*Inn on right side of stage. Benches, chairs, table in front of inn; sign bearing picture of His Majesty, George III, hangs over the door of the inn. Opposite the inn,* RIP'S *house, on the tumble-down porch of which are a bench and a tub, at which* DAME VAN WINKLE *is washing vigorously. In front of the inn,* NICHOLAS VEDDER, VAN BRUMMEL, BROM DEUTCHER, *and other men are sitting, smoking pipes. Man seen coming down the road, upper left.*]

BROM DEUTCHER. I wonder who that is coming down the road. It is probably some traveler. Now we shall hear the news. [*Enter* TRAVELER.]

TRAVELER. Good morning, friends! I have traveled a long distance, and this July weather is hot. [WAITER *brings in a jug of milk.* TRAVELER *drinks, and all sit quietly smoking.*]

NICHOLAS VEDDER. What is the news, traveler?

TRAVELER. Here's a paper; you may read for yourselves. I must hasten on my way. Thank you for your hospitality. [*Exit* TRAVELER.]

NICHOLAS VEDDER. A paper! Read, Van Brummel — you're the schoolmaster. [VAN BRUMMEL *takes the paper from* NICHOLAS VEDDER *and begins to look it over.*]

NICHOLAS VEDDER. Read it aloud! Let us hear the news, too!

VAN BRUMMEL. Let me see — April twentieth — Why, this paper is only three months old!

BROM DEUTCHER. Good! Read! Read the news!

VAN BRUMMEL. Well, what would you like to hear? Here is the shipping, the Indian uprising, the Stamp Act — [*Noise of children outside.*]

NICHOLAS VEDDER. There, that's Rip Van Winkle —
no reading news now! [RIP *enters with dog and troop of
noisy children, all talking and singing. One child is on his
shoulders, one is clinging to his coat.* YOUNG RIP *and* JUDITH
with other children. All are dancing and shouting. RIP *is
dancing and singing with the children. The children crowd
so closely about him that he can hardly move. The dog joins
in the noise.* NEIGHBOR WOMAN *enters from inn door with
water pail over her arm. She stands in the doorway of the inn.*]

NEIGHBOR WOMAN. Oh, there's Rip Van Winkle! You'll
get a pail of water for me, won't you, Rip?

RIP VAN WINKLE. Yes, we'll get the pail of water, eh?
Won't we, children? Come on! [*He takes the pail.*]

GRETCHEN. [*She sees* RIP *as she raises herself from the wash-
tub.*] What are you doing now, you good-for-nothing, you!
[*Children run away, behind inn, except* YOUNG RIP *and*
JUDITH.]

RIP VAN WINKLE. Oh, just going for water for a neighbor
woman.

GRETCHEN. You're always ready to help someone else.
I wish you'd help your wife once in a while and not always
attend to some one else's business!

RIP VAN WINKLE. Oh, Gretchen, my darling!

GRETCHEN. Your darlin', indeed! Then why don't you
stay at home, and not spend all your time at the inn here,
playing with children and neglecting your own boy Rip and
little Judith? [YOUNG RIP *and* JUDITH *run to their mother.*
GRETCHEN *goes into the house.* NEIGHBOR WOMAN *picks up
her pail.* RIP VAN WINKLE *shrugs his shoulders and casts
his eyes up. Then crosses to the inn. Children tiptoe back
fearfully and gather about* RIP *again.*]

CHILDREN. Is she gone? [*They peer about fearfully and
sneak back to* RIP.] Rip, tell us a story. Tell us a story

about witches and goblins and Indians. [RIP *gets a stool from the porch and the children crowd about him.*]

RIP VAN WINKLE. Yes, I'll tell you a story. Once there was a man — [*Thunder peal is heard. The children move closer, as the thunder frightens them.*]

CHILDREN. Oh, Rip! Hear that! Hear the thunder!

RIP VAN WINKLE. Why, don't you know what that is? That's Hendrick Hudson and his famous crew, playing nine-pins in the Kaatskills. [*More thunder.*]

CHILDREN. Oh, Rip! What a noise they make!

RIP VAN WINKLE. Yes, they are jolly fellows. They sail the broad sea over, through storm and danger. Then every twenty years they come back to the mountains. Hear their balls rolling! [*Heavy peal of thunder.*] That's Hendrick Hudson himself, the Flying Dutchman! [GRETCHEN *comes out of the house and down to Rip and children as they are talking.*]

GRETCHEN. Here you are again, telling stories that mean nothing! Why don't you attend to your farm? [*Children steal noiselessly out of sight behind inn.*] It's the worst kept farm in all the country around. The fences are falling down, the cows are astray, and there are more weeds than cabbages in the garden! Acre by acre your farm has dwindled away to almost nothing! Yet you can't take care of even that! And just look at your children! Your son is begotten in your own image! And he is growing up as lazy and as idle as you are! You spend all your time at the inn! You gossip and fill the children's heads with fairy stories and ruin them! As for me, I live on nothing! [GRETCHEN *goes hastily and angrily to the porch of* RIP VAN WINKLE'S *house.* RIP *slinks after her and stands near the door, watching her. He holds his old soft hat in his hands and fingers it nervously, turning it around and around.*]

RIP VAN WINKLE. Here, Gretchen — [*Putting his hand in his game bag.*] I'll give you all I have. It's only a small partridge that I shot this morning. I tried to get you a squirrel, but everything went wrong. No luck at all. [GRETCHEN *takes the partridge and looks at it in contempt. Throws it on the floor. This frightens the dog, whose tail droops to the ground.* GRETCHEN *takes the broom and chases the dog off the porch.*]

GRETCHEN. Lazy dog! Lazy dog, you! You are the cause of your master's idleness! You are two good-for-nothing, worthless creatures! Off with you! Off with you both! [*The dog springs off the porch, yelping, and runs back of the house.* RIP *puts on his cap and gets his gun, which is just inside the door of the house.*]

RIP VAN WINKLE. Well, I'll go, Gretchen. The outside of the house is the only place for me, and I must be off up the mountain for something to eat. [RIP *goes off up the road. He whistles for* WOLF. GRETCHEN, *although still angry, stops and looks after him, half in fear, and then enters the house. As soon as she is out of sight, the dog sneaks out from behind the house and follows* RIP, *who is whistling for him from behind the inn.*]

CURTAIN

ACT II

SCENE: *The Kaatskills.*

[*Green knoll down left center of stage, back stage a sort of amphitheater, surrounded by rocks. Enter* RIP *and the dog, toiling and panting.*]

RIP VAN WINKLE. Here, Wolf, let us rest a little on this green knoll. [*Takes a chunk of bread from his bag and gives it to* WOLF. *Pats the dog's head.*] Poor Wolf, thy mistress leads thee a dog's life of it. Never mind, my lad, while I live thou shalt never want a friend to stand by thee. But come, we have scrambled up to one of the highest peaks of the Kaatskill Mountains. It will be dark long before we can reach the village. And never a squirrel to stop the terrors of Dame Van Winkle's tongue! [RIP *and dog start down the mountain.* RIP *hears a voice calling.*]

VOICE. Rip Van Winkle! Rip Van Winkle! [RIP *looks around about him, startled. Hears the same cry again.*] Rip Van Winkle! Rip Van Winkle! [*There comes in sight a short, squarely built old fellow, with thick, bushy hair, and gray beard. He carries on his shoulder a stout keg, that seems heavy. He makes signs to* RIP *to assist him with the load.*]

RIP VAN WINKLE. How do you do? How do you do? [*Pause as* RIP *waits for an answer. None from stranger.*] You live up here, I suppose? You're pretty well? You're carrying something, eh? It's pretty good? [*Pantomime on the part of the stranger, indicating that keg is heavy, that* RIP *is to come and help him, and that there is something good to drink in the keg.*] It's heavy, is it? Is it heavy? It's a stout keg! Oh, you want me to carry it? [OLD MAN *assents in pantomime.* RIP *shyly and distrustfully takes the keg on his shoulder.* RIP *and the* OLD MAN *go off stage down left, the dog following. As soon as* RIP, *the* OLD MAN *and* DOG *disappear,* HENDRICK HUDSON *and his men appear from behind the rocks, and silently engage in a game of ninepins. Thunder now loud and close at hand.* RIP, OLD MAN *and* DOG *enter upper right.* RIP *starts with surprise.* DOG *slinks close to his master's legs and jumps with each peal of thunder.* RIP *takes off his hat and looks about him in fear and wonder, then addresses the group, turning from one to another.*] How do you do? How do you do? Oh — here's another one! Or are you the same one? No-o, you're not the same one — you're another one! How do you do? I said *How do you do!* [*No answer.*] How do you do? You heard me, eh? [*A few of them nod their heads.*] Oh, you can hear, huh? But you can't talk, huh? You're dumb — Oh, too bad — can't talk! My wife, Gretchen, she's no relation of yours! You're all brothers? Maybe this is a family party. Well, you're a melancholy pleasure party! Wolf and I had better go home. You'll excuse me, gentlemen! [RIP *starts away, but is frightened by the entrance of more men.* OLD MAN *who carried keg up the mountain opens keg and pours the contents into flagons. Makes signs for* RIP *to wait on the company.* RIP *obeys in fear and trembling.* RIP *watches the crew drinking; no one offers* RIP *any.*] Oh, no, thank you — I don't drink — [*Pause.*] — Not a very polite family. [*The crew return to the play of ninepins.* RIP *goes up to one of the flagons, and smells it. Sniffing.*] Umm — Good Hollands! Rip, you must be thirsty. You've come a long way up the mountains. Better try a little. [*Drinks and smacks his lips.*] Excellent Schnapps! Oh, what would Dame Van Winkle say to see me sitting here in such good company? [*Holding up flagon for toast.*] Well, here's to the health of all the company — to all the family and all the brothers! [*Drinks. Calls.*] Wolf! Wolf! Good dog, we must go home. [RIP *becomes suddenly drowsy. Lies slowly down and falls asleep. Dog, after turning around several times, lies down beside* RIP, *and also goes to sleep.*]

CURTAIN

ACT III

Scene 1

SCENE: *Same as Act II.*

[RIP *lying asleep on green knoll, at spot where he first saw the* OLD MAN *with the keg. Gun at his side.* RIP *very slowly wakes up, rubs his eyes, and looks about.*]

RIP VAN WINKLE. Surely I have not slept here all night! That old man with the keg! The mountain ravine! The wild retreat among the rocks! The woebegone party at ninepins! The flagon! Oh! That flagon! That wicked flagon! What excuse shall I make to Dame Van Winkle! [*Picks up his gun; one piece falls away.*] This rusty, worm-eaten old firelock is not my gun! [*Calling loudly.*] My gun! Ho! Ho! My gun! Who has taken my gun? Those grave roisterers of the mountain have put up a trick on us! They've robbed me of my gun! If I meet any of them, I'll demand my gun! [*Whistles.*] Wolf! Wolf! He must have strayed away, after a squirrel or a partridge! [*Whistles.*] Wolf! Wolf! [*Tries to get up. Moves with great difficulty. Twinges of pain follow every movement. Groans and exclamations.*] I am stiff in my joints! These mountain beds do not agree with me. If this frolic should lay me up with a fit of rheumatism, I shall have a blessed time with Dame Van Winkle! [RIP *walks with much difficulty. Looks into distance off stage, shading eyes with his hand. He is surprised at many sights. Whistles for his dog again.*] I am famished for want of breakfast! I must get home — I shall starve here. [*Starts down the mountain.*]

CURTAIN

Scene 2

SCENE: *Same as Act I but much changed by time.*

[*The inn sign is now the "Sign of George Washington" and the flagpole on the inn flies the Stars and Stripes. The porch of Rip's house has tumbled down. Before the curtain goes up, a crowd is heard applauding the* ORATOR. *Curtain goes up and shows* ORATOR *standing on a box, up stage left, speaking. Crowd is listening enthusiastically.*]

ORATOR. And shall the glorious freedom for which the heroes of '76 fought and died be thus betrayed into the hands of the aristocrats? Shall the rights of our citizens be left to the mercy of demagogues? Never! The people will never entrust their liberties to the grasping Federal party! To-day you will overthrow their tyranny by electing to Congress that loyal Democrat, that staunch defender of the peoples' rights, that brave and honored citizen of this place, Derrick Van Brummel! [*Applause.* ORATOR *begins to distribute ballots.*] Here, gentlemen, here are your ballots! [*The people crowd around* ORATOR *to get the ballots. Some step inside the inn to vote.* RIP *enters left, back. Troop of children follow at his heels, hooting, pointing at him, stroking their chins.* RIP *feels his chin, and is astonished at the length of his beard.*]

RIP VAN WINKLE. Why! My beard is a foot long! Everything is strange! I do not know these people or these houses! I believe I am bewitched! [*He looks about him.*] Surely this is my native village! There are the Kaatskill Mountains. There is the silver Hudson. That flagon last night has addled my poor head sadly! There is my house. [*He goes over to house and looks at it.*] It's fallen! It is in ruins! Is that my house? Yes, it must be. [*A dog that looks like* WOLF *snaps at him as he passes.*] My very dog has forgotten me! [*Goes into the house and calls out wildly.*] Gretchen! Gretchen! Children! Rip! Judith! [*No answer.* RIP *staggers out of the house.*] Gone — all gone! House gone! Wife! Children! [RIP *crosses to the inn. The crowd follows.* RIP *looks in amazement at the crowd which gazes at him in equal amazement.*] Union Hotel by Jonathan Doolittle! Flag! General Washington! [ORATOR *comes up to* RIP.]

ORATOR. On which side do you vote? [RIP *stares with a look of vacant stupidity.*]

A MEMBER OF THE CROWD. Are you a Federal or a Democrat? [RIP *stares without understanding.*]

SHERIFF. What brings you to the election with a gun on your shoulder and a mob at your heels? Do you mean to breed a riot in the village?

RIP VAN WINKLE. Alas! Gentlemen. I am a quiet man, a native of this place and a loyal subject of the King, God bless him!

ALL. A Tory! A Tory! A spy! A refugee! Away with him! Hustle him out! [RIP *is pushed to the back of the stage and stopped by the* SHERIFF *well up the stage.*]

RIP VAN WINKLE. I mean no harm, friends. I came here in search of some neighbors who used to keep this place.

ORATOR. Who are they? Name them!

RIP VAN WINKLE [*hesitatingly*]. Where's Nicholas Vedder?

ORATOR. Nicholas Vedder? Why, he's dead and gone these eighteen years!

RIP VAN WINKLE. Where is Brom Deutcher?

ORATOR. Oh, he went to the war. Some say he was killed at Stony Point — others that he was drowned at the foot of Anthony's Nose. I don't know — he never came back.

Rip Van Winkle. Where's the schoolmaster, Van Brummel?

Orator. He went to the war, too, and now he is a great man in Congress. We mean to elect him again. [*Cheers for* Van Brummel.]

Rip Van Winkle [*looking at the faces about him in a bewildered way*]. Does nobody here know poor Rip Van Winkle?

All. Oh, to be sure — there's Rip Van Winkle yonder, leaning against the inn porch.

Sheriff [*going up to* Rip]. Who are you, anyway, and what is your name?

Rip Van Winkle. God knows — I don't know — I'm not myself — I'm somebody else. That's me over yonder — No, no, that's somebody else, got into my shoes. I was myself last night, but I fell asleep in the mountains, and they've changed my gun and everything's changed, and I'm changed, and I can't tell who I am or what's my name! [*Bystanders nod and wink significantly and tap their heads.* Judith *pushes her way up to* Rip, *quieting a child in her arms.*]

Judith. Hush, Rip! Hush! The old man won't hurt you.

Rip Van Winkle. What is your name, my good woman?

Judith. Judith Gardenier.

Rip Van Winkle. And your father's name?

Judith. Ah, poor man! Rip Van Winkle was his name but it's twenty years since he left home, with his gun and his dog, and he has never been heard of since. His dog came home without him — but whether he was killed or carried off by the Indians, nobody can tell. I was then but a little girl.

Rip Van Winkle [*in a faltering voice*]. Where is your mother?

JUDITH. Oh, she died but a short time since. She broke a blood vessel in a fit of passion at a New England peddler. [RIP *catches his daughter and her child in his arms and looks in her face.*]

RIP VAN WINKLE. I am your father — young Rip Van Winkle once — old Rip Van Winkle now! [*Turning to the crowd.*] Does nobody know poor Rip Van Winkle? [*The* NEIGHBOR WOMAN, *now very aged, comes forward and peers into* RIP'S *face.*]

·NEIGHBOR WOMAN. Sure enough, it's Rip Van Winkle! It is himself! Welcome home again, old neighbor! Why, where have you been all these twenty long years?

RIP VAN WINKLE. Up in the mountains. [*All gather about* RIP.]

ALL. Rip Van Winkle! Sure enough, it's Rip Van Winkle! Welcome home!

ORATOR. Here's your ballot. We'll show you how to vote. [*All move toward the inn, some peering at* RIP *and touching their foreheads in a significant way.*]

JUDITH [*coming up to* RIP]. Come, father, come! Come home with me — you shall have the best of homes, and you can go in and out whenever you please!

CURTAIN

This photograph of a production of *Lucky Pehr* shows the scene at the seashore where Pehr meets Death.

CHAPTER XXXIII

THE FIRST THANKSGIVING DAY IN AMERICA

DURING the autumn a fifth grade had been studying the history of the early colonies of New England. In arranging the Thanksgiving program, the first Thanksgiving in America was naturally assigned to this group. The study of the history of the New England colonies had proceeded along the same lines as that of the Dutch colonies in New York, already alluded to in connection with *Rip Van Winkle*. The differences between the character of the Puritans and that of the Dutch settlers, the differences in their environments, the overmastering desire of the former for religious and political freedom, the deeply religious atmosphere in which they lived — were noted by the class. The members followed the story of the departure of the Pilgrims from Scrooby to the end of their first year in America. The Pilgrims' motive in leaving England, and then afterwards in moving on from Holland, was made clear. The account of their journey across the Atlantic in midwinter, the locating and building of their homes in the new country, the privation and sickness of that first winter, the treaty with Massasoit, and the plenteous harvest of the first summer — these were all studied. Many books were read which bore on the subject, and many stories of these times were retold.

The play *The First Thanksgiving Day in America* was written by the children. Suggestions and questions from

365

the teacher, and spirited discussions by the class helped to work out the details. The group decided to present three scenes: (1) the planning and preparation of the feast; (2) the welcoming of the Indian guests, the military drill, the games, and the Indian feast dance; (3) the feast. The dialogue was adapted from several books: Nina More's *Pilgrims and Puritans*, Drake's *On Plymouth Rock*, and, principally, Jane Austin's *Standish of Standish*. The boys and girls made a study of the costumes of the Pilgrims and of the Indians, and each child made his own headdress, whether Puritan or Indian. The girls also tried Puritan cooking; and the pumpkin pies for the feast were made by the sixth grade. At the same time, the second and third grades were reading about the thanksgiving feast of the Iroquois Indians, preparatory to presenting it in dramatic form. Thus the work of the two different classes ran side by side, and the two presentations took place on the same morning, a fact which added very much to the interest of the children.

THE PLAY

CHARACTERS

PRISCILLA	JOHN HOWLAND
MARY CHILTON	MILES STANDISH
ELIZABETH TILLEY	SQUANTO
MISTRESS BREWSTER	MASSASOIT
MISTRESS WHITE	SAMOSET
SENTINEL	QUADEQUINA
GOVERNOR BRADFORD	STEPHEN HOPKINS
ELDER BREWSTER	PILGRIMS
JOHN ALDEN	INDIANS

SOLDIERS

ACT I

SCENE: *A kitchen in the Common House, in Plymouth.*

[PRISCILLA *and* MARY *sprinkling linen.*]

MARY. Oh, Priscilla, girl, what thinkest thou is the news?

PRISCILLA. What is it? Speak quickly or I'll sprinkle thee rather than the linen. [*The girls play.* ELIZABETH *enters.*]

ELIZABETH. Priscilla! Mary! Mistress Brewster would have you in to see about noon meat.

PRISCILLA. But thy news, poppet! Thy news, quick!

MARY. Why, Governor Bradford hath resolved upon a day, or rather a week, of holidays and thanksgivings for the mercies God hath shown us. Think of it, Priss! A whole week of feasting and holidays.

PRISCILLA. Hm! It sounds well enow, but who is to make ready this feasting?

MARY. Why — all of us — and chiefly you, dear wench, for none can season a delicate dish or —

PRISCILLA. Aye, aye, I know that song full well; but dost really think, Mollie, that to do a good deal more and a good deal harder cooking than our wont will be so very sprightly a holiday?

MARY. But it will be doing our part to make holiday for the others.

PRISCILLA. Now then, if thou art not at thy old tricks of shaming my selfish forwardness.

ELIZABETH. And it is determined to send Squanto to invite King Massasoit and his train to the feast!

MARY. The Governor hath already ordered Masters Doty, Soule, and Latham to go afield to-morrow with their guns and to spend two days in gathering game.

PRISCILLA. Methinks another party should go to the beach to dig clams, for, though not so toothsome as venison and birds, it is a prey more surely to be come by.

ELIZABETH. The Elder saith the God of Jacob handeth us the clams as he did manna to those other children of his in the desert. At morning and at night we may gather them with certainty.

PRISCILLA. But they hold not sweet over Sunday; that is, if the day be hot!

MARY. And, Priscilla, we shall look to thee for marchpanes and manchets and plum porridge and possets and all manner of tasty cakes such as only thou canst bake.

PRISCILLA. All that I can do I will do blithely and steadfastly. Come, maids, to work!

CURTAIN

ACT II

SCENE: *Same as Act I.*

[*Table is placed in center, at which* PRISCILLA *and* ELIZABETH *are preparing for cooking. Fireplace at the left, at which* MARY *is stirring a kettle.* MISTRESS BREWSTER *and* MISTRESS WHITE *are seated on a bench at right peeling pumpkins for pies.*]

PRISCILLA. Bring in the turkeys and begin. [*She stands at the table and stuffs the turkeys.*] Oh, if only I had some chestnuts to stuff these turkeys with, they would taste more like the goose we had across the seas.

MARY. But their flavor is finer than the flavor our geese had. And here is one which will scale nigh twenty pounds!

ELIZABETH. Why don't you stuff them with beechnuts? There is a store of them at our house.

PRISCILLA. Why, beechnuts would be fine. Go and fetch some!

MARY. Priscilla, how are you going to cook the oysters?

PRISCILLA. In Leyden we used to cook them with bread crumbs and milk, but here we have no milk and no bread. I shall use biscuit crumbs and wine.

MARY. I have some scallop shells. Why not fill them with your compote and roast them in the ashes?

PRISCILLA. A wonderful idea! We can put one at each man's plate at the table. It will be a novelty and will set off the board famously!

ELIZABETH [*returns with the beechnuts*]. Oh, have you heard the news? King Massasoit and all of his braves are coming to the feast to-morrow! All your cooking will be needed.

MISTRESS WHITE. How providential that the Indians have always been so friendly to us.

MISTRESS BREWSTER. Yea, the Lord hath been very good to us.

MISTRESS WHITE. Verily hath He, Mistress Brewster. This is a happy autumn, after all our troubles.

MISTRESS BREWSTER. See our pleasant houses and the corn on the hills! We have happy homes here already.

PRISCILLA. But, oh, Mistress White, how unhappy were we last winter with the hunger and the cold and the sickness, and the unfinished houses.

MISTRESS BREWSTER. Aye, Priscilla, often did I wish for old England, its fertile fields, its merry villages — this is a cold and desolate land.

MARY. Truly! Only empty forests and desert sea all about us. There is little to talk about, and less to laugh about, but I think that happier times are coming.

MISTRESS BREWSTER. Yes, our homesickness is over.

We have houses, the earth smiles with the harvest, the Indians are our friends. The hand of God is spread over us to keep us.

ELIZABETH. But best of all, here is no king to persecute us, to say "I am the Lord's Anointed! Think as I think, worship as I worship!" We walk now in the light of our own hearts!

MISTRESS BREWSTER. Verily our blessings are manifold! It is exceeding good that to-morrow we give thanks unto the Lord!

CURTAIN

ACT III

SCENE: *Out of doors. Fort up stage to left. House up stage to right, showing front.*

[*When the curtain rises, a weary* SENTINEL *is pacing back and forth. He pauses often to look and listen. Hears a soft, birdlike whistle, which is repeated twice.*]

SENTINEL. That is the Indian call. They are coming to the feast. [*Goes back to the fort to announce their arrival.* GOVERNOR BRADFORD *comes out of the fort.* ELDER BREWSTER *comes out of the Common House. They exchange greetings.*]

ELDER BREWSTER. Good morning, Governor Bradford.

GOVERNOR BRADFORD. Good morning to you, Elder Brewster. [*They talk together.* JOHN ALDEN *comes out of the Common House, together with* JOHN HOWLAND, *carrying wood for a fire. They select a place to make the fire, well towards the middle of the stage, front.*]

JOHN ALDEN. This is the best place for the fire, is it not? There will be room round about it to sit and smoke the pipe of peace.

JOHN HOWLAND. It is a good place, but methinks a fire

will hardly be needed long — not after the sun is up.   [*They lay the wood for the fire and light it as they speak.*]

JOHN ALDEN.   Saw you ever such perfect weather in November?   It is like summer.

JOHN HOWLAND.   Squanto says it is the Indian Summer.

GOVERNOR BRADFORD [*speaking to the two young men*]. The Captain waiteth for you!   [*Exit the two* JOHNS.]

ELDER BREWSTER.   Come the savages so soon?

GOVERNOR BRADFORD.   Yes, and Miles is ever ready betimes.   Hark!   [*Indian whoops, off stage, distant, and a succession of unearthly shrieks, with which the guests announce both their arrival and their festive spirit.* MILES STANDISH *and* SOLDIERS *come out of fort.* PILGRIMS *come on stage from all sides.   Indian whoop is heard off stage, close at hand.* INDIANS *come on stage.   They are bearing presents for the* PILGRIMS.   *There are as many* INDIANS *as stage will allow.* SQUANTO *introduces, in pantomime,* MASSASOIT, SAMOSET, *and* QUADEQUINA, *to* GOVERNOR BRADFORD, MILES STAND-ISH, *and* ELDER BREWSTER.   *Introductions and interchange of compliments in truly regal style, in pantomime.*]

GOVERNOR BRADFORD.   Welcome, King Massasoit!   And welcome to your followers!   Seat yourselves about the fire. [*They sit.*]   The troops will now proceed with the military drill, under the direction of Captain Miles Standish.   [*Drill. All spectators seated during drill.*]

QUADEQUINA [*aside to* MASSASOIT].   If they have be-guiled us here to destroy us —

MASSASOIT.   Can'st not tell an eagle from a carrion crow? Would Winslow or the Sword or the Chief of the powwow do this?   Peace, my brother!

GOVERNOR BRADFORD.   We will now test our skill at arrow shooting.   Both Indians and Pilgrims will take part. Then will follow the Indian feast dance.

[*Arrow shooting.   Indian feast dance.   All spectators seated during dance.*]

ELDER BREWSTER [*aside to* GOVERNOR BRADFORD *as the dance proceeds*].   Are the heathen creatures practicing their incantations and warlock work in our very midst? [*Turning to* STEPHEN HOPKINS.]   Stephen Hopkins, thou knowest their devices — how is it?

STEPHEN HOPKINS.   Nay, Brother, it is a feast dance, a manner of thanksgiving.

GOVERNOR BRADFORD [*rising, at the conclusion of the dance*]. Squanto, invite our brothers to the feast our women have prepared.

CURTAIN

ACT IV

SCENE: *Same as Act III, with long table set front and middle of stage.*

[PRISCILLA *and other women are busy at table, which they are loading with the things prepared for the feast.   Clam broth, roasts of meat, manchets (sandwiches), bowls of salad set off with wreaths of autumn leaves, great baskets of grapes, white and purple, baskets of native plums (three colors: black and white and red), turkey, oyster scallops, nuts, pumpkin pies, and cakes.* GOVERNOR BRADFORD *comes to table, with* MILES STANDISH *and* MASSASOIT.   INDIANS *and* PILGRIMS *place themselves around the table.* SQUANTO *motions to an* INDIAN, *who brings in a bushel basket full of popcorn and pours it on the table.* PILGRIMS *exclaim, as it is the first popcorn they have seen.   As they stand about the table the* PILGRIMS *sing the One Hundredth Psalm, to the tune of "Old Hundred."*]

ELDER BREWSTER.   It is fitting, friends, that we should close this Thanksgiving week with a song of praise to Him who upheld us through the sad afflictions of the winter for which He beforehand prepared us.   Through the summer He has kept us in warmth, and now as winter approacheth again He hath well provided us plenteous harvests, and hath given us, in this strange land, King Massasoit and his braves for friends and helpers.   Verily, the Lord hath been good to us in all our ways and blessed our outgoings and incomings, for which let His Holy Name have praise forever.   [PILGRIMS *sing the Doxology.*]

CURTAIN

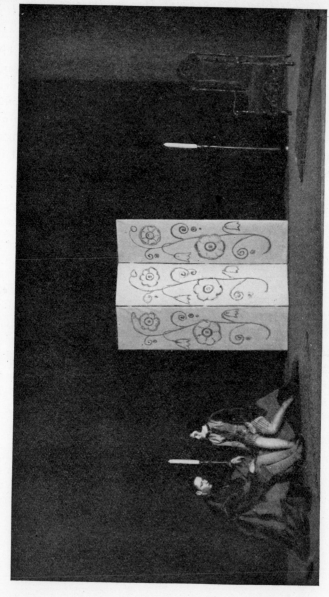

A scene from *Twelfth Night*, showing an apartment in the Duke's palace

CHAPTER XXXIV

OLD PIPES AND THE DRYAD

How the Play Was Made

THE sixth grade which produced the following play was studying early Greek history — the myth-making period. Many old Greek and Latin stories and some tree myths were read, among the latter the modern story *Old Pipes and the Dryad*, by Frank R. Stockton. As soon as the children had read this, they proposed to play it. Then the class reread the story carefully to see whether it was the right kind of material for dramatization. Each child took home a copy of the story and studied it for himself. The children finally decided that the effort was worth making.

Next they retold the story in as few words as possible, rejecting everything not suitable for their purpose, but retaining the natural order of incidents and thus holding the whole together. The following summary of the events of the story was written on the board and considered as a unit.

Old Pipes, helped up the hill by the children, discovers that his pipes are no longer heard by the cattle. He resolves to return the wages just paid to him.

Release of the Dryad. Old Pipes made twenty years younger.

The cave of the Echo Dwarfs. The angry Echo Dwarf vows vengeance. He steals the pipes and attempts to shut the Dryad up again in her tree.

The Dryad shuts the Echo Dwarf in the tree, restores the pipes to Old Pipes, and roams the forest for the remainder of the summer.

The mother of Old Pipes is made twenty years younger.

The discovery of the Dryad's tree by the children.

The Dryad kisses Old Pipes and his mother again, lets the Echo Dwarf out, and goes back to the warmth and comfort of her tree.

Then the presentation of these different incidents was discussed. The school was at the time without stage, curtains, scenery, or properties of any kind — even without a platform. Everything had to be planned and made. Next the details were reviewed very carefully, and many things were rejected as impossible under the circumstances. The children drew on the blackboard the scenes as they would like to have them and sketched the characters in costume, each giving his opinion freely and illustrating his ideas with chalk. They made drawings of the mountains, the rocky path, and the dryad tree. Many of the plans for the scenery were so elaborate that it was impossible to carry them out.

As the scenery and action were worked out, the dialogue developed. Each child contributed: one proposed a speech; the others considered and criticized. The final result in each case was written on the blackboard. The whole now took shape on the stage. After the first full rehearsal the children felt that something was wrong, and they were discouraged. The next morning, before school, while they were talking the matter over, one remarked, "There is too much talk and too little acting in this story for a play. It drags out too long." They then decided that they would *act* — and talk only when speech was absolutely necessary. The dialogue was eliminated wherever it was possible to substitute action.

There was still great dissatisfaction with the result. Some of the pupils were even ready to give up the play. Then they made the discovery that the struggle between the good and

the evil forces in the play was not great, that the story itself was not sufficiently dramatic. "There is not trouble
enough here for a play," said one. "Things just go on.
Enough does not happen." "Well," returned another, "let
us make more trouble. We don't need to have it just as it
is in the story." A variety of plans were suggested, but
finally it was agreed that the Echo Dwarf was the mischief-
maker, that the contention was between the Dryad and him,
and that he might be allowed to plan a greater revenge and
to carry his plans farther than in the story without inter-
fering with the final outcome. He must steal the pipes, try
to destroy them, hide them, and proceed in his attempt to get
the Dryad back into her tree again. The Dryad must discover the plot just in time, and, after shutting the Dwarf up
in the tree, find the pipes and put all things right again.

One of the greatest difficulties was to end the play in a
way satisfactory to the children. They would not consider
at all the conclusion given in the story — that the Dryad's
tree should be torn down and no one should ever know what
became of her. To them, this outraged all sense of right,
and besides, there was no necessity for it — it was just
"tacked on." At first, they proposed to conclude by leaving the Dryad free. Later they decided that this would not
be satisfactory. They objected to shutting her up again,
but at last concluded that this was best, since the tree was
her home, since she *wanted* to go back into it and could shut
herself in, and since she knew that Old Pipes would let her
out when the summer came again. In the final version, as
she goes to her tree, she kisses Old Pipes and his mother,
who are enjoying their evening meal outside the cottage,
leaving them each thirty years younger than they were at the
beginning of the play.

No other meaning to this story than what lay on the surface was ever discussed. The children spoke of the characters as real persons and of the incidents as real happenings. However, as the time drew near for presenting the play and the pupils realized more and more the joy of the Dryad in her own happiness and her delight in giving happiness to others, they called her the spirit of Spring, of Youth, of Life, and of Joy.

The costumes were all simple, designed by the children, and constructed for the most part out of materials at hand. Old Pipes wore a hunter's dress; the Dryad, a soft Greek robe; the Dwarfs, gray one-piece suits, with pointed cap and shoes; the Mother of Old Pipes, the dress of an old German woman; and the children, the dress of German peasants, for somehow they had the impression that this was a German tale.

THE PLAY [1]

CHARACTERS

OLD PIPES	MOTHER
LARGE BOY	DRYAD
SMALL BOY	ECHO DWARF
GIRL	DWARFS

ACT I

SCENE: *A rocky path.*

[*A large oak tree at left. Cottage at right. Rustic seat and small table outside. Enter* OLD PIPES *with two* BOYS *and a* GIRL — BOYS *holding* OLD PIPES' *arms and helping him along;* GIRL *pushing him from behind. He sinks exhausted on the seat. The children sit on the ground about him. They pull pieces of bread from their pockets and eat.*]

[1] The play is dramatized from Frank Stockton's story of the same name, and is used here with the special permission of Charles Scribner's Sons, New York, publishers of Mr. Stockton's story.

The production of *Old Pipes and the Dryad* from which this photograph is taken, is a more recent one than that described in the text. Here the cottage of Old Pipes is merely suggested by the lattice at the side of the stage. The trees are made of unbleached cotton cloth dyed to suggest the colors of the bark of oaks. The cyclorama of blue Canton flannel, when lighted, gives a splendid illusion of distant sky.

OLD PIPES.   I am very tired to-night.   I don't know that I could have climbed up this steep path to my home if you had not helped me.   [*Gives each of the children a copper coin.*] I am sorry I tired you so much.

LARGE BOY.   Oh, that would not have tired us, if we had not been high up on the mountains for the cattle to-day.

OLD PIPES [*in great surprise*].   Had to go high up on the mountains for the cattle!   What do you mean?   [GIRL *goes behind* PIPES, *puts her hand on her mouth, and makes all sorts of signs to the* BOYS *to stop.   They do not notice her.*]

SMALL BOY.   Why, you see, sir, that, as the cattle can't hear your pipes now, the chief villager has hired us to drive them down from the mountain every night.

OLD PIPES [*in great distress*].   How long have you done this?   [GIRL *tries to stop the* BOYS, *as before.*]

LARGE BOY.   Almost a year now.   I think ever since the people felt that the cattle could not hear your pipes.   We have not heard the echoes for a long time.   But we are rested now and must go home.   Good night, sir.   [*The children go, the* GIRL *scolding the* BOYS *all the way out.*]

GIRL.   It was a secret.   The old man did not know that the cattle can't hear him, and you have made him unhappy.

OLD PIPES [*after sitting a while silent and in deep trouble*]. Mother!   Mother!   [*Goes to the latticed window, where she sits spinning, and shouts again.*]   Mother!   Mother!   [MOTHER *comes hobbling out; she is very deaf, and* OLD PIPES *speaks very loudly as both move toward the seat.*]   Mother, did you hear what those children said?

MOTHER [*speaking in* OLD PIPES' *ear*].   Children!   I did not know that any children were here.

OLD PIPES.   Why, they say that the cattle can't hear my pipes any more, and the villagers are paying me for nothing.

MOTHER [*shouting*]. They can't hear you! Why, what's the matter with the cattle?

OLD PIPES. Nothing's the matter with the cattle. The matter is with me and my pipes. But one thing is certain; if I do not earn the wages, I shall not take them. [*Takes money from a bag that hangs at his side and counts it out.*]

MOTHER [*very angry*]. You piped the best you could, and what are we to do without the money?

OLD PIPES. I don't know, but I shall go straight down to the village and give back the money they paid me to-day. [*Starts off.* MOTHER *goes into the house, grumbling.*]

MOTHER. Foolish! Foolish! What are we to do without the money?

OLD PIPES [*dropping wearily under a tree*]. I cannot go to-night, I am too tired. But to-morrow — [*Leans heavily against the tree. A tapping is heard.* OLD PIPES *listens. It is heard again. He listens. A voice is heard.*]

DRYAD. Let me out! Let me out!

OLD PIPES [*springing to his feet*]. This must be a dryad tree, and she wants to get out! I'll let her out if I can. It is summer time, and the moon rises to-night before the sun goes down. I must find the key, and if I do I shall surely turn it. [*He goes all around the tree trying to turn every little bit of bark that he finds sticking out. One turns quite around.*] Here it is! [*A large part of the side of the tree is pushed open, and a beautiful* DRYAD *steps quickly out. She stands motionless, looking out over the mountains and all before her.*]

DRYAD. Lovely! Lovely! How good of you to let me out! I am exceedingly happy, most thankful! [*Kisses him on both cheeks.*] Oh, it's glorious! Glorious! What can I do for you, my kind friend?

OLD PIPES [*who has been gradually straightening up since receiving the* DRYAD'S *kiss, is standing with eyes and mouth wide open, hardly able to speak for surprise*]. Well! Well! I am glad that I let you out, but I must tell you that I turned the key because I wanted to see a dryad. I knew that your people lived in the trees and that you were happy to come out in the summer time. Now I am glad that I let you out, because you are so happy; but if you want to do something for me, you can take this money down to the chief villager. It is the money paid me for calling the cattle home from the mountains. It is more than a year now since I have been able to make them hear my pipes, and I can't receive pay for what I cannot do.

DRYAD [*taking the money*]. To the village! I will go any place for you. Often, in my tree, I have heard the sweet notes of your pipes. [*Moves away, looking at the beautiful things about her.*]

OLD PIPES [*following her to the entrance, watching her as far as he can see*]. Now I have seen a dryad! [*Begins to move toward the house and notices how light and free he feels. Swings his arms about and goes quickly to the house.*] Why! I feel quite rested. I can walk quite easily! My! I feel unusually strong, and I am very hungry! I shall go home and eat my supper and to-morrow go to the forest and cut some fuel for Mother. [*Exit.*]

[*Curtain drops for a moment to denote a lapse of time.*]

[*The next evening. Enter* OLD PIPES, *carrying a large armful of wood. He crosses the stage and begins to pile it up against the side of the cottage.*]

OLD PIPES. There, Mother, I have done a fine day's work. If I keep on this way, we shall have plenty of fuel for next winter. Now it is time to call the cattle home. I must get my pipes. [*Goes into the cottage and comes out, followed by his* MOTHER.]

MOTHER. What are you going to do now? If you will not take the money, why will you pipe?

OLD PIPES. I am going to play for my own pleasure. [*Plays a strong, full note. A faint echo is heard.*] Ha! Ha! What has happened to my pipes? [*Plays again.*] They must have been stopped up of late, but they are as clear and good as ever! [*Plays again. Echo is heard as before.* OLD PIPES *looks up toward the mountains.*] See, Mother! See! The cattle are coming down as they used to do. [*Rising as the truth flashes upon him.*] Oh, I see it all now, Mother! I had forgotten that a kiss from a dryad makes one ten years younger. She kissed me twice. I *am* really younger. Look! Mother, look! [*Begins a joyous dance across the stage to show his* MOTHER *how young he is.*] Come, come, Mother, come! She must kiss you too! [*Tries to pull her with him.*] Well, then, I'll find her and bring her to you. [*Dances off the stage in search of the* DRYAD.]

MOTHER [*looking after him in astonishment*]. He's bewitched! O Pipes! Pipes! When will you be old enough to have ordinary common sense? [*Turns toward the cottage.*] He's bewitched!

CURTAIN

ACT II

SCENE: *Cave of the Echo Dwarfs.*

[*Rocks lying all about. Dwarfs of all sizes running about playing. One echoes back the sound of laughter that comes from the distance. Another, the sound of a blacksmith's hammer. Another, the call of a voice. One big, fat, lazy-looking* DWARF *is lying on a rock, sound asleep. The notes of* OLD PIPES' *pipes sound in the distance. They all stop to listen and, when it is repeated, run to wake the big* DWARF. *He rolls to his feet and begins to echo back the notes of the pipes. He is very angry at being disturbed, and as soon as the piping stops, moves about shaking his head and fists and grinding his teeth.*]

ECHO DWARF. I thought those pipes had stopped forever. I have been deceived. I'll go and find out how long this is to last. I will find the piper himself. [*Starts to run off. Meets the* DRYAD.] Ho! Ho! What are you doing here? How did you get out of your tree?

DRYAD. Doing! I am being happy! That's what I'm doing. I was let out by the good old man who plays the pipes to call the cattle home, and I've kissed him and made him young enough to play as well as ever.

ECHO DWARF [*pale with anger, moves toward her in a threatening way*]. And you are the cause of this great evil that has come upon me? You are the wicked creature who has again started this old man upon his career of pipe playing? What have I ever done to you that you should condemn me for years and years to echo back the notes of those wretched pipes?

DRYAD [*laughing merrily*]. What a funny little fellow you are! Anyone would think that you had been condemned to toil from morning till night. Fie upon you, Echo Dwarf! You are lazy and selfish, and that is what is the matter with you. Instead of grumbling, you should rejoice at the good fortune of the old man, who has regained so much of his strength and vigor. Go home, do your work, and learn to be generous, and then you may be happy. Good-by! [*Moves off in the direction of the forest.*]

ECHO DWARF [*growing more angry and more savage, dances about, shakes his fist, and shouts at the* DRYAD]. Insolent creature! I'll make you suffer for this! You shall find out what it is to heap injury and insult upon one like me. I have earned my rest by long years of toil. [*Follows her, and*

then turns back.] I'll find the piper, steal his pipes, and hide
them!

CURTAIN

ACT III

SCENE: *Same as Act I.*

[*Enter* ECHO DWARF *from behind the cottage. He looks all
about.* OLD PIPES *comes out, looking about.* DWARF *grinds
his teeth and motions that he would like to kill* OLD PIPES, *but
runs after him and stops him.*]

ECHO DWARF. What are you looking for, old man?

OLD PIPES. I am looking for a Dryad whom I let out of
her tree. She kissed me twice and made me young enough
to call the cattle home again, and I want her now on account
of my old mother. I want to ask her to make my mother
younger, as she did me. When I was old myself, I did not
notice how feeble mother was. Now it shocks and grieves
me.

ECHO DWARF [*his eyes glistening*]. That's a noble idea!
But you know a dryad can make no person younger but the
one who lets her out of the tree. But then, that is easy. You
must find the Dryad, tell her what you want, and ask her to
step inside her tree. You shut her in and run for your
mother. She will open it, let the Dryad out, and you will
have your wish.

OLD PIPES. Good! good! I will go at once, but I must
first get my pipes, lest I should be late in returning. [*Exit.*]

ECHO DWARF [*rubbing his hands in glee*]. She is quite
foolish enough to do it. Then, when he goes for his mother,
I'll take a stone and break off the key, so nobody can ever
turn it again. She shall see! She shall see! [*Enter* OLD
PIPES.] Take me with you; you can carry me on your
shoulder, and I'll help you. [OLD PIPES *picks him up.*

The DWARF *snatches the pipes and begins to bend and bite them. They move on. Soon the* DWARF *catches sight of the* DRYAD *in the distance. Before she enters,* OLD PIPES *discovers his loss, and is hunting for the pipes when the* DRYAD *enters.*] Oh, there she is! Put me down. Don't tell her I suggested the plan. [OLD PIPES *puts him down. He runs off with the pipes and hides but watches and listens.*]

OLD PIPES. I have been searching everywhere for you. Mother looks so old and feeble. Will you go into your tree for a few minutes, and I'll run and bring her to open it. Then kiss her as you did me just after you come out.

DRYAD [*looking sadly at* OLD PIPES]. I should dislike it dreadfully, but if you wish it — [*Moves toward the tree and enters.*] I have thought of making you happier, and I have waited about your cottage many days for your mother. Yet she does not come out, and a dryad cannot enter a house. If you can, get her to come out. [*The* ECHO DWARF *grows so anxious that he moves into sight. The* DRYAD *sees him.*] Did you think of this plan of shutting me up yourself?

OLD PIPES [*hesitating*]. No, no; a dwarf, whom I met, proposed it to me.

DRYAD. Oh, I see through it all. It is the scheme of that miserable Echo Dwarf, your enemy and mine. Where is he? [DWARF *hides.* OLD PIPES *looks about.*] There he is. [OLD PIPES *sees him. The* DWARF *tries to escape, but the* DRYAD *catches him and drags him to the tree.*] We will put him in here. [OLD PIPES *helps to thrust him in.*] Now we will shut him up, and I shall be safe from his mischief for the rest of the time that I am free. [*She shuts the door. There is a clicking sound of bark.*] There, no more need to be afraid of him.

OLD PIPES. Oh, my pipes! The rascal has stolen them! [*Both search all about and at last discover them under a rock.*

OLD PIPES *busies himself repairing them.* DRYAD *helps him.* OLD PIPES *blows on his pipes and makes no noise at first. Then they sound loud and clear. The* DWARF *echoes back the notes from the tree.*]

OLD PIPES [*looking toward the tree*]. That wicked Dwarf would have ruined my pipes. Now he will have to stay in the tree until the Dryad wants to go back herself.

CURTAIN

ACT IV

SCENE: *Same as Act III.*

[*Light snow on ground. Wood piled at door of house.* OLD PIPES *comes out of the house for wood.* DRYAD *enters from back.*]

DRYAD [*shivering*]. It is cold! [*Turns to* OLD PIPES.] Before I go into my tree for the winter, will you not once more ask your mother to come out and meet me?

OLD PIPES. Oh, it's no use. We must find some other way. She does not believe in dryads. She has forbidden me even to speak the name to her again. She says that I have been bewitched by a sorceress. [*Exit* DRYAD. OLD PIPES *returns to house. Enter* GIRL *and* SMALL BOY *racing after the* LARGE BOY. *He drops, breathless, under the oak tree.*]

LARGE BOY. Ha ha! you did not catch me, after all! [*A knocking is heard in the tree. All listen. Again the knocking is heard, and also the voice of the* DWARF, *pleading.*]

DWARF [*from the tree*]. Let me out! Let me out! [*All start up.*]

LARGE BOY. Oh, this is a dryad tree, like the one OLD PIPES found. Let's let her out. [*Hunts for the key.*]

GIRL [*pulling him away from the tree*].　No, no, what are you thinking about?　I am the oldest here, and I am only thirteen.　Do you want us all to be turned into crawling babies again?

LARGE BOY.　I want to see her!　I want to see her!

SMALL BOY [*tugging at larger one*].　No, no; every kiss from a dryad makes one ten years younger, and I am only nine. Where would I be?　[*Both pull at* LARGE BOY.]

GIRL.　Are you crazy?　Run! run! run!　[*All run as fast as their legs can carry them.　Enter* MOTHER.]

MOTHER.　Alas!　Alas!　The time has come when I am too old to work.　I have grown utterly useless.　Someone else will have to cook and sew for my son.　I wonder where he is.　[*Looks for him, but sinks exhausted into the chair, and soon falls asleep.　The* DRYAD *enters, steps up lightly, and kisses the* MOTHER *on both cheeks.*]

DRYAD.　Now Old Pipes has his wish, and he will be happy.　[*Disappears.*]

MOTHER [*waking, yawns, stretches herself*].　My, how a little sleep does refresh one!　It is astonishing how well I feel!　[*Moves about quite easily, and, finding that she can walk without her cane, drops it, and turns quickly toward the cottage.*]　I must hurry.　My son will be here in a few minutes, and his supper must be ready.　[*Exit* MOTHER. *Enter* OLD PIPES *with his pipes.*]

OLD PIPES.　This is the last time that I shall call the cattle down this year.　The nights are growing colder, the mountains are bare, and the winter will soon be here.　[*Sits and begins to play.　Echo is heard from the tree.　Enter* MOTHER. *She brings forward the little table and sets the supper on it; then seats herself beside* OLD PIPES, *and, with a smile, watches the cattle coming down.　Both begin to eat. Enter* DRYAD.]

DRYAD [*shivering*]. The night winds chill me. How happy they look there together. But I do not believe it will hurt them to be a little younger. [*Steps up lightly and kisses each of them once. The* MOTHER *kisses her son.* DRYAD *shivers again.*] I must get back into my comfortable home in the oak. [*Goes to the tree, turns the key, and calls to the* DWARF.] Come out! Winter is coming. I want the shelter of the tree myself. The cattle have come down for the last time this year, the pipes will sound no more, and you can go to your rocks and have a holiday until next spring. [ECHO DWARF *skips out, and runs away among the rocks.*] Now he can break the key, it does not matter. Another will grow out in the spring, and I know that when the warm days are here next year Old Pipes will come and let me out. [*Shivers again, wraps her robe about her, enters the tree, and pulls the door after her.*]

CURTAIN

A setting for *Twelfth Night* showing a room in Olivia's house.

CHAPTER XXXV

THE KNIGHTING OF RICHARD NEVILLE

How the Play was Made

At the time this play was made, the students were studying the Norman Conquest. The teacher's plan was, as far as possible, to present historical events through literary channels. The character of Richard Cœur de Lion, as shown in Scott's *The Talisman* and *Ivanhoe*, was contrasted with his character as shown in the history text. His story was introduced by the tales of the Angevin kings, found by the children in literary sources to which they were directed by the instructor. Each pupil was then asked to bring in the best account he could find of the story of Thomas à Becket. In studying the reign of King John, the death of Prince Arthur, and the dissolution of the Angevin kingdom, the class read aloud the fourth act of *King John*. Selected parts from *The Talisman* were also read. The information concerning the earlier kings was written up by different members of the group in the form of short stories and brought into class. In connection with those about Richard I, the class made some study of the three crusades and of chivalry. They studied illustrations by . Doré and the geography of the country through which the Crusaders traveled. Imaginary journeys over the routes were made. Drawings of castles, of knights in full armor, and designs for decorations of costumes, shields, and swords were made by the children in the art department. All of this study brought them into touch with the great leaders of the crusades, with their spirit and purpose, and with the world-wide results of these movements.

These seventh- and eighth-grade students in their study of chivalry had established a fairly intimate acquaintance with knighthood. The ideal knight appealed to their love of adventure and to their awakening sense of character values and social obligations. A knight had to be pure in heart, truthful, pledged to right the wrong, to protect the weak, and to fulfill the other vows of knighthood. The children were fascinated also by the knight's sword, his shield, his pennant, and the richness and brilliant color of his clothing, and of his horse's caparison. These classes had read aloud prose, poetry, and drama; they had in imagination ridden with these knights on their quests, had battled with them in the crusades, and tilted with them in their tournaments, and they were so full of the subject of knighthood that a play, which they felt they could write themselves, was the natural fruit of their intensive and enthusiastic study. The writing and acting of *The Knighting of Richard Neville* gratified their love of romance, their longing for adventure, and their fondness for ceremony. No doubt the rough, playful English humor, as expressed by Bennet the Butler, had its own peculiar charm for them and appealed to their appreciation of horseplay and tricks.

THE PLAY

CHARACTERS

COOK.
SCULLERY MAID.
BENNET, *the king's butler.*
HERALD

WILLIAM THE CONQUEROR.

RICHARD NEVILLE, *a young esquire of* WILLIAM THE CONQUEROR.

SIR ROBERT D'ARCY, *a friend of Richard's father.*

SIR BRIAN GUILDFORD, *one of* WILLIAM THE CONQUEROR'S *knights.*

KNIGHTS, LADIES, COURTIERS, PAGES, ETC.

ACT I

SCENE: *A kitchen in* WILLIAM THE CONQUEROR'S *palace. London, the February after the Conquest.*

[*The* COOK *and her* SCULLERY MAID *are at work.* *Enter* BENNET, *the butler.*]

BENNET [*going to the fire to warm his hands*]. Well met, Cookie dear! Beshrew me, but 'tis pitiless cold in the chapel! [*He blows on his fingers.*]

COOK [*a sharp-voiced woman*]. You're always a-cold these days, Bennet. Why needs thee be in chapel so early? Are thy sins too heavy to wait for afternoon?

BENNET. Odds my life, dame, you're too busy down here with your messes to hear the news. Wot you not this is the day of young Dickon's knighting?

COOK [*a little angry because she doesn't know the news*]. I wot only that you're in my way, Sir Bottle-washer!

SCULLERY MAID [*eagerly*]. Pray, how came he by his honor, Sir Butler?

BENNET [*with one eye on the* COOK, *who pretends not to listen*]. Well, bratling, this is the way of it, and you must know. Young Richard was born to luck, just as you were born to the dish clout. He serves the Duke, and you serve Dame Cookie here. He goes to battle and you scrub the pots. And so you see it was at Senlac, when our side was pressing the stubborn English hard, that Duke William's horse went down all in a tangle. Lucky young Richard was just behind and covered the Duke with his shield till the Duke could free himself of his nag. Just as the Duke got up — "Crack!" went Dickon's shield, and then the Duke knocked down an English churl who was about to chop off Dickon's head. "Tit for tat, *Sir* Richard!" roared the Duke. And our Dickon was pulled back wounded. And now that we're safe in London and the Duke is king, Dickon's *Sir* is to be made good. [*To the* COOK, *who has stopped her work to listen.*] It's a brave tale, eh, Cookie? [*Meditatively rubbing his chin and sighing.*] I only wish I had been in Dickon's place at the battle!

COOK [*banging a saucepan.* BENNET *jumps*]. Sooth, it is a pity, so it is!

BENNET [*strutting like a turkey*]. You'd be glad to see me a knight, wouldn't you, Cookie? Your friend, Sir Bennet, the Butler! [*He makes her a sweeping bow as she angrily turns her back.*]

SCULLERY MAID. Oh, sir, will you not tell me what a man doth ere he may be made knight?

BENNET. Ah, Pottlekins, there is where I should fail; for it is no joke an a man be in earnest. Three whole days is the service. First you must take a bath, and in February that chills to the bone! Ugh! Dickon didn't tarry long in his tub, I warrant you. Gramercy, the warder in the castle yard, said he could hear Dickon's teeth chatter. But oh, you should have seen the beautiful tabard his uncle gave him! White samite it was, fine as an altar cloth. Then you must go to Canterbury and win the archbishop's blessing. And then [*impressively pointing his finger at the open-mouthed* SCULLERY MAID] you must, without a bite of supper to keep the sides of your stomach apart, you must watch all night in the chapel with only a candle alight at the altar, and pray, and pray, and pray. Methinks *I* should pray only for one of Cookie's good fat roasted capons.

SCULLERY MAID. And wasn't Richard Neville afraid in the dark, sir?

BENNET. Afraid? In God's chapel? Why for should he fear aught save his past sins? No, no, Dickon's a good youth. I've known him six years. But this morning, when Father Priest and I went to fetch him, he was blue as a peacock with hunger and cold. And the priest prayed and put on Dickon's three robes — a white one to signify his purity, a red one to signify the blood he must shed for the Church, and a black one, showing that he must die some day. But this evening he will be made a knight by the King himself!

SCULLERY MAID [*dropping her cloth*]. Oh, sir, is he a handsome youth?

COOK [*giving* SCULLERY MAID *a push*]. Here, Brat! — To your work! And you, Bennet, make a truce with your tongue! [*She pushes him out of the kitchen.*]

CURTAIN

ACT II

SCENE: *In the hall of the* KING'S *palace.*

[*Ladies and courtiers grouped about the throne. Enter the* KING, *brusquely, and takes his seat. All bow. The king's* HERALD *approaches.*]

HERALD. The King, of his good will, is about to confer knighthood upon the young esquire, Richard Neville, for bravery in battle!

KING [*in a loud voice*]. Richard, my son, stand forth! [RICHARD, *clad in a close-fitting jacket, belt, and hose, steps slowly forward into the open space before the* KING. *A sword is hanging about* RICHARD'S *neck. He drops on one knee.*] Richard Neville, you have done bravely in battle. You have acted as if you were already a true knight. And do you now swear to be brave and upright, to be liberal to the poor, to protect the widow and the orphan, to succour the afflicted, to fight to the end for God and your king and country?

RICHARD. Aye, sire, I do.

KING. Let him be armed.

SIR ROBERT [*a hale old knight, the friend of* RICHARD'S *dead father, approaches, lifts the sword from* RICHARD'S *neck, and gives it to a priest, who lifts it up for a blessing*]. My dear lad, thou hast been a true son of thy father. He will be proud of thee. Take, therefore, this sword. It was his, and it served him well in many a hard day. And now it is thine in turn. I pray you may always do as he did, and you will do well.

RICHARD [*takes the sword and kisses the cross hilt reverently*]. I thank you, sir.

KING. The spurs, Guildford!

GUILDFORD [*approaches with the gilt spurs and fastens them on* RICHARD'S *heels. Then rising*]. I trust Richard Neville will so conduct himself that these spurs shall never be hacked off in shame and degradation.

KING [*rising and drawing his own sword, holds it aloft for a moment, then, stepping down from the dais, he touches* RICHARD'S *shoulder lightly three times*]. Rise, Sir Richard Neville, and may thy pennon soon become a banner.

CURTAIN

CHAPTER XXXVI

THE DEPARTURE

How the Play Was Made

As an example of the dramatization of a portion of a great novel, the little play called *The Departure* on the following pages will perhaps serve fairly well. It was made by a group of tenth-grade pupils. If one will read, in connection with *The Departure*, the first and second chapters of Thackeray's *Vanity Fair*, he will perceive the character and amount of work that was necessary to put Thackeray's leisurely telling of Becky Sharp's farewell to Miss Pinkerton's academy into dramatic form suitable to stage presentation. Numerous changes, rearrangements, elaborations, and additions had to be effected. Among these are the following: Thackeray gives much exposition through description and comment — for example, the paragraph in Chapter I of *Vanity Fair* describing Amelia Sedley. Thackeray's exposition had to be condensed and placed where it would not hamper the audience's interest in plot development. Digression and comment were eliminated. They are permissible in a novel but have no place in a one-act play. Amelia Sedley and not Becky Sharp is stressed in Chapter I of the novel, but as Amelia is not the center of interest in the play the pupils changed the emphasis. The interview in Chapter II, in which Becky annoys Miss Pinkerton by conversing in French, is placed with the incidents related in Chapter I. In the novel Miss Jemima gives Becky the

dictionary after she has entered the carriage. In order
to preserve unity of place and time, the pupils had the dictionary given Becky before she left the house. Moreover, Becky's
revolutionary utterances about Napoleon, which were

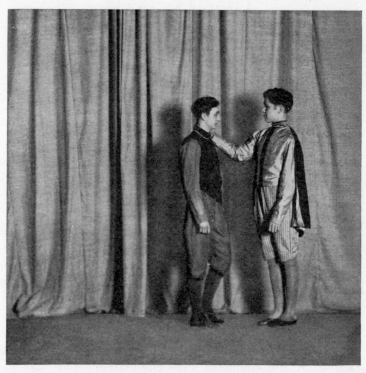

A scene from *Twelfth Night:* a street.

really given in the coach, and the destruction of the dictionary are used in the dramatization before Becky's departure. In several instances dialogue had to be invented.
For example, Thackeray does not tell what was actually
said in way of good-by to Amelia by her fellow students.
Therefore the pupils created conversation.

The Play

Characters

Miss Pinkerton, *principal of the academy for young ladies, Chiswick Mall; pompous, austere, Minerva-like.*

Miss Jemima Pinkerton, *her sister; good-natured, timid, little.*

Miss Amelia Sedley, *a wealthy pupil about to leave the academy; charming, gentle, and generous.*

Miss Rebecca Sharp, *an articled pupil; slight in person, sandy-haired, temperamental.*

Time: *A sunshiny morning in June, about 1812.*

Scene: *The drawing-room at Miss Pinkerton's academy, Chiswick Mall.*

[*The front-door bell rings as the curtain rises.* Miss Pinkerton *is seated at a desk, writing.* Miss Jemima *is standing by a window looking out over some geranium pots.*]

Miss Jemima. It is Mrs. Sedley's coach, sister. Sambo, the black servant, has just rung the bell; and the coachman has a new red waistcoat.

Miss Pinkerton. Have you completed all the necessary preparations incident to Miss Sedley's departure, Miss Jemima?

Miss Jemima. The girls were up at four this morning, packing her trunks, sister. We have made her a bow-pot.

Miss Pinkerton. Say a *bouquet*, sister Jemima. 'Tis more genteel.

Miss Jemima. Well, a booky as big almost as a hay-stack. I have put up two bottles of the gillyflower water for Mrs. Sedley and the receipt for making it, in Amelia's box.

Miss Pinkerton [*rising*]. I trust, Miss Jemima, you

have made a copy of Miss Sedley's account. [MISS JEMIMA *hands her a sheet of paper which she has been holding in her hand.*]

MISS PINKERTON [*as she takes it*]. This is it, is it? [*She looks it over with care.*] Very good — ninety-three pounds, four shillings. Be kind enough to address it to John Sedley, Esquire, and to seal this billet which I have written to his lady.

MISS JEMIMA [*taking the letter*]. How flattered Mrs. Sedley will feel to receive one of your precious autographed epistles! I remember well the beautiful letter of condolence that you wrote after Miss Birch died of the scarlet fever. If anything could have consoled Mrs. Birch for her daughter's loss, it would have been the pious and eloquent composition with which you announced the event.

MISS PINKERTON. I did only my duty.

MISS JEMIMA [*looking at the letter*]. May I read it?

MISS PINKERTON. You may do so. Mayhap it will help to elevate your standards of literary judgment.

MISS JEMIMA [*sits down and reads the letter*]. "The Mall, Chiswick, June 15, 1812. Madam, After her six years' residence at the Mall, I have the honor and happiness of presenting Miss Amelia Sedley to her parents, as a young lady not unworthy to occupy a fitting position in their polished and refined circle." [*Deeply impressed.*] How beautifully phrased! [MISS PINKERTON *shows by her manner that she considers her letter little short of a masterpiece.* MISS JEMIMA *continues her reading.*] "Those accomplishments which become her birth and station will not be found wanting in the amiable Miss Sedley, whose *industry* and *obedience* have endeared her to her instructors, and whose delightful sweetness of temper has charmed her *aged* and her *youthful* companions. In music, in dancing, in orthography, in every variety of embroidery and needlework, she will be found to have realized her friends' *fondest wishes*." [*Looking up from the letter*.] Amelia is well nigh perfect! Indeed, she is!

MISS PINKERTON. Not perfect. Miss Sedley has some obvious weaknesses. One of her deficiencies, I have felt it my duty to call to the attention of her parents. Read on, sister Jemima.

MISS JEMIMA [*reading*]. "In geography there is still much to be desired; and a careful and undeviating use of the blackboard for four hours daily during the next three years is recommended as necessary to the acquirement of that dignified *deportment* and *carriage*, so requisite for every young lady of *fashion*. In the principles of religion and morality, Miss Sedley will be found worthy of an establishment which has been honored by the presence of *The Great Lexicographer* and the patronage of the admirable Mrs. Chapone. In leaving the Mall, Miss Amelia carries with her the hearts of her companions and the affectionate regards of her mistress, who has the honor to subscribe herself, Madam, your most obliged humble servant, Barbara Pinkerton." It is most felicitous. You seldom write a letter, but when you do, what a rare favor!

MISS PINKERTON. I reserve my epistles for truly momentous occasions. There is a postscript regarding Rebecca Sharp, you may read that also.

MISS JEMIMA. "P.S. Miss Sharp accompanies Miss Sedley. It is particularly requested that Miss Sharp's stay in Russell Square may not exceed ten days. The family of distinction with whom she is engaged desire to avail themselves of her services as governess as soon as possible." [*Under her breath*.] Poor Becky!

MISS PINKERTON. Now seal the letter, Jemima, and address the account to Mr. Sedley. [MISS JEMIMA *does as she is bid.*] It is entirely fitting that Mr. Sedley and his lady should feel highly honored that their daughter has been permitted to receive her education at the academy where Dr. Samuel Johnson, The Great Lexicographer, once paid a visit.

Miss Jemima. That is indeed true.

Miss Pinkerton. Miss Jemima, get the Dictionary from the cupboard. I shall follow my invariable custom of presenting one of dear Dr. Johnson's Dictionaries to each scholar departing from the Mall. [Miss Pinkerton *seats herself at the desk.* Miss Jemima *gets two copies from the cupboard, one of which she hands to* Miss Pinkerton. Miss Pinkerton *inscribes and autographs it.* Miss Jemima, *with a rather dubious and timid air, hands her sister the second copy.*] For whom is this, Miss Jemima?

Miss Jemima [*trembling slightly and turning her back on her sister*]. For Becky Sharp. She's going too.

Miss Pinkerton [*with emphasis*]. *Miss Jemima!* Are you in your senses? Replace the Dictionary in the closet and never venture to take such a liberty in the future.

Miss Jemima. Well, sister, it's only two-and-ninepence, and poor Becky will be miserable if she don't get one.

Miss Pinkerton. Rebecca Sharp is a mere articled pupil. I've done quite enough for her without conferring upon her the high honors which deservedly belong to Miss Amelia Sedley as the daughter of a wealthy and influential London merchant. Never venture, I pray you, to associate their names again. [Miss Jemima *replaces the Dictionary.*] Send Miss Sedley instantly to me. Direct Sambo to take the luggage to the coach; order Miss Sharp to assist. [Miss Jemima *trots off, exceedingly flurried and nervous.* Miss Pinkerton *gets a decanter of wine and a dish of seed-cakes and places them on a table in the center of the room.*

Miss Sedley *enters. She wears a large bouquet and carries a bandbox and several small parcels. She curtsies to* Miss Pinkerton, *who beckons her to be seated.*]

Miss Pinkerton. Dear Miss Sedley, after six years' residence at Chiswick Mall, you are now about to venture forth to take up the duties and responsibilities devolving upon a young English gentlewoman of fashion. My dear, remember always the school that has nurtured you. Guide your life by its elegant standards and lofty teachings. Your many charming qualities, my dear, have endeared you to our hearts. Pray accept this little token of our loving esteem. [*She hands her the Dictionary.*]

Miss Sedley. Oh, thank you, Miss Pinkerton.

Miss Pinkerton. May this precious volume remind you constantly of Chiswick Mall and the academy which Dr. Samuel Johnson honored with his august presence. On the fly-leaf of the Dictionary is a copy of the famous Lexicographer's "lines addressed to a young lady on quitting Miss Pinkerton's school." And now, my dear, you must partake of a seedcake and refresh yourself with a sip of wine. [*She pours some wine into a glass and hands it to Amelia, and places the plate of seedcakes beside her.*]

Miss Jemima [*outside*]. You'll go in and say good-by to Miss Pinkerton, won't you, Becky?

Miss Sharp [*outside*]. I suppose I must. [Miss Sharp *knocks at the door.*]

Miss Pinkerton. Come in. [Miss Sharp *enters, curtsies, goes straight up to* Miss Pinkerton, *and speaks in perfect French.*]

Miss Sharp. Mademoiselle, je viens vous faire mes adieux. [Miss Pinkerton, *not understanding a word of French, bites her lips, waves a hand in way of adieu, and gives* Miss Sharp *an opportunity of shaking one of her fingers.*]

MISS PINKERTON. Miss Sharp, I wish you good morning. [MISS SHARP *folds her hands, with a frigid smile, bows, and quite declines to accept the proffered honor.*]

MISS PINKERTON [*with an indignant toss of her venerable, Roman-nosed, and turban-crowned head*]. For five-and-thirty years, I have never seen the individual who has dared in my own house to be so rude to me. Miss Sharp, you are quite devoid of any sense of gratitude, gratitude due me as your benefactress. I have nourished a viper in my bosom!

MISS SHARP. A viper — a fiddlestick! [MISS PINKERTON *nearly faints with astonishment.*] You took me in because I was useful. There is no question of gratitude between us. I hate this place, and I'm glad I'm leaving it for good and ever.

MISS PINKERTON. Are you aware, Miss Sharp, that you are addressing Miss Pinkerton? [BECKY *shrugs her shoulders and laughs.* MISS PINKERTON *struggles to hide her anger, and turns to* AMELIA]. Heaven bless you, my child! [*She embraces* AMELIA, *scowling the while over* AMELIA'S *shoulder at* BECKY SHARP.] Now Amelia, I shall summon your fellow students that they may bid you farewell. When you have quite finished your refreshments, join us in the hall. [*She goes out. In a moment* MISS JEMIMA *enters.*]

MISS JEMIMA [*going to* AMELIA *and giving her a small package*]. It's some sandwiches, my dear. You may be hungry, you know.

MISS SEDLEY. Thank you. It is most kind and thoughtful of you.

MISS JEMIMA. You will excuse me now — I must go and make certain that Sambo has arranged your flowers, presents, trunks, and bonnet boxes in the carriage. I will make sure, Miss Sharp, that your small cowskin trunk is with

Miss Sedley's luggage. [*She hesitates a moment, and then goes to the cupboard and gets a Dictionary.*] And Becky, Becky Sharp, here's a book for you that my sister — that is, I — Johnson's Dictionary, you know; you must not leave without that. Perhaps, Becky, you would better put it under your cloak until you are in the carriage. [*She hands* MISS SHARP *the Dictionary.*] Good-by! God bless you! [MISS JEMIMA *goes out.* MISS SHARP *angrily throws the Dictionary on the floor.*]

MISS SEDLEY. Oh, Rebecca, how can you do so?

MISS SHARP. I hate the whole house! I hope I may never set eyes on it again! I wish it were in the bottom of the Thames, I do; and if Miss Pinkerton were there, I wouldn't pick her out, that I wouldn't. Oh, how I should like to see her floating in the water yonder, turban and all, with her train streaming after her, and her nose like the beak of a wherry.

MISS SEDLEY. Hush, oh, please, hush!

MISS SHARP. Why, do you think Miss Pinkerton will come in and punish me by making me stay in this black hole? Indeed, she won't. She's too glad to get rid of me.

MISS SEDLEY. Be silent, Rebecca, please be silent.

MISS SHARP. I hope she will hear me and know that I hate her with all my soul. For two years I have had only insults and outrage from her. I have been treated worse than any servant in the kitchen. I have never had a friend or a kind word, except from you. I have been made to tend the little girls in the lower schoolroom, and to talk French, until I grew sick of my mother tongue. But talking French to Miss Pinkerton is capital fun, isn't it? She doesn't know a word of French and is too proud to confess it. I believe it is that which has made her part with me, and so thank heaven for French. *Vive La France! Vive l'Empereur!*

A setting for *Twelfth Night* showing Olivia's garden.

Vive Bonaparte! [*She runs to* AMELIA *and embraces her ecstatically.*]

AMELIA. Oh, Rebecca, Rebecca, for shame!

MISS SHARP. I know that to say "Long live Bonaparte" here in England is as much as to say "Long Live Lucifer." Still I say "Long live *l'Empereur! Vive la France!*"

MISS SEDLEY. How can you, how dare you have such wicked, revengeful thoughts? [MISS PINKERTON'S *voice is heard outside.*]

MISS PINKERTON. Come, Amelia, all the dear friends, all the young ladies, and the dancing master are here in the hall ready to bid you farewell.

MISS SEDLEY. Yes, Miss Pinkerton.

MISS PINKERTON. Miss Sharp, bring Miss Amelia's bandbox and parcels instantly. [REBECCA *frowns;* AMELIA *puts down her glass, picks up some of her parcels, and goes out.* MISS SHARP *gathers up the remaining parcels and the bandbox.*]

MISS PINKERTON [*impatiently and loudly*]. Miss Sharp, did you hear me call?

MISS SHARP [*quite out of temper*]. There's that old vixen again. I shall be happy when I've seen and heard the last of her. [*She sees the Dictionary, picks it up, and in a sudden burst of anger tears it to pieces. While she is doing this, those in the hall are bidding* AMELIA *good-by. Among the speeches heard are:* "Here is a little present for you, Amelia." "Send your letters under cover of my grandpapa, the Earl of Dexter." "Write every day, you dear darling Amelia! When I write to you, I shall call you Mamma." [*Good-byes, kisses, and* AMELIA'S *declarations of thanks punctuate these speeches. The sound of their voices diminishes as they leave the hall and go out to the coach.*]

MISS SHARP [*throwing the torn leaves of the Dictionary about the room.*] Revenge may be wicked, but it's natural. [*She*

tosses the mutilated and empty covers on the floor.]   I'm no
angel.   [*She exits hastily with the box and packages.   In a few
moments the bang of the front door is heard as* BECKY *slams it
behind her.   Enter* MISS JEMIMA.   *She sees the paper strewn
about.*]

MISS JEMIMA.   Well, I never!   [*What has occurred slowly
dawns upon her.   She picks up the covers and the torn leaves.*]
What an audacious young minx!

CURTAIN

PART IV

BIBLIOGRAPHY

A LIST OF PLAYS AND BOOKS RELATED
TO THE DRAMA[1]

FULL-LENGTH PLAYS

Modern American Drama

The Arrow Maker, by Mary Austin.

A drama in three acts.

Houghton.

9 M.   9 W.   Others.

A hut and two exteriors.

Indian costumes.

Royalty, twenty-five dollars.

This tragic story of a heroic medicine woman is recommended
for the reading list of the senior high school.

White Wings, by Philip Barry.

A play in three acts.

French.

14 M.   2 W.

Two exteriors.

American costumes of 1895, 1907, and 1915.

Royalty on application to the publisher.

"This was generally conceded by the critics to be one of the
most charming and subtle comedies ever written by an American.
It has to do with the passing of an epoch in American civilization.
. . . The story tells the novel if pathetic effort of a whole family
of white wings (street cleaners) to maintain the dignity of their

---

[1] It is needless to state that these lists are far from complete.   The compiler
offers it as a suggestion merely.

profession in the face of opposition from the advance of the automobile." (Publisher's notice.)

This play is difficult for high schools to stage. It should, however, prove delightful reading to students of the twelfth grade.

You and I, by Philip Barry.
>A comedy in three acts.
>French.
>Two interiors.
>Modern costumes.
>Royalty, fifty dollars.

The problem deals with an artist of limited income and a fixed standard of living who tries to gain the full realization of his ideals and abilities and not to defer marriage unreasonably long.

You and I is the ninth prize play written by a student of Prof. George Baker's "47 Workshop" class at Harvard and is an interesting play for the reading list of the eleventh and twelfth grades.

The Goose Hangs High, by Lewis Beach.
>A comedy in three acts.
>Little; Baker; French.
>7 M. 6 W.
>One interior.
>Modern costumes.
>Royalty, fifty dollars.

Their father's grave financial problems bring the three thoughtless, selfish Ingals children to their senses. The play brings out the inherent fineness of modern American boys and girls.

This excellent comedy of present-day American life is enjoyed by the senior high school and is good for presentation.

The Return of Peter Grimm, by David Belasco.
>A play in three acts.
>In *Modern American Plays*, edited by George P. Baker (Harcourt); and in *Representative Plays by American Dramatists*, edited by Montrose J. Moses (Dutton).
>8 M. 3 W.

One interior.

Modern costumes.

Royalty on application to the author.

Peter Grimm wishes his niece, Catherine, to marry Frederick Grimm. To please her uncle, she promises to do so. Death suddenly overtakes Peter Grimm. His perturbed spirit then hovers about the house, for Peter now knows that the marriage he longed for is a mistake. Finally, with a young, sensitive, dying lad as the medium of communication, he gets his message to Catherine. "There is more in this play to commend than central characterization. Deft touch after touch makes us swiftly feel that we are on the borderland between the real and the unreal; and the difficult atmosphere, once created, is perfectly sustained." (George P. Baker.)

This is suitable reading in the eleventh and twelfth grades but rather unsuited to presentation.

The Yellow Jacket, by J. Harry Berimo and George C. Hazelton.

A Chinese play done in the Chinese manner in three acts.

Houghton.

14 M.   12 W.

Chinese interior.

Chinese costumes.

Royalty on application to the publisher.

Much liked by mature students. It is difficult but not impossible for seniors to stage.

Wappin' Wharf, by Charles S. Brooks.

A comedy in two acts.

Harcourt.

6 M.   3 W.

One simple interior.

Pirate costumes.

Royalty on application to the publisher.

Here is a worth-while pirate story, readily presented by high-school students.

Queen Victoria, by David Carb and Walter Prichard Eaton.
A play in seven episodes.
Dutton.
12 M.   4 W.   Extras.
Four interiors.
Costumes of Queen Victoria's day.
Royalty on application to the publisher.
Students of the twelfth grade enjoy reading this historical drama.

The Beggar on Horseback, by Marc Connelly and George S. Kaufman.
A fantastic comedy in three acts.
Boni & Liveright; French.
22 M.   7 W.
Several interiors and exteriors.
Modern and fantastic costumes.
Royalty on application to the publisher.
A young composer, in love with a poor girl, dreams that he has married a rich woman for the sake of her money.   The scenes presenting the distorted vision show the artist as a slave to wealth and to an uncongenial family.

The satire and romance of this drama are interesting to pupils of the senior class.   Production would be most difficult.

He and She, by Rachel Crothers.
A domestic drama in three acts.
In *Representative American Plays*, edited by Arthur H. Quinn (Century).
3 M.   5 W.
Two interiors.
Modern costumes.
Royalty on application to the publisher.
A husband and wife both submit designs for a frieze.   The wife wins the large reward, and a domestic schism seems imminent. The welfare of their seventeen-year-old daughter makes the wife realize that her first duty is to her home.   She gives up the prize.

This play, one of the best written by an American dramatist, will be enjoyed by some of the twelfth graders.

The Shepherd, by Olive Tilford Dargan.
A play in three acts.
Scribner.
14 M. 5 W. Others.
One interior (a peasant house in Russia).
Russian costumes of 1905.
Royalty on application to the publisher.
The play gives a most interesting story of a brave fellow's struggle to curb mob violence, and is well worth study and presentation in the upper senior high school.

The Detour, by Owen Davis.
A play in three acts.
French; Little.
5 M. 4 W.
One interior, one exterior.
Modern costumes.
Royalty on application to the publisher.
"A simple picture of life as it is lived on a Long Island farm." (Owen Davis.)
This well-worked-out study of a brave woman's attempt to free herself and her daughter from the stupefying effects of a rural environment is excellent reading for the senior high school. It might prove a good play for thoughtful twelfth graders to present.

Icebound, by Owen Davis.
A play in three acts.
Longmans.
6 M. 6 W.
Two interiors.
Modern costumes.
Royalty, twenty-five dollars.
This realistic study of northern Maine small-town folk has a place on the eleventh- and twelfth-grade reading list.

The Family Upstairs, by Harry Delf.
A comedy of American life in three acts.
French.
4 M.   5 W.
One interior.
Modern costumes.
Royalty on application to the publisher.
An over-officious and anxious mother meddles in the love affair
of her daughter and nearly disrupts matters.
This drama might easily be acted, although it is more frequently
reserved for the high-school reading list.

The Road to Yesterday, by Beulah M. Dix and Evelyn G. Suther-
land.
A comedy of fantasy in four acts.
French.
8 M.   6 W.
Three interiors.
Modern and Elizabethan costumes.
Royalty, twenty-five dollars.
A young girl dreams she is living in the days of Shakespeare.
She goes through thrilling experiences.   The play is much liked
by the senior high school.

The Rose of Plymouth Town, by Beulah M. Dix and Evelyn G.
Sutherland.
A romantic comedy in four acts.
Dramatic Publishing Society.
4 M.   4 W.
One interior, one exterior.
Costumes of the period of 1622 in New England.
Royalty, ten dollars.
This is a pleasant and not too difficult comedy for presentation.
Miles Standish is introduced into the romance.

The Lost Pleiad, by Jane Dransfield.
A poetic fantasy in two acts.
Little.

10 M. 8 W. Extras.

One simple exterior. The play lends itself admirably to outdoor performance.

Greek costumes.

Royalty on application to the publisher.

The play is based on the myth of the Pleiad who came to earth to marry a mortal. Several high schools have found this excellent for presentation.

Minick, by Edna Ferber and George S. Kaufman.

A comedy in three acts.

Doubleday; Baker.

6 M. 9 W.

One interior.

Modern costumes.

Royalty, twenty-five dollars.

Old man Minick takes up his residence with his son and daughter-in-law. He soon finds that their interests clash hopelessly. The old man takes matters into his own hands and goes to join some of his cronies at a home for the aged. Eleventh and twelfth graders enjoy reading this amazingly truthful portrayal of middle-class American home life.

Beau Brummel, by Clyde Fitch.

A play in four acts.

French.

12 M. 7 W. Extras.

Five interiors, one exterior.

English costumes of the eighteenth century.

Royalty, twenty-five dollars.

The title part in this tragic story was made famous by Richard Mansfield. The drama is good reading for the senior high school. Since the characterizations are subtle, the play is difficult for secondary-school presentation.

Nathan Hale, by Clyde Fitch.

A play in four acts.

Baker.

11 M.   4 W.   1 J.

Three interiors, a tent, two exteriors.

Costumes of the revolutionary period.

Royalty, ten dollars.

This is an admirable serious play for the senior high school to present.

Children of the Moon, by Martin Flavin.

A play in three acts.

French; Brentano's.

5 M.   3 W.

One interior.

Modern costumes.

Royalty, twenty-five dollars.

A tragic study of a selfish mother who uses fear of inherited insanity as an argument to prevent her daughter marrying the man she loves.

This play has its place on the twelfth-grade reading list.   It is not suitable for high-school presentation.

Miss Lulu Bett, by Zona Gale.

An American comedy of manners in three acts.

Appleton.

4 M.   5 W.

Two interiors, one exterior.

Modern costumes.

Royalty, twenty-five dollars.

Winner of the Pulitzer drama prize in 1921.

"A milestone in American Drama."   (Thomas Dickinson.)

"She was depicting uninspired American life (almost for the first time in our literature) and she held fast to the ideals of American family conversation."   (Robert C. Benchley.)

The story is woven around Lulu, a colorless household drudge, living in the house of her sister and brother-in-law.

Although not suitable for high-school presentation, this makes an interesting play for the twelfth-grade reading list.

Master Will of Stratford, by Louise A. Garnett.

A Midwinter-Night's Dream in three acts with a prologue and an epilogue.

Macmillan.

17 M.   10 W.   Others.

One exterior, one interior.

Elizabethan costumes.

Royalty on application to the publisher.

This faithful picture of Shakespeare as a lad is excellent drama for senior-high-school presentation.

A Poor Little Rich Girl, by Eleanor Gates.

"A fairy play of to-day" in three acts.

French.

17 M.   7 W.

Two interiors, four exteriors.

Fanciful costumes.

Royalty, twenty-five dollars.

"At once a work of genuine fancy and sound art, and a work standing to the wholesome credit of the all too scantily filled ledger of imaginative American dramatic writing." (George Jean Nathan.)

The staging of this play presents several physical difficulties.

Alice in Wonderland, by Alice Gerstenberg.

A comedy in three acts.

Allyn and Bacon; Little.

13 M.   4 W.

Four interiors, three exteriors.

Royalty, twenty-five dollars.

This dramatization of Lewis Carroll's *Alice's Adventures in Wonderland* and *Through a Looking-Glass* contains good acting material for the junior high school.

Inheritors, by Susan Glaspell.

A play in three acts.

Dodd.

10 M.   6 W.

Two interiors.

Modern costumes.

Royalty, twenty-five dollars.

The drama tells the story of Madeline Morton's efforts to carry on her father's ideal of freedom of thought.   It belongs in the twelfth-grade reading list.

So This is London, by Arthur Goodrich.

A comedy in three acts.

French.

7 M.   4 W.

Three interiors.

Modern costumes.

Royalty, twenty-five dollars.

An American and an English family, brought together in consequence of the engagement of a son and daughter, have their foolish notions regarding one another dispelled.

Its presentation is wholesome in the senior high school.

Caponsacchi, by Arthur Goodrich and Rose A. Palmer.

A play in three acts and an epilogue based on Robert Browning's poem, "The Ring and the Book."

Appleton.

21 M.   5 W.   Extras.

Four interiors, two exteriors.

Seventeenth-century Italian costumes.

Royalty on application to the publisher.

"I am very glad that this play is being published, as it deserves the permanent form of print."   (William Lyon Phelps.)

Some of the most intelligent of the twelfth grade will care to read this play.

In Abraham's Bosom, by Paul Green.

Drama in seven scenes.

McBride.

9 M.   3 W.

Three interiors, two exteriors.

Costumes of about 1885.

Royalty on application to the publisher.

This study of negro life in the eastern section of North Carolina won the Pulitzer prize in 1927. It merits a place on the reading list of the twelfth grade.

Captain Applejack, by Walter Hackett.

A farcical comedy in three acts.

French.

6 M. 5 W.

Two interiors.

Modern and fantastic costumes.

Royalty on application to the publisher.

Ambrose Applejack longs for adventure and love. His wish is fulfilled without the trouble of leaving his own home. The stirring quality of the play, with its crooks, pirates, and theatricality, makes a great appeal to high-school boys. The play has been presented many times by amateurs.

Hell-Bent fer Heaven, by Hatcher Hughes.

A play in three acts.

French.

5 M. 2 W.

One interior (the Hunt home in the Carolina Mountains).

Mountaineers' costumes.

Royalty on application to the publisher.

This vivid, tragic drama of mountain life, which won the Pulitzer Prize in 1924, is appealing reading for young people of the twelfth grade. It is not recommended for school presentation.

Dulcy, by George S. Kaufman and Marc Connelly.

A comedy in three acts.

French; also in Cohen's *Longer Plays by Modern Authors,* Putnam.

8 M. 3 W.

One interior.

Modern costumes.

Royalty, twenty-five dollars.

Dulcy, a talkative woman, in her eagerness to be of help, gets matters into an almost hopeless state of confusion.

Not only is this play good reading for the senior high school, but a senior class would find it worth-while light comedy to present.

Merton of the Movies, by George Kaufman and Marc Connelly.
A comedy in four acts.
French.
21 M. 6 W.
Two exteriors, three interiors.
Modern costumes.
Royalty, twenty-five dollars.

This satire of the cinema affords interesting reading for the senior high school but is difficult to stage.

The Show-Off: A Transcript of Life, by George Kelly.
A comedy in three acts.
French.
6 M. 3 W.
One interior.
Modern costumes.
Royalty on application to the publisher.

"I might as well begin boldly and say that *The Show-Off* is the best comedy which has yet been written by an American. . . . George Kelly builds up the case for Aubrey Piper by countless small strokes. By degrees he opens up the heart of the man. There he stands — liar, braggart, egotist, but the consistency of his faults colors them with magnificence." (Heywood Broun.)

This characterization makes good reading for the senior high school and is well worth presentation by juniors or seniors.

Craig's Wife, by George Kelly.
A drama in three acts.
French.
5 M. 6 W.
One interior.

Modern costumes.

Royalty on application to the publisher.

"People who live to themselves, Harriet, are generally left to themselves." (*Miss Austen*, one of the characters in the play.)

Although too mature for high-school production, many twelfth-grade students enjoy reading it.

Caliban by the Yellow Sands, by Percy MacKaye.

A community masque of the art of the theater devised and written to commemorate the tercentenary of the death of Shakespeare.

Doubleday.

A very large cast of characters.

The setting of the entire masque is architectural and scenic, not a background of natural landscape as in the case of most outdoor pageants.

Elaborate costumes representing many nations and many periods.

Royalty on application to the publisher.

Although extremely well conceived and written, this masque is probably too long and intricate for most high-school students.

The Canterbury Pilgrims, by Percy MacKaye.

A comedy in four acts.

Macmillan.

43 M. 7 W. Others.

Two interiors, two exteriors.

Early English costumes.

Royalty on application to the publisher.

Here is a costume play, based on Chaucer's *Canterbury Tales*, often presented by high schools.

Jeanne D'Arc, by Percy MacKaye.

A tragedy in five acts.

Macmillan.

33 M. 9 W. Others.

Two interiors, four exteriors.

French costumes of the early fifteenth century.

Royalty on application to the publisher.

This is not only interesting reading, but it might well be staged by senior-high-school students.

Kinfolk of Robin Hood, by Percy MacKaye.

A play in four acts.

French.

23 M.   7 W.

One interior, two exteriors.

Old English costumes.

Royalty, ten dollars.

Written for production by a boys' school, this pleasant telling of the adventures of the famous outlaw takes about one hour and a half to act.   It is worth-while material for eighth- and ninth-grade presentation.

Sanctuary, by Percy MacKaye.

A bird masque.

Stokes.

4 M.   2 W.   Others.

The scene is the sylvan glade of a bird sanctuary.

Fanciful costumes.

Royalty on application to the publisher.

"This masque was written for the dedication of the bird sanctuary of the Meriden Bird Club of Meriden, New Hampshire." (Author.)

A few of the more mature members of the senior high school enjoy reading this.

The Scarecrow; or, The Glass of Truth, by Percy MacKaye.

A tragedy of the ludicrous in four acts.

Macmillan.

10 M.   6 W.

Two interiors.

New England costumes of the late seventeenth century.

Royalty on application to the publisher.

"In *Mosses from an Old Manse*, the Moralized Legend, 'Feather-top,' relates, in some twenty pages of its author's inimitable style, how Mother Rigby, a reputed witch of old New England days, converted a corn-patch scarecrow into the semblance of a fine gentleman of the period; how she dispatched this semblance to 'play its part in the great world, where not one man in a hundred,' she affirmed, 'was gifted with more real substance than itself.' " (Author.) This play is recommended for reading in the senior high school, and it should be an excellent drama for older students to present.

A Thousand Years Ago, by Percy MacKaye.

A romantic comedy in four acts.

French.

9 M. 2 W. Extras.

Fantastic settings.

Chinese and fancy costumes.

Royalty, fifty dollars.

"The present play is an original comedy, of which certain elements in the plot have been suggested by the old Persian tale which is the theme of the eighteenth-century Italian comedy *Turandotte*, by Carlo Gozzi, translated into German by Friedrich Schiller. It is not a revision or rewriting of that work. It is an entirely new play." (Author.)

Washington; The Man Who Made Us, by Percy MacKaye.

A ballad play in prologue, three acts, and epilogue.

Knopf.

29 M. 9 W. Extras.

Numerous settings.

Costumes of the Revolutionary War period.

Royalty on application to the publisher.

"Theme — the relation of the will of Washington to the world's will." (Author.)

This play is long and difficult to stage; but, if judiciously cut, it can be acted by older high-school students.

Cranford, by Marguerite Merington.

A comedy in three acts from Mrs. Gaskell's famous story.

Duffield.

1 M.   9 W.

One interior.

English costumes of the time of King William the Fourth.

Royalty on application to the publisher.

This comedy is easy to present in any grade from the ninth through the twelfth.

The King's Henchman, by Edna St. Vincent Millay.

Play in three acts.

Harper.

19 M.   15 W.   1 J.   Extras.

Numerous settings.

Early English costumes.

Royalty on application to the publisher.

"*The King's Henchman* is a lyric drama of Saxon England, a play of rare beauty dealing with a story of profound passion and treacherous love." (Publisher's notice.)

This is for the reading list of the more intelligent members of the twelfth grade.

The Lamp and the Bell, by Edna St. Vincent Millay.

Historical verse in five acts.

Appleton; Harper; Baker.

13 M.   21 W.   8 J.   Others.

Numerous settings.

Costumes of the Elizabethan period.

Royalty, twenty-five dollars.

This rather spectacular and elaborate play is suitable for presentation in the twelfth grade by a group of girls.

The Great Divide, by William Vaughn Moody.

A play in three acts.

Houghton.

10 M.   3 W.   1 J.

Two interiors, one exterior (difficult).

Royalty on application to the publisher.

"They [*The Great Divide* and *The Faith Healer*] are now generally recognized as among the most encouraging signs of the possibility of an American drama that shall be at once popular, powerful, and worthily conceived." (John M. Manly.)

This is recommended for reading only in the last year of the high school.

Fashion, by Anna Cora Mowatt.

A comedy in five acts.

French.

8 M. 5 W.

Simple, old-fashioned interiors.

American costumes of 1850.

No royalty.

Senior-high-school students take keen delight in acting this play, which is one of our best examples of mid-nineteenth-century American melodrama.

Beyond the Horizon, by Eugene G. O'Neill.

A play in three acts.

Boni & Liveright.

6 M. 4 W.

One interior, two exteriors.

Modern costumes.

Royalty on application to the publisher.

O'Neill has given us here a serious and powerful portrayal of a young New England artist's struggle to rise above his farm environment. This proves a most valuable drama for study in the twelfth grade.

The Emperor Jones, by Eugene G. O'Neill.

A tragic play in eight scenes.

Appleton; Boni & Liveright.

3 M. 1 W. Many minor characters.

One interior, six exteriors.

West Indian costumes.

Royalty on application to the publisher.

"The action of the play takes place on an island in the West Indies as yet not self-determined by the White Mariner. The form of native government is, for the time being, an empire."

This tragedy makes challenging reading for ninth-, tenth-, eleventh-, and twelfth-grade students. It is difficult to present but possible if done with very simplified settings.

Marco Millions, by Eugene O'Neill.

A play in a prologue, three acts, and an epilogue.

Boni & Liveright.

29 M.   2 W.   Others.

Eight interiors, three exteriors.

Royalty on application to the publisher.

"It is finely imaginative; it persuades to the recognition of the beauty that surrounds us, wholly missed by the large race of Babbitts." (George P. Baker.)

The play is highly recommended for the reading list of the twelfth grade.

The Piper, by Josephine P. Peabody.

A poetic drama in four acts.

Houghton; French.

14 M.   5 W.   5 J.   Others.

Two exteriors, one cavern.

German costumes of 1284.

Royalty, twenty-five dollars.

Based on the story which Robert Browning used in his poem, the play is much liked by high-school students of all ages. If simply staged, it is most appropriate to high-school needs.

The Wolf of Gubbio, by Josephine P. Peabody.

A comedy in three acts.

Houghton.

13 M.   8 W.   3 J.   Others.

Two exteriors (difficult).

Italian costumes of 700 years ago.

Royalty on application to the publisher.

This leisurely but charming telling of the story of Saint Francis of Assisi has a place on the reading list of the senior high school.

The Jazz Singer, by Samson Raphaelson.

A comedy drama in three acts.

Brentano's.

15 M.   5 W.

One interior, one "back stage" of the Music Box Theatre, New York.

Modern costumes.

Royalty on application to the publisher.

"American life, in this year 1925, consists essentially of surfaces. . . . In seeking a symbol of the vital chaos of America's soul, I find no more adequate one than jazz.   I hear jazz, and I am given a vision of cathedrals and temples collapsing and, silhouetted against the setting sun, a solitary figure, a lost soul, dancing grotesquely in the ruin. . . . Thus do I see the jazz singer. . . . I have used a Jewish youth as my protagonist, because the Jews are determining the nature and scope of jazz more than any other race.   You find the soul of a people in the songs they sing.   You find the meaning of the songs in the souls of the minstrels who create and interpret them.   In *The Jazz Singer* I have attempted an explanation of the soul of one of these minstrels." (Author.)

Most interesting reading for eleventh- and twelfth-grade students, it is possible of production by skillful high-school seniors.

Clarence, by Booth Tarkington.

A comedy in four acts.

French.

5 M.   5 W.

Two interiors.

Modern costumes.

Royalty, twenty-five dollars.

Clarence's humble and obscure share in the World War was driving mules in Texas. Later, as employee in the wealthy Wheeler household, he brings harmony out of seemingly hopeless discord.

This admirable comedy of American life is excellent material in the senior high school for reading and for acting.

Intimate Strangers, by Booth Tarkington.
> A comedy in three acts.
> French.
> 4 M.   4 W.
> Two interiors.
> Modern costumes.
> Royalty, twenty-five dollars.

A lawyer meets at a small, forlorn railway station an attractive woman who, like himself, is stranded by the storm. The lawyer visits the lady's house. Intimacy grows and also keen concern on the man's part regarding the woman's age. Though a charming comedy, delightfully written, the story is rather slender. It forms pleasant reading for students of the senior high school

Come Out of the Kitchen, by A. E. Thomas.
> A comedy in three acts.
> French.
> 6 M.   5 W.
> Three interiors.
> Modern costumes.
> Royalty, twenty-five dollars.

The story is written around a Virginia family, who, finding themselves financially embarrassed, decide to rent their magnificent home to a rich Yankee. One of the conditions stipulates that a competent staff of white servants should be engaged. One of the daughters of the house conceives the madcap idea that she, her sister, and two brothers shall act as the domestic staff. This entertaining comedy is worthy of presentation in the senior high school.

The Copperhead, by Augustus Thomas.

A drama in four acts.

French.

7 M.   4 W.

One exterior, one interior.

Costumes of 1861 and 1903.

Royalty, twenty-five dollars.

The plot concerns a man who, under orders of President Lincoln, became a spy.   Hated and maligned for many years, he was at last revealed in his true character, a loyal hero.

Especially appropriate is this for study and presentation in upper grades of the senior high school.

Oliver Goldsmith, by Augustus Thomas.

A comedy in three acts.

French.

18 M.   6 W.

Three interiors.

Costumes of 1775.

Royalty, twenty-five dollars.

A place on the senior-high-school reading list should be given to this drama.

Sun-Up, by Lula Vollmer.

A play in three acts.

Longmans.

7 M.   2 W.

One simple cabin interior.

Mountaineer costumes.

Royalty, fifty dollars.

The scene of this gripping drama is a typical mountain cabin in western North Carolina.   The play brings home the futility and horror of hatred and warfare.   Splendid reading for senior-high-school students. It is difficult to act but not impossible for serious-minded young people.

The Home-Makers, by Maude B. Vosburgh.
A play of the Pilgrims in three acts.
French.
10 M.   6 W.   6 J.
Two simple sets.
Costumes of the period.
No royalty.
"Dramatic material from the original Pilgrim narratives and
letters is here condensed into situation, and dialogue that retains
the pithy mother-wit and rhythmical vigor of the early Stuart
speech." (Publisher's notice.)
Good material for the junior high school.

Snow White and the Seven Dwarfs, by Jessie Braham White.
A fairy-tale play in seven scenes.
French.
13 M.   11 W.   Extras.
Settings are easily managed.
Fairy costumes.
Royalty, twenty-five dollars.
This very lovely telling of the famous old fairy tale was produced
with great success by Winthrop Ames at his Little Theatre, New
York.   High-school students of all ages enjoy presenting this play.

Modern English Drama

The Admirable Crichton, by Sir James M. Barrie.
A comedy in four acts.
Scribner; French.
8 M.   6 W.   Extras.
Two interiors, one exterior.
Modern costumes.
Royalty, fifty dollars.
Lord Loam and his family are wrecked on a desert island.
Crichton, the family butler, becomes, by right of ability, their
leader.   He announces his engagement to Lord Loam's eldest

daughter just as a rescue ship is sighted. This remarkable study of social equality is one of the few modern comedies worthy of careful study and presentation by senior-high-school students.

Alice-Sit-by-the-Fire, by Sir James M. Barrie.
    A comedy in three acts.
    Scribner; French.
    4 M.   5 W.
    Two interiors.
    Modern costumes.
    Royalty on application to the publisher.
    In this charming play which girls of the senior class enjoy reading, a romantic adolescent daughter tries frantically to save her wise mother from an imaginary danger.

Dear Brutus, by Sir James M. Barrie.
    A comedy in three acts.
    Scribner; French.
    5 M.   6 W.
    One interior, one exterior.
    Modern costumes.
    Royalty on application to the publisher.
    Dear Brutus deals with the theme: What would we do with our lives if we had another chance?
    Too difficult for high-school students to act, it is excellent for the senior-class reading list.

A Kiss for Cinderella, by Sir James M. Barrie.
    A comedy in three acts.
    Scribner.
    9 M.   8 W.   Others.
    Four interiors, one exterior.
    Modern costumes.
    Royalty on application to the publisher.
    A poor girl with suppressed desires has, in her dream, a Cinderella experience.
    Here is a good play for senior-high-school presentation.

Mary Rose, by Sir James M. Barrie.
A play in three acts.
Scribner.
5 M.   3 W.
One interior, one exterior.
Modern costumes.
Royalty on application to the publisher.
In this serious comedy, beautifully worked out, the elfin-like Mary Rose mysteriously disappears.   After a time her spirit returns to its old haunts and to its loved ones.
Although rather too subtle in its hidden meanings to be enjoyed by all, some mature seniors take great pleasure in reading it.

Peter Pan, by Sir James M. Barrie.
A fairy play.
Scribner.
Numerous characters including several children.
Various and difficult settings.
Modern and fanciful costumes.
Royalty on application to the publisher.
This entrancing fairy play belongs on the reading lists of the junior and senior high schools.   If judiciously cut and simply staged, it is excellent for presentation by the older students.

Quality Street, by Sir James M. Barrie.
A comedy in four acts.
Scribner; French.
7 M.   6 W.   Several children.
One interior.
Costumes of the period of the Napoleonic War.
Royalty on application to the publisher.
Here is an excellent comedy for senior-class presentation, particularly for girls' schools.

What Every Woman Knows, by Sir James M. Barrie.
A comedy in four acts.
Scribner; French.

6 M.   4 W.   Extras.

Four interiors.

Modern Scottish costumes.

Royalty on application to the publisher.

Maggie Shand, who thinks she lacks charm, shows her Scottish canniness when she saves her husband from the mesmerism of self-conceit and a shallow woman's pretty face. This brilliant play is splendid material for study in the senior class, but almost too difficult for high-school presentation.

The Great Adventure, by Arnold Bennett.

A play of fancy in four acts.

Doran; Baker.

15 M.   3 W.

Four interiors.

Modern costumes.

Royalty, twenty-five dollars.

A highly sensitive artist, Ilom Carve, weary of adulation, disappears. His valet dies. His body is mistaken for that of his master and is buried at Westminster Abbey.

Juniors and seniors find this particularly interesting reading.

The Title, by Arnold Bennett.

A comedy in three acts.

Doran.

4 M.   4 W.

One interior.

Modern costumes.

Royalty on application to the publisher.

The Title deals with English class feeling and makes worth-while material for the twelfth-grade reading list.

What the Public Wants, by Arnold Bennett.

A comedy in four acts.

Doran.

8 M.   5 W.

Two interiors.

Modern costumes.

Royalty on application to the publisher.

The story of a newspaper publisher who changes his practice of printing "what the public wants." It may be read by the more mature seniors.

Milestones, by Arnold Bennett and Edward Knoblock.

A comedy in three acts.

Doran; Baker.

10 M.   5 W.

One interior.

English costumes of 1860, 1885, and 1912.

Royalty, twenty-five dollars.

"A contrast between three generations. A study in the clash which is ever in progress between the generous audacities of youth and the jealous cautions of old age." (Publisher's announcement.)

This play is for the eleventh- and twelfth-grade reading list since the characterization is too difficult for actors of high-school age.

Hobson's Choice, by Harold Brighouse.

Comedy in three acts.

French.

7 M.   5 W.

Three interiors.

Modern costumes.

Royalty, twenty-five dollars.

"An epitome of Lancashire life, or at any rate of that stratum defined in England as 'the lower middle class,' that class which Henry Horatio Hobson would proclaim as 'the backbone of society.'" (B. Iden Payne.)

For the senior-high-school reading list. Older high-school pupils find pleasure in presenting this *genre* comedy.

Magic, by Gilbert K. Chesterton.

A fantastic comedy in a prelude and three acts.

Putnam.

6 M.   1 W.

Modern costumes.

One interior.

Royalty on application to the publisher.

"Mr. Chesterton calls his play a fantastic comedy. It is a blend of the real and the unreal, of the tangible and the impalpable. The perversities of individuals and the failings of the age take shape in the atmosphere of conjury in which the play is steeped." (Publisher's notice.)

This makes an interesting play for the twelfth-grade reading list.

A Bill of Divorcement, by Clemence Dane.

A drama in three acts.

Macmillan.

5 M. 4 W.

One interior.

Modern costumes.

Royalty on application to the publisher.

This tragic drama considers the problem of an English household in which the master of the home has been incapacitated by shell shock and mental derangement. Although not suited to amateur presentation, it will prove interesting to some seniors because of its excellence as a play.

The Mollusc, by Hubert Davies.

A comedy in three acts.

Baker.

2 M. 2 W.

One interior.

Modern costumes.

Royalty, twenty-five dollars.

A story of an attempt to reform a woman who works hard to indulge her mollusclike laziness. This play is liked by senior high-school students. It is well worth presenting if one feels justified in spending upon such a small cast the time necessary to produce a play.

Crossings, by Walter de la Mare.
  A fairy play.
  Knopf.
  11 M.   10 W.   Children.   Others.
  Three interiors, one exterior.
  The costumes are modern and fanciful.
  Royalty on application to the publisher.
  This fascinating story of how four motherless children spent two weeks alone at "Crossings" appeals to the same audience that loves *Peter Pan.*   It is delightful when staged.

Abraham Lincoln, by John Drinkwater.
  Play in six scenes.
  Houghton.
  37 M.   10 W.   Extras.
  Six interiors.
  Costumes of 1865.
  Royalty on application to the publisher.
  "In using for the purpose of drama a personality of so wide and recent a fame as that of Abraham Lincoln, I feel that one or two observations are due to my readers and critics.   First, my purpose is not that of the historian but of the dramatist...... Secondly, my purpose is, again, that of the dramatist, not that of the philosopher. .... My concern is with the profoundly dramatic interest of his character, and with the inspiring example of a man who handled war nobly and with imagination." (Author.)
  This play is highly recommended for study and presentation in the senior high school.

Robert E. Lee, by John Drinkwater.
  A play in nine scenes.
  Houghton.
  18 M.   3 W.
  Five interiors, four exteriors.
  Costumes of 1865.
  Royalty on application to the publisher.
  A well-written historical play for the senior high school.

Mixed Marriage, by St. John Ervine.
>A drama in four acts.
>Macmillan.
>4 M.   2 W.
>One interior.
>Modern costumes.
>Royalty on application to the publisher.
>This stern portrayal of race hatred is fitted only for the reading
list of the twelfth grade.

Hassan, by James Elroy Flecker.
>A play in five acts.
>Knopf.
>26 M.   6 W.   Others.
>Three interiors, one exterior.
>Oriental costumes.
>Royalty on application to the publisher.
>Hassan of Bagdad makes the Golden Journey to Samarkand.
>"*Hassan*, for sheer pleasure of reading, is not excelled by any
other contemporary play." (Laurence Stallings.)
>It is a delightful play for the twelfth-grade reading list.

Change, by John O. Francis.
>A play in four acts.
>Doubleday.
>8 M.   3 W.
>One interior.
>Modern Welsh costumes.
>Royalty on application to the publisher.
>"The tragic conflict of ideals of two generations which have
grown irreparably apart in social and economic views." (Sterling
A. Leonard.)
>This is a drama for the twelfth-grade list.

Justice, by John Galsworthy.
>A tragedy in four acts.
>Scribner.
>17 M.   1 W.   Extras.

Six interiors.

Modern costumes.

Royalty on application to the publisher.

"The economic structure of society on any basis requires the keeping of certain compacts. It cannot endure such a breaking of these compacts as Falder is guilty of when he changes the figures on the cheque. Yet by the simple march of events it is overwhelmingly proven that society here stamps out a human life not without its fair possibilities — for eighty-one pounds." (Ludwig Lewisohn.)

This belongs on the reading list of the more thoughtful twelfth graders.

Loyalties, by John Galsworthy.

A drama in three acts.

Scribner.

16 M.   3 W.

Five interiors.

Modern costumes.

Royalty on application to the publisher.

This splendidly written, thrilling tragedy begins with the discovery of the fact that a wealthy young Jew, guest at the country house of a distinguished Englishman, has been robbed of a large sum of money. The drama discusses seriously various types of loyalty. It is heartily recommended for reading and study in the senior class.

The Mob, by John Galsworthy.

A drama in four acts.

Scribner.

14 M.   6 W.   Extras.

Three interiors, two exteriors.

Modern costumes.

Royalty on application to the publisher.

The play deals with the tragic consequences which followed a man's unwelcome voicing of his objections to an unjust war. It belongs on the reading list of the senior class.

The Pigeon, by John Galsworthy.

A fantasy in three acts.
Scribner.
12 M.   2 W.
One interior.
Modern costumes.
Royalty on application to the publisher.
A generous but unwise artist is fleeced again and again by
various undeserving social misfits.   The reading list of the serious-
minded seniors should include this selection.

The Silver Box, by John Galsworthy.

A comedy in three acts.
Scribner.
11 M.   5 W.   2 J.   Others.
Three interiors.
Modern costumes.
Royalty on application to the publisher.
In this profoundly moving study of the unjust discrimination of
the English court, money and influence save a rich man's son, and
lack of money and influence send a poor workingman to prison.
A great play for twelfth-grade students to read and study.   It is
not suited to high-school presentation.

Strife, by John Galsworthy.

A drama in three acts.
Scribner.
Three interiors, one exterior.
22 M.   7 W.   1 J.   Extras.
Modern costumes.
Royalty on application to the publisher.
This tragic play deals with the labor problem.   For the reading
list of the eleventh and twelfth grades.   It is excellent for study
but too unrelieved in its seriousness for presentation by immature
and inexperienced actors.

Engaged, by W. S. Gilbert.
> Farcical comedy in three acts.
> French.
> 5 M. 5 W.
> One interior, one exterior.
> Modern costumes.
> No royalty.
> This very amusing, old-fashioned comedy by the great English humorist W. S. Gilbert deserves a place on the reading list of the senior high school.

The Voysey Inheritance, by Harley Granville-Barker.
> A play in five acts.
> Little.
> 10 M. 8 W.
> Two interiors.
> Modern costumes.
> Royalty on application to the publisher.
> "The inheritance is a dishonored name and a dishonest business." (Sterling A. Leonard.)
> The play is recommended for the reading list of the twelfth grade.

Pickwick, by Cosmo Hamilton and Frank C. Reilly.
> A play in three acts.
> Putnam.
> 37 M. 13 W. Extras.
> Five interiors, two exteriors.
> Old English costumes.
> Royalty on application to the publisher.
> This delightful play "freely based upon the *Pickwick Papers* by Charles Dickens," is excellent for study and presentation in the eleventh and twelfth grades.

Tilly of Bloomsbury, by Ian Hay.
> A comedy in three acts.
> French.

9 M. 7 W.

Two interiors.

Modern costumes.

Royalty, twenty-five dollars.

A wholesome and entertaining story of the love affair of a poor girl whose overanxious family nearly wrecked her chance of wedding the wealthy young fellow she genuinely loved, through a ridiculous attempt to appear other than they really were.

This play is a welcome addition to the reading list of the senior high school, and can be presented by juniors and seniors with pleasure and profit.

The Chinese Lantern, by Laurence Housman.

A play in three acts.

French.

12 M. 2 W.

One interior.

Chinese costumes.

Royalty, twenty-five dollars.

Since the author catches some of the atmosphere of China, the play is effective and charming for eleventh and twelfth grades to present.

Prunella; or, Love in a Dutch Garden, by Laurence Housman and Harley Granville-Barker.

A fantasy in three acts.

Little.

11 M. 10 W. Others.

One exterior.

Fanciful costumes.

Royalty on application to the publisher.

"This exquisite little fantasy . . . is full of quaint invention, humor, irony, and pathos." (William Archer.)

The play is probably too difficult for high-school production, but belongs on the reading list of the eleventh and twelfth grades.

The Manœuvers of Jane, by Henry Arthur Jones.

A comedy in four acts.

French.

9 M.   11 W.

Three interiors.

Modern costumes.

Royalty on application to the publisher.

Jane's not overscrupulous attempts to get her own way are replete with humorous complications. The play is good fun for tenth-, eleventh-, and twelfth-grade students to read. Because of its character, the comedy is perhaps not for high-school presentation.

Mary Goes First, by Henry Arthur Jones.

A comedy in three acts and an epilogue.

French.

8 M.   4 W.

One interior.

Modern costumes.

Royalty, twenty-five dollars.

This comedy of manners gives an entertaining story of an Englishwoman's struggle to win social position. The play is too typically English to appeal to most high-school pupils. Because of its excellent technique, it has a place on the reading list of the twelfth grade.

The Servant in the House, by Charles Rann Kennedy.

A play in five acts.

Harper.

5 M.   2 W.

One interior.

Modern dress and one native Eastern costume.

Royalty, twenty-five dollars.

The discordant household of an English vicar is transformed by the influence of the vicar's brother disguised as an Indian butler. This modern morality is recommended for senior-class reading, study, and presentation because of its story, technique, and ethics.

The Winterfeast, by Charles Rann Kennedy.
   A drama in five acts.
   Harper.
   5 M.   2 W.
   One interior.
   Icelandic costumes.
   Royalty on application to the publisher.
   The scene of this tragic drama is Iceland, and the time is A.D.
1020.   It is interesting reading for the twelfth grade.

The Tragedy of Nan, by John Masefield.
   A tragedy in three acts.
   Macmillan.
   8 M.   6 W.
   One interior.
   Modern costumes.
   Royalty on application to the publisher.
   "One of the most poignantly tragic of modern plays;   the
mercilessness of weak and selfish people crushes out a beautiful
life." (Sterling A. Leonard.)
   Although on the reading list of advanced high-school pupils, the
play is not for presentation.

The Tragedy of Pompey the Great, by John Masefield.
   A tragedy in three acts.
   Macmillan.
   18 M.   4 W.   Extras.
   Two interiors, one deck of a vessel.
   Royalty on application to the publisher.
   This finely told story of the defeat of the brave Pompey by
Cæsar should be placed on the reading list of the twelfth grade.

If I Were King, by Justin H. McCarthy.
   A play in four acts.
   French.
   20 M.   9 W.
   Three interiors, one exterior.

Royalty, twenty-five dollars.

The scene of this spectacular, romantic play is laid in the reign of Louis the Eleventh. The plot deals with the adventures of François Villon.

This play might be added to the reading list of the eleventh and twelfth grades.

The Dover Road, by A. A. Milne.
> A comedy in three acts.
> French.
> 6 M.   4 W.
> One interior.
> Modern costumes.
> Mr. Latimer, interested in the problems of his fellows, stops couples eloping from London to Paris. He manages to detain them long enough to give them a chance to become really acquainted with each other. As a result the elopement is usually called off.
> Twelfth graders enjoy reading this quaint comedy.

The Great Broxopp, by A. A. Milne.
> A comedy in a prologue and three acts.
> Putnam.
> 5 M.   6 W.
> Four interiors.
> Modern costumes.
> Royalty on application to the publisher.
> The wealthy James Broxopp to please his family retires. Inactivity makes him most miserable. His wife realizing the cause of his unhappiness permits sharpers to get the Broxopp fortune. Broxopp goes back to the business world and regains his joy in living. The play affords enjoyable reading for senior high school and could doubtless be presented by juniors and seniors.

Mr. Pim Passes By, by A. A. Milne.
> A comedy in three acts.
> French.

3 M. 4 W.

One interior.

Modern costumes.

Royalty, fifty dollars.

Mr. Pim, a mellow but somewhat muddle-headed old fellow, stops for a short time at the Mardens' and makes a statement that causes great consternation in the household.

This amusing play of character is much enjoyed by eleventh and twelfth grades.

The Romantic Age, by A. A. Milne.

A comedy in three acts.

French; Knopf.

5 M. 4 W.

One interior, one exterior.

Modern costumes.

Royalty, fifty dollars.

The extravagantly romantic ideas of a young girl are tempered by the logic of her lover. A whimsical, slender, well-written comedy, it appeals primarily to young high-school girls. The play is often presented by amateurs but is probably not fitted for production in most secondary schools.

The Truth About Blayds, by A. A. Milne.

A comedy in three acts.

French.

4 M. 4 W.

One interior.

Modern costumes.

Royalty on application to the publisher.

The Blayds-Conway family is astonished to learn that the famous poet, Oliver Blayds, has built his reputation upon a lie. The family readjustment furnishes the story of the play. This tragi-comedy makes interesting reading for high-school students who are genuinely interested in fine drama. The play is difficult to act but not impossible for advanced and gifted pupils.

When Bunty Pulls the Strings, by G. Moffet.
A comedy in three acts.
Sanger and Jordan.
5 M.   5 W.   Extras.
One interior, one exterior.
Scottish costumes.
Royalty on application to the publisher.
The canniness of the Scots is the theme of this comedy.   It is
enjoyed by young people of the eleventh and twelfth grades.

Wings Over Europe, by Robert Nichols and Maurice Browne.
A play in three acts.
Covici-Friede.
16 M.
One interior.
Modern costumes.
Royalty on application to the publisher.
Francis Lightfoot, a poetic young scientist, says to the British
cabinet, "I can turn wood into gold, liberate mankind from the
slavery of matter and the necessity of work, or blow the whole world
to smithereens — what are you going to do about it?"   This phil-
osophic melodrama belongs on the reading list of the twelfth grade.

Sherwood; or, Robin Hood and the Three Kings, by Alfred Noyes;
School and Acting Edition, by J. Milnor Dorey.
A play in five acts.
Stokes.
15 M.   6 W.   1 J.   Extras.
Four exteriors.
Old English costumes.
Royalty, thirty-five dollars.
Alfred Noyes, the well-liked English poet, has here written a
play which students of the high school enjoy presenting.

Disraeli, by Louis N. Parker.
A play in four acts.
Dodd.
14 M.   7 W.

Three interiors.

Costumes of Queen Victoria's day.

Royalty, twenty-five dollars.

"This is not an historical play, but only an attempt to show a picture of the days — not so very long ago — in which Disraeli lived and some of the racial, social, and political prejudices he fought against and conquered." (Author.) This play, which George Arliss made famous by his splendid acting, is worth study and presentation in the twelfth grade.

Joseph and His Brethren, by Louis N. Parker.

A pageant play in four acts.

Dodd.

37 M. 16 W. Extras.

Five interiors, six exteriors.

Biblical costumes.

Royalty on application to the publisher.

Some of the tenth and eleventh graders will like this play.

Pomander Walk, by Louis N. Parker.

A romantic comedy in three acts.

French.

10 M. 8 W.

One exterior.

Costumes, of the late eighteenth century.

Royalty, twenty-five dollars.

A charming wholesome comedy, difficult to stage, it is particularly enjoyed by girls of the twelfth grade.

Herod, by Stephen Phillips.

A tragedy in three acts.

Dodd.

12 M. 6 W.

One interior.

Biblical costumes.

Royalty on application to the publisher.

The reading list of the most advanced seniors should contain this play.

Ulysses, by Stephen Phillips.
A drama in prologue and three acts.
Macmillan.
20 M. 11 W. Extras.
One interior, six exteriors.
Ancient Greek costumes.
Royalty on application to the publisher.
Wisely cut, this play can be profitably presented by twelfth graders.

The Farmer's Wife, by Eden Phillpotts.
A comedy in three acts.
Brentano's.
10 M. 11 W.
Two interiors.
Modern costumes.
Royalty on application to the publisher.
A lonely widower confides to his housekeeper his intention of proposing to one of the five available women in the neighborhood. The play, in a most humorous manner, then shows the poor man's disappointment as one after another of these eligibles turns him down. He is accepted at last by a lady he had thought ineligible, and all ends happily. This amusing comedy of English rural life makes interesting and worth-while reading for the eleventh and twelfth grades.

The Amazons, by Sir Arthur Wing Pinero.
A farce in three acts.
Baker.
7 M. 5 W.
One interior, one exterior.
Modern costumes.
Royalty, ten dollars.
"Lady Castlejordan, greatly desiring a boy, is sent three girls, one after another. As the best way out of the difficulty, she gives her girls boys' names and dresses, educates, and otherwise brings them up as boys. This answers very well so long as they are

children, but when the three 'right men' turn up, mamma's careful plans go astray." (Publisher's notice.) This is good reading material for the high school, but it is rather too slender to receive the considerable amount of time necessary for presentation.

The Big Drum, by Sir Arthur Wing Pinero.
    A comedy in four acts.
    Baker.
    12 M.   5 W.
    Three interiors.
    Modern costumes.
    Royalty, ten dollars.
    This story is of the love affair of a brilliant writer who is financially unsuccessful. The play is fitted for twelfth-grade students who are genuinely interested in the work of this great modern dramatist. It is not suited to high-school presentation.

Dandy Dick, Sir Arthur Wing Pinero.
    A farce in three acts.
    Baker.
    7 M.   4 W.
    Two interiors.
    Modern costumes.
    Royalty, ten dollars.
    The Reverend Augustus Judd, hoping to win money enough to restore the tower of his church, bets upon a horse owned by his sport-loving sister. A most diverting farce results. Senior-high-school students greatly enjoy reading the play.

The Thunderbolt, Sir Arthur Wing Pinero.
    A drama in four acts.
    Baker.
    10 M.   9 W.
    Three interiors.
    Modern costumes.
    Royalty, ten dollars
    The play deals with the reaction of an English provincial family

to money. The drama is too mature in subject-matter for presentation in the high school but the compiler of this bibliography uses *The Thunderbolt* in the twelfth grade as an example of excellent technique.

Trelawny of the "Wells," by Sir Arthur Wing Pinero.
A comedietta in four acts.
Dramatic Publishing Co.
14 M. 9 W.
Three interiors.
Costumes of 1860.
Royalty, ten dollars.
Trelawny of the "Wells" tells the vicissitudes which beset the love affair of Rose Trelawny, a successful actress, and Gower, the scion of an aristocratic theater-hating family. Incidentally the play gives a memorable picture of the old-fashioned oratorical actors at the time when they were being supplanted by the new school of realism.
Here is an excellent play for senior-class presentation.

Florence Nightingale, by Edith G. Reid.
A drama in three acts.
Macmillan.
8 M. 6 W. Extras.
Two interiors, two exteriors.
Costumes of the last half of the nineteenth century.
Royalty on application to the publisher.
"In the play I have been obliged for the purposes of the stage to condense certain events in her life into special periods." (Author.)
This biographical play may be placed on the reading list of the eleventh and twelfth grades.

Androcles and the Lion, by George Bernard Shaw.
A play in a prologue and two acts.
Brentano's.
16 M. 2 W. Extras.

Two interiors, two exteriors.

Costumes of the early Christian era.

Royalty on application to the publisher.

In this comedy, which at times seems to border on farce, Shaw considers the problem of creed and religion. It is an excellent play for study and presentation in the twelfth grade.

Arms and the Man, by George Bernard Shaw.

A comedy in three acts.

Brentano's

4 M.   3 W.

Two interiors, one exterior.

Bulgarian and Serbian costumes of 1885.

Royalty on application to the publisher.

"In *Arms and the Man,* Shaw has no moral or social or historical or philosophical credo to state. He has an amusing and gay plot to give his audiences. His chocolate soldier is a delightful human being, but Shaw does not, as he does in his later plays, use the personal charm of his characters to make an audience listen to their author's ideas. (Fanny Butcher.)

This delicious satire on war makes delightful reading for the twelfth grade.

Cæsar and Cleopatra, by George Bernard Shaw.

A drama in five acts.

Brentano's.

30 M.   4 W.

Three interiors, four exteriors.

Costumes of the period.

Royalty on application to the publisher.

"Mr. Shaw's idea of what might have happened the year of Cæsar's meeting with Cleopatra, when she was a flapper of sixteen and he a partly bald old gentleman of fifty." (Burns Mantle.)

This romantic play has a definite place on the twelfth-grade reading list. It is almost too difficult to set and act for high-school presentation. With simple staging and expert actors it might be done creditably.

Candida, by George Bernard Shaw.

A comedy in three acts.

Brentano's.

4 M.   2 W.

One interior.

Modern costumes.

Royalty on application to the publisher.

The play deals with the complications which arise in the household of Reverend James M. Morell when his wife mothers an adolescent poet.   It finds a place on the reading list of the more serious seniors.

Captain Brassbound's Conversion, by George Bernard Shaw.

A comedy in three acts.

Brentano's.

12 M.   1 W.   Extras.

Two interiors, one exterior.

Modern costumes.

Royalty on application to the publisher.

This clever English comedy of modern life can be placed on the reading list of the twelfth grade.

The Devil's Disciple, by George Bernard Shaw.

A melodrama in four acts.

Brentano's.

10 M.   5 W.

Four interiors, one exterior.

Costumes of the Revolutionary War period.

Royalty on application to the publisher.

Richard Dudgeon, hater of sentimentality and Puritanical hypocrisy, professed disciple of the devil, in order to save the life of Pastor Anderson allows himself to be made a prisoner through a mistake in identity.   Even when sentenced to die as a spy he refuses to make himself known.   It is a powerful play for the eleventh and twelfth grades to read.

Pygmalion, by George Bernard Shaw.

A comedy in five acts.

Brentano's.

9 M.   7 W.

One exterior, two interiors.

Modern costumes.

Royalty on application to the publisher.

Professor Higgins, a specialist in phonetics, proves to his sceptical friend, Colonel Pickering, that he can teach an illiterate cockney flower girl to behave and talk like a lady.   This brilliant comedy could be acted by skillful twelfth-grade students.

Saint Joan, by George Bernard Shaw.

A chronicle play in six scenes and an epilogue.

Brentano's.

21 M.   2 W.   Extras.

Six interiors, one exterior.

Early fifteenth-century costumes.

Royalty on application to the publisher.

If cut judiciously and staged simply, this brilliant historical drama can well be presented by experienced and talented twelfth graders.

You Never Can Tell, by George Bernard Shaw.

A comedy in four acts.

Brentano's.

6 M.   4 W.

Two interiors, one exterior.

Modern costumes.

Royalty on application to the publisher.

This farcical exposé of parents and children is difficult to act and difficult to stage; however, occasionally a gifted and intelligent group of twelfth graders has given it with a considerable measure of success.

The Two Virtues, by Alfred Sutro.

A comedy in four acts.

French.

3 M.   5 W.

Two interiors.

Modern costumes.

Royalty, twenty-five dollars.

This well-written comedy of manners is for the reading list of the most advanced high-school students.

Outward Bound, by Sutton Vane.
A play in three acts.
Boni & Liveright.
6 M.   3 W.
One interior.
Modern costumes.
Royalty on application to the publisher.

The play presents an interesting dramatic situation. The majority of the characters on an outward-bound ship are dead. The fate of the travelers to the undiscovered country is skillfully worked out.

It offers interesting reading for juniors and seniors and it is suitable for presentation.

The Importance of Being Earnest, by Oscar Wilde.
Comedy in three acts.
French; Baker; Putnam.
5 M.   4 W.
Two interiors, one exterior.
Modern costumes.
Royalty, thirty-five dollars.

Twelfth-grade students immensely enjoy reading this clever and scintillating farce-comedy, but it is too sophisticated for high-school presentation.

The Melting Pot, by Israel Zangwill.
A drama in four acts.
Macmillan; French.
5 M.   5 W.
Two interiors, one exterior.
Modern costumes.
Royalty, twenty-five dollars.

This serious study of race prejudice and the making of an American has been frequently presented by high schools.

Modern Irish Drama

The Golden Apple, by Lady Gregory.
A play in three acts.
Putnam.
11 M. 4 W. Extras.
Numerous interiors and exteriors.
Fanciful costumes.
Royalty, twenty-five dollars.
Ninth and tenth grades enjoy acting this fairy story for younger children.

The Dragon, by Lady Gregory.
A wonder play in three acts.
Putnam.
8 M. 6 W.
One interior.
Fanciful costumes.
Royalty, twenty-five dollars.
The tale seems a trifle long-drawn-out. Nevertheless, the play has been presented successfully many times by high-school actors.

The Drone, by Rutherford Mayne.
A comedy in three acts.
Maunsel.
6 M. 3 W.
One interior.
Modern Irish costumes.
Royalty on application to the publisher.
A somewhat interesting tale of Irish life; it may be placed on the reading list of the senior high school.

The Turn of the Road, by Rutherford Mayne.
A play in two scenes and an epilogue
Maunsel
7 M. 3 W.
One interior.
Modern Irish costumes.

Royalty on application to the publisher.

A talented Irish lad is driven from home by his unsympathetic father because he refuses to give up his violin and devote himself to tilling the soil.

It takes about an hour and three quarters to act and is well worth presentation in the senior high school.

The Whiteheaded Boy, by Lenox Robinson.

A comedy in three acts.

Putnam; French.

5 M. 7 W.

One interior.

Modern Irish costumes.

Royalty, fifty dollars.

An Irish family attempts to make a genius of a stupid son, but they are outwitted.

Here is a good comedy for presentation in the senior class.

Deirdre of the Sorrows, by John M. Synge.

A poetic tragedy in three acts.

Luce.

8 M. 3 W.

Two interiors, one exterior.

Early Irish costumes.

Royalty on application to the publisher.

This beautiful dramatization of the tragic legend of Deirdre belongs on the reading list of the twelfth grade.

The Playboy of the Western World, by John M. Synge.

A comedy in three acts.

Luce.

7 M. 5 W. Extras.

The scene is a rough country public-house.

Modern Irish costumes.

Royalty on application to the publisher.

Here is related the effect of hero worship upon a timid, poetic Irish lad who struck at his tyrannical father with a loy.

This beautifully written play commends itself to study and presentation by twelfth graders.

The Well of the Saints, by John M. Synge.
A drama in three acts.
Luce.
4 M.   3 W.   Extras.
Two country roadsides.
Irish costumes of a century or more ago.
Royalty on application to the publisher.
The story of a blind beggar and his wife to whom sight brought sad disillusionment is told with haunting poetic beauty.   It will be enjoyed by a few of the more artistic and serious twelfth graders.

MODERN EUROPEAN DRAMA

The Dybbuk, by S. Ansky.
A dramatic legend in three acts.
Boni & Liveright.
22 M.   13 W.   Extras.
Two interiors, one exterior.
Ancient Jewish costumes.
Royalty on application to the publisher.
This powerful dramatic telling of an ancient legend of the Jewish people is too mature for high-school students, except perhaps a few seniors.

R. U. R., by Karel Capek.
A fantastic melodrama in four acts.
Doubleday; Baker.
9 M.   4 W.   Extras.
Three interiors.
Modern and fanciful costumes.
Royalty for the Doubleday text on application to the publisher; no royalty for the Baker text.
The Rossum Company manufactures artificial beings that are like human beings except that they have no souls.   These machine-

made men are taught to use arms. At length they revolt, and the world is swept of all mankind save one man. The problem of the repopulation of the world then has to be solved. A good play for reading, study, and presentation in the eleventh and twelfth grades.

The Inspector-General, by Nikolai V. Gogol. Translated by Constance Garnett.
>A comedy in five acts.
>Knopf.
>19 M.   5 W.   Extras.
>Two interiors.
>Modern Russian costumes.
>Royalty on application to the publisher.

Twelfth-grade students enjoy reading and producing this amusing exposure of dishonesty and graft among officials. Since the date of its first presentation this comedy has not been absent from the theaters of Russia.

The Squabbles of Chioggia, by Carlo Goldoni. Translated from the Italian by Charles Lemmi.
>A comedy in three acts.
>*The Drama*, August 1914.
>9 M.   5 W.
>Two interiors, two exteriors.
>Venetian costumes of 1750.
>Royalty on application to the publisher.

"Let us not forget those sturdy fisher-folk of *The Squabbles of Chioggia* who want 'to dance, and sing, and have a good time,' as Lucretia says, but who cheerfully risk their lives at sea to earn their daily bread. They squabble, but when trouble becomes at all serious, the men face each other on the open square, disdaining all scheming and subterfuge; and if the women gossip and tittle-tattle, they, too, when the matter becomes serious, can bravely force back tears, and take harsh consequences for the common good." (Charles Lemmi.) Here is an interesting light comedy for the eleventh and twelfth grades.

Hannele, by Gerhart Hauptmann. Rendered into English verse by
Charles H. Meltzer.
A dream poem.
Doubleday.
6 M. 11 W. Others.
The scene is a room in an almshouse.
Modern and fanciful costumes.
Royalty on application to the publisher.
"Here is the country almshouse and the wretched creatures in
it; here is a poor, abused little girl who is brought there to die.
The play follows her last hours and presents her feverish and fan-
tastic thought." (Edward E. Hale, Jr.)
This play made a profound impression when first produced. It
should interest serious-minded twelfth-grade readers.

The Sunken Bell, by Gerhart Hauptmann. Freely rendered into
English verse by Charles H. Meltzer.
A fairy play in five acts.
Doubleday.
6 M. 7 W. 2 J. Extras.
Two interiors, one exterior.
Fanciful costumes.
Royalty on application to the publisher.
"*The Sunken Bell*, strictly considered, is more a poetic work
than a drama .... For my own part I incline to regard Heinrich,
the bell-founder, as a symbol of Humanity struggling painfully
toward the realization of its dream of the ideal truth and joy and
light and justice. (Frank Chouteau Brown.)
The twelfth-grade reading list should contain this masterpiece.
The play is too difficult for presentation by any high-school pupils
other than a select group of unusually able seniors.

The Weavers, by Gerhart Hauptmann.
A social drama in five acts.
Viking Press.
26 M. 12 W. 2 J. Extras.
Five interiors, one exterior.

German costumes of 1840.

Royalty on application to the publisher.

This very great and tragic play, depicting a revolt among some Silesian weavers, belongs on the reading list of the most serious seniors.

A Doll's House, by Henrik Ibsen.

A drama in four acts.

Scribner; Appleton; Baker; French; Macmillan.

4 M. 4 W. 3 Children.

One interior.

Late nineteenth-century Scandinavian costumes.

No royalty.

Nora Helmar, who has been treated as if she were an irresponsible child by her father and by her husband, learns through bitter experience that a doll's house can never be a real home. The play is not suited to high-school presentation, but is used by the compiler of this bibliography in the senior-class drama course as an example of superior technique.

An Enemy of the People, by Henrik Ibsen.

A drama in five acts.

Scribner; Baker; French.

9 M. 2 W.

Four interiors.

Late nineteenth-century costumes.

No royalty.

"A scientist who insists on making known and setting to work to remedy the evils and wrongs of his community has to reckon with the people." (Sterling A. Leonard.) This belongs on the senior-class reading list.

John Gabriel Borkman, by Henrik Ibsen.

A drama in four acts.

Scribner.

3 M. 5 W.

Two interiors, one exterior.

Late nineteenth-century costumes.

Royalty on application to the publisher.

This is a drab picture of a disappointed man who broods in the upper chamber of his house and of his wife and her sister, who struggle to rescue the son from the tragic atmosphere of the gloomy home. The play is for the reading list of seniors.

The Lady from the Sea, by Henrik Ibsen.

A drama in four acts.

Scribner.

5 M. 3 W. Extras.

Two interiors, three exteriors.

Late nineteenth-century costumes.

No royalty.

The theme of the play "is the psychological development of an idle woman who has nothing particular to occupy her life" (R. F. Sharp). *The Lady from the Sea*, if it has any place in the high school, belongs on the twelfth-grade reading list.

The Master Builder, by Henrik Ibsen.

A tragedy in three acts.

Baker; Macmillan.

4 M. 3 W. Extras.

One interior, one exterior.

Late nineteenth-century costumes.

No royalty.

Hilda Wangel inspires Halvard Solness, a noted architect and builder, who has lost something of his fearlessness and vision, to climb the heights of a new steeple. He loses his life but frees his soul. This difficult but masterly play is not beyond the comprehension of the members of the twelfth grade.

Peer Gynt, by Henrik Ibsen.

A dramatic poem.

Scribner; Baker.

25 M. 6 W. Others.

Numerous settings.

Norwegian costumes of the beginning and middle of the nineteenth century.

No royalty.

"In *Brand,* the hero is an embodied protest against the poverty of spirit and half-heartedness that Ibsen rebelled against in his countrymen. In *Peer Gynt* the hero is himself the embodiment of that spirit." (P. H. Wicksteed.)

The adventures of this highly imaginative egotist make interesting reading for the more experienced high-school pupils.

The Betrothal, by Maurice Maeterlinck. Translated by Alexander T. de Mattos.

A fairy play in five acts and eleven scenes.

Dodd.

12 M. 12 W. Children, and others.

Numerous interiors and exteriors. Some of the exteriors are merely decorated curtains.

Fanciful costumes.

Royalty on application to the publisher.

This sequel to *The Blue Bird* is interesting reading for ninth, tenth, and eleventh grades.

The Blue Bird, by Maurice Maeterlinck. Translated by Alexander T. de Mattos.

A fairy play in six acts.

Dodd.

A large number of characters.

Numerous scenes.

Fanciful costumes.

Royalty on application to the publisher.

Tyltyl and Mytyl, two peasant children, accompanied by the Dog, Cat, Bread, Water, Sugar, and others, go in search of the Blue Bird or Happiness. The compiler of this list of plays feels that this exquisite fairy play, which grips the imagination when read, loses not a little of its force and charm when staged as a whole. (The forest scene makes a charming little play in itself for the seventh, eighth, or ninth grade.)

Pelleas and Melisande, by Maurice Maeterlinck.
A poetic drama in five acts.
Dodd; Boni and Liveright.
6 M.   2 W.   Extras.
Numerous interiors and exteriors.
Costumes of the Middle Ages.
Royalty on application to the publisher.
This idyllic tragic story of love, if used in the high school at all, should be placed on the reading list of the oldest students.

The Swan, by Ferenc Molnar.   English text by Benjamin Glazer.
A comedy in three acts.
Boni & Liveright.
9 M.   8 W.   Extras.
Three interiors.
Modern Austrian costumes.
Royalty on application to the publisher.
"Here is a romantic comedy in the high mood, and a fancy, a wit, and an imagination that glows and gleams." (James Craig.) This well-written comedy is liked by twelfth graders.

Chantecler, by Edmond Rostand.   Translated by Gertrude Hall.
A play in four acts.
Duffield.
Many characters.
Numerous and difficult settings.
Fanciful costumes.
Royalty on application to the publisher.
In this delightful extravaganza, Rostand shows himself to be an interpreter of life as well as a poet.   Chantecler believes that it is his clarion note that calls the sun and brings the day.   A golden hen pheasant tries in vain to win his love and make him forget his duty.   Enraptured over the song of a nightingale, Chantecler forgets to crow, but the sun rises and Chantecler's dream of power is dispelled.
Every senior-high-school reading list should contain this play. Although it is too difficult for presentation as a whole, nevertheless some individual scenes are readily staged and acted.

Cyrano de Bergerac, by Edmond Rostand. Translated by Brian
    Hooker.
  An heroic comedy in five acts.
  Holt.
  29 M. 10 W. Extras.
  Two interiors, three exteriors.
  French costumes of the middle of the seventeenth century.
  Royalty on application to the publisher.
  "The English text has turned alive under his (Brian Hooker's)
hands and kindled itself into a veritable poem. It conveys from
one language to another the spontaneity, the rapture of the origi-
nal." (Clayton Hamilton.)
  This is the translation which Walter Hampden uses. This great
play should be read by every twelfth grader. It is probably too
difficult for high-school presentation.

L'Aiglon, by Edmond Rostand. Translated by Louis N. Parker,
    Harper; translated by Basil Davenport, Yale University
    Press.
  A romantic tragedy in six acts.
  19 M. 6 W. Others.
  Three interiors, two exteriors.
  Costumes of Napoleon's day.
  Royalty on application to the publisher.
  "L'Aiglon, the youngest son of Napoleon, is imprisoned by his
father's enemies. The young duke, eager to emulate the deeds
of his illustrious father, tries in vain to gain his freedom.
  The play is too difficult for presentation save by the most skill-
ful twelfth-grade pupils. It has, without doubt, a place on their
reading list.

The Romancers, by Edmond Rostand.
  A comedy in three acts.
  Baker.
  5 M. 1 W. Extras.
  One garden set.

Costumes of the seventeenth and eighteenth century.

No royalty.

A boy and a girl make love over the garden wall that separates their fathers' estates. Their parents pretend to oppose the match. Many humorous complications follow. This simple fantasy is easy to perform. The first act is a unit in itself and is often presented as a one-act play. *The Romancers* is recommended for presentation in the ninth and tenth grades.

The Cradle Song, by Gregorio Martinez Sierra. Translated by John
   G. Underhill.

A comedy in two acts and an interlude.

Dutton.

4 M.   10 W.   Extras.

Two interiors.

Modern Spanish and nuns' costumes.

Royalty on application to the publisher.

This is a leisurely told but exquisitely lovely story of the change wrought among a group of Spanish Dominican nuns through their care of a baby girl. This makes a splendid play for thoughtful high-school students to present and is admirably suited to a cast entirely of girls.

The Romantic Young Lady, by G. Martinez Sierra.   English version by Helen and Harley Granville-Barker.

A comedy in three acts.

French.

5 M.   6 W.

Two interiors.

Modern costumes.

Royalty, fifty dollars.

This quaint and charming tale of the romantic adventure of a novelist whose hat was blown through the window and into the room of a charming young Spanish girl is a delightful comedy for the reading list of the eleventh and twelfth grades. It might well be considered as material for presentation.

The Hraun Farm, by Jóhann Sigurjónsson. Translated by Henninge
     K. Schanche.
     A drama in three acts.
     In *Short Plays by Representative Authors,* Macmillan.
     4 M.   8 W.   3 J.
     Three exteriors.
     Present day Icelandic costumes.
     Royalty on application to the translator.
     "In *The Hraun Farm* (*hraun* meaning a field covered with
volcanic stone) the reader is reminded of the ancient tribal people
in the terrible struggle of the father between love for his land and
love for his child." (Alice M. Smith.) An interesting Icelandic
play for the reading list of the ninth, tenth, eleventh, and twelfth
grades.

Lucky Pehr, by August Strindberg.
     A drama in five acts.
     Appleton.
     33 M.   5 W.   Extras.
     Four interiors, three exteriors.
     Costumes of the Middle Ages.
     Royalty on application to the publisher.
     This allegorical play deals with somewhat the same sort of
material as that used by Ibsen in *Peer Gynt.* Pehr seeks many
years, in many places, and among various people for happiness and
success. He wins at length. The play is difficult to present, but
if cut a little and staged simply, it is most effective and fitting for
twelfth graders.

The Jesters, by Miguel Zamacois. Adapted from the French by
     John N. Raphael.
     A simple story in four acts of verse.
     Brentano's.
     12 M.   2 W.
     Two interiors, two exteriors.
     Sixteenth-century French costumes.
     Royalty on application to the publisher.

This charming play is well placed on the reading list of the twelfth grade.

Eighteenth-Century English Drama

The Good-Natured Man, by Oliver Goldsmith.
  A comedy.
  Putnam; Dramatic Publishing Co.
  11 M.   5 W.
  Two interiors, an inn garden.
  Eighteenth-century costumes.
  No royalty.
  A few twelfth-grade students will read this.

She Stoops to Conquer, by Oliver Goldsmith.
  A comedy in five acts.
  Many editions.   Stage version, Baker.
  15 M.   4 W.
  Two interiors, one exterior.
  Costumes of the eighteenth century.
  No royalty.
  Senior-high-school pupils still find pleasure in presenting this old-fashioned comedy.

The Critic; or, A Tragedy Rehearsed, by Richard B. Sheridan.
  A comedy in three acts.
  French.
  20 M.   7 W.
  Three interiors.
  Costumes, 1777 and Elizabethan.
  No royalty.
  The play has sufficient merit to warrant presentation by twelfth graders.

The Rivals, by Richard B. Sheridan.
  A comedy in five acts.
  Many editions.   Acting edition, French; Baker.
  8 M.   4 W.

Five interiors, three exteriors.
Costumes of the eighteenth century.
No royalty.
This comedy is splendid for senior-high-school classes to present.

The School for Scandal, by Richard B. Sheridan.
A comedy in five acts.
Many editions; acting version, Baker.
12 M.   4 W.   Extras.
Several interiors.
Costumes of the eighteenth century.
No royalty.
A presentation of this admirable comedy of manners would be
an excellent project for any twelfth grade.

Seventeenth-Century French Drama

L'Avare (The Miser), by Molière.   Translated by Curtis H. Page,
    Putnam; by Katherine P. Wormeley, Little.
A comedy in five acts.
10 M.   4 W.
One interior.
French costumes of Louis XIV period.
No royalty.
"His *Miser* especially, in which the contest between father
and son destroys all natural piety, is of unusual grandeur and in
a high sense tragic." (Goethe.) This play belongs on the twelfth-
grade reading list.

Le Bourgeois Gentilhomme (The Tradesman Turned Gentleman),
    by Molière.   Translated by Curtis H. Page, Putnam; by
    Katherine P. Wormeley, Little.
A comedy-ballet in five acts.
11 M.   4 W.   Extras.
French costumes of Louis XIV period.
No royalty.

"*The Tradesman Turned Gentleman* is perhaps the best of the many court entertainments, uniting music, dancing, and comedy, which Molière furnished for the diversion of King Louis.... For us, however, the chief interest of the play lies in its characters and its humor.... Molière has given us, once for all, the eternal comedy of the snob." (Curtis H. Page.)

This is one of the plays which is thoroughly worth the time necessary for twelfth graders to get it ready for presentation.

Don Juan; ou, le Festin de Pierre (Don Juan; or, The Stone Guest), by Molière. Translated by Curtis H. Page, Putnam; by Katherine P. Wormeley, Little.

A comedy in five acts.

12 M. 3 W. Extras.

Three interiors, three exteriors.

French costumes of Louis XIV period.

No royalty.

"The essential character of his [Molière's] *Don Juan* is not sensuality: it is power unaccompanied by any sense of duty or responsibility." (Curtis H. Page.)

Probably, with a few judicious cuts, this play could be acted by intelligent twelfth graders.

Les Femmes Savantes (The Learned Ladies), by Molière. Translated by Curtis H. Page, Putnam; by Katherine P. Wormeley, Little.

A comedy in five acts.

8 M. 5 W.

One interior.

French costumes of Louis XIV period.

No royalty.

"*The Learned Ladies* ended the war begun by *The Affected Misses*, against intellectual snobbishness, bad taste, and affectation of all sorts." (Curtis H. Page.)

This fine example of high comedy belongs on the reading list of the twelfth grade.

Le Malade Imaginaire (The Imaginary Invalid), by Molière. Translated by Curtis H. Page, Putnam; by Katherine P. Wormeley, Little.

A comedy in three acts.

16 M. 7 W. Extras.

Two interiors, two exteriors. Possible to stage with draperies only.

French costumes of Louis XIV period.

No royalty.

This last play of the great French dramatist makes a mirthful comedy for presentation by the eleventh or twelfth grade.

Le Médecin Malgré Lui (The Doctor by Compulsion), by Molière. Translated by Curtis H. Page, Putnam; by Katherine P. Wormeley, Little.

A comedy in three acts.

8 M. 3 W.

Simple setting.

French costumes of Louis XIV period.

No royalty.

"In *The Doctor by Compulsion* he produced what is on the whole the best of his many farces; and a really good farce is almost as rare as a good comedy of character." (Curtis H. Page.)

Senior-high-school students do well to study and present this play.

Le Misanthrope (The Misanthrope), by Molière. Translated by Curtis H. Page, Putnam; by Katherine P. Wormeley, Little.

A comedy in five acts.

8 M. 3 W.

Simple setting.

Costumes of Louis XIV period.

No royalty.

"*Le Misanthrope* is a manly protest against the empty conventionalities of civilization — the shams, the gauds, the trifles, the insincerities of which modern society so often seems to be made up." (Brander Matthews.)

This play, considered by many of the French critics as Molière's masterpiece, assuredly has its place on the twelfth-grade reading list.

Les Precieuses Ridicules (The Affected Misses), by Molière.
> Translated by Curtis H. Page, Putnam; by Katherine P. Wormeley, Little.

A comedy in one act.

6 M.   3 W.   Extras.

One interior.

French costumes of Louis XIV period.

No royalty.

"A piquant and telling satire upon the affectations of literary culture then prevalent." (Brander Matthews.)

Pupils of the eleventh and twelfth grades will enjoy presenting this short play.

Elizabethan Drama

The Knight of the Burning Pestle, by Francis Beaumont and
> John Fletcher.   (Arranged for presentation by Delta Upsilon Society of Harvard University), Dutton; in *Chief Elizabethan Dramatists*, edited by William A. Neilson, Houghton.

A farce in five acts.

19 M.   5 W.   Others.

Interiors, streets, and forest.

Elizabethan costumes.

No royalty.

Some of the twelfth grade will care to read this play.

The Shoemaker's Holiday, by Thomas Dekker.

A comedy.

> Scribner; also in *Chief Elizabethan Dramatists*, edited by William A. Neilson, Houghton.

17 M.   4 W.

Simple settings.

Elizabethan costumes.

No royalty.

This Elizabethan comedy can be placed on the twelfth-grade reading list.   It is better suited to college than to high-school performance.

The Honourable History of Friar Bacon and Friar Bungay, by
    Robert Greene.
A comedy.
In *Chief Elizabethan Dramatists*, edited by William A. Neilson,
Houghton; Dutton.
25 M. 4 W. Others.
Elizabethan costumes.
No royalty.
It is possible for twelfth-grade students to present this Eliza-
bethan play effectively.

The Sad Shepherd, by Ben Jonson.
A poetic idyl in three acts.
Dutton.
17 M. 6 W. Others.
A forest.
Robin Hood costumes.
No royalty.
This Robin Hood story is readily produced by skillful twelfth
graders. It can be done out of doors.

The Spanish Tragedy; or, Hieronimo Is Mad Again, by Thomas
    Kyd.
Tragedy.
In *Chief British Dramatists*, edited by Brander Matthews and
Paul R. Lieder; in *Chief Elizabethan Dramatists*, edited by William
A. Neilson, Houghton.
Very large group of characters.
Simple settings.
Costumes of the sixteenth century.
No royalty.
A few pupils of the twelfth grade will read this play.

Alexander and Campaspe, by John Lyly.
A romantic comedy in five acts.
Oxford.
24 M. 2 W.
Two interiors, one exterior.

Costumes of the period.

No royalty.

This play can be adapted for presentation by twelfth-grade pupils.

Endymion: The Man in the Moon, by John Lyly.

Allegory.

In *Chief Elizabethan Dramatists*, edited by William A. Neilson, Houghton.

15 M. 8 W.

Simple setting.

Costumes of the period.

No royalty.

This play is read by a very few twelfth graders.

The Jew of Malta, by Christopher Marlowe.

Tragedy.

In *Chief Elizabethan Dramatists*, edited by William A. Neilson Houghton.

16 M. 6 W. Others.

Simple setting.

Costumes of the period.

No royalty.

A few of the twelfth grade will read this play.

Tamburlaine, Part I, by Christopher Marlowe.

Chronicle.

In *Chief Elizabethan Dramatists*, edited by William A. Neilson, Houghton.

21 M. 4 W. Others.

Simple setting.

Costumes of the period.

No royalty.

This is valuable reading for the advanced members of the twelfth grade.

The Tragical History of Dr. Faustus, by Christopher Marlowe.

Tragedy.

In *Chief Elizabethan Dramatists*, edited by William A. Neilson,

Houghton; in *Little Theatre Classics*, *First Series*, edited by Samuel A. Eliot, Little.

16 M. 2 W. Others.

Simple setting.

Costumes of the period.

No royalty.

A wisely cut version of Dr. Faustus could be presented by expert twelfth graders.

The Old Wives' Tale, by George Peele.

Comedy.

In *Chief Elizabethan Dramatists*, edited by William A. Neilson, Houghton.

13 M. 6 W. Others.

Simple setting.

Costumes of the period.

No royalty.

A very few twelfth-grade pupils will read this play.

*As You Like It.

 Comedy of Errors.

 Coriolanus.

*Hamlet.

 Henry V.

*Julius Cæsar.

 King John.

*Macbeth.

*The Merchant of Venice.

*A Midsummer-Night's Dream.

 Richard II.

 Richard III.

 Romeo and Juliet.

*The Taming of the Shrew.

*The Tempest.

*Twelfth Night.

* Shakespeare's plays are so well known that it is unnecessary to give any data regarding them. Those starred are especially recommended for presentation in the senior high school.

Pre-Shakespearean Drama

Abraham and Isaac, Anonymous.

A miracle play.

In *Representative English Plays*, edited by John S. P. Tatlock, Century; in *Little Theatre Classics*, edited by Samuel A. Eliot, Little; in *Chief British Dramatists*, edited by Brander Matthews and Paul Robert Lieder, Houghton.

Five characters.

Simple setting.

Biblical and period costumes.

No royalty.

This is excellent for senior-high-school students to present.

Everyman, Anonymous.

Morality play.

In *Representative English Plays*, edited by John S. P. Tatlock, Century; in *Everyman, With Other Interludes*, Dutton; acting versions published by French and by Houghton.

5 M. 12 W.

A simple setting.

Period costumes.

No royalty.

This beautiful old religious play is splendid and effective drama for senior-high-school production. It takes about an hour and a half to act, and it can be done by a cast entirely of boys or entirely of girls.

Gammer Gurton's Needle, Anonymous.

A farce.

French (a modern adaptation by Colin Campbell); in *Portmanteau Adaptations*, by Stuart Walker, Appleton.

6 M. 4 W.

One exterior.

Period costumes.

No royalty.

Gammer Gurton loses her precious needle. When she is told

that it has been stolen by a neighbor, a most amusing fight ensues. The modern adaptation of this lively farce is good material for ninth, tenth, or eleventh grades to present either within doors or without. The playing time is about one hour.

Noah's Flood, Anonymous.

A miracle play.

In *Representative English Plays*, edited by John S. P. Tatlock, Century.

5 M.   4 W.

Simple setting.

Period costumes.

No royalty.

A few students in the twelfth grade will care to read this.

The Second Shepherd's Play, Anonymous.

A miracle play.

In *Chief British Dramatists*, edited by Brander Matthews and Paul R. Lieder, Houghton; in *Representative English Plays*, edited by John S. P. Tatlock, Century.

4 M.   3 W.

Simple setting.

Period costumes.

No royalty.

The twelfth-grade reading list should include this title.

Master Pierre Patelin, translated by R. T. Holbrook.

Farce.

Baker.

4 M.   1 W.

Simple setting.

French costumes about 1465.

No royalty.

The play is concerned with the crooked dealings of a clever lawyer.

Tenth-, eleventh-, or twelfth-grade students find great fun in acting this famous old French farce, which takes about an hour and a half to play.

Ralph Roister Doister, by Nicholas Udall.
Comedy in five acts.
In *Chief British Dramatists*, edited by Brander Matthews and
Paul R. Lieder, Houghton; French.
12 M.   5 W.
Simple setting.
English costumes of middle of sixteenth century.
No royalty.
This is a rollicking and amusing comedy which some of the more
advanced twelfth-grade students will read with delight.

Classical Greek Drama

Agamemnon, by Æschylus.   Translated by Gilbert Murray.
Tragedy.
Oxford.
4 M.   2 W.   Chorus.
The scene is the Palace of Atreus.
Costumes of the period.
No royalty.
This splendid translation is recommended for the twelfth-grade
reading list.

The Frogs, by Aristophanes.   Translated by Gilbert Murray.
Comedy.
Oxford.
9 M.   3 W.   Others.
Simple setting.
Costumes of the period.
No royalty.
Here is another great play for the twelfth-grade list.

Alcestis, by Euripides.   Translated by Gilbert Murray.
Tragedy.
Oxford; Baker publishes a text with instructions for production.
7 M.   3 W.   Chorus.
No setting necessary.
Greek costumes.

No royalty.

Since Gilbert Murray's translation is most beautiful, some students of the twelfth grade will enjoy it.

Iphigenia in Tauris, by Euripides. Translated by Gilbert Murray.

Romantic drama.

Oxford.

5 M.   2 W.   Chorus.

Exterior of a barbaric Temple.

Greek costumes.

No royalty.

"It is a delightful play; subtle, ever-changing, full of movement and poignancy....And after all, the adventure of Euripides is not quite like that of the average romantic writer.   It is shot through by reflection, by reality, and by sadness.   There is a shadow that broods over 'Iphigenia,' though it is not the shadow of death.   It is exile, homesickness." (Gilbert Murray.)

Twelfth-grade students are capable of giving an excellent presentation of this great Greek play.

The Medea, by Euripides.   Translated by Gilbert Murray.

Tragedy.

Oxford.

5 M.   2 W.   Chorus and others.

Simple setting.

Greek costumes.

No royalty.

This play has a place on the reading list of the twelfth grade.

The Trojan Women, by Euripides. Translated by Gilbert Murray.

Tragedy.

Oxford.

3 M.   5 W.   Chorus.

One simple setting.

Greek costumes.

No royalty.

This forceful tragedy showing the horrors of war has a place on the twelfth-grade reading list.

Antigone, by Sophocles. Translated by Lewis Campbell.
  Tragedy.
  Oxford; Baker publishes an acting version.
  5 M. 3 W. Chorus.
  Simple setting.
  Greek costumes.
  No royalty.
  Well prepared twelfth-grade students will find this a splendid
play to produce. The Mendelssohn music is frequently used.

COLLECTIONS OF SHORT PLAYS

   I. *Allison's Lad and Other Plays*, by Beulah M. Dix. Holt.
  II. *Another Treasury of Plays for Children*, edited by Mont-
       rose J. Moses. Little.
 III. *The Atlantic Book of Junior Plays*, edited by Charles
       Swain Thomas. Atlantic.
  IV. *The Atlantic Book of Modern Plays*, edited by Sterling
       A. Leonard. Atlantic.
   V. *Contemporary One-Act Plays*, edited by B. Roland Lewis.
       Scribner.
  VI. *Echoes of the War*, by Sir James M. Barrie. Scribner.
 VII. *Five Plays*, by Lord Dunsany. Little.
VIII. *Half Hours*, by Sir James M. Barrie. Scribner.
  IX. *The Junior Play Book*, edited by Helen Louise Cohen.
       Harcourt.
   X. *A Miracle of St. Anthony and Other Plays*, by Maurice
       Maeterlinck. Boni & Liveright.
  XI. *More One-Act Plays by Modern Authors*, edited by Helen
       Louise Cohen. Harcourt.
 XII. *More Portmanteau Plays*, by Stuart Walker. Appleton.
XIII. *One-Act Plays*, compiled and edited by George A. Gold-
       stone. Allyn and Bacon.
 XIV. *One-Act Plays by Modern Authors*, edited by Helen
       Louise Cohen. Harcourt.

XV. *One-Act Plays for Secondary Schools, First Series*, selected and edited by James P. Webber and Hanson H. Webster. Houghton.

XVI. *One-Act Plays of To-day*, edited by Joseph W. Marriott. Dodd.

XVII. *One-Act Plays of To-day, Second Series*, edited by Joseph W. Marriott. Dodd.

XVIII. *Plays for Classroom Interpretation*, edited by Edwin Van B. Knickerbocker. Holt.

XIX. *Plays in Prose and Verse*, by William Butler Yeats. Macmillan.

XX. *Plays of Gods and Men*, by Lord Dunsany. Luce.

XXI. *Plays Old and New*, selected and edited by Stella B. Finney. Allyn and Bacon.

XXII. *Portmanteau Adaptations*, by Stuart Walker. Appleton.

XXIII. *Portmanteau Plays*, by Stuart Walker. Appleton.

XXIV. *Representative One-Act Plays by American Authors*, edited by Margaret G. Mayorga. Little.

XXV. *Seven Short Plays*, by Lady Gregory. Luce.

XXVI. *Short Plays by Representative Authors*, edited by Alice M. Smith. Macmillan.

XXVII. *Short Plays for Junior and Senior High Schools*, selected and edited by James P. Webber and Hanson H. Webster. Houghton.

XXVIII. *Short Plays from Dickens*, by Horace B. Browne. Scribner.

XXIX. *Short Plays of Various Types*, edited by Milton M. Smith. Merrill.

XXX. *Six Plays*, by Rachel L. Field. Scribner.

XXXI. *Three Welsh Plays*, by Jeannette Marks. Little.

XXXII. *A Treasury of Plays for Children*, edited by Montrose J. Moses. Little.

XXXIII. *Twelve Plays*, by Edwin Van B. Knickerbocker. Holt.

SHORT PLAYS

Mrs. Pat and the Law, by Mary Aldis.

Baker; Duffield; XXIV.[1]

2 M.   2 W.   1 J.

Scene: a simple interior.

Modern costumes.

Royalty, five dollars.

Mrs. Pat, a long-suffering Irish washerwoman, is persuaded to invoke the law against her drink-loving husband. When the police arrive she relents.

This little comedy with underlying seriousness is liked by pupils of the senior high school.

Carved Woman, by Hartley B. Alexander.

XI.

2 M.   1 W.

Scene: draperies.

American Indian costumes.

Royalty on application to the publisher.

In this dramatic fragment Hartley B. Alexander, professor of philosophy and authority on Indian culture, has given the Orpheus and Eurydice myth as it is expressed in legendary lore of our Northwest Indians. A few of the more serious-minded students of the senior class will enjoy reading this poetic masque. Possibly a few will care to act it before a specially selected audience.

Love of One's Neighbor, by Leonid Andreyev.

In *Fifty Contemporary One-Act Plays*, Appleton.

15 M.   7 W.   1 J.

Scene: a wild place in the mountains.

Modern dress of several nationalities.

Royalty on application to the publisher.

This brilliant comedy, satirizing brotherly love, interests the senior high school particularly.

[1] The Roman numbers refer to the list of collections of short plays immediately preceding this list.

Colombine, by Reginald Arkell.
XV.
4 M.   1 W.   1 J.
Scene: Roman camp.
Fantastic costumes.
Royalty on application to the publisher.
This charming fantasy is a delight to the more poetic pupils of the high school.

The Postscript, by Emile Augier.
French.
1 M.   2 W.
Scene: a modern interior.
Modern costumes.
No royalty.
"One of the brightest and most brilliant little one-act comedies in any language, and to be warmly recommended to American readers." (Brander Matthews.)   It is best placed on the reading list of the eleventh and twelfth grades.

Gringroire, by Theodore De Banville.
Dramatic Publishing Co.
4 M.   2 W.
Scene: an interior.
Louis XI costumes.
No royalty.
This poetic comedy well merits presentation.

Catherine Parr, by Maurice Baring.
In *Diminutive Dramas*, Houghton; Baker.
1 M.   1 W.
Scene: the breakfast chamber in the palace of Henry VIII.
Elizabethan costumes.
Royalty, five dollars.
This brilliant trifle, showing an altercation between King Henry the Eighth and Catherine Parr, is easily acted by senior-high-school students.

The Greek Vase, by Maurice Baring.

In *Diminutive Dramas*, Houghton.

2 M.

Scene: a garret.

Modern costumes.

Royalty on application to the publisher.

An art collector selfishly urges a sick artist to sell a precious vase.

This brief play, most serious in its story, is very well written.   It is interesting to senior-high-school students.

Barbara's Wedding, by Sir James M. Barrie.

VI.

4 M.   2 W.

Scene: a sitting room in an English country cottage.

Modern costumes.

Royalty on application to the publisher.

A bewildered old colonel, who sees visions of the past, is unable to comprehend the tragic changes brought about by the World War. This pathetic picture is as fine a thing as Barrie has done. It should be read and studied in the twelfth grade.   Presentation requires great sincerity and much skill.

The New Word, by Sir James M. Barrie.

2 M.   2 W.

Scene: an English dining room.

Modern costumes.

Royalty on application to the publisher.

The New Word deals with the father-and-son complication. The World War, which made people know many new things, caused a father and son to realize that they were not antagonistic but deeply attached to each other.   Some of the more discriminating students will appreciate this play, one of the very best that Barrie has written.

The Old Lady Shows Her Medals, by Sir James M. Barrie.
VI.
2 M. 4 W.
Scene: a basement room.
Modern costumes.
Royalty on application to the publisher.

A childless charwoman, who feels that she has no part in the World War, pretends to have a son at the front. She is exposed. This is perhaps the best of the war plays. Its deep insight into character, genuine comedy, and sharp pathos render it fine stuff for senior-high-school students to study and stage.

Rosalind, by Sir James M. Barrie.
VIII.
1 M. 2 W.
Scene: the parlor of a cottage by the sea.
Modern costumes.
Royalty on application to the publisher.

Rosalind, an actress, who is really "forty and a bittock," reveals her age to a romantic young English fellow in order to cure his infatuation for her.

This sparkling comedy is delightful for the eleventh- and twelfth-grade reading list. It requires rare skill to present it. Now and then there is a twelfth-grade group that can act it with success.

The Twelve-Pound Look, by Sir James M. Barrie.
V; VIII.
2 M. 2 W.
Scene: the living room of an English city residence.
Modern costumes.
Royalty on application to the publisher.

A woman gains economic independence and freedom from a selfish, unimaginative husband. On the eve of being knighted the man is astonished to perceive the look of revolt in the eyes of his second wife.

This is a difficult comedy to act, but it is assuredly worth while for twelfth-grade students to attempt.

A Well-Remembered Voice, by Sir James M. Barrie.

VI.

4 M. 2 W.

Scene: an artist's studio.

Modern costumes.

Royalty on application to the publisher.

A young man who was killed in the war returns and speaks, not to his mother who has resorted to spiritualistic mediums for a message from her son, but to his skeptical father. This play is interesting reading for the eleventh and twelfth grades.

The Will, by Sir James M. Barrie.

VIII.

6 M. 1 W.

Scene: a lawyer's office.

Modern costumes; also costumes of the times of Queen Victoria and of King Edward.

Royalty on application to the publisher.

The three short acts of this play extend over a considerable period of time, and they show in a most poignant manner the ill effect of success and money upon two lives in particular. This is an extraordinarily satisfying short play for twelfth-grade students to study and present.

The Clod, by Lewis Beach.

Doubleday; French.

4 M. 1 W.

Scene: a simple interior.

Civil War costumes.

Royalty, ten dollars.

An ignorant woman, nervously and physically exhausted, kills two Southern officers who bully her beyond endurance. This little masterpiece should be on the reading list of the high school. It is a full-bodied and enthralling tragedy for twelfth graders to study and present.

No Smoking, by Jacinto Benavente.
   Scribner; *Drama*, Feb. 1917.
   2 M.   2 W.
   Scene: a compartment on a European train.
   Modern costumes.
   Royalty on application to the publisher.
   A man goes to the smoking compartment.   An officious woman,
thinking he has left the train, throws his luggage out of the rail-
way carriage.
   This amusing trifle is fun to act at some occasion of minor im-
portance.

The Stepmother, by Arnold Bennett.
   Doran; XVI; XXXIII.
   2 M.   2 W.
   Scene: a luxuriously furnished modern interior.
   Modern costumes.
   Royalty on application to the publisher.
   This farce comedy satirizes, in the author's brilliant style, the
popular lady novelist.   Eleventh- and twelfth-grade girls especially
enjoy reading it.

The Riding to Lithend, by Gordon Bottomley.
   IV.
   9 M.   9 W.
   Scene: the hall of Gunnar's house, Lithend, in South Iceland,
A. D. 900.
   Royalty on application to the publisher.
   "*The Riding to Lithend* is an Icelandic play taken out of the
noblest of the Sagas. . . . [It] is a fight, one of the greatest fights in
legend. . . . The subject is stirring, and Mr. Bottomley takes it
into the very high region of poetry, giving it a purport beyond that
of the original teller of the tale. . . . [The play] is not a representation of life; it is a symbol of life." (Lascelles Abercrombie.)
   This poetic drama is worth reading and acting in the senior
high school.

Rose of the Wind, by Anna Hempstead Branch.

Houghton.

2 M. 2 W.

Scene: a cobbler's cottage.

Fantastic costumes.

Royalty on application to the publisher.

This charming fairy play is effective for presentation in the ninth and tenth grades especially. Song and dance are required.

The Shoes That Danced, by Anna Hempstead Branch.

XV.

3 M. 5 W. 1 J.

Scene: Watteau's Studio.

Fantastic costumes.

Royalty on application to the publisher.

This poetic, fanciful play is enjoyed by many senior-high-school students.

The Change-House, by John Brandane.

XI.

3 M. 2 W. Extras.

Scene: a large room in the Change-House.

Scottish costumes of the year 1752.

Royalty on application to Baker.

Iain Dubh learns that Callum is about to be hanged for a murder which Iain himself unintentionally committed. He struggles against heroic odds to rescue the condemned man. The political background of animosity between the Redcoats and the Highlanders is well pictured in this drama. The play is recommended for study and for presentation in the eleventh and twelfth grades.

Followers, by Harold Brighouse.

IX; XV; XVI.

A "Cranford" sketch.

1 M. 3 W.

Scene: the parlor of Miss Lucinda Baines at Cranford.
English costumes of 1859.
Royalty on application to French.
Miss Baines says no to the man she loves. After twenty-five years in India, he returns and again offers his hand. Believing that she is now too old for romance, she again says no and good-by. Softened by the catastrophe of her own life, she begins to sympathize with and to aid the young lovers about her.
This charming and somewhat pathetic bit of life delights the older members of the senior high school. It is recommended for study and for presentation.

Lonesome-Like, by Harold Brighouse.
In *Representative One-Act Plays by British and Irish Authors,* Little; Baker; IV; XVII.
2 M.   2 W.
Scene: interior of a Lancashire cottage.
Modern costumes.
Royalty, five dollars.
"A shy young engineer is suffering from loneliness since the death of his mother a year before. Failing in his all too clumsy love affair, he turns to an old woman, disabled by rheumatism and about to be taken to the poorhouse, and adopts her as his mother." (Ben Iden Payne.)
This is an unusually well-written one-act play of rural life. Eleventh and twelfth grades act it with much success.

The Maid of France, by Harold Brighouse.
French; XIV.
3 M.   2 W.
Scene: a village square on Christmas Eve during the World War.
Military costumes.
Royalty, five dollars.
This patriotic drama should be on the reading list of the senior high school. It is most impressive and effective when acted.

The Price of Coal, by Harold Brighouse.

French.

1 M.   3 W.

Scene: the living room of a Lanarkshire collier's cottage.

Modern costumes.

Royalty, five dollars.

This one-act drama, which gives a vivid picture of the dreadful hazards of the miner's life, rightly belongs on the drama list of the senior high school.   It needs talented and genuinely emotional seniors to present it faithfully.

The Bank Account, by Howard Brock.

Brentano's.

1 M.   2 W.

Scene: a rather shabby living room.

Modern costumes.

Royalty on application to the publisher.

A hard-working clerk each week gives his wife three dollars out of his meager salary to invest in a Coöperative Bank.   At the end of twelve years he learns that his frivolous wife has squandered the entire sum and that his hope of buying a little farm and of escaping from the bondage of his clerkship is blasted.

This is suitable for the reading list of the senior high school.

Joint Owners in Spain, by Alice Brown.

Macmillan; Baker.

4 W.

Scene: a chamber in an old ladies' home.

Old-fashioned modern costumes.

Royalty, five dollars.

Two cantankerous old women, inmates of an old ladies' home, because they have made life miserable for every one who has ever lived with them, are placed together in one room to work out their problem.

The faithful character drawing in this little comedy makes it popular for ninth, tenth, eleventh, and twelfth grades to present.

The Little King, by Witter Bynner.

Knopf; XXVII.

2 M. 1 W. 2 J.

Scene: a room in the Temple at Paris.

French costumes of the last part of the eighteenth century.

Royalty on application to the publisher.

This finely written drama shows the tremendous bravery of the imprisoned boy-king of France, Louis XVII. Here is a play that has a place on the reading list of the ninth, tenth, eleventh, and twelfth grades. It is somewhat difficult to act but merits the effort.

The Little Stone House, by George Calderon.

Baker.

5 M. 2 W.

Scene: a Russian living room.

Russian costumes.

Royalty, five dollars.

A mother, believing her son dead, makes great sacrifices to save money to erect a small mausoleum in his memory. When the son returns, and she learns that he is a base convict, she turns him over to the police.

This powerful play is not too difficult for expert twelfth graders to present.

The Dumb and the Blind, by Harold Chapin.

French.

2 M. 2 W.

Scene: a simple interior.

Modern costumes.

Royalty on application to the publisher.

Concerning this realistic picture of a bargeman's family in the slums of London, Mr. William Archer writes: "A veritable master-piece in its way — a thing Dickens would have delighted in.... We feel that the dumb has spoken and the blind has seen." This might well be placed on the reading list of the eleventh and twelfth grades.

The Philosopher of Butterbiggens, by Harold Chapin.
  French; IV; XXI.
  2 M. 1 W. 1 J.
  Scene: a tenement kitchen-living room.
  Modern costumes.
  Royalty, ten dollars.
  This particularly splendid comedy deals with a Scottish family living in a suburb of Glasgow. It is a most worth-while play for study and for staging.

What Men Live By, by Virginia Church.
  III.
  5 M. 4 W. 3 J.
  Scene: a basement room.
  Russian costumes.
  Royalty on application to the publisher.
  This well-made adaptation of Tolstoi's famous story is suited to the needs and tastes of the eighth and ninth grades.

Love in a French Kitchen. Translated and adapted from the old
    French by Colin Clements and John M. Saunders.
  French; *Poet Lore*, Winter, 1917.
  1 M. 2 W.
  Scene: an interior.
  Mediæval French costumes.
  Royalty, ten dollars.
  This play, one of the most famous of the masterpieces of old French farce, is read with enjoyment by students of the senior high school. It is vastly amusing when acted by advanced members of the twelfth grade.

Suppressed Desires, by George Cram Cook and Susan Glaspell.
  Baker; XXIV.
  1 M. 2 W.
  Scene: an interior.
  Modern costumes.
  Royalty, ten dollars.

This satirical farce-comedy shows an over-ardent practitioner of psychoanalysis taking her own medicine. It is enjoyed by eleventh and twelfth grades and is fairly well worth presenting.

The Lord's Prayer, by François Coppée. Translation by Mary Aldis.
XV.
3 M. 3 W. Soldiers.
Scene: a simple room.
French costumes of 1871.
Royalty, three dollars. (French publishes a translation of this play under the title *Pater Noster*. There is no royalty for this edition.)
This drama depicts an incident of the Paris Commune in 1871. It has a place on the reading list of the senior high school.

The Violin Maker of Cremona, by François Coppée.
Dramatic Publishing Co.; III.
3 M. 1 W. Extras.
Scene: a violin maker's shop at Cremona.
Italian costumes of 1750.
No royalty.
This charming little romance tells the story of two worthy young men who contest for the hand of a beautiful girl. It is interesting for the ninth and tenth grades to read and present.

Peggy, by Rachel Crothers.
Baker.
2 M. 4 W. 1 J.
Scene: a room in an old house, a short distance out of Philadelphia.
Modern costumes.
Royalty, ten dollars.
A dancer makes a great sacrifice for the love of her stepson. This absorbing short play by one of America's most successful dramatists may be placed on the reading list of the senior high school. The characterizations are difficult for amateurs, but twelfth graders might act it with a measure of effectiveness.

The Play of Saint George, by J. M. C. Crum.
  Baker; III.
  13 M. 6 W. Others.
  No special scenery is required. Singing adds greatly to the effectiveness of the play, but it is not absolutely necessary.
  Old English costumes.
  No royalty.
  This farce, based on the old legend of the patron saint of England, was written by the Reverend J. M. C. Crum for some English school children. Its infectious fun and its simplicity help to render it good play material for American seventh and eighth graders.

On Vengeance Height, by Allan Davis.
  French; XXXIII.
  2 M. 2 W.
  Scene: the interior of a rude cabin.
  Modern mountaineer costumes.
  Royalty, five dollars.
  This tragic story of a blood feud in the Tennessee Mountains belongs on the list of dramas read in the senior high school. It is not beyond the acting ability of some of the more advanced students.

Allison's Lad, by Beulah M. Dix.
  I; XVIII; XXIV.
  6 M.
  Scene: an upper chamber of an English village inn.
  English costumes of 1648.
  Royalty on application to the publisher.
  A young soldier, who seems to inherit cowardly traits from his father, is brought to a sense of his duty by an old friend and admirer of his mother. The courageous manner in which the boy faces death proves that he is fundamentally his mother's son. This is a very good play for eighth, ninth, tenth, and eleventh grades to study and present.

The Captain of the Gate, by Beulah M. Dix.

I; IV.

6 M.

Period costumes.

Scene: an upper chamber of the gatehouse, a dimly-lit apartment, built of stone.

Royalty on application to the publisher.

This tragic incident in the invasion of Ireland by Cromwell profoundly interests boys of the senior high school. It is difficult to act, but it is quite possible and thoroughly worth while for serious-minded students.

The Dark of the Dawn, by Beulah M. Dix.

I; XXIX.

4 M.

Scene: a simple interior.

Costumes of the time of the Thirty Years' War.

Royalty on application to the publisher.

This dramatic episode appeals strongly to boys of the eighth, ninth, and tenth grades.

The Maker of Dreams, by Oliphant Down.

Baker; French; XIV; XVI; XXIX.

2 M.   1 W.

Scene: a room in an old cottage.

Fantastic costumes.

Royalty, eight dollars.

Pierrot, blinded by the praise given him for his songs, seeks love afar and fails to appreciate the affection of Pierrette. The Maker of Dreams opens Pierrot's eyes. This fantasy is a great favorite with senior-high-school pupils. Presentation is not difficult for serious actors. The person playing Pierrot must have a good singing voice. Baker furnishes the musical score for one dollar and fifty cents.

Pierrot of the Minute, by Ernest Dowson.

Baker; In *Fifty Contemporary One-Act Plays*, Appleton; XIV.

1 M.   1 W.

Scene: a glade in the Parc du Petit Trianon.

Fantastic costumes.

No royalty.

This dramatic fantasy in one act "illustrates the idea that, while the artist is ephemeral, his art endures." (Publisher's comment.) This delicate, beautifully written play by one of the modern English poets is not beyond the abilities of twelfth-grade pupils. It is admirably suited to out-of-doors presentation.

X = O: A Night of the Trojan War, by John Drinkwater.

XV.

6 M.

Scene: a Greek tent and the Trojan walls.

Greek and Trojan costumes.

Royalty on application to the publisher.

This poetic tragedy brings home forcibly the human cost of war. This should be on the list of plays to be studied. Eighth graders are not too immature to be introduced to it. The staging offers difficulties, but they are not insurmountable.

The Poor House, by Louise Driscoll.

XI.

2 M.   2 W.

Scene: a kitchen.

Modern costumes.

Royalty on application to the publisher.

An elderly spinster, in order to keep her shiftless nephew out of the reformatory, gives the money which she had saved to gain admittance to the Home for Aged Women. This pathetic picture of an over-indulgent woman is suitably placed on the reading list of the senior high school.

The Evil Kettle, by Lord Dunsany.

French; II.

1 M.   1 W.

Scene: an interior.

Costumes of the eighteenth century.

Royalty on application to the publisher.

This comedy, about the discovery of steam, pleases ninth graders.

Fame and the Poet, by Lord Dunsany.

IV.

2 M.   1 W.

Scene: a poet's room in London.

Modern costumes.

Royalty on application to the publisher.

For ten years a poet worships Fame and offers his songs at her altars.   One evening the fair lady appears, and the poet is sadly disillusioned.   This satirical comedy is fittingly placed on the reading list of the senior high school.   If acted, it is suited only to mature seniors.

The Glittering Gate, by Lord Dunsany.

VII.

2 M.

Scene: a lonely place near the Gate of Heaven.

Modern costumes.

Royalty on application to the publisher.

Jim and Bill, lately burglars, now both dead, try in vain to force their way into heaven.   This is a notable little play for the reading list of the ninth grade and the senior high school.

The Gods of the Mountains, by Lord Dunsany.

VII.

10 M.   Extras.

Scene: one interior, one exterior.

Fanciful costumes.

Royalty on application to Little, Brown and Company.

Seven beggars pretend to be gods; for a time they seem to meet with success, but at length they are punished by being turned into stone.   This richly symbolic play in three short acts is highly recommended for study and presentation in the senior high school.

The Golden Doom, by Lord Dunsany.

In *Representative One-Act Plays by British and Irish Authors,* Little; VII; XVIII.

10 M.   A boy and a girl.

Scene: outside the King's great door in Zericon, before the fall of Babylon.

Period costumes.

Royalty on application to the publisher.

"In *The Golden Doom* the fate of an empire and a little boy's desire for a new plaything become linked as facts of equal importance in the web of fate." (Edwin Björkman.) Here is a play which merits study and presentation in the eighth and ninth grades, or even in the senior high school.

King Argimēnēs and the Unknown Warrior, by Lord Dunsany.

VII.

11 M. 4 W. Extras.

First scene: the slave-fields of King Darniak; second scene: the throne hall of King Darniak.

The time is long ago.

Period costumes.

Royalty on application to the publisher.

King Argimēnēs, deposed and enslaved by King Darniak, while digging in the slave-fields unearths a great sword. His courage returns; he leads a revolt, overthrows the false dynasty, and again comes into his own. This is one of the immensely satisfying short plays for study and presentation in the senior high school.

The Lost Silk Hat, by Lord Dunsany.

VII; XIII.

5 M.

Scene: a fashionable street in London.

Modern costumes.

Royalty on application to the publisher.

This zestful comedy is slight in plot but is replete with excellent character drawing and amusing satire. It is good reading for the senior high school. Presentation requires considerable skill on the part of the actors.

A Night at an Inn, by Lord Dunsany.

XVI; XX; XXIX.

8 M.

Scene: a room in an old inn.

Modern and fanciful costumes.

Royalty on application to the publisher.

Four thieves steal a huge ruby from an idol's eye. They are confident that through strength and cleverness they can outwit all pursuers. They kill three priests of the idol, but finally the idol itself appears, and death is the portion of the robbers. This is one of the best one-act tragedies. It is justly popular in the senior high school for study and for presentation.

The Prince of Stamboul, by Lord Dunsany.

XXVII.

3 M. 2 W. 1 J.

Scene: a room in a cottage.

Modern costumes.

Royalty on application to the publisher.

A little girl who is very ill greatly desires to hear Tommy Tiddler play "Home Sweet Home" on his flute. The Prince, a great violinist, plays for the sick girl without effecting a cure. Tommy Tiddler is sent for, and the child's life is saved. This is a play for the reading list of the eighth, ninth, and tenth grades. The fact that it requires actors who are musicians rules it out of the list of plays suggested for general presentation.

The Queen's Enemies, by Lord Dunsany.

XX.

9 M. 2 W. Extras.

Scene: an underground temple in Egypt.

Egyptian costumes of the Sixth Dynasty.

Royalty on application to the publisher.

The Queen invites her enemies to a banquet in a great room under the Nile. Having protested her eagerness for a reconciliation, she has the waters of the Nile let into the chamber, and her guests meet with a terrible death. This tale of tragic horror is much liked by pupils of the senior high school. The staging, for one thing, rules it out of the list of plays suggested for general presentation.

The Tents of the Arabs, by Lord Dunsany.
XX.
A play in two short acts.
5 M. 1 W.
Scene: outside the gate of the city of Thalanna.
Arabian costumes.
Royalty on application to the publisher.
The King of Thalanna, weary of his so-called power, willingly surrenders his throne and as a humble camel driver follows the call of the desert.
The superb beauty and the literary excellence of this romance recommend it for study and for staging in the senior high school.

Hearts Enduring, by John Erskine.
XI.
1 M. 1 W.
Scene: the interior of a hut.
Costumes of the time of the Crusades.
Royalty, five dollars.
Professor Erskine's brief tragic episode tells of a Crusader who returns to find his wife a victim of a loathsome disease. It belongs on the reading list of the senior high school.

Nerves, by John Farrar.
III.
9 M.
Scene: a mess hall.
Modern costumes.
Royalty on application to the publisher.
A sensitive young fellow, under the horrible strain of war, for a time loses his nerve. Then in a supreme effort to prove his bravery to his comrades, he makes a solo flight, brings down one of the enemy, but loses his own life. This tragedy should be on the list of plays to be read in the ninth grade and in the senior high school. A performance of *Nerves* on Armistice Day would be a fitting way of bringing home to young people the cost of war.

'Op-O'-Me-Thumb, by Frederick Fenn and Richard Pryce.

In *Representative One-Act Plays by British and Irish Authors,* Little; XVII.

1 M.   5 W.

Scene: the working room at a laundry in Soho.

Modern costumes.

Royalty, ten dollars.

A charming little cockney laundress makes believe that she has a rich and handsome lover in the owner of an uncalled-for package. At length the man appears, and she has a rude awakening.

This humorous and pathetic play merits study and presentation in the senior high school.

Campbell of Kilmhor, by J. A. Ferguson.

French; IV; XVI.

4 M.   2 W.   Soldiers.

Scene: the interior of a lonely cottage.

Costumes of the period of Mary Stuart.

Royalty, five dollars.

This stirring patriotic drama of the time of Mary Stuart is worthy of study and presentation.   It is not too subtle for ninth and tenth graders.

The Fifteenth Candle, by Rachel L. Field.

III.

2 M.   3 W.

Scene: a small dark room in the basement of a city block.

Modern costumes.

Royalty, ten dollars where admission is charged; five dollars where it is not.

This is a play of tenement life.   An Italian immigrant girl battles against her father's greed in order that her younger sister may continue her training in art.   Eighth, ninth, and tenth graders enjoy reading this play.

Three Pills in a Bottle, by Rachel L. Field.

XXX.

4 M.   3 W.   1 J.

Scene: a simple interior.

Fantastic costumes.

Royalty, ten dollars where admission is charged; five dollars where it is not.

A little sick boy from his window makes friends with passers-by. Each allows his soul to visit the child. This fantasy has been deservedly popular with high-school students. The ninth and tenth grades are especially good years in which to study and present it.

"Voices," by Hortense Flexner.

XXIV.

2 W.

Scene: the main street of Domrémy, in front of the church sacred to Jeanne D'Arc.

Modern French peasant costumes.

Royalty on application to the publisher.

The spirit of Jeanne d'Arc appears to Yvonne, a peasant girl, and tells her that not the sword but a host of women, actuated by pitying hearts, will overthrow tyranny and end warfare. This extremely short poetic drama is of value for study and presentation in the senior year of the high school.

The Man Who Married a Dumb Wife, by Anatole France.

Lane; XXI.

14 M.   4 W.

Scene: a large room in a French home.

French costumes of the Middle Ages.

Royalty on application to Dodd, Mead and Company.

Judge Botal summons famous physicians to heal his wife of dumbness. Shortly after her cure he seeks a remedy for her loquacity. This is one of the very best short farces in any language, and Mr. Curtis Hidden Page has made a splendid translation. Senior-high-school students stage and act the play with particular zest and profit.

A Way Out, by Robert Frost.

XI.

2 M.

Scene: a bachelor's kitchen-bedroom in an old farmhouse.

Modern costumes.

Royalty on application to the publisher.

The tragic death of a New England recluse at the hands of a criminal is done with the same weird realism and power which the great New England poet has shown in many of his famous narrative poems. The eleventh and twelfth grades enjoy reading this play, but it is perhaps too tragic for high-school presentation.

By Ourselves, by Ludwig Fulda.

XXVI.

3 M.   2 W.

Scene: a dining room.

Modern costumes.

Royalty on application to the publisher.

A self-centered husband and a pleasure-loving wife, after a few months of married life, find that they are drifting apart. A reconciliation is brought about in a novel manner.

This social satire is interesting reading in the senior high school. Twelfth graders are capable of presenting it with telling effect.

The Brink of Silence, by Esther E. Galbraith.

XXIV; XXIX.

4 M.

Scene: inside a log house on a rocky island far down in the Antarctic.

Modern costumes.

Royalty on application to the publisher.

This play reveals the heroic sacrifice of an unfortunate explorer for his wife and son. It appeals particularly to boys of the junior high school. Staging offers few difficulties.

The Neighbors, by Zona Gale.

Huebsch.

2 M.   6 W.

Scene: simple interior.

Modern costumes.

Royalty on application to the publisher.

A poor woman assumes the care of an orphan.   The neighbors in their desire to help forget their petty disputes and work together in perfect harmony.

This comedy of village life is well worth performance and ninth, tenth, eleventh, and twelfth grades alike enjoy it.

Uncle Jimmy, by Zona Gale.

French.

3 M.   5 W.

Scene: the back dooryard of two adjoining homes.

Modern costumes.

Royalty on application to the publisher.

This comedy gives an amusing portrait of middle-class people living in a small town in Wisconsin.   It is fittingly placed on the reading list of the ninth, tenth, and eleventh grades.   It offers opportunities for excellent characterization.

The Little Man, by John Galsworthy.

XIV; XVI.

9 M.   2 W.

First scene: the departure platform of an Austrian railway station; second scene: a second-class compartment of a corridor carriage; third scene: an arrival platform.

Modern costumes.

Royalty on application to the publisher.

This farcical morality, which has for its central idea universal brotherhood, is admirably suited to senior-high-school study and presentation.   The settings are readily suggested by the use of simple screens and draperies.

The Sun, by John Galsworthy.

IV.

2 M.   1 W.

Scene: a stile by a river.

Modern costumes.

Royalty on application to the publisher.

A soldier discharged because of wounds encounters his rival for the hand of a young woman.   This vivid, terse picture of the days immediately after the World War may well be placed on the reading list of the eleventh and twelfth grades.

Overtones, by Alice Gerstenberg.

Longmans.

4 W.

Scene: a fashionable drawing-room.

Modern costumes.

Royalty, ten dollars where admission is charged; five dollars where it is not.

A jealous society woman and the wife of a struggling artist converse politely, while their dual selves reveal to the audience the turmoil and anxiety in the minds of the two women.   This is a very well-conceived and skilfully executed one-act play.   It is mature and somewhat sophisticated for high-school use, but twelfth-grade girls enjoy it and often present it with notable success.

The Pot Boiler, by Alice Gerstenberg.

Longmans.

5 M.   2 W.

No particular setting required.

Modern costumes.

Royalty, ten dollars where admission is charged; five dollars where it is not.

In this rather amusing satire on playwriting, an author conducts a rehearsal.   Students of the eleventh and twelfth grades often enjoy working out the presentation of this play without the aid of an adult.

The Unseen, by Alice Gerstenberg.

Longmans; XIII.

1 M.   2 W.

Scene: a dining room.

Modern costumes.

Royalty, ten dollars where admission is charged; five dollars where it is not.

The Unseen presents a confused Swedish maid, an architect contesting for a large prize, an ambitious wife, and a happy solution for all.

This is interesting reading for the ninth and tenth grades.

Trifles, by Susan Glaspell.

Baker.

3 M.   2 W.

Scene: a kitchen.

Modern costumes.

Royalty, ten dollars.

"*Trifles* is a tragedy; yet the audience sees neither the tragic deed nor the persons concerned. A man appears to have been murdered in a lone farmhouse, and his wife is under arrest on suspicion. A country attorney, the sheriff, and a farmer are fussing about in search of evidence against her; while two women friends, finding a slain canary and a broken bird cage, divine the whole story of a woman driven to desperation by cruelty and neglect." (Publisher's notice.)

This is a really great one-act play. Twelfth-grade students should study it even if they do not act it.

Back of the Yards, by Kenneth Sawyer Goodman.

Stage Guild.

3 M.   2 W.

Scene: an interior.

Modern costumes.

Royalty on application to the publisher.

This powerful play dealing with the problem of the city boy and the street gang is suitable both for reading and for presentation in the senior year.

Dust of the Road, by Kenneth Sawyer Goodman.

Longmans; Stage Guild; XIII.

A Christmas morality in a modern setting.

3 M. 1 W.

Scene: the living room of a comfortable and fairly prosperous Middle-Western farmer.

Modern costumes.

Royalty, five dollars where admission is charged; two dollars and a half where it is not.

On Christmas Eve a tramp prevents a man and woman from stealing money intrusted to them. This is an effective play for senior-high-school students to present.

The Game of Chess, by Kenneth Sawyer Goodman.

Stage Guild; XXXIII.

4 M.

Scene: a wainscoted room.

Modern Russian costumes.

Royalty on application to the publisher.

A Russian aristocrat by clever strategy brings about the death of a workman who came to slay him. A powerful gripping drama for twelfth-grade boys to present.

The Bellman of Mons, by Dorothy R. Googins.

III.

6 M. 5 W. 2 J. Others.

First scene: a market-place in ancient Mons; second: the interior of a cowherd's cottage.

Costumes of ancient Belgium.

Royalty on application to the publisher.

The play, in three short acts, tells how a peasant lad broke the curse of silence which for a hundred years rested on the great organ of Mons Cathedral. Eighth and ninth graders particularly find this drama worthy for study and presentation.

The Impertinence of the Creature, by Cosmo Gordon-Lennox.

French; in *Representative One-Act Plays by British and Irish Authors*, Little.

1 M.   1 W.

Scene: a boudoir leading from a London ballroom.

Modern costumes.

Royalty, five dollars.

Lady Millicent, at a ball where she knows no one, rebukes a gentleman who follows her from room to room. She finds at length that he is Herbert Barwell, the noted explorer, and that he has been requested by the hostess, his sister, to take Lady Millicent down for supper. This little comedy takes about ten minutes to act. It serves well a twelfth grade which wishes to do a slight but entertaining duologue.

Rococo, by Harley Granville-Barker.

Little.

3 M.   3 W.

Scene: drawing-room of an English vicarage.

Modern costumes.

Royalty on application to the publisher.

This zestful comedy, which depicts the physical and verbal struggles of a clergyman and his relatives to gain possession of a rococo vase, has a place on the reading list of the eleventh and twelfth grades.

The Last of the Lowries, by Paul Green.

French; XI.

1 M.   3 W.

Scene: a kitchen.

Modern costumes.

Royalty, five dollars.

It tells the story of the last member of the Lowry family and his death on the occasion of his return home to see his mother and family. This folk drama about the Croatan outlaws of Robeson County, North Carolina, is interesting reading for the senior high school.

Damer's Gold, by Lady Gregory.

Putnam; French.

4 M.   1 W.

Scene: a simple interior.

Irish costumes.

Royalty, five dollars.

This lively comedy in two short acts has for its subject the greed of relatives.   It is well suited for reading and presentation in the ninth, tenth, or eleventh grade.

The Gaol Gate, by Lady Gregory.

French; XXV.

1 M.   2 W.

Scene: outside the gate of Galway Gaol.

Irish costumes.

Royalty, five dollars.

A country woman comes to the prison gate to inquire after her son.   She is told by the gatekeeper that he was hanged a few hours previously.   This pathetic little play has a place on the reading list of the senior high school.

Hyacinth Halvey, by Lady Gregory.

French; V; XXV.

4 M.   2 W.

Scene: outside the post office in the little town of Cloon.

Modern Irish peasant costumes.

Royalty, five dollars.

The tenacity of reputation is the theme in this delightful comedy of Irish life.   It is enjoyed in the ninth and tenth years most thoroughly.

The Jackdaw, by Lady Gregory.

French; XXV.

4 M.   2 W.

Scene: the interior of a small shop.

Modern Irish peasant costumes.

Royalty, five dollars.

This delightful comedy of Irish life is recommended for study and for presentation in the ninth grade or in the senior high school.

The Rising of the Moon, by Lady Gregory.

French; XV; XVII; XXV; XXIX.

4 M.

Scene: the side of a quay in a seaport town.

Modern Irish costumes.

Royalty, five dollars.

Adherence to the letter of the law versus loyalty to an ideal is the subject of this play. This comedy is perfect for study and presentation anywhere from the eighth grade up.

Spreading the News, by Lady Gregory.

French; IV; XIV; XVIII; XXI; XXIV; XXV; XXVI.

7 M. 3 W.

Scene: the outskirts of a fair green in Ireland.

Modern Irish peasant costumes.

Royalty, five dollars.

Gossip and its fruition are the subject of this well-nigh perfect Irish farce-comedy. Ninth, tenth, and eleventh grades especially enjoy the study and presentation of this play.

The Traveling Man, by Lady Gregory.

French; XXV; XXVII; XXXII.

1 M. 1 W. 1 Boy.

Scene: a cottage kitchen.

Modern Irish peasant costumes.

Royalty, five dollars.

An impatient woman turns from her door a stranger whom she finds playing with her little son. After he has gone, she realizes that she has turned away the King of the World. This very brief but lovely play is excellent for eighth and ninth grades to present. It fits the Christmas season beautifully.

The Workhouse Ward, by Lady Gregory.
>French; XIII; XXV.
>2 M. 1 W.
>Scene: a ward in Cloon workhouse.
>Modern Irish peasant costumes.
>Royalty, five dollars.

This well-written farce-comedy reveals the innate loyalty of two old Irish paupers, who, from their adjacent beds in the workhouse, hurl abusive language and even more substantial things at each other. This play contains splendid character study. It can readily be presented by ninth graders or by students of the senior high school.

The Valiant, by Holworthy Hall and Robert Middlemass.
>Longmans.
>5 M. 1 W.
>Scene: the warden's room in a prison.
>Modern costumes.
>Royalty, ten dollars.

A young man about to be hanged is visited by his sister. She fails to recognize him, and in order that his mother shall never know that her son has been a murderer, he makes the girl believe that her brother died the death of a hero on the battlefield. This intensely gripping play is good acting material for twelfth-grade boys. It is a great favorite on the reading list of the senior high school.

Will o' the Wisp, by Doris F. Halman.
>Baker; XVIII; XXIV.
>4 W.
>Scene: "the interior of a farmhouse at the end of things."
>Modern costumes.
>Royalty, ten dollars.

A will-o'-the-wisp leads a poet to find among the moors inspiration for his songs. The poet marries, and his rich wife causes him to forget his art. The will-o'-the-wisp leads her out beyond the cliff head to her death. Experience indicates that eleventh- and twelfth-grade girls find pleasure in acting this fanciful play.

The Burglar Who Failed, by St. John Hankin.
In *Dramatic Works*, Vol. III, Mitchell Kennerley.
1 M.   2 W.
Scene: an English bedroom.
Modern costumes.
Royalty on application to the publisher.
A sports-loving English girl discovers a burglar under her bed.
The genuine humor and the clever character drawing in St. John Hankin's little play make it popular material for presentation in the senior high school.

The Florist Shop, by Winifred Hawkridge.
Baker; in *The Harvard Dramatic Club, 1st Series*, Brentano's.
3 M.   2 W.
Scene: interior of a florist's shop.
Modern costumes.
Royalty, ten dollars.
Maude, the sentimental bookkeeper in Slovsky's flower shop, through a quaint scheme brings about the marriage of a long-engaged couple.   Here is a play which never fails to interest young people of the senior high school.   It is admirable comedy for twelfth graders to stage.

The Wonder Hat, by Ben Hecht and Kenneth Sawyer Goodman.
Stage Guild; XXIV.
3 M.   2 W.
Scene: a park by moonlight.
Fanciful costumes.
Royalty on application to the publisher.
Punchinello sells to Harlequin the wonder hat which renders the wearer invisible.   The consequence is the vast confusion of Columbine, Pierrot, and Margot.
This brilliant, fantastic burlesque is worthy material for twelfth graders to present.

Modesty, by Paul Hervieu.

French; V.

2 M.   1 W.

Scene: an interior.

Modern costumes.

No royalty.

A young woman declares that she will accept the hand of the man who tells her frankly what he thinks of her. One of her suitors takes her at her word. The result is not precisely what the young man had been led to expect.

This amusing satirical comedy is much enjoyed by the senior high school. It is good fun when well acted.

Martha's Mourning, by Phoebe Hoffman.

Baker; XXIV.

3 W.

Scene: a simple interior.

Modern costumes.

Royalty, five dollars.

The story deals with the death-bed repentance of a miserly old woman.

This well-written one-act play has a place on the twelfth-grade reading list.

Moonshine, by Arthur Hopkins.

French; V.

2 M.

Scene: a simple interior.

Modern costumes.

Royalty, five dollars.

A revenue officer matches wits with desperate moonshiners and makes a clever get-away.

Ninth-, tenth-, eleventh-, and twelfth-grade students love to read and to act this thrilling play written by a man who knows the professional stage at first hand.

The Dear Departed, by Stanley Houghton.

French; XI; XVII.

3 M.   2 W.   1 Girl of ten.

Scene: the sitting room of a small house in a lower-middle-class district of a provincial town.

Modern costumes.

Royalty, five dollars.

This study of hypocrisy is justly popular.   Senior-high-school pupils act it with excellent effect.

The Fifth Commandment, by Stanley Houghton.

In *Five One-Act Plays,* French.

2 M.   2 W.

Scene: a simple interior.

Modern costumes.

Royalty on application to the publisher.

A selfish mother ruins her daughter's chance of marriage.   This serious play is interesting reading for many seniors.

Bethlehem, by Laurence Housman.

Macmillan.

13 M.   2 W.   Others.

Scene: Act I, a bare field; Act II, the inn-stable.

Biblical costumes.

Royalty on application to the publisher.

This poetic story of the Nativity is admirable for presentation in the senior high school. It can be staged with draperies for a background. Song and instrumental music play an important part in the performance.

The Mouse Trap, by William Dean Howells.

French.

1 M.   6 W.

Modern costumes.

Scene: an interior.

No royalty.

This amusing but somewhat ancient farce may perhaps claim a place on the reading list of the ninth and tenth grades.

The Nativity, by Douglas Hyde.
In *Poets and Dreamers*, by Lady Gregory, Murray.
7 M.   3 W.
Scene: just outside the stable where Jesus was born.
Biblical costumes.
Royalty on application to the publisher.
This exquisite telling of the story of two Irish peasant women who sought the cradle of the Christ child is admirable drama for junior- or senior-high-school students to study and present.

The Twisting of the Rope, by Douglas Hyde.
IX.
2 M.   3 W.
Scene: a room in a farmer's house.
Irish peasant costumes.
Royalty on application to the publisher.
This amusing little Irish folk play is enjoyed by boys of the junior high school particularly.   Presentation is very simple.

The Ghost of Jerry Bundler, by W. W. Jacobs and Charles Rock.
French.
7 M.
Scene: the interior of an old-fashioned inn.
Modern costumes.
Royalty, five dollars.
A group of men at an old English inn are discussing ghosts.   The statement is made that the place is supposed to be haunted by the spirit of Jerry Bundler.   One of the men declares that he has no fear of ghosts, and to test his statement, another member of the party dresses up like a ghost.   A tragedy follows.   Some versions of the play give a happy ending, but this tends to spoil the unity of the drama.
Ninth-grade and senior-high-school students enjoy reading and acting this rather gruesome but effective play.

The Monkey's Paw, by W. W. Jacobs and Louis N. Parker.
French; XVII.   *
3 M.   1 W.

Scene: a simple interior.

Modern costumes.

Royalty, ten dollars.

Senior-high-school students enjoy reading this grim mystery play.

The Goal, by Henry Arthur Jones.

Doran.

4 M. 2 W.

Scene: a richly furnished apartment.

Modern costumes.

Royalty on application to the publisher.

The great English dramatist pictures in his most masterful style the last half hour of the life of an iron-willed bridge builder. It should appear on the reading list of the twelfth grade.

The Flattering Word, by George Kelly.

French.

2 M. 3 W.

Scene: a simple interior.

Modern costumes.

Royalty, ten dollars.

This is a satire showing the power of flattery on a narrow and prejudiced mind. It has sufficient merit to place it on the reading list of the senior high school, and makes a pleasing comedy for presentation at the general assembly.

My Lady's Lace, by Edward Knoblock.

French; XV.

2 M. 2 W.

Scene: the exterior of a small Dutch house of about 1660.

Dutch costumes.

Royalty, ten dollars.

The plot involves a lovely young girl who, to escape marriage with a young man of her autocratic father's choice, sets a trap which reveals her suitor's mercenary and base nature.

This striking episode, from Mr. Knoblock's long play, *My Lady's Dress*, belongs on the reading list of the ninth, tenth, eleventh, and twelfth grades. It is effective for presentation.

Lima Beans, by Alfred Kreymborg.
French; Longmans; XXIV.
2 M.   1 W.
Scene: an interior.
Fantastic costumes.
Royalty, ten dollars.
This famous one-act, free-verse play is highly recommended to senior-high-school pupils for presentation. The staging as well as the acting permits of much originality and display of artistic taste.

Manikin and Minikin, by Alfred Kreymborg.
French; Longmans; V; XV; XXI.
1 M.   1 W.
Scene: the mantelshelf, with clock and two candlesticks.
Eighteenth-century costumes.
Royalty, ten dollars.
This fantastic comedy makes an effective little play for presentation in the senior high school.

Mr. Sampson, by Charles Lee.
French.
1 M.   2 W.
Scene: the kitchen of a cottage on a moorland in the West Country.
Modern costumes.
Royalty, five dollars.
Mr. Sampson proposes marriage to the two Stevens sisters. As he has no preference he says to them, "Be so kind as to settle it up between yourselves ——"
This play requires skilful characterization, but twelfth graders enjoy acting it, and audiences share in the enjoyment.

Jephthah's Daughter, by Elma E. Levinger.
French; III; IX; XXI.
5 M.   6 W.   Extras.
Scene: before the house of Jephthah, on the road to Mizpah.

Biblical costumes.

No royalty.

This well-constructed drama, founded on the Bible story, received a prize in one of the contests conducted by the Drama League of America. It merits careful reading and study in the ninth and tenth grades. It can be presented by a small group, or it can well be staged as a pageant play.

The Silver Lining, by Constance D'Arcy Mackay.

XXVI; XXIX.

2 M. 1 W.

Scene: a library.

English costumes of the year 1778.

Royalty on application to the publisher.

This diminutive comedy gives an incident in the life of Fanny Burney. It is well suited to the interests of the eighth and ninth grades, and fits well on the school assembly program.

Gettysburg, by Percy MacKaye.

French; IV; XIV.

1 M. 1 W.

Scene: a woodshed.

Modern rural costumes.

Royalty, ten dollars.

Percy MacKaye tells his story in rhythmic verse. It has a place on the reading list of the ninth and tenth grades.

Kinfolk of Robin Hood, by Percy MacKaye.

French; III.

27 M. 7 W.

Scene: two interiors and one exterior.

Old English costumes.

Royalty, ten dollars.

This romantic play, in four brief acts, is based on an old English ballad. It is admirable for boys of the junior high school to present. Curtains can be used in place of scenery.

Sam Average, by Percy MacKaye.
Duffield; V; XXIV.
3 M. 1 W.
Scene: an intrenchment in Canada, near Niagara Falls.
Costumes of 1814.
Royalty, ten dollars.
Sam Average keeps a soldier loyal to his cause. This play is effective on the stage and is liked by many senior-high-school students.

Washington and Betsy Ross, by Percy MacKaye.
French.
3 M. 2 W.
Scene: an interior.
American Colonial costumes.
Royalty, ten dollars.
This play has been especially arranged by Mr. MacKaye to form one of the scenes in his long play, *Washington, the Man Who Made Us.* It is a delightful episode, complete in itself, and deals with the making of our first flag.
The play is valuable for reading and for presentation particularly in the ninth and tenth grades.

A Fan and Two Candlesticks, by Mary MacMillan.
Appleton.
3 M. 1 W.
Scene: a simple interior.
Colonial costumes.
Royalty on application to the publisher.
This rococo bit of the Georgian period written in rhymed couplets is attractive to high-school students.

The Blind, by Maurice Maeterlinck.
Dodd.
7 M. 6 W.
Scene: an ancient Norland forest.
Priestly and ancient costumes.
Royalty on application to the publisher.

A priest who has led a party of blind persons into a wood suddenly dies. This masterful bit of tragic symbolism is best placed on the reading list of the more mature seniors.

The Death of Tintagiles, by Maurice Maeterlinck.

X.

6 W. 1 J.

Scene: Act I, the top of a hill overlooking a castle; Act II, a room in the castle; Act III, the same room; Act IV, a corridor; Act V, before a great iron door in a gloomy vault.

Fanciful costumes.

Royalty on application to the publisher.

This is an affecting little play in five short acts about a child in the grasp of a powerful queen and her devoted sisters' vain attempts to rescue her.

The mysticism and maturity of this drama put it beyond the appreciation of high-school students except, perhaps, a few seniors.

The Interior, by Maurice Maeterlinck.

X.

4 M. 5 W.

Scene: an old garden. At the back is a house with large windows through which a room is distinctly visible.

Modern costumes.

Royalty on application to the publisher.

This is another of Maeterlinck's short mystical tragedies. It may be placed on the reading list of the more devoted drama lovers of the senior class.

The Intruder, by Maurice Maeterlinck.

X; XIV.

Scene: a dimly lighted room in an old country house.

Modern costumes.

Royalty on application to the publisher.

The mystery of the coming of death is the theme of this great symbolic play. The beauty and the significance of the drama make it valuable reading for thoughtful high-school students.

The Miracle of St. Anthony, by Maurice Maeterlinck.

X.

11 M.   4 W.

First scene: an entrance hall of an old homestead; second: a living room.

Modern French provincial costumes.

Royalty on application to the publisher.

In this clever satire, St. Anthony appears to a seemingly grief-stricken group and offers to bring back the deceased. This play may be placed on the reading list of the senior class but is not appropriate for high-school presentation.

The Merry Merry Cuckoo, by Jeannette Marks.

XXIV; XXVI; XXXI.

3 M.   2 W.

Scene: a garden.

Modern costumes.

Royalty on application to the publisher.

A devoted old Welsh wife is willing to risk the salvation of her soul to give her husband happiness during his dying hours. This is a very beautiful play for the senior high school to read and study. If presented it must be done by rarely sympathetic and sincere actors.

The Locked Chest, by John Masefield.

XXVI.

3 M.   1 W.   Extras.

Scene: a room in Iceland, in the ninth or tenth century.

Ancient Icelandic costumes.

Royalty on application to the publisher.

This memorable play shows how a brave woman, in spite of a cowardly husband and a brutal enemy, saves the life of her cousin. Pupils of the ninth grade and of the senior high school enjoy reading this play. Eleventh and twelfth grades find it excellent for presentation.

The Red Turf, by Rutherford Mayne.
Maunsel.
4 M.   1 W.
Scene: a peasant kitchen in the bog lands in the West of Ireland.
Irish costumes.
Royalty on application to the publisher.
A dispute over the ownership of land leads to tragedy.   This grim but faithful picture belongs on the reading list of the senior high school.   Presentation of it is within the scope of seniors.

The Bishop's Candlesticks, by Norman McKinnel.
French.
3 M.   2 W.
Scene: a simple interior.
French costumes of 1800.
Royalty, five dollars.
This dramatization of an incident in Victor Hugo's *Les Miserables* is good acting material for the eighth, ninth, tenth, eleventh, and twelfth grades.

Tradition, by George Middleton.
French; V.
1 M.   2 W.
Scene: an interior.
Modern costumes.
Royalty, five dollars.
Pupils in the eleventh and twelfth grades can in a measure appreciate this study of a father's attempt to crush the artistic ambitions of his wife and daughter.

Aria da Capo, by Edna St. Vincent Millay.
Appleton.
4 M.   1 W.
Scene: "A stage set for a Harlequinade, a merry black and white interior."
Harlequinade and shepherd costumes.
Royalty, fifteen dollars.

In this weird fantasy, Pierrot, Columbine, two shepherds, and Cothurnus (masque of tragedy) give searching glimpses into the mysteries of human experience.

This splendidly conceived and written play, with its deep philosophy, is most valuable drama for serious-minded seniors to study and present.

Two Slatterns and a King, by Edna St. Vincent Millay.
Appleton.
2 M.   2 W.
No special setting.
Fanciful costumes.
Royalty on application to the publisher.
This jolly trifle in verse, called by Miss Millay a Moral Interlude, is excellent for study and presentation in the junior high school.

The Artist, by A. A. Milne.
French; XI.
1 M.   1 W.
Scene: the hall of a country cottage.
Modern costumes.
Royalty, ten dollars.
This most gay, sparkling, and somewhat sophisticated consideration of the whimsicalities of the artistic temperament is best appreciated in the twelfth grade.   It is good acting material.

The Boy Comes Home, by A. A. Milne.
French; XV; XVI.
2 M.   3 W.
Scene: a room furnished in heavy mid-Victorian style.
Modern costumes.
Royalty, ten dollars.
A young man returning from the World War and his profiteering uncle have a turbulent half-hour of readjustment.

The senior-high-school reading list is the place for this so-called comedy.

The Man in the Bowler Hat, by A. A. Milne.
French.
4 M.   2 W.
Scene: an interior.
Modern costumes.
Royalty, ten dollars.
This extravagant comedy contains enough of Milne's charm and whimseys to place it on the reading list of the senior high school.

The Wurzel-Flummery, by A. A. Milne.
French; XIV.
3 M.   2 W.
Scene: the morning room of an English town house.
Modern costumes.
Royalty, ten dollars.
Two rival members of Parliament are offered fifty thousand pounds if they will change their names to Wurzel-Flummery. A clever and amusing complication results.
This rather slight but brilliantly written comedy is enjoyed by pupils of the ninth and tenth grades particularly.

A Roadhouse in Arden, by Philip Moeller.
Knopf.
4 M.   2 W.
Scene: a room in a tavern.
Elizabethan costumes.
Royalty on application to the publisher.
The Shakespeare and Bacon controversy and several Shakespeare characters are treated most cleverly in this somewhat sophisticated comedy. With the cutting of a few lines, the play is enjoyable material for presentation in the eleventh and twelfth grades.

On the Shelf, by Christopher Morley.
Longmans.
4 M.   4 W.

Scene: on the shelf of a public library.

Modern and fanciful costumes.

Royalty, ten dollars.

"When the curtain rises the audience sees a small section of this shelf enormously magnified. The backs of eight volumes are visible. From out of these come the characters to enact their story." (Comment by the publisher.)

This unique comedy, in which an author and the children of his brain converse, can be staged effectively by eleventh and twelfth graders.

Thursday Evening, by Christopher Morley.

Longmans; Baker.

1 M. 3 W.

Scene: a kitchen.

Modern costumes.

Royalty, ten dollars.

A very young couple indulge in a foolish quarrel. Their two mothers, who are visiting them, overhear the wrangling and pretend to take part. As a result the young husband and wife defend each other and harmony is restored.

Eleventh and twelfth grades like to read this little play. It has been presented with a measure of success.

The Crumbs That Fall, by Lockart North (Philip Hubbard).

Baker.

8 M.

Scene: a part of the dining room of the Straggler's Club, Piccadilly, on the evening of Founder's dinner.

The gentlemen are in dinner jackets.

Royalty, ten dollars.

A blown electric-light fuse, a jostled arm, and a lost pearl lead to an unexpected revelation.

This theatrically effective play is suggested for the reading list of the ninth and tenth grades especially.

The Melon Thief, by Shiegeyoshi Obata.
> French.
> From a mediæval Japanese farce in three scenes.
> 2 M.
> Scene: the countryside.
> Japanese costumes.
> Royalty, five dollars.
> This jolly farce is enjoyed by ninth and tenth graders especially.

Ile, by Eugene O'Neill.
> Boni & Liveright; IV; XIII.
> 4 M. 1 W. 1 J.
> Scene: a cabin on board a whaling ship.
> Modern costumes.
> Royalty on application to the publisher.
> This grim, powerful story of a lonely woman driven to madness because of her husband's greed belongs on the reading list of the senior high school. It is too difficult and tragic for presentation before the senior year.

In the Zone, by Eugene O'Neill.
> Boni & Liveright; XXIV.
> 9 M.
> Scene: the seamen's forecastle of a British tramp steamer.
> Modern costumes.
> Royalty on application to the publisher.
> This most realistic portrayal of the unjust suspicions of a group of rough seamen in the submarine zone during the World War merits a place on the reading list of the eleventh and twelfth grades.

Where the Cross Is Made, by Eugene O'Neill.
> Boni & Liveright; XI.
> 6 M. 1 W.
> Scene: a room fitted up like a captain's cabin.
> Modern costumes.
> Royalty on application to the publisher.

"An old sea captain watches for the return of his ship sent long ago to find pirate treasure. The ship is lost and his mind is gone, but he sees the drowned men enter with the treasure. His son catches the madness, but the daughter remains sane and bears the brunt of the tragedy." (Publisher's notice.)

High-school students, from the ninth grade up, enjoy reading this gruesome but impressive tale. Twelfth graders might produce it effectively.

The Rushlight, by Monica Barry O'Shea.

Drama, November 1917.

1 M.   2 W.

Scene: the main room of a cottage in Ireland.

Present-day Irish costumes.

Royalty on application to the publisher.

A condemned Irish revolutionist can save his life provided he will betray his comrades. The boy's mother, rather than have her son a traitor, burns the evidence in the rushlight which hangs in front of the statue of the Virgin.

This well-written play is rightly placed on the drama list of the senior high school. It is very effective if sincerely acted.

Over the Hills, by John Palmer.

XXXIII.

2 M.   2 W.

Scene: a comfortable interior.

Modern costumes.

Royalty on application to the publisher.

When a restless husband imagines that he would love to live close to nature and rough it, his desire is granted. He is soon surfeited and returns to his wife and fireside. This comedy may be added to the senior-high-school reading list.

A Minuet, by Louis N. Parker.

French; III.

2 M.   1 W.

Scene: the living room in the jailer's quarters in the prison of the Conciergerie.

French costumes during the time of the "Reign of Terror."
Royalty, ten dollars.

This is a brief lyric drama of the bravery of a Marquis and his
wife as they await a summons to the guillotine. It is highly
recommended for study and presentation in the junior high school.

Fortune and Men's Eyes, by Josephine Preston Peabody.
French; XIV.
8 M.   2 W.
Scene: an interior.
Elizabethan costumes.
Royalty, ten dollars.

This poetic drama, written with great distinction by the author
of *The Piper*, concerns itself with Shakespeare and Mary Fytton.
The senior-high-school reading list may well contain this play.

Two Crooks and a Lady, by Eugene Pillot.
French; Brentano's; XVIII.
3 M.   3 W.
Scene: a library in an old Fifth Avenue mansion.
Modern costumes.
Royalty, ten dollars.

This very popular detective play tells how an elderly woman,
confined to her chair because of paralysis, outwits two thieves.

It is worth a place on the reading lists of the ninth grade and
of the senior high school.

Playgoers, by Sir Arthur Wing Pinero.
French.
2 M.   6 W.
Scene: an interior.
Modern costumes.
Royalty, five dollars.

This comedy, written by one of the most expert modern playwrights, is a most amusing satire on so-called society people who
insist upon trying to force culture on their employees.

The senior-high-school play list may well claim this comedy.

The Widow of Wasdale Head, by Sir Arthur Wing Pinero.
Little.
5 M.　1 W.
Scene: a room in an inn.
Costumes of the time of George III.
Royalty on application to the publisher.
This expertly written fantastic ghost story has a place on the
reading list of the senior high school.

A Dollar, by David Pinski.
French; V.
6 M.　2 W.
Scene: an exterior.
Modern costumes.
Royalty, five dollars.
This fantastic comedy by the great Yiddish dramatist is popular
with the older students of the high school.

A Sunny Morning, by Serafin and Joaquin Alvarez Quintero.
XV.
2 M.　2 W.
Scene: a retired part of a park in Madrid, Spain.
Modern Spanish costumes.
Royalty on application to the publisher.
An elderly man and woman meet by chance in the park and
recall the romantic happenings of their early days.　This excellent
translation from the Spanish merits a place on the reading list
of the ninth, tenth, and eleventh grades.　It is charming when
presented by sympathetic actors.

Judge Lynch, by J. W. Rogers, Jr.
French.
2 M.　2 W.
Scene: an exterior.
Modern costumes.
Royalty, ten dollars.

This tense, tragic drama tells the story of a negro who pays the penalty for a crime which he did not commit.

Judge Lynch is the winner of the David Belasco Cup in the 1924 National Little Theatre Tournament.

The play should be on the reading list of the senior high school. If presented, it will be most effective when done in the twelfth grade.

The Forfeit, by T. B. Rogers.
    IX; XXXIII.
    3 M. 2 W.
    Scene: the business office of a jeweler.
    Modern costumes.
    Royalty on application to Holt.

A confidential clerk steals a valuable jewel. Aided by the girl he loves, he succeeds in saving his reputation but pays a great price for his folly.

The play absorbs the interest of the senior high school and is effective in presentation.

The Knave of Hearts, by Louise Saunders.
    Longmans; IV.
    Fifteen characters, all of whom may be played by girls if it is so desired.
    Scene: the pleasant kitchen of the King of Hearts.
    Fanciful costumes.
    Royalty, ten dollars where admission is charged; five dollars where it is not.

The play gives an ingenious explanation of why the Knave stole the tarts. Eighth- and ninth-grade pupils enjoy both reading and presenting it.

Poor Maddelena, by Louise Saunders.
    Scribner; XXXIII.
    2 M. 1 W.
    Scene: the land of fantasy.

Pierrot and Pierrette costumes and also Italian peasant clothes.
Royalty on application to the publisher.

The author has given, in the three very brief acts of her play, a novel and delightful turn to the familiar Pierrot-Pierrette story.

The more æsthetic members of the senior high school enjoy reading the play, and it is lovely in presentation.

O'Flaherty, V. C., by George Bernard Shaw.
    Brentano's.
    2 M. 2 W.
    Scene: the door of an Irish country house in a park, in the summer of 1915.
    Modern Irish costumes.
    Royalty on application to the publisher.

This brilliant satire on war, which the author states was "a recruiting poster in disguise," reads and acts remarkably well. It is a favorite of the older students.

'Lijah, by Edgar Valentine Smith.
    Baker.
    3 M. 1 W.
    Scene: the living room of a Southern colonial mansion.
    Modern costumes.
    Royalty, ten dollars.

This comedy, awarded the first prize by the Birmingham Little Theatre in 1925, gives an effective picture of Southern hospitality. A once rich planter entertains two business men from the North. He makes great personal sacrifices in order to hide his poverty from his guests.

This drama is well placed on the reading list of the senior high school, and is doubtless worthy of presentation.

The Little Father of the Wilderness, by Austin Strong and Lloyd
    Osbourne.
    French; XI.
    6 M. 1 W. Extras.
    Scene: an antechamber of the Palace of Versailles.

Costumes of the time of Louis XV.

Royalty, ten dollars.

Père Marlotte, a Jesuit priest, goes to Versailles. He supposes that the king has summoned him in order to reward him for his services in the wilderness of America. He finds that Louis has sent for him in order to decide a wager which he had made on the height of Niagara Falls. The play ends fortunately for the Jesuit priest.

The quality and content of this drama recommend it for reading and even for presentation in the eleventh or twelfth grade.

The Far-Away Princess, by Hermann Sudermann.

French; V.

2 M. 7 W.

Scene: a veranda of an inn.

Modern costumes.

No royalty.

A student who worships a princess from afar meets but does not recognize her. He tells her his secret, and she confides to him her ideals.

This distinguished piece of writing, by one of the greatest of the German dramatists, should be placed on the senior-high-school list of plays for study and for possible presentation.

The Man on the Kerb, by Alfred Sutro.

French; XXVI.

1 M. 1 W.

Scene: an underground room.

Modern costumes.

Royalty, five dollars.

The Man on the Kerb pictures with unflinching fidelity the struggle of an unfortunate English family against hopeless poverty.

This gripping human tragedy should be studied with scrupulous care by all eleventh- and twelfth-grade students of the art of the drama. The play is too tragic for young people to present.

A Marriage Has Been Arranged, by Alfred Sutro.
French; XVII.
1 M.   1 W.
Scene: an interior.
Modern costumes.
Royalty, five dollars.
This well-written and rather mature comedy probably has a place on the reading list of the more advanced seniors.

Riders to the Sea, by John M. Synge.
In *Representative One-Act Plays by British and Irish Authors*, Little; IV; XIV.
1 M.   3 W.   Others.
Scene: a cottage kitchen.
Modern Irish costumes.
Royalty on application to the publisher.
Synge, with wonderful understanding, portrays the tragedy of an old woman of western Ireland, whose men folk have all been lost at sea.
This is one of the few perfect plays.   It should be read and studied by all tenth-, eleventh-, and twelfth-grade students. Presentation is difficult but not impossible for sympathetic twelfth graders.

The Shadow of the Glen, by John M. Synge.
Luce.
3 M.   1 W.
Scene: a cottage kitchen in Ireland.
Modern Irish costumes.
Royalty on application to the publisher.
A suspicious old husband pretends death in order to test his lonely wife's loyalty and love.   This powerful, grim play is read with satisfaction by seniors.

The Post Office, by Rabindranath Tagore.
XXVI.
8 M.   2 J.   Extras.

Scene: an interior.

Present-day costumes of India.

Royalty on application to the publisher.

A little lad of India because of ill health is condemned to a life of inactivity. Through his active imagination he makes a new world for himself.

This play of unusual spiritual beauty and gentle pathos is read and enjoyed by many pupils of the senior high school. If presented it should be done by a select group for a select audience.

Beauty and the Jacobin, by Booth Tarkington.

Harper; XIV.

3 M. 2 W.

Scene: a garret in a rusty lodging house in northern France.

French costumes of the year 1793.

Royalty on application to the publisher.

An incident in the French Revolution. This witty, tense scene is enjoyed by the senior high school. Effective presentation depends largely upon the acting of one individual.

The Trysting Place, by Booth Tarkington.

Baker; IX.

4 M. 3 W.

Scene: an interior.

Modern costumes.

No royalty.

The trysting place is an out-of-the-way corner of a hotel lounge, and the trysters range in age from sixteen to sixty.

This rather amusing farce is enjoyed by high-school students.

The Boor, by Anton Tchekov.

French; V; XIII.

2 M. 1 W.

Scene: the reception room of a Russian country estate.

Modern Russian costumes.

No royalty.

A domineering lieutenant and a positive young widow are the main characters in this broad comedy of Russian country life. Ninth graders as well as pupils of the senior high school get much fun out of a presentation of this play.

A Marriage Proposal, by Anton Tchekov.
French; III; XXXIII.
2 M. 1 W.
Scene: the reception room in a Russian country home.
Modern Russian costumes.
No royalty.
This brilliant farce is justly popular with senior-high-school pupils. It is splendid stage material.

The Swan Song, by Anton Tchekov.
XXVI.
2 M.
Scene: on the stage of a country theater in Russia.
Modern Russian costumes.
Royalty on application to the publisher.
Tchekov, the great Russian dramatist, in *The Swan Song,* gives a glimpse into the life of an actor who has just finished his farewell performance. This powerful play is doubtless too difficult for young people to present. It is, however, admirable for study in the senior high school.

The Falcon, by Alfred, Lord Tennyson.
XV; XXIX.
2 M. 2 W.
Scene: an Italian cottage.
Italian costumes.
No royalty.
The Falcon was written in 1879 for Mr. and Mrs. Kendal, two well-known English actors.
This dramatic telling of an old story may well be added to the reading list of the senior high school. Presentation is both possible and worth while.

Sham, by Frank G. Tompkins.
  Appleton; XIII.
  3 M.   1 W.
  Scene: a darkened room.
  Modern costumes.
  Royalty on application to the publisher.
  A burglar is caught in the act of robbing a house.   In a most amusing manner he shows himself a man of taste and culture, and cleverly exposes the affectations and shams of the man and woman who own the house.   This play is popular in the senior high school.

The Rider of Dreams, by Ridgley Torrence.
  XXVI.
  2 M.   1 W.   1 J.
  Scene: a room used for kitchen, dining room, and laundry by a colored family.
  Modern costumes.
  Royalty on application to the publisher.
  When a negro with an uncontrolled imagination gets into bad company and steals, a wise old mulatto takes the culprit in hand and makes him turn over a new leaf.
  This admirable negro folk drama surely belongs on the reading list of the senior high school.   It is well worth presentation.

Miss Maria, by Maude B. Vosburgh.
  French.
  1 M.   4 W.   4 J. (not speaking parts)
  Scene: a sitting room.
  New England costumes of about 1860.
  No royalty.
  A middle-aged gentlewoman loses her money in wild-cat schemes. She plans to open a school; but a romance develops, and she marries an old friend.
  This excellent dramatization from Margaret Deland's *Old Chester Tales* is pleasant reading, especially for the girls of the senior high school.

The Birthday of the Infanta, by Stuart Walker.
II; III; XXII.
5 M.   2 W.
Scene: a royal balcony overlooking a garden.
Spanish costumes of the sixteenth century.
Royalty on application to the author.
This skilful dramatization of Oscar Wilde's lovely and touching story is admirable for study and presentation in either the junior or senior high school.

The Lady of the Weeping Willow Tree, by Stuart Walker.
Appleton; XII.
2 M.   4 W.
Scene: two simple interiors.
Japanese costumes.
Royalty on application to the publisher.
This Japanese legend, beautifully told in three very brief acts, has for its theme the reward of perfect faith.   It well deserves a place on the reading list of the eleventh and twelfth grades. When sincerely and artistically acted, it is most effective.

Nevertheless, by Stuart Walker.
XV; XXIII.
1 M.   1 Girl.   1 Boy.
Scene: a room just upstairs.
Modern costumes.
Royalty on application to the publisher.
This slender but pleasing little comedy about the encounter of two children with a burglar interests eighth- and ninth-grade pupils particularly.   It is easy to present.

Sir David Wears a Crown, by Stuart Walker.
XXII.
13 M.   5 W.
Scene: a gateway to the King's Castle.
Fanciful costumes.
Royalty on application to the publisher.
This is a sequel to *Six Who Pass While the Lentils Boil.*

Six Who Pass While the Lentils Boil, by Stuart Walker.
 XXIII; XXVI; XXXII.
 6 M. 2 W.
 Scene: a simple setting.
 Fanciful costumes.
 Royalty on application to the publisher.
 We have in this charming fantasy one of the few plays which is
quite right in content and in form for very young people. Eighth
and ninth graders love to act this play for their classmates and
for the younger grades.

The Twig of Thorn, by M. J. Warren.
 Baker.
 6 M. 7 W.
 Scene: one interior.
 Modern Irish peasant costumes.
 No royalty.
 "Oonah breaks the first blossom from the thorn tree at the
crossroads and puts herself in the power of 'the good people' — the
fairies. The minstrel Aileel takes the curse upon himself and thus
saves Oonah for her lover." (Publisher's notice.) This play of
Irish folklore is liked particularly by ninth and tenth graders.

The Old Peabody Pew, by Kate Douglas Wiggin.
 French.
 1 M. 8 W.
 Scene: a church interior.
 Old-fashioned costumes.
 Royalty, five dollars.
 This pleasant New England romance is easily acted by senior-
high-school students. It plays about an hour and a quarter.

Confessional, by Percival Wilde.
 Holt; XIII.
 3 M. 3 W.
 Scene: a cottage parlor.
 Modern costumes.
 Royalty on application to Baker.

Percival Wilde deals searchingly with the effect of a bribe upon the actions of a family reputed thoroughly honorable. This serious drama is recommended for the reading list of the senior high school. It is effective in production.

The Traitor, by Percival Wilde.
French.
6 M.
Scene: a tent.
Modern uniforms.
Royalty, ten dollars.
The ruse by which a traitor is discovered makes effective drama. This play is liked by senior-high-school students.

The Unseen Host, by Percival Wilde.
XV.
3 M.
Scene: an improvised hospital in Paris.
Modern costumes.
Royalty on application to Baker.
The beauty and the mysticism of this brief picture of the death of a young soldier of the World War guarantees it a place on the reading list of the senior high school.

Where but in America, by Oscar M. Wolff.
Baker; V; XXIV; XXIX; XXXIII.
1 M.   2 W.
Scene: a dining room.
Modern costumes.
Royalty, five dollars.
"Humorous satire on conditions in America where servants are sometimes more well-to-do than the people who employ them. The young couple are about to buy a home and find that their servant's lover is the man from whom they are about to purchase." (*Plays for High Schools and Colleges.*) This extremely popular play is for the reading list of the senior high school. Eleventh and twelfth graders find profit in presenting it.

Cathleen Ni Houlihan, by William Butler Yeats.
XIX.
2 M.   3 W.   1 Boy.
Scene: the interior of a cottage close to Killala.
Irish costumes of 1798.
Royalty on application to the publisher.
This symbolic play presents in a beautifully poetic fashion
Ireland's ardent desire for freedom.
The senior-high-school students, as well as ninth graders, do
well to study and act this gem.

The Hour-Glass, by William Butler Yeats.
XIX.
4 M.   2 W.   2 J.
Scene: a simple interior.
Irish and fanciful costumes.
Royalty on application to the publisher.
This morality play of genuine artistry and dramatic effective-
ness is highly recommended for use in the ninth grade and in the
senior high school.

The King's Threshold, by William Butler Yeats.
XIX.
9 M.   4 W.   Extras.
Scene: steps before a palace.
Fanciful costumes.
Royalty on application to the publisher.
This verse play, which tells how a poet regained for his fellow
artists rightful honor, is liked by the older members of the high
school. It can be acted effectively by a cast composed entirely
of girls.

The Land of Heart's Desire, by William Butler Yeats.
In *Representative One-Act Plays by British and Irish Authors,*
Little; IV; XIX.
3 M.   2 W.   1 J.
Scene: an Irish kitchen.
Irish costumes.

Royalty, five dollars.

The Land of Heart's Desire is one of the loveliest of the short poetic tragedies. Its story is from Irish folklore. Although this play is frequently recommended for junior-high-school reading and study, nevertheless the compiler of this drama list believes that its maturity of meaning renders it more appropriate for study in the senior high school. Effective production depends upon careful understanding and most sympathetic presentation.

A Pot of Broth, by William Butler Yeats.

XIX.

2 M. 1 W.

Scene: a kitchen.

Irish peasant costumes.

Royalty on application to the publisher.

This is a humorous, deftly written trifle about a clever tramp. It is ideal for junior-high-school use.

Deirdre, by William Butler Yeats.

XIX.

5 M. 4 W.

Scene: a guest house in a wood.

Fanciful Irish costumes.

Royalty on application to the publisher.

This poetic, tragic story of the last scene in the life of Deirdre of the Sorrows is appreciated by some of the older students. It belongs on the reading list of the senior class.

Books Related to the Art of the Theater[1]

ANDERSON, MADGE. — *The Heroes of the Puppet Stage.* Harcourt. 1923.

ANDREWS, CHARLTON. — *The Drama To-day.* Lippincott. 1913. "There is no brief compendium of the drama to-day, as it is practised, not only in England and America but also upon the continent. It is to supply the need of such a manual that the present treatise has been written." (Preface by the Author.)

[1] Intended primarily for special assignments.

—— *Technique of Play Writing.* Home Correspondence School, Springfield, Mass. 1915.

ANDREWS, HARRY LEE, and WEIRICK, BRUCE. — *Acting and Play Production: A Manual for Classes, Dramatic Clubs, and Little Theaters.* Longmans. 1925.

ARCHER, WILLIAM. — *Play-Making. A Manual of Craftsmanship.* Dodd. 1912. "I make bold to say that Mr. Archer's is the best book that has yet been written in our language, or in any other, on the art and science of playmaking." (Brander Matthews.)

ARVOLD, ALFRED G. — *The Little Country Theatre.* Macmillan. 1922.

ASHDOWN, CHARLES H. — *Armour and Weapons in the Middle Ages.* Brentano's. 1925.

BAKER, GEORGE PIERCE. — *Dramatic Technique.* Houghton. 1919. "Why, however, is it impossible that some time should be saved a would-be dramatist by placing before him, not mere theories of play-writing, but the practice of dramatists of the past, so that what they shared in common, and where their practice differed, may be clear to him? That is all this book attempts. To create a dramatist would be a modern miracle." (Preface by the Author.)

BARRY, IRIS. — *Let's Go to the Movies.* Payson & Clarke. 1927. "Going to the pictures is nothing to be ashamed of. I should like to discuss why we do slink into the cinema and what happens to us there. . . . It [cinematography] is already a dramatic art: the finest films are lovely to the eye as they are moving to the emotions." (Introduction by the Author.)

BATCHELDER, ERNEST A. — *Design in Theory and Practice.* Macmillan. 1927.

BATES, ESTHER WILLARD. — *The Art of Producing Pageants.* Baker. 1925.

——*Pageants and Pageantry.* Ginn. 1912. "The following chapters summarize briefly the experience of some years in producing and writing amateur plays and pageants." (Preface by the Author.)

BEEGLE, MARY P., and CRAWFORD, JACK R. — *Community Drama and Pageantry.* Yale University Press. 1916. "This book is offered as a preliminary survey of some of the technical questions involved in writing and staging pageants and community drama. The main purpose has been to make the suggestions as practical as possible." (Preface by the Authors.)

BELLINGER, M. — *A Short History of the Drama.* Holt. 1927.

BOSWORTH, HALLIAM. — *Technique in Dramatic Art. A Delineation of the Art of Acting by Means of Its Underlying Principles and Scientific Laws. With Technical Instruction in the Art of Play Production and Public Speaking.* Macmillan. 1926.

BOWEN, CYRIL. — *Practical Hints on Stage Costume, including Instruction and Patterns for Making Hats, Boot Tops, Sword Belts, Lace Ornaments, Ballet Skirts, etc.* French.

BOYD, ERNEST. — *The Contemporary Drama of Ireland.* Little. 1917. The author undertakes a discussion of Irish drama, Irish dramatists, and the theaters of Ireland.

BRANDES, GEORGE. — *William Shakespeare, a Critical Study.* Macmillan. 1924.

BURLEIGH, LOUISE. — *The Community Theatre in Theory and Practice.* Little. 1917. "In these chapters it is the aim of the author to consider the social quality of the dramatic art, the emotional needs of an ordinary community, and to point out that each may have its greatest opportunity for perfection through a theatre based upon those principles upon which democratic institutions must be built." (Introduction by the Author.)

BURTON, RICHARD. — *How to See a Play.* Revised Edition. Macmillan. 1929. "The would-be playwright can learn his trade, even as another, and must, to succeed. And the spectator . . . the necessary coadjutor with player and playwright in theater success, can also become an adept in his part of this co-operative result." (Preface by the Author.) This is an excellent text for use in the twelfth grade.

CALTHROP, DION CLAYTON. — *English Costumes*. Macmillan. 1923.

CALVERT, LOUIS. — *Problems of the Actor*. Holt. 1918. This is a most helpful volume by an artist of many years' experience on the professional stage.

CHALMERS, HELENA. — *Clothes: On and Off the Stage*. Appleton. 1928. "She gives a detailed account, copiously illustrated, of the history of dress from the Stone Age to the present day. Every type of garment and accessory is named, tabulated, and described. There are chapters on cutting and manufacture of costumes, head-dresses, and shoes. The materials available in every age and country are listed, and modern substitutes suggested." (Frances Park in *Theatre Arts Monthly*.)

CHANDLER, FRANK W. — *Aspects of Modern Drama*. Macmillan. 1915.

CHENEY, SHELDON. — *The Art Theatre: Its Character as Differentiated from the Commercial Theatre; Its Ideals and Organization; and a Record of Certain European and American Examples*. Knopf. 1925.

—— *The Open-Air Theatre*. Argus. 1918.

—— *Stage Decoration*. With 256 illustrations. Day. 1928. "The first book in English to present a complete study of the development of stage decoration and stage forms, with illustrations from the Greeks to Constructivism. More than a mere treatise on decoration, *Stage Decoration* not only reviews the evolution of stage form but considers its significance in relation to modern production." (Publisher's announcement.)

—— *The Theatre: Three Thousand Years of Drama Acting and Stage-craft*. Longmans. 1929. "Mr. Cheney, with a boundless enthusiasm and freshness, sees all the stage of the past with his vision as a sensitive theatre-goer, and this makes his book one of unique value." (Walter Prichard Eaton in the New York *Herald Tribune*.)

CHUBB, PERCIVAL, and Others. — *Festivals and Plays in Schools and Elsewhere*. Harper. 1912. Contents: 1, Festivals; 2, Musical Festivals; 3, School Exercises and Recreations.

CLARK, BARRETT H. — *European Theories of the Drama*. Appleton. 1918. "An attempt to set before the reader the development of the theory of dramatic technique in Europe from Aristotle to the present time. It has been my purpose to select such texts as have been influential in shaping the technical form of plays. Sometimes the doctrine appears as criticism of particular work, sometimes as the playwright's own theory of his art, and sometimes as a history, a summing up of the dramatic product of a particular epoch." (Introduction by the Author.)

—— *A Study of the Modern Drama*. Appleton. 1925. The volume contains valuable commentary on the drama from Ibsen to the present day.

COOK, HENRY CALDWELL. — *The Play Way: An Essay in Educational Method*. Stokes. 1917. An account of the work done at the Pearse School at Cambridge, England.

COQUELIN, BENOIT C. — *The Actor and His Art*. Columbia University. Republished 1928.

CRAFTON, ALLEN, and ROYER, JESSICA. — *Acting*. Crofts. 1926.

CRAIG, EDWARD GORDON. — *On the Art of the Theatre*. Dodd. 1925. "Most people begin with the theory and go on — if they go on — to carry their theory into practice. Mr. Gordon Craig has done a better thing, and, having begun by creating a new Art of the Stage on the actual boards of the theatre, has followed up his practical demonstration by a Book of Theory, in which he explains what he has done, telling us also what he hopes to do." (Arthur Symons.) "Craig's best-known and most consulted work." (Sheldon Cheney.)

—— *The Theatre-Advancing*. Little. 1919.

—— *Towards a New Theatre. Forty Designs for Stage Scenes, with Critical Notes by the Inventor*. Dodd. 1925.

CRAWFORD, MARY CAROLINE. — *The Romance of the American Theatre*. Little. 1925. "The dominant personalities of the American stage from the earliest days are presented in this valuable and comprehensive survey of the American Theatre." (Publisher's notice.)

CURTIS, ELNORA W. — *The Dramatic Instinct in Education*. Introduction by G. Stanley Hall. Houghton. 1914. "An effort has been made to present the different phases in which dramatic instinct finds outlet, and to unify the many ordinary forms, perhaps unrecognized until brought into psychological relation with those more commonly understood as its expression." (Preface by the Author.) This book has an excellent bibliography.

DE GOVEIA, CLARENCE J. — *The Community Playhouse: A Manual on Its Organization and Maintenance*. Viking Press. 1923.

DICKINSON, THOMAS H. — *The Case of the American Drama*. Houghton. 1915. Contents: The New Theatre in the Light of History; The Social Sanction of Dramatic Art; the Present Situation of the Stage in America; The Theatre in the Open; Festivals and Pageantry; The Promise of an American Drama.

—— *The Insurgent Theatre*. Viking Press. 1917. "In this book it has been my purpose to treat the recent events of the non-commercial theatre as these refer to organization and management." (Preface by the Author.) This book contains a chapter on The Little Theatre and one on The Children's Theatre.

—— *Playwrights of The New American Theatre*. Macmillan. 1925.

DOLMAN, JOHN, JR. — *The Art of Play Production*. Harper. 1929.

DRINKWATER, JOHN. — *The Art of Theatre-Going*. Houghton. 1927. "The purpose of this book is chiefly to define some general principles of the theatre by means of examples drawn from my own experience as an actor, producer, dramatist, and playgoer. In order to make these examples as precise as possible I have, as an Englishman, necessarily had to confine my attention for the most part to the English theatre as I have known it in my own lifetime." (Preface by the Author.) It contains two chapters on the cinema.

DUKES, ASHLEY. — *Drama.* Holt. 1927. Contents: Nature of the Drama; Varieties of Drama; The Dramatist; The Actor; The Producer; The Scene; The Playhouse; Drama Present and Future.

EATON, WALTER PRICHARD. — *The Actor's Heritage: Scenes from the Theatre of Yesterday and the Day Before.* Little. 1924.

ERVINE, ST. JOHN. — *How to Write a Play.* Macmillan. 1928. "In this book Mr. Ervine, who is himself a successful dramatist and dramatic critic, tells the apprentice author something of the way in which a dramatist does his work." (Publisher's notice.)

EVREINOV, NICOLAS. — *The Theatre in Life.* Edited and Translated by Alexander I. Nazaroff. Brentano's. 1927.

FRY, EMMA V. — *Educational Dramatics: A Handbook on the Educational Player Method.* Noble. 1917.

FUCHS, THEODORE. — *Stage Lighting.* Little. 1929. This practical handbook contains over three hundred illustrations and diagrams.

GRANVILLE-BARKER, HARLEY. — *The Exemplary Theatre.* Little. 1922.

GREGORY, LADY. — *Our Irish Theatre.* A Chapter of Autobiography. Putnam. 1913.

GRIMBALL, ELIZABETH B., and WILLS, RHEA. — *Costuming a Play: Inter-Theatre Arts Handbook.* Century. 1925. This handbook "endeavors to give correct and practical information and costume plates as a basis for individual development and artistic variations in the designing and making of costumes." (Foreword by the Authors.)

HAMILTON, CLAYTON M. — *Conversations on Contemporary Drama.* Macmillan. 1924.

—— *Problems of the Playwright.* Holt. 1917.

—— *Studies in Stagecraft.* Holt. 1914. "*The Theory of the Theatre* dealt chiefly with principles inherited by the present from the past: but *Studies in Stagecraft* deals chiefly with principles that seem destined to be bequeathed by the present to the future." (Preface by the Author.)

—— *The Theory of the Theatre.* Holt. 1914.

HENIGER, ALICE M. HERTS. — *The Kingdom of the Child.* With an Introduction by G. Stanley Hall. Dutton. 1918. Contents: 1, Drama in Education; 2, Children as Actors.

HENNEQUIN, ALFRED. — *The Art of Playwriting: Being a Practical Treatise on the Elements of Dramatic Construction. Intended for the Playwright, the Student, and the Dramatic Critic.* Houghton. 1910.

HERTS, ALICE MINNIE. — *The Children's Educational Theatre.* Harper. 1911.

HILLEBRAND, HAROLD N. — *Writing the One-Act Play: A Manual for Beginners.* Knopf. 1925.

HILLIARD, EVELYNE; McCORMICK, THEODORA; and OGLEBAY, KATE. — *Amateur and Educational Dramatics.* Macmillan. 1917. Endorsed by the Educational Dramatic League. Contents: 1, Drama in Education; 2, Amateur Theatricals.

HORNBLOW, ARTHUR. — *A History of the Theatre in America, from Its Beginnings to the Present Time.* Lippincott. 1919. In two volumes.

HUGHES, GLENN. — *The Story of the Theatre: A Short History of Theatrical Art from Its Beginning to the Present Day.* French. 1928. "This book is intended primarily for students of the theatre; secondarily, for the general reader. So far as the writer knows, it represents the first attempt in English to summarize in one volume the main events of theatrical history from the earliest times to the present." (Preface by the Author.)

ISAACS, EDITH J. R., ed. — *Theatre: Essays on the Arts of the Theatre.* Little. 1927. "Thirty-one essays by leading theatre artists and critics on the arts, the theory and practice of the modern theatre. An attempt to restate theatre values in the light of modern practice, especially in the American theatre, from 1917 to 1927, the ten most creative years of its long and varied history." (*Theatre Arts Monthly.*)

JONES, HENRY ARTHUR. — *The Foundations of a National Drama. A Collection of Lectures, Essays, and Speeches, Delivered and Written in the Years 1896–1912.* (Revised and corrected, with additions.) Doubleday. 1913. "My one wish has been to spread amongst playgoers a knowledge of those facts and conditions and rules which will help to develop an intellectual drama in England, and make our theatre an object of national pride and esteem, the admiration instead of the contempt of Europe." (Preface by the Author.)

JOSEPH, HELEN H. — *A Book of Marionettes.* Viking Press. Revised edition 1929.

KELLY, FRANCIS M., and SCHWABE, RANDOLPH. — *Historic Costume: A Chronicle of Fashion in Western Europe, 1490–1790.* Scribner. 1925. This volume is splendidly illustrated.

KROWS, ARTHUR E. — *Equipment for Stage Production: A Manual of Scene Building.* Appleton. 1928.

—— *Play Production in America.* Holt. 1916. "In a measure, this book tells what the theatre is trying to do; but it has another aim, elevated for the time into a vital issue, to tell, quite literally, how the theatre is trying to do it." (Preface by the Author.)

LAWRENCE, WILLIAM J. — *The Elizabethan Playhouse and Other Studies.* Lippincott. 1912–13.

LEE, JOSEPH. — *Play in Education.* Macmillan. 1915. "My aim in this book is to present a true picture of the child. . . . 'Play,' to grown people, signifies something of secondary importance. To the child, upon the other hand, play is the most important thing there is. It is primary, comes first in interest, represents real life; it is what all the rest is for." (Introduction by the Author.)

LEWIS, B. ROLAND. — *The Technique of the One-Act Play: A Study in Dramatic Construction.* Luce. 1918. "The writing of this volume has been prompted by two things. One is the conviction that the principles of writing the one-act play can be taught with a large measure of profit to the earnest playwright; and the other is the strong belief that the devotee of the drama will welcome a volume dealing with a study of the principles of dramaturgy as operative in the shorter dramatic product." (Preface by the Author.)

LEWISOHN, LUDWIG. — *The Drama and the Stage.* Harcourt. 1922.

—— *The Modern Drama: An Essay in Interpretation.* Viking Press. 1915.

MACGOWAN, KENNETH. — *The Theatre of Tomorrow.* Boni & Liveright. 1921. The book contains 8 illustrations in color and thirty-two in half-tone.

—, and JONES, ROBERT EDMOND.—*Continental Stagecraft.* Harcourt. 1922. Eight illustrations in color, thirty-two in half tone. "This book is a record of impressions gained from ten weeks of travel through the theaters of France, Sweden, Czecho-Slovakia, and Austria during April, May, and June 1922." (Prefatory note by Kenneth Macgowan.)

MACKAY, CONSTANCE D'ARCY.— *Costumes and Scenery for Amateurs: A Practical Working Handbook.* Holt. 1915.

—— *How to Produce Children's Plays.* Holt. 1915. Contents: 1, Children's Plays; 2, Drama in Education. Here is also a bibliography of books that will be of help to dramatic directors.

—— *The Little Theatre in the United States.* Holt. 1917. "This book aims to give a complete survey of one of the newest, freest, most potent, and democratic forces in the art of the American stage — the Little Theatre." (Preface by the Author.)

MacKaye, Percy.— *The Civic Theatre in Relation to the Redemption of Leisure: A Book of Suggestion.* Argus. 1912.

—— *The Playhouse and the Play and Other Addresses Concerning the Theatre and Democracy in America.* Macmillan. 1909. "Of the five essays here included, the first concerns itself with the conditioning influences of the theatre upon the drama; the second, with a possible goal for our native drama; the third, with the civic status of the dramatist's profession; the fourth, with the needs of leadership; the fifth, with art as public service." (Introduction by the Author.)

Malone, Andrew E.— *The Irish Theatre:* 1896–1928. Scribner. 1928.

Matthews, Brander.— *A Book About the Theatre.* Scribner. 1916. The author discusses, among other things, the limitations of the stage, the dramatization of novels, operas, dance, pantomime, puppet-plays, and shadow-pantomime.

—— *On Acting.* Scribner. 1914.

—— *Playwrights on Playmaking and Other Studies of the Stage.* Scribner. 1923.

—— *The Principles of Playmaking; and Other Discussions of the Drama.* Scribner. 1919.

—— *Rip Van Winkle Goes to the Play: And Other Essays on Plays and Players.* Scribner. 1926.

—— *A Study of the Drama.* Houghton. 1910. "This book is a study of the technique of the drama. It is intended, not for those who want to write plays, but for those who wish to learn how plays are written now, and how they were written in the past." (Prefatory note by the Author.)

McCandless, Stanley R. — *Glossary of Stage Lighting.* Theatre Arts. "Contains full information on general terms of stage lighting, location of lights, types of instruments, switchboard, and accessories." (Publisher's notice.)

McIsaac, Frederick J. — *The Tony Sarg Marionette Book.* Illustrated by Tony Sarg. Viking Press. 1921.

MILLS, WINIFRED H. and DUNN, LOUISE M. — *Marionettes, Masks, and Shadows.* Illustrated by Corydon Bell. Doubleday. 1927. This excellent volume contains a concise statement of the history of marionettes; chapters on the making of marionettes, marionette plays and stages, scenery and kindred topics. The second part of the book discusses masks, how made and when used. The final section deals with making and producing of the various types of shadow plays. There are numerous lists of books and copious illustrations.

MITCHELL, ROY. — *Shakespeare for Community Players.* Dutton. 1919.

—— *The School Theatre: A Handbook of Theory and Practice.* Brentano's. 1925.

MODERWELL, HIRAM K. — *The Theatre of To-day.* Dodd. 1927. "This book is intended as a description and explanation of the new forces which have entered theatrical production in the last ten years, judged in the light of their probable historical importance as well as of their growing contemporary influence." (From the Author's foreword.) This volume has an excellent introduction and bibliography of books of the theater by John Mason Brown and thirty-two illustrations. It is an excellent book for teachers to own.

MORGAN, ARTHUR E. — *Tendencies of Modern English Drama.* Scribner. 1923.

MOSES, MONTROSE J. — *The American Dramatist.* Little. 1925. "There is no book treating distinctively of the American dramatist and his work. This volume is therefore designed to meet a want which some day will be felt, though at present the literary critic contents himself in the belief that there is no American drama, and there never has been. Be this as it may, the activity has none the less existed, and no literary treatise has dealt with it properly." (Preface by the Author.)

MOULTON, RICHARD G. — *Shakespeare as a Dramatic Artist: A Popular Illustration of the Principles of Scientific Criticism.* Oxford. 1906.

—— *Shakespeare as a Dramatic Thinker: A Popular Illustration of Fiction as the Experimental Side of Philosophy.* Macmillan. 1907.

NATHAN, GEORGE JEAN. — *The Critic and the Drama.* Knopf. 1922. Contents: Æsthetic Jurisprudence; Drama as an Art; The Place of the Theatre; The Place of Acting; Dramatic Criticism; Dramatic Criticism in America.

NICOLL, ALLARDYCE. — *British Drama: An Historical Survey from the Beginnings to the Present Time.* Crowell. 1925. "This book could not be, and is not intended to be, exhaustive. It attempts to trace the history of our theatre from its most primitive origins in the Middle Ages to the present day, and for this purpose it deals rather with tendencies than with individuals." (Preface by the Author.)

—— *The Development of the Theatre: A Study of Theatrical Art from the Beginnings to the Present Day.* Harcourt. 1927. "Almost invaluable to the student because of its unified collection of plans and pictures and comments, combining in one volume material scattered hitherto in a hundred places, some of them difficult to get at." (Walter Prichard Eaton.) This volume contains two hundred and seventy-one illustrations.

NORTHRUP, BELLE, and GREEN, ANNA L. — *Historic Costume Plates.* Bureau of Publication, Teachers College, Columbia University, New York. Short description of historic fashions with index and suggestions for using the accompanying thirty plates.

OVERTON, GRACE SLOAN. — *Drama in Education: Theory and Technique.* Century. 1926. "This book is intended as a text for courses emphasizing the value and use of the dramatic method in secular and religious education." (Preface by the Author.)

PELLEW, CHARLES E. — *Dyes and Dyeing.* McBride. 1913.

PEPPARD, HELEN M. — *The Correction of Speech Defects.* Macmillan. 1925.

PHELPS, WILLIAM LYON. — *Essays on Modern Dramatists*. Macmillan. 1921.

—— *The Twentieth Century Theatre: Observations on the Contemporary English and American Stage*. Macmillan. 1918.

PICHEL, IRVING. — *Modern Theatres*. Harcourt. 1925. Well illustrated. "To-day . . . hundreds of community houses are being erected .... Practically all of them will include stages and auditoriums. At the same time, hundreds of new school buildings are being planned, and these, too, will have stages .... But, unless architects have at their disposal much more technical knowledge of the producers' requirements than in the past, it is certain that most of these theatres and auditoriums and stages will be bad — as are the auditoriums and stages in most existing schools. It is to forestall some of the commonest mistakes that this book is written — to describe them in detail, and to set up against them the ideal features toward which designers of such structures should strive." (Introduction by the Author.)

—— *On Building a Theatre: Stage Construction and Equipment for Small Theatres, Schools, and Community Buildings*. Theatre Arts. 1920. Eighty pages and twenty-two illustrations.

PLAYGROUND AND RECREATION ASSOCIATION OF AMERICA. — *Community Drama. Suggestions for a Community-wide Program of Dramatic Activities*. Century. 1926. "In preparing this book the Association has kept in mind the needs of the community workers all over the country who, without special training in dramatic work, but with an appreciation of the values of drama to the individual and the community, are helping churches, schools, and other groups in their dramatic activities." (Foreword.)

QUINN, ARTHUR H. — *A History of the American Drama*. Harper. 1923. Two volumes. Illustrated. "The authoritative and picturesque story of the evolution of our drama from the Civil War to the present day, with a complete bibliography and play list." (Publisher's notice.)

RACINET, AUGUSTE. — *Le Costume Historique*. Paris. 1888. Six volumes. The book is most valuable.

RUSSELL, MARY M. — *How to Produce Plays and Pageants: A Guide to Their Preparation and Production for Church and Community*. Doubleday. 1923.

SAYLER, OLIVER M., ed. — *Max Reinhardt and his Theatre*. Brentano's. 1924. Fifty-seven color plates and one hundred and sixty-four black-and-white illustrations. "The most exhaustive book concerning the problems of the stage that has ever been issued in this country. It is a volume that no one who desires authoritative information on this, the most important phase of modern dramatic development, can afford to be without." (Paul R. Martin, *Chicago Journal of Commerce*.)

—— *Our American Theatre*. Brentano's. 1923. Twenty-five illustrations. "My motive, as I have indicated more than once in the succeeding chapters, has been to sketch the highlights of this period (fifteen years) and, so far as possible, as I aimed to do in *The Russian Theatre*, to make our American Theatre live through intimate studies of the men and women who have been responsible for its record." (Preface by the Author.)

—— *The Russian Theatre*. Brentano's. 1922. "The book is worthy to present to our people the most energetic and intense stage that, in over a century, mankind has anywhere produced." (Introduction by Norman Hapgood.)

SHAY, FRANK. — *The Practical Theatre: A Manual for Little Theatre, Community Players, Amateur Dramatic Clubs, and Other Independent Producing Groups*. Appleton. 1926. It contains "a little-theatre working library."

SHERINGHAM, GEORGE and SAVER, JAMES. — "Design in the Theatre Community." *The Studio*, special winter number, 1927–28.

SIMONS, SARAH E., and ORR, CLEM I. — *Dramatization: Selections from English Classics Adapted in Dramatic Form*. Scott. 1913. "It is the aim of this volume to give practical suggestions for the dramatization of high school classics." (Preface by the Authors.)

STANISLAVSKY, CONSTANTIN. — *My Life in Art.* Little. 1924. "Young people can learn from him (Stanislavsky) how hard and how long they must work to educate themselves for the theatre, how many difficulties they will have to conquer, how much knowledge they must acquire in order to earn the right to work conscientiously in the theatre at all, how much severe, cold self-criticism and analysis they must use to perfect themselves. That is one of the values which should heartily recommend this book to everybody working in the theatre." (Richard Boleslavsky, *Theatre Arts Monthly*.)

STRATTON, CLARENCE. — *Producing in Little Theatres.* Holt. 1921. "A model manual, sane and sensible, helpful and practical.... A word of praise must be given the many illustrations ... selected to adorn the book .... Immediately helpful." (Brander Matthews.)

—— *Theatron.* Holt. 1929. This excellent record of the modern stage in all its branches is illustrated with some two hundred photographs of artists' sketches, model sets, lighting plans, and other technicalities of the art.

TAYLOR, EMERSON G. — *Practical Stage Directing for Amateurs: A Handbook for Amateur Managers and Actors.* Dutton. 1916. Contents: The Choice of a Play; Organization; Rehearsing; The Amateur Actor's A. B. C.; Make-up; The Stage and the Scenery.

WAUGH, FRANK A. — *Outdoor Theatres: The Design, Construction, and Use of Open-Air Auditoriums.* Badger. 1917.

WILDE, PERCIVAL. — *The Craftsmanship of the One-Act Play.* Little. 1923.

WISE, CLAUDE M. — *Dramatics for School and Community.* Appleton. 1923. Comprehensive information on lighting, setting, make-up, costuming, staging, directing, pageants, and an excellent bibliography make this book worth while.

YOUNG, AGNES BROOKS. — *Stage Costuming.* Macmillan. 1927. This excellent text gives valuable information on textiles and textures, the making of patterns, methods of dyeing, the special nature of costume sewing, the making of armor, jewelry, wigs, footwear, and masks, the effect of stage lights upon color values, and character costuming. The volume contains a reference bibliography for period costumes and numerous helpful illustrations.

YOUNG, STARK. — *The Flower in Drama: A Book of Papers on the Theatre.* Scribner. 1923. It contains an excellent chapter on acting.

—— *The Theatre.* Doran. 1927. A study of the arts of the theater.

—— *Theatre Practice.* Scribner. 1926. "This volume undertakes to consider not dramatists and plays alone but rather the arts of acting too, of theatrical design and production and such special phases and problems of these as illusion, stage movement, tempo, realistic and poetic methods, the voice, music, color and lights, and furthermore, such artists, designers, producers, directors, and playwrights as illustrate and embody the principles considered." (Preface by the Author.)

VALUABLE PERIODICALS ON THE ART OF THE THEATER

The Drama. Sponsored by the Drama League of America. The New York office is at 116 West 39th Street.

The Mask. Published quarterly in Florence, Italy. It can be ordered through Brentano's, New York.

Theatre Arts Monthly. Published monthly by Theatre Arts, Inc., 119 West 57th Street, New York.

Theatre Guild Magazine. Published by Theatre Guild Magazine, Inc., 302 West 45th Street, New York.

Theatre Magazine. Published monthly by Theatre Magazine Company, 2 West 45th Street, New York.

LIST OF PUBLISHERS

Allyn & Bacon — 11 E. 36th St., New York.

Appleton — D. Appleton & Company, 29–35 W. 32nd St., New York.

Argus — Argus Books, Inc., 434 S. Wabash Ave., Chicago.

Atlantic — Atlantic Monthly Press, Inc., 8 Arlington St., Boston.

Badger — Richard G. Badger (The Gorham Press), 100 Charles St., Boston.

Baker — Walter H. Baker Company, 41 Winter St., Boston.

Boni & Liveright — 61 W. 48th St., New York.

Brentano's — Fifth Ave. & 27th St., New York.

Century — Century Company, 353 Fourth Ave., New York.

Columbia Univ. — Columbia University Press, Columbia University, New York.

Covici, Friede — Covici, Friede, Inc., 79 W. 45th St., New York.

Crofts — F. S. Crofts & Company, 66 Fifth Ave., New York.

Crowell — T. Y. Crowell Company, 393 Fourth Ave., New York.

Day — John Day Company, Inc., 25 W. 45th St., New York.

Dodd — Dodd, Mead & Company, Inc., 443 Fourth Ave., New York.

Doran—Publications acquired by Doubleday, Doran.

Doubleday — Doubleday, Doran & Company, Inc., Garden City, Long Island, New York.

Drama — The Drama League of America, 59 E. Van Buren St., Chicago.

Dramatic — Dramatic Publishing Company, 542 S. Dearborn St., Chicago.

Duffield — Duffield & Company, 200 Madison Ave., New York.

Dutton — E. P. Dutton & Company, Inc., 681 Fifth Ave., New York.

French — Charles French, Inc., 52 W. 45th St., New York.

Ginn — Ginn & Company (Athenæum Press), 15 Ashburton Pl., Boston.

Harcourt — Harcourt, Brace & Company, 383 Madison Ave., New York.

Harper — Harper & Brothers, 49 E. 33d St., New York.

Holt — Henry Holt & Company, 1 Park Ave., New York.

Home Correspondence School, 129 Worthington St., Springfield, Mass.

Houghton — Houghton Mifflin Company (Riverside Press, Cambridge), 2 Park St., Boston.

Kennerley — Mitchell Kennerley, New York. Publications acquired by Argus.

Knopf — Alfred A. Knopf, 730 Fifth Ave., New York.

Lane — John Lane, London (Dodd is the American agent).

Lippincott — J. B. Lippincott Company, 227–231 E. Washington Square, Philadephia.

Little — Little, Brown & Company, 34 Beacon St., Boston.

Longmans — Longmans, Green & Company, 55 Fifth Ave., New York.

Luce — John W. Luce & Company, 212 Summer St., Boston.

Macmillan — The Macmillan Company, 60 Fifth Ave., New York.

Maunsel — Maunsel & Company, Ltd., 96 Mid. Abbey Street, Dublin, Ireland.

McBride — Robert M. McBride & Company, 17 W. 16th St., New York.

Merrill — Charles E. Merrill Company, 381 Fourth Ave., New York.

Noble — Noble & Noble, 76 Fifth Ave., New York.

Oxford — Oxford University Press, 114 Fifth Ave., New York.

Payson & Clarke — Payson and Clarke, Ltd. Now Brewer & Warren, Inc., 6 E. 53rd St., New York.

Putnam — G. P. Putnam's Sons (Knickerbocker Press), 2–4 W. 45th St., New York.

Scott — Scott, Foresman & Company, 623–633 S. Wabash Ave., Chicago.

Scribner — Charles Scribner's Sons, 597 Fifth Ave., New York.

Stage Guild — Stage Guild, 917 Railway Exchange Bldg., Chicago.

Stokes — Frederick A. Stokes Company, 443-447 Fourth Ave., New York.

Theatre Arts — Theatre Arts, Inc., 119 W. 57th St., New York.

Viking — Viking Press, Inc., 30 Irving Place, New York.

Yale University Press — Yale University Press, 386 Fourth Ave, New York.

INDEX

Abraham and Isaac, 477
Abraham Lincoln, 151, 438
acting out, 11
Admirable Crichton, The, 153 ff,
　157, 155, 432
admission fee, 34
Adventures of Tom Sawyer, The,
　10
Æschylus, 479
Affected Misses, The, 473
Agamemnon, 479
Aiglon, L', 466
Alcestis, 479
Aldis, Mary, 483
Alexander, Hartley B.,
Alexander and Campaspe, 474
Alice in Wonderland, 172, 419
Alice-Sit-by-the-Fire, 433
Allison's Lad, 128, 495
Amazons, The, 450
Ames, Winthrop, 208, 209
Andersen, Hans Christian, 20
Andreyev, Leonid, 483
Androcles and the Lion, 151, **152,**
　266, **288,** 297, 312, 452
Angevin kings, 391
animal stories, 94 ff.
announcement of acts, 188
Ansky, S., 459
anthology, individual, 81
Antigone, 481
Appia, 154

Apple Blossoms in the Spring, 81
appreciation, 31 ff., 46
Aria da Capo, **133, 138,** 523
Ariel's Song, 81
Aristophanes, 479
Arkell, Reginald, 484
Arliss, George, 108
Arms and the Man, 453
Arrow Maker, The, 411
Arthurian legends, 42, 76, 91 ff.
Artist, The, 524
assemblies, daily, 60
As You Like It, 168 ff., **171**
audience, 145, 159
auditorium, 199, 207 f.
Augier, Emile, 484
Austin, Jane, 366
Austin, Mary, 411
Australia, 6
Autumn, 81
autumn festival, 213 ff.
Avare, L', 470
Awakening of Brynhild, The, 90

Babylon, feasts of, 214
Back of the Yards, 507
balcony, 208
Ballad of Robin Hood, The, 76
ballads, 76, 89
Bank Account, The, 491
Barbara's Wedding, 485
Baring, Maurice, 484 f.

Barrie, Sir James M., 128, 130, 153, 154, 432 ff., 485 ff.
Barry, Philip, 411 f.
Barrymore, John, 168
Bates, Esther W., 144
battens, 158, 203
Bavarian harvest custom, 215, 219f.
Beach, Lewis, 128, 412, 487
beards, 187
Beau Brummel, 417
Beaumont, Francis, 473
Beauty and the Beast, 19
Beauty and the Jacobin, 535
Beegle, Mary P., 144
Beggar on Horseback, A, 414
Beginnings of Art, 6
Belasco, David, 156, 412
Bellman of Mons, The, 508
Benavente, Jacinto, 488
Ben Hur, 116
Bennett, Arnold, 435 f., 488
Benrimo, J. Harry, 413
Bethlehem, 515
Betrothal, The, 464
Beyond the Horizon, 427
Bible, 42, 86, 87, 116, 226 f.
Big Drum, The, 451
Bill of Divorcement, A, 437
Birthday of the Infanta, The, 538
Bishop's Candlesticks, The, 523
Blind, The, 520
blood in children's plays, 24
Bluebells, 81
Blue Bird, The, 464
Boats Sail on the River, 78
Book of Nursery Rhymes, A, 64
boomerang, 204
Boor, The, 535
Boots and His Brothers, 21

borders, lighting, 195 f.
Bottomley, Gordon, 488
Boucicault, Dion, 350
Bourgeois Gentilhomme, Le, 54, 470
Boy Comes Home, The, 524
Boy's King Arthur, The, 91
Branch, Anna Hempstead, 489
Brandane, John, 489
Bremen Town Musicians, The, 74, 94
Briar Rose, 72
Brighouse, Harold, 147, 436, 489 ff.
Brink of Silence, The, 504
Brooks, Charles S., 413
Brown, Alice, 491
Browne, Maurice, 491
Browning, Robert, 81
bunch lights, 198
Burglar Who Failed, The, 513
Burne-Jones, 117
Burton, Richard, 128
Butterfly dance, 6
Bynner, Witter, 492
By Ourselves, 504

Cæsar, 102
Cæsar and Cleopatra, 453
Calderon, George, 492
Caliban by the Yellow Sands, 423
Calvert, Louis, 110
Campbell of Kilmhor, 502
Candida, 454
Canterbury Pilgrims, The, 423
capacity of school auditorium, 208
Capek, Paul, 459
Caponsacchi, 420
Captain Applejack, 421
Captain Brassbound's Conversion, 454

Captain of the Gate, The, 496
Carb, David, 414
Carroll, Albert, **234**
Carved Woman, 483
casting, 42 f., 106, 273
casts, advantages of multiple, 106, 114, 117
Cat and the Mouse in Partnership, The, 21
Catherine Parr, **59,** 484
Cathleen Ni Houlihan, 128, **129,** 541
Cat That Walked by Himself, The, **96,** 97 ff.
ceiling of school stage, 203
Celtic stories, 92
Change, 439
Change House, The, 489
Chantecler, 465
Chapin, Harold, 492 f.
character, 18 f., 22, 27
character parts, make-up for, 186 ff.
charades, 136
Chekov. *See* Tchekov
Chesterton, Gilbert K., 436
Chicago Institute, 97
Children of the Moon, 418
children's plays, 16 ff., 20 f., 24, 63 ff., 179 f., 184
children's theater, 47, 49
Child's Garden of Verses, 78
Chinese Lantern, The, 443
chivalry, 391
Christmas, 120, 144, 147, 202
Chubb, Percival, 144
Church, Virginia, 493
Cinderella, 19, 22
civic theater, 131
Clarence, 429
classic drama, 157, 479 ff.

Clements, Colin, 493
Clod, The, 128, 191, 487
coach, professional, 124
colonial party, 236
Colonists, 233 ff., 345, 365
color, 184, 206
color medium in lighting, 196
Columbine, 484
comedy, 27
Come Out of the Kitchen, 430
community drama, 131
Confessional, The, 539
Conkling, Hilda, 79
Connelly, Marc, 414, 421 f.
Continental Stagecraft, 193
Cook, George Cram, 493
Cook County Normal School, 336
Coppée, François, 494
Copperhead, The, 431
Correggio, 119
costume, 132, 136, 348, 378, 179 ff., 183
costume room, 204
Course of Study, 345
Cradle Song, The, **frontis., 7,** 467
Craig, Gordon, 131, 154, 156
Craig's Wife, 422
Cranford, 426
Crawford, Jack R., 144
Critic, The; or a Tragedy Rehearsed, 469
Crothers, Rachel, 414, 494
Crum, J. M. C., 495
Crumbs That Fall, 526
Crusaders, 391
Cuchulain, 92
curtain calls, 188
curtains as setting, 126, 169, 175, 177, 203, 274 ff., 322, 348 f.

curtains, stage, 149, 206 f.
cycle, 84
cyclorama, 149, 156, 175, 187, 196, 203
Cyrano de Bergerac, 466

Daffodils, The, 81
Dalcroze, Émile-Jaques, 54
Damer's Gold, 510
dance, 5
Dandy Dick, 451
Dane, Clemence, 437
Dargan, Olive Tilford, 415
Dark of the Dawn, The, 496
Dasant, Sir George Webbe, 69
David and Goliath, 87
Davies, Hubert, 437
Davis, Owen, 415
Day Dream, The, 73
daylight, playing in, 181
Dear Brutus, 433
Dear Departed, The, 515
Death of Sigmund, The, 90
Death of Tintagiles, The, 521
de Banville, Theodore, 484
Decoration Day exercise, 100 f.
Defoe, Daniel, 85
Deirdre, 542
Deirdre of the Sorrows, 458
Dekker, Thomas, 473
de la Mare, Walter, 79, 81, 438
Delf, Harry, 416
Departure, The, 397
depth of school stage, 203
Detour, The, 415
Development of the United States, 1787–1865, 100 ff.
Devil's Disciple, The, 454
Dewey, John, 137

dialogue, 17 f., 110, 183, 251, 268, 337, 351, 376, 397
dimmers, 198 f.,
Dionysus, feast of, 214 ff.
director, place of, 114
disastrous ending, 22
Disraeli, 130, 448
divided stage, 161
Dix, Beulah Marie, 128, 494 f., 416
Doctor by Compulsion, The, 472
Dollar, A, 530
Doll's House, The, 21, 130, 462
Don Juan; ou le Festin de Pierre, 471
doors, 175, 204
Doré, Gustave, 391
double period, 12 f.
Dover Road, The, 446
Down, Oliphant, 496
Dowson, Ernest, 496
Dragon, The, 457
Drake, Samuel Adams, 366
drama, 1, 5, 26, 31, 116, 130 ff., classic, 479 ff.
    eighteenth-century English, 469 ff.
    Elizabethan, 473 ff. *See* Shakespeare and Shakespearean plays
    modern, 1, 411 ff.
    pre-Shakespearean, 476 ff;
    school, 44
    seventeenth-century French, 470 ff. *See* Molière
drama club, 125, f.
drama course, 100, 124, 127, 132 ff.
dramatic analysis, 29
dramatic construction, principles of, 29
dramatic impulse, 1 ff., 4 f., 8, 13, 16, 30 ff., 63 ff., 134

dramatic play, 10, 13 ff., 75
dramatic training, 34, 52, 54
Dransfield, Jane, 416
Drawing of Odin's Sword out of the Branstock, The, 90 f.
Dresden Royal Opera House, 119
dressing rooms, 204 f.
Drinkwater, John, 151, 438, 497
Driscoll, Louise, 497
Drone, The, 457
Dulcy, 421
Dumb and the Blind, The, 492
Duncan, John, 250
Dunsany, Lord, 128, 130, 496 ff.
Dust of the Road, 508
Dybbuk, The, 459

Eaton, Walter Prichard, 414
education, purposes of, 24, 136 ff.
effects, stage, 188, 191 ff.
eighteenth-century English drama, 469 ff.
electrical equipment, 193, 199
Elementary School Teacher, 92, 102
Elizabethan drama, 473 ff.
Elizabethan stage, 163, 166 f.
Elsie books, 11
Émile, 85
emotional outlet, 57
Emperor Jones, The, 427
Endymion: The Man in the Moon, 475
Enemy of the People, An, 462
Engaged, 442
English drama. *See* drama
English Fairy Tales, 69
English harvest home, 214, 218
epic, 76

equipment, electrical, 193, 199
   lighting, 194 ff.
Erskine, John, 501
Ervine, St. John, 439
Euripides, 151, 479 f.
Everyman, 159, 477
Evil Kettle, The, 497
expression, art, 27
expression, dramatic, 4, 6, 9, 14, 31, 52 f., 54 ff., 67
exteriors, settings for, 187

fable, 95
Faerie Queen, The, 81
fairies, 22
Falcon, The, 536
Fame and the Poet, 498
Family Upstairs, The, 416
Fan and Two Candlesticks, A, 520
Far-Away Princess, The, 533
farce, 159
Farmer's Wife, The, 450
Farrar, John, 501
Fashion, 427
Faust, 49
Faustus, The Tragical History of Doctor, 475
fear, vicarious experience of, 24
Feet of the Young Men, The, 81
Femmes Savantes, Les, 471
Fenn, Frederick, 502
Ferber, Edna, 417
Ferdiad, 93
Ferguson, J. A., 502
Field, Rachel L., 502 f.
Fifteenth Candle, The, 502
Fifth Commandment, The, 515
Finding of the Grape, The, 215 ff.
fine arts, 137

First Thanksgiving Day in America, The, 75, 214, 365 ff.
Fiske, Mrs., 154
Fitch, Clyde, 417
fixed units in lighting, 195
Flavin, Martin, 418
Flecker, James Elroy, 439
Fletcher, John, 473
Flexner, Hortense, 503
flood lamps, 197, 201
floor of school stage, 203
Florist Shop, The, **77**, **84**, 513
flowers, presentation of, 188
Fly Away, Fly Away Over the Sea, 78
folk stories as material for children's plays, 19
Followers, 489
footlights, 197, 202
For Better or Worse, 142 ff.
foreign languages and dramatic expression, 56 f.
Forfeit, The, 531
Forging of the Sword, The, 90
Fortune and Men's Eyes, 529
Fortuny lighting system, 131
Forum, school, 125 f.
frames for lights, 198
France, Anatole, 503
Francis, John O., 439
French drama, seventeenth-century, 470 ff. *See* Molière
Froebel, 5
Frog dance, 6
Frogs, The, 479
Frost, Robert, 81, 504
Fulda, Ludwig, 504

Galbraith, Esther E., 504
Gale, Zona, 418, 505

gallery for lighting, 198
Galsworthy, John, 130, 153, 439 ff., 505 f.
Game of Chess, The, 508
Gammer Gurton's Needle, 159, **477**
Gaol Gate, The, 510
Garnett, Louise, A., 419
Gates, Eleanor, 419
gelatin frame, 196, 198
Gerstenberg, Alice, 419, 506 f.
gesture, 53 f., 111 f.
Getting of the Horse Greyfell, The, 90
Getting of the Treasure, The, 90
Gettysburg, 519
Ghost of Jerry Bundler, The, 516
Gilbert, W. S., 442
Glaspell, Susan, 419, 493, 507
Glass of Truth, The, 424
Glittering Gate, The, 498
Goal, The, 517
Gods of the Mountain, The, 498
Gogol, Nikolai V., 460
Golden Apple, The, 457
Golden Doom, The, 498
Golden Numbers, 79
Goldoni, Carlo, 460
Goldsmith, Oliver, 469. *See Oliver Goldsmith*
Goodman, Kenneth Sawyer, 507 f., 513
Good-Natured Man, The, 469
Goodrich, Arthur, 420
Goose Hangs High, The, 412
Gordon-Lennox, Cosmo, 509
Granville-Barker, Harley, 442 f., 509
Great Adventure, The, 435
Great Broxopp, The, 446

Great Divide, The, 426
Greek festival, 215, 217 f.
Greek games, 325
Greek history, 375
Greek life and literature, 324
Greek plays, 88, 479
Greek Vase, The, 485
Green, Paul, 420, 509
Greene, Robert, 474
Gregory, Lady, 27, 92, 128, 130, 457, 510 ff.
gridiron, 203
Grimm brothers, 19, 22, 69, 72, 265
Gringoire, 484
Grosse, Edmund, 6

Hackett, Walter, 421
Hall, Holworthy, 512
Hall, Jennie, 88, 91
Halloween, 251
Halman, Doris F., 512
Hamilton, Cosmo, 442
Hamlet, 163 ff., **164, 167**
Hampden, Walter, 154, 168
Hankin, St. John, 513
Hannele, 461
Hans in Luck, 25
happy ending, 22, 24
Harris, Joel Chandler, 237, 260
Harrison, Geneva, **167**
Hassan, 439
Hauptmann, Gerhart, 461
Hawkridge, Winifred, 513
Hawthorne, Nathaniel, 321
Hay, Ian, 442
Hazelton, George C., 413
He and She, 414
Heart of Oak books, 265
Hearts Enduring, 501

Hecht, Ben, 513
height of school stage, 203
Hell-Bent fer Heaven, 421
Henty, George Alfred, 18
Herod, 449
hero tales, 83
Hervieu, Paul, 514
Hieronimo Is Mad Again, 474
Hillman and the Housewife, The **17**
historical plays, costume in, 183
history and school drama, 28, 102
Hobson's Choice, 436
Hoffman, Phoebe, 514
Holbrook, R. T., 159, 478
"Holy Night," 119
Home Book of Verse for Young People, The, 79
Home Makers, The, 432
Honourable History of Friar Bacon and Friar Bungay, The, 474
Hopkins, Arthur, 514
Horses of the Sea, The, 78
Horween, Arnold, **167**
Houghton, Stanley, 515
Hour-Glass, The, 104, 128, 541
Household Stories, 69, 72
House That Jack Built, The, 71
Housman, Laurence, 443, 515
Howells, William Dean, 515
How to See a Play, 128
Hraun Farm, The, 468
Hubbard, Philip, 526
Hughes, Hatcher, 421
humor, 25, 39 f., 64, 74
Hunchback Weaver, The, 69
husking bee, 103, 222 ff.
Hyacinth Halvey, 510
Hyde, Douglas, 116, 516
hymns, 81

Ibsen, Hendrik, 21, 130, 462 f.
Icebound, 415
Idylls of the King, 91
If I Were King, 445
I Know a Bank, 81
Ile, 527
Iliad, The, 88
Imaginary Invalid, The, 472
imitation, 4 f., 8 f., 10, 12 f.
Impertinence of the Creature, The, 509
Importance of Being Earnest, The, 456
In Abraham's Bosom, 420
Indians, 214 f., 217 f., 366
industries, dramatization of, 74 f.
Inheritors, 419
inscenierung, 186
Inspector-General, The, 460
Interior, The, 521
interiors, setting for, 187
intervals between acts, 187
In the Zone, 527
Intimate Strangers, 430
Intruder, The, 521
Iphigenia in Tauris, 480
Irish theater, 27, 104, 131, 457 ff.
Irving, Washington, 345
Is the Moon Tired?, 78
Ivanhoe, 28, 391

Jack Be Nimble, 66 ff.
Jackdaw, The, 510
Jackman, Dean, 336
Jacob, 86
Jacobs, Joseph, 69
Jacobs, W. W., 142, 516
James, Professor, 12
Jazz Singer, The, 429

Jeanne d'Arc, 423
Jefferson, Joseph, 350
Jephthah's Daughter, 518
Jesters, The, 468
Jesus, 5
Jew of Malta, The, 475
jingles. *See* rhymes and jingles
Joan of Arc, 147 ff. *See Jeanne d'Arc*
John Gabriel Borkman, 462
Joint Owners in Spain, 491
Jones, Henry Arthur, 130, 444, 517
Jones, Robert Edmond, 154, 193
Jonson, Ben, 474
Joseph, 87 f.
Joseph and His Brethren, 449
Judge Lynch, 530
Julius Cæsar, 55, 181
Jungle Book, The, 94, 96
junior high school, 26 ff., 100 ff.
Justice, 439
Just-So Stories, 96

Kangaroo dance, 6
Kaufman, George S., 414, 417, 421 f.
Keith, Ian, 164
Kelly, George.E., 422, 517
Kennedy, Charles Rann, 153, 444 f.
kindergarten, 25
Kinfolk of Robin Hood, 424, 519
King Argimēnēs and the Unknown Warrior, 499
King John, 391
King Lear, 21
King's Henchman, The, 426
King's Threshold, The, 541
Kipling, Rudyard, 80, 94, 96
Kiss for Cinderella, A, 433

Knave of Hearts, The, 531
knighthood, 391 ff.
Knightly Legends of Wales, 91
Knighting of Richard Neville, 92, 391 ff.
Knight of the Burning Pestle, The, 473
Knoblock, Edward, 436, 517
Kreymborg, Alfred, 518
Krows, Arthur Edwin, 194, 209
kuppelhorizont, 131
Kyd, Thomas, 474

laboratory method, 31
lacquer, lamps dipped in, 196
Lady from the Sea, The, 463
Lady of the Weeping Willow, The, 538
Laertes, Polonius' advice to, 136
Lamp, The, 92
Lamp and the Bell, The, 426
Land of Heart's Desire, The, 541
Lang, Andrew, 64 f.
Lanier, Sidney, 91
large classes, dramatic expression in, 67
Last of the Lowries, The, 510
Latin stories, 375
Lear, Edward, 64
Learned Ladies, The, 471
learning a rôle, 107
Lee, Charles, 518
Levinger, Elma E., 518
Lewis, B. Roland, 128
lighting, 47, 119 f., 120, 131, 149, 156, 175, 186, 193 ff., 206, 278 f.
light plot for *The Merchant of Venice,* 200
'Lijah, 532

Lima Beans, 518
Lionel of Orkney, 92
literary drama, 19, 26 ff., 104 f., 145 ff.
literary taste, 25
literature as a factor in education, 30, 41 f., 68, 83, 134
Little Father of the Wilderness, The, 532
Little King, The, 492
Little Man, The, 505
Little Red Riding Hood, 24
Little Stone House, The, 492
Little Theatre, 208 f.
little-theater movement, 131
Locked Chest, The, 522
Lonesome-Like, 490
long play, 4, 128 ff., 150
Lord's Prayer, The, 494
Lost Pleiad, The, 416
Lost Silk Hat, The, 499
Love in a Dutch Garden, 443
Love in a French Kitchen, 493
Love of One's Neighbor, 483
Loyalties, 151, 440
Lucky Pehr, **194,** 201, **322, 336, 344, 364,** 468
Luke, St., 116
Lyly, John, 474 f.
lyric, 76

Mabie, Hamilton W., 36
Mabinogion for Boys, 91
Macgowan, Kenneth, 193
Mackay, Constance D'Arcy, 579
MacKaye, Percy, 423 ff., 519 f.
MacMillan, Mary, 520
Maeterlinck, Maurice, 464 f., 520 ff.

magic, 22, 24
Magic, 436
Maid of France, The, 147 ff., 196, 490
make-believe, 9, 45, 67
Maker of Dreams, The, 496
make-up, 184
Malade Imaginaire, Le, 472
Man from Home, The, 123
Manikin and Minikin, 518
Man in the Bowler Hat, The, 525
Manœuvers of Jane, The, 444
Man on the Kerb, The, 533
Man Who Married a Dumb Wife, The, 503
Marco Millions, 428
Mark Twain, 10
Marks, Jeanette, 522
Marlowe, Christopher, 475
Marriage Has Been Arranged, A, 534
Marriage Proposal, A, 128, 536
Martha's Mourning, 514
marvellous, children's love of, 22
Mary Goes First, 444
Mary Rose, 434
Masefield, John, 445, 522
masks, 99
masques, 131
Master Builder, The, 463
Master Pierre Patelin, 159 ff., 160, 220, 478
Master Will of Stratford, 419
Matthews, Brander, 161
Mayne, Rutherford, 151, 457, 522
McCarthy, Justin, 445
mechanical accessories, 181
Medea, The, 480
Médecin Malgré Lui, Le, 472

Melon Thief, The, 527
Melting Pot, The, 456
memorization, voluntary, 82
Merchant of Venice, The, 172 ff., **173, 174, 176**, 183 f., 188 ff., 200 f.
Merington, Marguerite, 426
Merry Adventures of Robin Hood, The, 89
Merry Adventure with Midge the Miller, The, 89
Merry, Merry Cuckoo, The, 522
Merton of the Movies, 422
Middle Ages, stage of the, 161
Middlemass, Robert, 512
Middleton, George, 523
Midsummer Night's Dream, A, **23**, 45
Milestones, 436
Millay, Edna St. Vincent, 426, 523 f.
Milne, A. A., 79, 446 f., 524 f.
Milton, John, 81
miniature stage, 106, 184
Minick, 417
Minuet, A, 529
Miracle of St. Anthony, The, 522
Misanthrope, Le, 472
Miser, The, 470
Miss Lulu Bett, 418
Miss Maria, 537
Mixed Marriage, 439
Mob, The, 440
model of setting, 183
model stage, 106, 184
modern drama, 1, 411 ff.
Moderwell, Hiram K., 163, 193
Modesty, 514
Moeller, Philip, 525

Moffett, G., 448
Molière, 54, 130, 151, 470 ff.
Mollusc, The, 437
Molnar, Ferenc, 465
Monkey's Paw, The, 516
Moody, William Vaughn, 426
Moonshine, 514
moral values, 19, 21, 27
More, Nina, 366
Morley, Christopher, 525 f.
Morris, William, 90
Mother Goose, 64 ff.
Moulton, Richard G., 31
Mouse Trap, The, 515
moving pictures, 49 ff., 131
Mowatt, Anna Cora, 427
Mowgli, 97
Mr. Pim Passes By, 446
Mr. Sampson, 205, 518
Mrs. Pat and the Law, 483
Mr. Wolf Makes a Failure, 96 ff.

narrative poems, 76
Nathan Hale, 417
Nativity, The, 104, 116 ff., 516
natural light, 195
Neighbors, The, 505
Nerves, 501
Nevertheless, 538
New England, 75, 365, 214 ff.
New Word, The, 485
New York, 75
Nichols, Robert, 448
Night at an Inn, A, 33, 128, 499
Noah's Flood, 478
non-realistic setting, 168, 172 ff., 177 f.
Nonsense Books, 64
Norman Conquest, 391

Norse literature and ideals, 90
North, Lockart, 526
Norton, Charles Eliot, 265
Nose Tree, The, 265 ff.
No Smoking, 488
notation of lighting scheme, 201
novel, dramatization of a selection from a, 397
Now We Are Six, 79
Noyes, Alfred, 448
Nursery Rhyme Book, The, 64

Obata, Shiegeyoshi, 527
Odyssey, The, 42, 76, 88
offstage effects, 188
O'Flaherty, V. C., 532
Old Lady Shows Her Medals, The, 486
Old Peabody Pew, The, 539
Old Pipes and the Dryad, 83, 375 ff., 379
Old Wives' Tale, 476
Old Woman and Her Sixpence, The, 69 ff.
Oliver Goldsmith, 431
On Building a Theatre, 193 f., 203
one-act play, 128, 144, 481 ff.
O'Neill, Eugene G., 427 f., 527
On May Morning, 81
On Plymouth Rock, 366
On the Shelf, 525
On Vengeance Height, 495
open-air theater, 131
'Op-O'-Me-Thumb, 502
oral reading, 36
oratory, 102
organization of drama course, 124
Oriental feasts, 214
original plays, 141

origin of English drama, 116
Orr, William, 144
Osbourne, Lloyd, 532
O'Shea, Monica Barry, 528
Other Wise Man, The, 116
outdoor setting, 89, 338, 172
Outward Bound, 456
Over the Hills, 528
Overtones, 156, 506
Owl, The, 81

pageantry, 131, 144, 226 ff.
paint shop, 204
Palestine, 86
Palmer, George W., 88
Palmer, John, 528
Palmer, Rose A., 420
pantomime, 6, 8, 53 f., 68, 113,
  136, 351
Paradise of Children, The, 321
Parker, Col. Francis W., 5, 58
Parker, Louis N., 448 f., 516, 528
Parker School, Francis W., 124,
  164, 199
passage under stage, 204
Pasture, The, 81
Peabody, Josephine P., 428, 529
Peacock Pie, 79
Peele, George, 476
Peer Gynt, 463
Peggy, 494
Pelleas and Melisande, 465
personality, assumed, 12
perspective, 172, 187
Pestalozzi, 5
Peter Pan 434
Peters, Rollo, 168
Phillips, Stephen, 449 f.
Phillpotts, Eden, 450

Philosopher of Butterbiggens, The,
  493
Pichel, Irving, 193 f., 203
Pickwick, 442
pictures, use of in preparing a play,
  117
*Pierre Patelin. See Master Pierre
  Patelin*
Pierrot of the Minute, 496
Pigeon, The, 441
Pilgrims, 365 ff.
Pilgrims and Puritans, 366
Pillot, Eugene, 529
Pinero, Sir Arthur Wing, 130, 151,
  450 ff., 529 f.
Pine-Tree Shillings, The, 233 ff.
Pinski, David, 530
Piper, The, 428
Pippa's Song, 81
Playboy of the Western World, The,
  151, 458
Playgoers, 529
playmaking, 14 ff., 25, 28, 56, 86,
  141 ff., 213 ff., 226 ff., 233 ff.,
  250 ff., 260, 336 ff., 345 ff.,
  365 f., 375 ff., 397 f., 391 f., 321 ff.
Play of St. George, The, 495
Play Production in America, 193,
  209
playwright, qualifications of, 28
plot, 18 ff.
Poems by a Little Girl, 79
poetic justice, 22, 24
poetry for children, 76, 79 f., 82
Polonius, 118, 136
Pomander Walk, 449
Poor House, The, 497
Poor Little Rich Girl, A, 419
Poor Maddelena, 531

Popular Tales from the Norse, 69
portable lamps, 197
positions on the stage, **274**
Post Office, The, 534
Postscript, The, 484
Posy Ring, The, 79
Pot Boiler, The, 506
Pot of Broth, The, 104, 542
Precieuses Ridicules, Les, 473
pre-Shakespearean drama, 477 ff.
Price of Coal, The, 491
primitive peoples, 6, 8, 213
Prince of Stamboul, The, 500
problems for children's plays, 21
production of school plays, 33, 114,
    132, 134, 144, 153
professional coach, 124
professional theater, 44 ff., 51, 130
project method, 14, 336 ff.
prompt book, 188, 201
properties, 158 f., 188, 203
proscenium, 202
*Prunella; or Love in a Dutch
    Garden,* 443
Pryce, Richard, 502
psalms, 81
psychology, 35, 94
Psychology, 137
Pygmalion, 454
Pyle, Howard, 89

Quality Street, **32**, 434
Queen's Enemies, The, 500
Queen Victoria, 414
Quintero, Serafin, and Joaquin
    Alvarez, 530

Rainbow Gold, 79
Ralph Roister Doister, 479

Raphaelson, Samuel, 429
reading skill, 56
realistic performance, 168
Red Turf, The, **109**, 523
rehearsal, 106, 108, 110 f., 113
Reid, Edith G., 452
Reilly, Frank C., 442
Reinhardt, Max, 131, 154
religion, 26
Return of Peter Grimm, The, 412
Revere, Paul, 102
revolving stage, 131
Reynard the Fox, 95
rhymes and jingles, 17, 63, 76
Richard Cœur-de-Lion, 391
Rider of Dreams, The, 537
Riders of the Sea, 128, 534
Riding to Lithend, The, 488
Riley, James Whitcomb, 65
Rip Van Winkle, 75, 89, 345 ff.
Rising of the Moon, The, **128**, 511
Rivals, The, 469
Roadhouse in Arden, A, 525
Road to Yesterday, The, 416
Robert E. Lee, 438
Robin Hood, 76, 89, 424, 448
Robin Hood and the Three Kings,
    448
Robinson, Lenox, 458
Robinson Crusoe, 42, 85 ff.
Rock, Charles, 516
Rococo, 509
Rogers, J. W., Jr., 530
Rogers, T. B., 531
rôle, learning a, 107 f.
Romancers, The, 466
romances, 76, 83
Romantic Age, The, 447
Romantic Young Lady, The, 467

Roosevelt, Theodore, 92
Rosalind, 486
Rose of Plymouth Town, The, 416
Rose of the Wind, 489
Rossetti, Christina, 65, 78
Rostand, Edmond, 465 f.
Rousseau, J. J., 85
rundhorizont, 156, 203
R. U. R., 459
Rushlight, The, 528

Sabine, Dean, 209
Sacrifice of Isaac, The, 159
Sad Shepherd, The, 474
Saint Joan, 455
Sam Average, 520
Sanctuary, 424
Saunders, John M., 493
Saunders, Louise, 531
Scammon Gardens, 338
Scarecrow, The, 424
scenario of *The Magic Gifts*, 271
scenery, non-realistic, 149
Scherz, Thea J., 57
school drama and the professional
    stage, 44 ff.
School for Scandal, The, 130, 470
school theater, 202 ff.
Scott, Dr. Colin, 336
Scott, Sir Walter, 281, 391
screens, 155 f., 177, **182**, 278,
    325
seating in school auditorium, 208 f.
Second Shepherd's Play, The, 478
Seeonee Wolf Pack, 97
selection of players see casting
semi-conventional setting, 172
senior high school, 30 ff., 125 ff.,
    141 ff., 145 ff., 180

Servant in the House, The, 130, 153,
    234, 444
setting, 111, 118 f., 120, 126, 131,
    136 ff., 169 ff., 172, 177, 181,
    183, 273 ff.
Shadow of the Glen, The, 534
Shakespeare and Shakespearean
    plays, 21, 28, 81, 130, 151, 163 ff.,
    172 ff., **173**, **174**, **176**, 177 ff.,
    183 ff., 200 f., **374**, **390**, 391,
    398, **406**, 476
Sham, 537
Shaw, George Bernard, 130, 151,
    452 ff., 532
*Sheep and the Pig That Set Up
    Housekeeping, The*, 69
Shepherd, The, 415
Sheridan, Richard Brinsley, 130,
    469 f.
*Sherwood; or Robin Hood and the
    Three Kings*, 448
She Stoops to Conquer, 469
Shoemaker and the Elves, The,
    69
Shoemaker's Holiday, The, 473
Shoes That Danced, The, 489
Shooting Match at Nottingham, The,
    89
short plays, 128, 144, 481 ff.
Show Off, The, 422
Siegfried, 90
Sierra, Gregorio Martinez, 467
Sigurd the Volsung, 76, 90 f.
Sigurjonsson, Johann, 468
Silver Box, The, 441
Silver Lining, The, 519
Sing Song, 78
Sir David Wears a Crown, 538
Sir Patrick Spens, 76

Six Who Pass While the Lentils Boil, 539

Slaying of Fafnir, The, 90

Sleeping Beauty, The, 22, 72 f.

sliding stage, 131

Smith, Edgar Valentine, 532

Smith, Nora Archibald, 79

smoke, stage, 98

Snow White and the Seven Dwarfs, 48, 52, 53, 204, 432

social customs, play-making as a mode of studying, 103

social studies, dramatization of, 74

Sohrab and Rustum, 76

Sophocles, 481

So This Is London, 420

Spanish Tragedy; or Hieronimo Is Mad Again, The, 474

speech. *See* dialogue

Spenser, Edmund, 81

spotlights, 198, 201, 206

Spreading the News, 104, 511

Squabbles of Chioggia, The, 460

stage, 131, 161, 163, 166 f., 202 f.

stage arrangement, 97, 106, 158, 161, 275, 276, 277, 280, 323, 326, 349, 350

staging, 117, 273 ff., 322., 348 ff.

Standish of Standish, 366

"Star of Bethlehem, The," 107

Stars, 81

Stepmother, The, 488

steps, use of proscenium, 202

Stevenson, Burton Egbert, 79

Stevenson, Robert Louis, 18, 78, 80

Stockton, Frank R., 375

Stone Guest, The, 471

stories as material for play-making, 19 ff., 69, 83 ff.

story, essentials of well-constructed, 20 f.

Strife, 441

Strindberg, August, 201, 468

strips, lighting, 198

Strong, Austin, 532

Studies in Education, 57, 66, 88, 117

Study of the Drama, A, 161

stylization, 163

Sudermann, Hermann, 533

Sun, The, 506

Sunken Bell, The, 461

sunlight, reproduction of, 195

Sunny Morning, A, 530

Sun-Up, 431

Suppressed Desires, 493

Sutherland, Evelyn G., 416

Sutro, Alfred, 455, 533 f.

Swan, The, 465

Swan Song, The, 536

Swiss Family Robinson, The, 11

switchboard for school stage, 198 f.

symbolism in *The Ugly Duckling,* 20

symbols, 9 f.

Synge, John M., 128, 130, 151, 458 f., 534

Tabernacles, feast of, 214

Tagore, Rabindranath, 534

Tales from the Fjeld, 69

Talisman, The, 391

Tamburlaine, Part I, 475

Tarkington, Booth, 429 f., 535

tastes and standards, 135 f.

Tchekov, Anton, 128, 535 f.

teacher of drama, 29, 35 ff., 110

Teasdale, Sara, 79, 81

technique, 20, 40 f., 130, 267 ff., 352

Technique of the One-Act Play, The, 128

Tennyson, Alfred, Lord, 73, 81, 91, 134, 536

Tents of the Arabs, The, 501

text, use of at rehearsal, 108

Thackeray, William Makepeace, 397

Thanksgiving, 75, 213 f., 226 ff., 229, 365 ff.

Theatre of To-day, The, 163, 193

Theatre of Tomorrow, The, 193

theater, school, 202 ff.

This Singing World, 79

Thomas, A. E., 430

Thomas, Augustus, 431

Thousand Years Ago, A, 425

Three Billy Goats Gruff, The, 69, 71 f., 94

Three Pills in a Bottle, 503

Thunderbolt, The, 130, 451

Thursday Evening, 526

Tilly of Bloomsbury, 212, 442

toilet accommodations, 204

Tom Pinch, 182, 185

Tompkins, Frank G., 537

Torrence, Ridgley, 537

Tradesman Turned Gentleman, The, 470

Tradition, 523

tragedy, 27

Tragedy of Nan, The, 445

Tragedy of Pompey the Great, The, 445

Tragical History of Dr. Faustus, The, 475

tragic literature, 24

training, results of dramatic, 52

training for teacher of dramatics, 35 ff.

Traitor, The, 540

trap door, 204

Traveling Man, The, 511

Treasure Island, 18

Trelawny of the "Wells," 151, 452

Trifles, 507

Trojan Women, The, 480

Truth about Blayds, The, 447

try-out system, 107

Trysting Place, The, 535

Turn of the Road, The, 122, 151, 457

Twelfth Night, 177 ff., 374, 390, 398, 406

Twelve-Pound Look, The, 128, 486

Twig of Thorn, The, 539

Twisting of the Rope, The, 515

Two Crooks and a Lady, 529

Two Slatterns and a King, 524

Two Virtues, The, 455

Udall, Nicholas, 479

Ugly Duckling, The, 20

Ulysses, 134

Ulysses, 450

Uncle Jimmy, 505

Uncle Remus, 96, 260

University of Chicago School of Education, 88, 336, 338

Unseen, The, 507

Unseen Host, The, 540

Untermeyer, Louis, 79

Valiant, The, 512

Van Dyke, Henry, 116

Vane, Sutton, 456

Vanity Fair, 397 ff.

ventilation of school auditorium, 208 f.

Vikings, The, 91

vintage feats, 214 f., 217 f.
Violin Maker of Cremona, The, 494
voice, 36, 137 ff.
"*Voices*," 503
Vollmer, Lulu, 431
Volsünga Saga, 92 f.
Vosburgh, Maude B., 432, 537
Voysey Inheritance, The, 442

wagon stage, 131
Walker, Stuart, 159, 538 f.
Wallace, Lew, 116
Wappin' Wharf, 413
Warren, M. J., 539
Washington and Betsy Ross, 520
Washington's birthday, 235
Washington; the Man Who Made Us, 425
Way Out, A, 504
Weavers, The, 461
Well of the Saints, The, 459
Well-Remembered Voice, The, 487
Welsh, Charles, 64
What Every Woman Knows, 434
What Men Live By, 493
What the Public Wants, 435
When Bunty Pulls the Strings, 448
When We Were Very Young, 79
Where but in America, 540
Where the Bee Sucks, 81
Where the Cross Is Made, 527
White, Jessie Braham, 432
Whiteheaded Boy, The, 458
White Wings, 411
Why the Bear is Stumpy-Tailed, 94
Widow of Wasdale Head, 530

Wiggin, Kate Douglas, 79, 539
wigs, 187
Wilde, Oscar, 456, 538
Wilde, Percival, 539 f.
Will, The, **33**, 154, 487
Will o' the Wisp, 512
Wind Has Such a Rainy Sound, The, 78
Wings over Europe, 448
Winterfeast, The, 445
Wolff, Oscar M., 540
Wolf of Gubbio, The, 428
Wonder Book, The, 321
Wonder Hat, The, 513
Woodman and the Goblins, The, 72, 74, 243 ff., 324
Wordsworth, William, 12, 81
Workhouse Ward, The, 512
world literature, 83 ff.
Wrath of Achilles, The, 88
Wurzel-Flummery, The, 525

X-O: A Night of the Trojan War, 497
X-ray reflector, 196

Yeats, William Butler, 22, 92, 128, 541 f.
Yellow Jacket, The, 413
Ye Spotted Snakes, 81
You and I, 412
You Never Can Tell, 455

Zamacois, Miguel, 468
Zangwill, Israel, 456